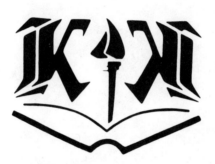

Limited Classical Reprint Library

AN EXPOSITION
OF THE
BOOKS OF CHRONICLES

by

W.H. Bennett, Litt.D., D.D.

Foreword by Dr. Cyril J. Barber

Klock & Klock Christian Publishers, Inc.
2527 Girard Avenue North
Minneapolis, Minnesota 55411

Originally published by
A. C. Armstrong and Son
London, 1908

ISBN: 0-86524-169-4

Printed by Klock & Klock in the U.S.A.
1983 Reprint

FOREWORD

It was John Milton who, in *Areopagitica*, wrote, "Books are not absolutely dead things, but do contain a potency of life in them to be as active as that soul was whose progeny they are; nay, they do preserve as in a vile the purest efficacy and extraction of that living intellect that bred them."

Two books of the Bible that are frequently ignored, as if they were lifeless appendages to the Books of Samuel and Kings, are I and II Chronicles. When their purpose and intent is properly understood, however, these Old Testament works are found to provide us with unique insights into the plan of God and His ways with mankind.

In the Septuagint the Books of Chronicles were inaccurately styled "Things Past Over or Omitted." It seems as if, even in this early period of Jewish history, this work was misunderstood and suffered from neglect.

In actual fact, the temple is central in the Books of Chronicles. Following the division of the kingdom, Judah is the only nation among God's people to which reference is made. Men and events take on significance only in relation to the temple and the worship of the Lord. Prominence is given to those aspects of history which illustrate the cultivation of the Mosiac legislation as a medium of spiritual blessing and the channel of prosperity for God's people.

The present publishers, in searching for a commentary on these important books, soon found that relatively little had been written on them. The only substantive work worthy of serious consideration was produced by William Henry Bennett who taught Old Testament Exegesis at the New College, London. Dr. Bennett later became principal of the Lancashire College in Manchester. He authored *The Life of Christ According to St. Mark*, and *The Religion of the Post-Exilic Prophets* while also contributing commentaries on Genesis, Exodus and the General Epistles in the *New Century Bible* and on the Book of Jeremiah in *The Expositor's Bible*, and the Book of Joshua in *The Temple Bible*. Other works published include *The Theology of the Old Testament* (1896), a *Primer of the Bible* (1897) and *Biblical Introduction* (1899 done in collaboration with W. F. Adeney).

In this present work, Dr. Bennett discusses questions of chronology and genealogy before focusing his attention on the spiritual teaching of the Books of Chronicles. His exposition is marked by a keen insight into the history of the times and the condition of God's people. As with men of the calibre of F. J. Delitzsch, J. G. Murphy and J. MacGregor, Dr. Bennett held to certain literary hypotheses regarding the composition of the text. Unlike these men, Professor Bennett allowed these presuppositions to influence certain aspects of his exposition. This tendency, however, is not sufficient to render his work valueless. In fact, those who are knowledgeable of such tendencies will find his treatment of I and II Chronicles exceedingly helpful.

While Dr. Bennett's exposition will need to be read with some caution, on account of his views regarding textual transmission, those who are seeking a clear and helpful exposition of the text will find that he provides them with rich insights that they can ill-afford to ignore. We all, at one time or another, need to remind ourselves of the words of Francis Bacon who, in his *Advancement of Learning*, wrote:

> ". . . the images of men's [genius] and knowledge remain in books, exempt from the wrong of time, and *capable of perpetual renovation.*"

No one need follow Dr. Bennett in his adherence to documentary theories of composition, *et cetera*. But they can and should "renovate" what he has written so that the "potency of life in them may be as active" as it was in him whose writings they now are privileged to handle.

Dr. Cyril J. Barber
Author, *The Minister's Library*

PREFACE

TO expound Chronicles in a series which has dealt with Samuel, Kings, Ezra, and Nehemiah is to glean scattered ears from a field already harvested. Sections common to Chronicles with the older histories have therefore been treated as briefly as is consistent with preserving the continuity of the narrative. Moreover, an exposition of Chronicles does not demand or warrant an attempt to write the history of Judah. To recombine with Chronicles matter which its author deliberately omitted would only obscure the characteristic teaching he intended to convey. On the one hand, his selection of material has a religious significance, which must be ascertained by careful comparison with Samuel and Kings; on the other hand, we can only do justice to the chronicler as we ourselves adopt, for the time being, his own attitude towards the history of Hebrew politics, literature, and religion. In the more strictly expository parts of this volume I have sought to confine myself to the carrying out of these principles.

Amongst other obligations to friends, I must specially mention my indebtedness to the Rev. T. H. Darlow, M.A., for a careful reading of the proof-sheets and many very valuable suggestions.

One object I have had in view has been to attempt to show the fresh force and clearness with which modern methods of Biblical study have emphasised the spiritual teaching of Chronicles.

CONTENTS

BOOK I

INTRODUCTION

BOOK II

GENEALOGIES

I CHRON. i.–ix., etc.

CHAPTER VIII

CHAPTER IX

CHAPTER X

CHAPTER XI

BOOK IV

THE INTERPRETATION OF HISTORY

2 CHRON. x.—end, etc.

CHAPTER I

CHAPTER II

CHAPTER III

CHAPTER IV

INDEX

(The larger figures in black type are the chief references)

1 Chronicles

BOOK I

INTRODUCTION

CHAPTER I

DATE AND AUTHORSHIP

CHRONICLES is a curious literary torso. A comparison with Ezra and Nehemiah shows that the three originally formed a single whole. They are written in the same peculiar late Hebrew style; they use their sources in the same mechanical way; they are all saturated with the ecclesiastical spirit; and their Church order and doctrine rest upon the complete Pentateuch, and especially upon the Priestly Code. They take the same keen interest in genealogies, statistics, building operations, Temple ritual, priests and Levites, and most of all in the Levitical doorkeepers and singers. Ezra and Nehemiah form an obvious continuation of Chronicles; the latter work breaks off in the middle of a paragraph intended to introduce the account of the return from the Captivity; Ezra repeats the beginning of the paragraph and gives its conclusion. Similarly the register of the high-priests is begun in 1 Chron. vi. 4-15 and completed in Neh. xii. 10, 11.

We may compare the whole work to the image in Daniel's vision whose head was of fine gold, his breast and arms of silver, his belly and his thighs of brass, his legs of iron, his feet part of iron and part of clay. Ezra and Nehemiah preserve some of the finest historical material in the Old Testament, and are our only

3

authority for a most important crisis in the religion of
Israel. The torso that remains when these two books
are removed is of very mixed character, partly borrowed
from the older historical books, partly taken down from
late tradition, and partly constructed according to the
current philosophy of history.

The date[1] of this work lies somewhere between the
conquest of the Persian empire by Alexander and the
revolt of the Maccabees, *i.e.*, between B.C. 332 and B.C.
166. The register in Neh. xii. 10, 11, closes with
Jaddua, the well-known high-priest of Alexander's
time ; the genealogy of the house of David in 1 Chron.
iii. extends to about the same date, or, according to
the ancient versions, even down to about B.C. 200.
The ecclesiastical system of the priestly code, established by Ezra and Nehemiah B.C. 444, was of such
old standing to the author of Chronicles that he introduces it as a matter of course into his descriptions
of the worship of the monarchy. Another feature
which even more clearly indicates a late date is the
use of the term " king of Persia " instead of simply
" the King " or " the Great King." The latter were
the customary designations of the Persian kings while
the empire lasted ; after its fall, the title needed to be
qualified by the name " Persia." These facts, together
with the style and language, would be best accounted
for by a date somewhere between B.C. 300 and B.C. 250.
On the other hand, the Maccabæan struggle revolu-
tionised the national and ecclesiastical system which
Chronicles everywhere takes for granted, and the silence
of the author as to this revolution is conclusive proof
that he wrote before it began.

---

[1] Cf. *Ezra* ; *Nehemiah* ; *Esther*, by Professor Adeney, in "Expositor's
Bible."

There is no evidence whatever as to the name of the author ; but his intense interest in the Levites and in the musical service of the Temple, with its orchestra and choir, renders it extremely probable that he was a Levite and a Temple-singer or musician. We might compare the Temple, with its extensive buildings and numerous priesthood, to an English cathedral establishment, and the author of Chronicles to some vicar-choral, or, perhaps better, to the more dignified precentor. He would be enthusiastic over his music, a cleric of studious habits and scholarly tastes, not a man of the world, but absorbed in the affairs of the Temple, as a monk in the life of his convent or a minor canon in the politics and society of the minster close. The times were uncritical, and so our author was occasionally somewhat easy of belief as to the enormous magnitude of ancient Hebrew armies and the splendour and wealth of ancient Hebrew kings ; the narrow range of his interests and experience gave him an appetite for innocent gossip, professional or otherwise. But his sterling religious character is shown by the earnest piety and serene faith which pervade his work. If we venture to turn to English fiction for a rough illustration of the position and history of our chronicler, the name that at once suggests itself is that of Mr. Harding, the precentor in *Barchester Towers*. We must however remember that there is very little to distinguish the chronicler from his later authorities ; and the term " chronicler " is often used for " the chronicler or one of his predecessors."

CHAPTER II

HISTORICAL SETTING

IN the previous chapter it has been necessary to deal
with the chronicler as the author of the whole
work of which Chronicles is only a part, and to go
over again ground already covered in the volume
on Ezra and Nehemiah; but from this point we can
confine our attention to Chronicles and treat it as a
separate book. Such a course is not merely justified,
it is necessitated, by the different relations of the
chronicler to his subject in Ezra and Nehemiah on the
one hand and in Chronicles on the other. In the
former case he is writing the history of the social and
ecclesiastical order to which he himself belonged, but
he is separated by a deep and wide gulf from the
period of the kingdom of Judah. About three hundred
years intervened between the chronicler and the
death of the last king of Judah. A similar interval
separates us from Queen Elizabeth; but the course of
these three centuries of English life has been an almost
unbroken continuity compared with the changing
fortunes of the Jewish people from the fall of the
monarchy to the early years of the Greek empire.
This interval included the Babylonian captivity and
the return, the establishment of the Law, the rise of
the Persian empire, and the conquests of Alexander.

The first three of these events were revolutions of supreme importance to the internal development of Judaism ; the last two rank in the history of the world with the fall of the Roman empire and the French Revolution. Let us consider them briefly in detail. The Captivity, the rise of the Persian empire, and the Return are closely connected, and can only be treated as features of one great social, political, and religious convulsion, an upheaval which broke the continuity of all the strata of Eastern life and opened an impassable gulf between the old order and the new. For a time, men who had lived through these revolutions were still able to carry across this gulf the loosely twisted strands of memory, but when they died the threads snapped ; only here and there a lingering tradition supplemented the written records. Hebrew slowly ceased to be the vernacular language, and was supplanted by Aramaic ; the ancient history only reached the people by means of an oral translation. Under this new dispensation the ideas of ancient Israel were no longer intelligible ; its circumstances could not be realised by those who lived under entirely different conditions. Various causes contributed to bring about this change. First, there was an interval of fifty years, during which Jerusalem lay a heap of ruins. After the recapture of Rome by Totila the Visigoth in A.D. 546 the city was abandoned during forty days to desolate and dreary solitude. Even this temporary depopulation of the Eternal City is emphasised by historians as full of dramatic interest, but the fifty years' desolation of Jerusalem involved important practical results. Most of the returning exiles must have either been born in Babylon or else have spent all their earliest years in exile. Very few can have been old enough to have

grasped the meaning or drunk in the spirit of the older
national life. When the restored community set to
work to rebuild their city and their temple, few of them
had any adequate knowledge of the old Jerusalem, with
its manners, customs, and traditions. "The ancient
men, that had seen the first house, wept with a loud
voice "[1] when the foundation of the second Temple
was laid before their eyes. In their critical and dis-
paraging attitude towards the new building, we may
see an early trace of the tendency to glorify and idealise
the monarchical period, which culminated in Chronicles.
The breach with the past was widened by the novel
and striking surroundings of the exiles in Babylon.
For the first time since the Exodus, the Jews as a
nation found themselves in close contact and intimate
relations with the culture of an ancient civilisation and
the life of a great city.

Nearly a century and a half elapsed between the
first captivity under Jehoiachin (B.C. 598) and the
mission of Ezra (B.C. 458); no doubt in the succeeding
period Jews still continued to return from Babylon to
Judæa, and thus the new community at Jerusalem,
amongst whom the chronicler grew up, counted
Babylonian Jews amongst their ancestors for two or
even for many generations. A Zulu tribe exhibited
for a year in London could not return and build their
kraal afresh and take up the old African life at the
point where they had left it. If a community of
Russian Jews went to their old home after a few years'
sojourn in Whitechapel, the old life resumed would be
very different from what it was before their migration.
Now the Babylonian Jews were neither uncivilised
African savages nor stupefied Russian helots; they

---

[1] Ezra iii. 12.

were not shut up in an exhibition or in a ghetto ; they settled in Babylon, not for a year or two, but for half a century or even a century ; and they did not return to a population of their own race, living the old life, but to empty homes and a ruined city. They had tasted the tree of new knowledge, and they could no more live and think as their fathers had done than Adam and Eve could find their way back into paradise. A large and prosperous colony of Jews still remained at Babylon, and maintained close and constant relations with the settlément in Judæa. The influence of Babylon, begun during the Exile, continued permanently in this indirect form. Later still the Jews felt the influence of a great Greek city, through their colony at Alexandria.

Besides these external changes, the Captivity was a period of important and many-sided development of Jewish literature and religion. Men had leisure to study the prophecies of Jeremiah and the legislation of Deuteronomy ; their attention was claimed for Ezekiel's suggestions as to ritual, and for the new theology, variously expounded by Ezekiel, the later Isaiah, the book of Job, and the psalmists. The Deuteronomic school systematised and interpreted the records of the national history. In its wealth of Divine revelation the period from Josiah to Ezra is only second to the apostolic age.

Thus the restored Jewish community was a new creation, baptised into a new spirit ; the restored city was as much a new Jerusalem as that which St. John beheld descending out of heaven ; and, in the words of the prophet of the Restoration, the Jews returned to a "new heaven and a new earth."[1] The rise of the

---

[1] Isa. lxvi. 22.

Persian empire changed the whole international system
of Western Asia and Egypt. The robber monarchies
of Nineveh and Babylon, whose energies had been
chiefly devoted to the systematic plunder of their
neighbours, were replaced by a great empire, that
stretched out one hand to Greece and the other to
India. The organisation of this great empire was the
most successful attempt at government on a large scale
that the world had yet seen. Both through the Persians
themselves and through their dealings with the Greeks,
Aryan philosophy and religion began to leaven Asiatic
thought ; old things were passing away : all things were
becoming new.

The establishment of the Law by Ezra and Nehemiah
was the triumph of a school whose most important and
effective work had been done at Babylon, though not
necessarily within the half-century specially called the
Captivity. Their triumph was retrospective : it not only
established a rigid and elaborate system unknown to
the monarchy, but, by identifying this system with the
law traditionally ascribed to Moses, it led men very
widely astray as to the ancient history of Israel. A
later generation naturally assumed that the good kings
must have kept this law, and that the sin of the bad
kings was their failure to observe its ordinances.

The events of the century and a half or thereabouts
between Ezra and the chronicler have only a minor
importance for us. The change of language from
Hebrew to Aramaic, the Samaritan schism, the few
political incidents of which any account has survived,
are all trivial compared to the literature and history
crowded into the century after the fall of the monarchy.
Even the far-reaching results of the conquests of
Alexander do not materially concern us here. Josephus

indeed tells us that the Jews served in large numbers
in the Macedonian army, and gives a very dramatic
account of Alexander's visit to Jerusalem ; but the
historical value of these stories is very doubtful, and in
any case it is clear that between B.C. 333 and B.C. 250
Jerusalem was very little affected by Greek influences,
and that, especially for the Temple community to which
the chronicler belonged, the change from Darius to
the Ptolemies was merely a change from one foreign
dominion to another.

Nor need much be said of the relation of the chronicler to the later Jewish literature of the Apocalypses
and Wisdom. If the spirit of this literature were
already stirring in some Jewish circles, the chronicler
himself was not moved by it. Ecclesiastes, as far as
he could have understood it, would have pained and
shocked him. But his work lay in that direct line of
subtle rabbinic teaching which, beginning with Ezra,
reached its climax in the Talmud. Chronicles is really
an anthology gleaned from ancient historic sources and
supplemented by early specimens of Midrash and
Hagada.

In order to understand the book of Chronicles, we
have to keep two or three simple facts constantly and
clearly in mind. In the first place, the chronicler was
separated from the monarchy by an aggregate of
changes which involved a complete breach of continuity
between the old and the new order : instead of a nation
there was a Church; instead of a king there were a high-
priest and a foreign governor. Secondly, the effects of
these changes had been at work for two or three
hundred years, effacing all trustworthy recollection
of the ancient order and schooling men to regard the
Levitical dispensation as their one original and antique

ecclesiastical system. Lastly, the chronicler himself belonged to the Temple community, which was the very incarnation of the spirit of the new order. With such antecedents and surroundings, he set to work to revise the national history recorded in Samuel and Kings. A monk in a Norman monastery would have worked under similar but less serious disadvantages if he had undertaken to rewrite the *Ecclesiastical History* of the Venerable Bede.

CHAPTER III

SOURCES AND MODE OF COMPOSITION

OUR impressions as to the sources of Chronicles are derived from the general character of its contents, from a comparison with other books of the Old Testament, and from the actual statements of Chronicles itself. To take the last first: there are numerous references to authorities in Chronicles which at first sight seem to indicate a dependence on rich and varied sources. To begin with, there are "The Book of the Kings of Judah and Israel,"[1] "The Book of the Kings of Israel and Judah,"[2] and "The Acts of the Kings of Israel."[3] These, however, are obviously different forms of the title of the same work.

Other titles furnish us with an imposing array of prophetic authorities. There are "The *Words*" of Samuel the Seer,[4] of Nathan the Prophet,[5] of Gad the Seer,[4] of Shemaiah the Prophet and of Iddo the Seer,[6]

---

[1] Quoted for *Asa* (2 Chron. xvi. 11); *Amaziah* (2 Chron. xxv. 26); *Ahas* (2 Chron. xxviii. 26).

[2] Quoted for *Jotham* (2 Chron. xxvii. 7) ; *Josiah* (2 Chron. xxxv. 26, 27).

[3] Quoted for *Manasseh* (2 Chron. xxxiii. 18).

[4] Quoted for *David* (1 Chron. xxix. 29).

[5] Quoted for *David* (1 Chron. xxix. 29) and *Solomon* (2 Chron. ix. 29).

[6] Quoted for *Rehoboam* (2 Chron. xii. 15).

13

of Jehu the son of Hanani,[1] and of the Seers[2];
"The *Vision*" of Iddo the Seer[3] and of Isaiah the
Prophet[4]; "The *Midrash*" of the Book of Kings[5] and
of the Prophet Iddo[6]; "The *Acts* of Uzziah," written
by Isaiah the Prophet[7]; and "The *Prophecy*" of
Ahijah the Shilonite.[8] There are also less formal
allusions to other works.

Further examination, however, soon discloses the
fact that these prophetic titles merely indicate different
sections of "The Book of the Kings of Israel and
Judah." On turning to our book of Kings, we find
that from Rehoboam onwards each of the references
in Chronicles corresponds to a reference by the book
of Kings to the "Chronicles[9] of the Kings of Judah."
In the case of Ahaziah, Athaliah, and Amon, the reference to an authority is omitted both in the books of
Kings and Chronicles. This close correspondence
suggests that both our canonical books are referring
to the same authority or authorities. Kings refers to
the "Chronicles of the Kings of Judah" for Judah, and
to the "Chronicles of the Kings of Israel" for the
northern kingdom; Chronicles, though only dealing
with Judah, combines these two titles in one: "The
Book of the Kings of Israel and Judah."

---

   [1] Quoted for *Jehoshaphat* (2 Chron. xx. 34).
   [2] Quoted for *Manasseh* (2 Chron. xxxiii. 19). "Seers," A.V., R.V.
Marg., with LXX.; R.V., with Hebrew text, "Hozai." The passage
is probably corrupt.
      [3] Quoted for *Solomon* (2 Chron. ix. 29).
      [4] Quoted for *Hezekiah* (2 Chron. xxxii. 32).
      [5] Quoted for *Joash* (2 Chron. xxiv. 27).
      [6] Quoted for *Abijah* (2 Chron. xiii. 22).
      [7] Quoted for *Uzziah* (2 Chron. xxvi. 22).
      [8] Quoted for *Solomon* (2 Chron. ix. 29).
      [9] Cf. pp. 17, 18.

In two instances Chronicles clearly states that its prophetic authorities were found as sections of the larger work. "The Words of Jehu the son of Hanani" were "inserted in the Book of the Kings of Israel," [1] and "The Vision of Isaiah the Prophet, the son of Amoz," is in the Book of the Kings of Judah and Israel. [2] It is a natural inference that the other "Words" and "Visions" were also found as sections of this same "Book of Kings."

These conclusions may be illustrated and supported by what we know of the arrangement of the contents of ancient books. Our convenient modern subdivisions of chapter and verse did not exist, but the Jews were not without some means of indicating the particular section of a book to which they wished to refer. Instead of numbers they used names, derived from the subject of a section or from the most important person mentioned in it. For the history of the monarchy the prophets were the most important personages, and each section of the history is named after its leading prophet or prophets. This nomenclature naturally encouraged the belief that the history had been originally written by these prophets. Instances of the use of such nomenclature are found in the New Testament, *e.g.*, Rom. xi. 2 : "Wot ye not what the Scripture saith in Elijah" [3] —*i.e.*, in the section about Elijah—and Mark xii. 26 : "Have ye not read in the book of Moses in the place concerning the bush ? " [4]

While, however, most of the references to "Words," "Visions," etc., are to sections of the larger work, we need not at once conclude that *all* references to authorities in Chronicles are to this same book. The

---

[1] 2 Chron. xx. 34.   [3] R.V. marg.
[2] 2 Chron. xxxii. 32. [4] R.V.

genealogical register in 1 Chron. v. 17 and the "lamentations" of 2 Chron. xxxv. 25 may very well be independent works. Having recognised the fact that the numerous authorities referred to by Chronicles were for the most part contained in one comprehensive "Book of Kings," a new problem presents itself : What are the respective relations of our Kings and Chronicles to the "Chronicles" and "Kings" cited by them ? What are the relations of these original authorities to each other ? What are the relations of our Kings to our Chronicles ? Our present nomenclature is about as confusing as it well could be ; and we are obliged to keep clearly in mind, first, that the "Chronicles" mentioned in Kings is not our Chronicles, and then that the "Kings" referred to by Chronicles is not our Kings. The first fact is obvious ; the second is shown by the terms of the references, which state that information not furnished in Chronicles may be found in the "Book of Kings," but the information in question is often not given in the canonical Kings.[1] And yet the connection between Kings and Chronicles is very close and extensive. A large amount of material occurs either identically or with very slight variations in both books. It is clear that either Chronicles uses Kings, or Chronicles uses a work which used Kings, or both Chronicles and Kings use the same source or sources. Each of these three views has been held by important authorities, and they are also capable of various combinations and modifications.

Reserving for a moment the view which specially commends itself to us, we may note two main tendencies of opinion. First, it is maintained that Chronicles

---

[1] *E.g.,* the wars of Jotham (2 Chron. xxvii. 7):

either goes back directly to the actual sources of Kings, citing them, for the sake of brevity, under a combined title, or is based upon a combination of the main sources of Kings made at a very early date. In either case Chronicles as compared with Kings would be an independent and parallel authority on the contents of these early sources, and to that extent would rank with Kings as first-class history. This view, however, is shown to be untenable by the numerous traces of a later age which are almost invariably present wherever Chronicles supplements or modifies Kings.

The second view is that either Chronicles used Kings, or that the " Book of the Kings of Israel and Judah " used by Chronicles was a post-Exilic work, incorporating statistical matter and dealing with the history of the two kingdoms in a spirit congenial to the temper and interests of the restored community. This "post-Exilic" predecessor of Chronicles is supposed to have been based upon Kings itself, or upon the sources of Kings, or upon both ; but in any case it was not much earlier than Chronicles and was written under the same influences and in a similar spirit. Being virtually an earlier edition of Chronicles, it could claim no higher authority, and would scarcely deserve either recognition or treatment as a separate work. Chronicles would still rest substantially on the authority of Kings.

It is possible to accept a somewhat simpler view, and to dispense with this shadowy and ineffectual first edition of Chronicles. In the first place, the chronicler does not appeal to the " Words " and " Visions " and the rest of his " Book of Kings " as authorities for his own statements ; he merely refers his reader to them for further information which he himself does not furnish. This " Book of Kings " so often mentioned

2

is therefore neither a source nor an authority of Chronicles. There is nothing to prove that the chronicler himself was actually acquainted with the book. Again, the close correspondence already noted between these references in Chronicles and the parallel notes in Kings suggests that the former are simply expanded and modified from the latter, and the chronicler had never seen the book he referred to. The Books of Kings had stated where additional information could be found, and Chronicles simply repeated the reference without verifying it. As some sections of Kings had come to be known by the names of certain prophets, the chronicler transferred these names back to the corresponding sections of the sources used by Kings. In these cases he felt he could give his readers not merely the somewhat vague reference to the original work as a whole, but the more definite and convenient citation of a particular paragraph. His descriptions of the additional subjects dealt with in the original authority may possibly, like other of his statements, have been constructed in accordance with his ideas of what that authority should contain ; or more probably they refer to this authority the floating traditions of later times and writers. Possibly these references and notes of Chronicles are copied from the glosses which some scribe had written in the margin of his copy of Kings. If this be so, we can understand why we find references to the Midrash of Iddo and the Midrash of the book of Kings.[1]

In any case, whether directly or through the medium of a preliminary edition, called "The Book of the Kings

---

[1] 2 Chron. xiii. 22 ; xxiv. 27. The LXX., however, does not read "Midrash" in either case ; and it is quite possible that glosses have attached themselves to the text of Chronicles.

of Israel and Judah," our book of Kings was used
by the chronicler. The supposition that the original
sources of Kings were used by the chronicler or this
immediate predecessor is fairly supported both by
evidence and authority, but on the whole it seems an
unnecessary complication.

Thus we fail to find in these various references to
the "Book of Kings," etc., any clear indication of the
origin of matter peculiar to Chronicles; nevertheless
it is not difficult to determine the nature of the sources
from which this material was derived. Doubtless some
of it was still current in the form of oral tradition when
the chronicler wrote, and owed to him its permanent
record. Some he borrowed from manuscripts, which
formed part of the scanty and fragmentary literature
of the later period of the Restoration. His genealogies
and statistics suggest the use of public and ecclesiastical
archives, as well as of family records, in which ancient
legend and anecdote lay embedded among lists of
forgotten ancestors. Apparently the chronicler harvested pretty freely from that literary aftermath that
sprang up when the Pentateuch and the earlier historical
books had taken final shape.

But it is to these earlier books that the chronicler
owes most. His work is very largely a mosaic of paragraphs and phrases taken from the older books. His
chief sources are Samuel and Kings; he also lays the
Pentateuch, Joshua, and Ruth under contribution. Much
is taken over without even verbal alteration, and the
greater part is unaltered in substance; yet, as is the
custom in ancient literature, no acknowledgment is
made. The literary conscience was not yet aware of
the sin of plagiarism. Indeed, neither an author nor
his friends took any pains to secure the permanent

association of his name with his work, and no great guilt can attach to the plagiarism of one anonymous writer from another. This absence of acknowledgment where the chronicler is plainly borrowing from elder scribes is another reason why his references to the " Book of the Kings of Israel and Judah " are clearly not statements of sources to which he is indebted, but simply what they profess to be : indications of the possible sources of further information.

Chronicles, however, illustrates ancient methods of historical composition, not only by its free appropriation of the actual form and substance of older works, but also by its curious blending of identical reproduction with large additions of quite heterogeneous matter, or with a series of minute but significant alterations. The primitive ideas and classical style of paragraphs from Samuel and Kings are broken in upon by the ritualistic fervour and late Hebrew of the chronicler's additions. The vivid and picturesque narrative of the bringing of the Ark to Zion is interpolated with uninteresting statistics of the names, numbers, and musical instruments of the Levites.[1]   Much of the chronicler's account of the revolution which overthrew Athaliah and placed Joash on the throne is taken word for word from the book of Kings ; but it is adapted to the Temple order of the Pentateuch by a series of alterations which substitute Levites for foreign mercenaries, and otherwise guard the sanctity of the Temple from the intrusion, not only of foreigners, but even of the common people.[2]   A careful comparison of Chronicles with Samuel and Kings is a striking object lesson in ancient historical composition.   It is

---

[1] Cf. 2 Sam. vi. 12–20 with 1 Chron. xv., xvi.
[2] Cf. 2 Kings xi. ; 2 Chron. xxiii.

an almost indispensable introduction to the criticism of the Pentateuch and the older historical books. The "redactor" of these works becomes no mere shadowy and hypothetical personage when we have watched his successor the chronicler piecing together things new and old and adapting ancient narratives to modern ideas by adding a word in one place and changing a phrase in another

CHAPTER IV

THE IMPORTANCE OF CHRONICLES

BEFORE attempting to expound in detail the religious significance of Chronicles, we may conclude our introduction by a brief general statement of the leading features which render the book interesting and valuable to the Christian student.

The material of Chronicles may be divided into three parts : the matter taken directly from the older historical books ; material derived from traditions and writings of the chronicler's own age ; the various additions and modifications which are the chronicler's own work.[1] Each of these divisions has its special value, and important lessons may be learnt from the way in which the author has selected and combined these materials.

The excerpts from the older histories are, of course, by far the best material in the book for the period of the monarchy. If Samuel and Kings had perished, we should have been under great obligations to the chronicler for preserving to us large portions of their

---

[1] The last two classes are not easily distinguished ; but the additions which introduce the Levitical system into earlier history are clearly the work of the chronicler or his immediate predecessor, if such a predecessor be assumed, or were found in somewhat late sources. This is also probably true of other explanatory matter.

ancient records. As it is, the chronicler has rendered invaluable service to the textual criticism of the Old Testament by providing us with an additional witness to the text of large portions of Samuel and Kings. The very fact that the character and history of Chronicles are so different from those of the older books enhances the value of its evidence as to their text. The two texts, Samuel and Kings on the one hand and Chronicles on the other, have been modified under different influences ; they have not always been altered in the same way, so that where one has been corrupted the other has often preserved the correct reading. Probably because Chronicles is less interesting and picturesque, its text has been subject to less alteration than that of Samuel and Kings. The more interested scribes or readers become, the more likely they are to make corrections and add glosses to the narrative. We may note, for example, that the name "Meribbaal" given by Chronicles for one of Saul's sons is more likely to be correct than "Mephibosheth," the form given by Samuel.[1]

The material derived from traditions and writings of the chronicler's own age is of uncertain historical value, and cannot be clearly discriminated from the author's free composition. Much of it was the natural product of the thought and feeling of the late Persian and early Greek period, and shares the importance which attaches to the chronicler's own work. This material, however, includes a certain amount of neutral matter : genealogies, family histories and anecdotes, and notes on ancient life and custom. We have no

---

[1] Cf. 2 Sam. iv. with 1 Chron. viii. 34, also 2 Sam. vii. 7 with 1 Chron. xvii. 6, and 2 Sam. xvii. 25 with 1 Chron. ii. 17. In both these instances Chronicles preserves the correct text.

parallel authorities to test this material, we cannot prove the antiquity of the sources from which it is derived, and yet it may contain fragments of very ancient tradition. Some of the notes and narratives have an archaic flavour which can scarcely be artificial; their very lack of importance is an argument for their authenticity, and illustrates the strange tenacity with which local and domestic tradition perpetuates the most insignificant episodes.[1]

But naturally the most characteristic, and therefore the most important, section of the contents of Chronicles is that made up of the additions and modifications which are the work of the chronicler or his immediate predecessors. It is unnecessary to point out that these do not add much to our knowledge of the history of the monarchy; their significance consists in the light that they throw upon the period towards whose close the chronicler lived: the period between the final establishment of Pentateuchal Judaism and the attempt of Antiochus Epiphanes to stamp it out of existence; the period between Ezra and Judas Maccabæus. The chronicler is no exceptional and epoch-making writer, has little personal importance, and is therefore all the more important as a typical representative of the current ideas of his class and generation. He translates the history of the past into the ideas and circumstances of his own age, and thus gives us almost as much information about the civil and religious institutions he lived under as if he had actually described them. Moreover, in stating its estimate of past history, each generation pronounces unconscious judgment upon itself. The chronicler's interpretation and philosophy

---

[1] Cf. Book II., Chap. IV.

of history mark the level of his moral and spiritual ideas. He betrays these quite as much by his attitude towards earlier authorities as in the paragraphs which are his own composition ; we have seen how his use of materials illustrates the ancient, and for that matter the modern, Eastern methods of historical composition, and we have shown the immense importance of Chronicles to Old Testament criticism. But the way in which the chronicler uses his older sources also indicates his relation towards the ancient morality, ritual, and theology of Israel. His methods of selection are most instructive as to the ideas and interests of his time. We see what was thought worthy to be included in this final and most modern edition of the religious history of Israel. But in truth the omissions are among the most significant features of Chronicles ; its silence is constantly more eloquent than its speech, and we measure the spiritual progress of Judaism by the paragraphs of Kings which Chronicles leaves out. In subsequent chapters we shall seek to illustrate the various ways in which Chronicles illuminates the period preceding the Maccabees. Any gleams of light on the Hebrew monarchy are most welcome, but we cannot be less grateful for information about those obscure centuries which fostered the quiet growth of Israel's character and faith and prepared the way for the splendid heroism and religious devotion of the Maccabæan struggle.

BOOK II

GENEALOGIES

CHAPTER I

NAMES

THE first nine chapters of Chronicles form, with a few slight exceptions, a continuous list of names. It is the largest extant collection of Hebrew names. Hence these chapters may be used as a text for the exposition of any spiritual significance to be derived from Hebrew names either individually or collectively. Old Testament genealogies have often exercised the ingenuity of the preacher, and the student of homiletics will readily recollect the methods of extracting a moral from what at first sight seems a barren theme. For instance, those names of which little or nothing is recorded are held up as awful examples of wasted lives. We are asked to take warning from Mahalalel and Methuselah, who spent their long centuries so ineffectually that there was nothing to record except that they begat sons and daughters and died. Such teaching is not fairly derived from its text. The sacred writers implied no reflection upon the Patriarchs of whom they gave so short and conventional an account. Least of all could such teaching be based upon the lists in Chronicles, because the men who are there merely mentioned by name include Adam, Noah, Abraham, and other heroes of sacred story. Moreover, such teaching is unnecessary and not altogether wholesome. Very few men who are at all capable of obtaining a permanent place in history need to be spurred on by sermons; and for most people the suggestion that a man's life is a failure unless he secures posthumous fame is false and mischievous. The Lamb's book of life is the only record of the vast majority of honourable and useful lives; and the tendency to self-advertisement is sufficiently wide-spread and spontaneous already: it needs no pulpit stimulus. We do not think any worse of a man because his tombstone simply states his name and age, or any better because it catalogues his virtues and mentions that he attained the dignity of alderman or author.

The significance of these lists of names is rather to be looked for in an opposite direction. It is not that a name and one or two commonplace incidents mean so little, but that they suggest so much. A mere parish register is not in itself attractive, but if we consider even such a list, the very names interest us and kindle our imagination. It is almost impossible to linger in a country churchyard, reading the half-effaced inscriptions upon the headstones, without forming some dim picture of the character and history and even the outward semblance of the men and women who once bore the names.

> "For though a name is neither
> . . . hand, nor foot,
> Nor arm, nor face, nor any other part
> Belonging to a man,"

yet, to use a somewhat technical phrase, it *connotes* a man. A name implies the existence of a distinct personality, with a peculiar and unique history, and yet, on the other hand, a being with whom we are linked in close sympathy by a thousand ties of common human nature and everyday experience. In its lists of what are now mere names, the Bible seems to recognise the dignity and sacredness of bare human life.

But the names in these nine chapters have also a collective significance : they stand for more than their individual owners. They are typical and representative, the names of kings, and priests, and captains ; they sum up the tribes of Israel, both as a Church and a nation, down all the generations of its history. The inclusion of these names in the sacred record, as the express introduction to the annals of the Temple, and the sacred city, and the elect house of David, is the formal recognition of the sanctity of the nation and of national life. We are entirely in the spirit of the Bible when we see this same sanctity in all organised societies : in the parish, the municipality, and the state ; when we attach a Divine significance to registers of electors and census returns, and claim all such lists as symbols of religious privilege and responsibility.

But names do not merely suggest individuals and communities : the meanings of the names reveal the ideas of the people who used them. It has been well said that "the names of every nation are an important monument of national spirit and manners, and thus the Hebrew names bear important testimony to the peculiar vocation of this nation. No nation of antiquity has such a proportion of names of religious import." [1] Amongst ourselves indeed the religious meaning of names has almost wholly faded away;

---

[1] Oehler, *Old Testament Theology*, i. 283 (Eng. trans.).

"Christian name" is a mere phrase, and children are named after relations, or according to prevailing fashion, or after the characters of popular novels. But the religious motive can still be traced in some modern names; in certain districts of Germany the name " Ursula " or "Apollonia" is a sure indication that a girl is a Roman Catholic and has been named after a popular saint.[1] The Bible constantly insists upon this religious significance, which would frequently be in the mind of the devout Israelite in giving names to his children. The Old Testament contains more than a hundred etymologies [2] of personal names, most of which attach a religious meaning to the words explained. The etymologies of the patriarchal names—"Abraham," father of a multitude of nations; "Isaac," laughter; "Jacob," supplanter; "Israel," prince with God—are specially familiar. The Biblical interest in edifying etymologies was maintained and developed by early commentators. Their philology was far from accurate, and very often they were merely playing upon the forms of words. But the allegorising tendencies of Jewish and Christian expositors found special opportunities in proper names. On the narrow foundation of an etymology mostly doubtful and often impossible, Philo, and Origen, and Jerome loved to erect an elaborate structure of theological or philosophical doctrine. Philo has only one quotation from our author: " Manasseh had sons, whom his Syrian concubine bare to him, Machir; and Machir begat Gilead." [3] He quotes this verse to show that recollection is associated in a subordinate capacity

---

[1] Nestle, *Die Israelitischen Eigennamen*, p. 27. The present chapter is largely indebted to this standard monograph.

[2] Nestle.

[3] 1 Chron. vii. 14.

with memory. The connection is not very clearly made
out, but rests in some way on the meaning of Manasseh,
the root of which means to forget. As forgetfulness
with recollection restores our knowledge, so Manasseh
with his Syrian concubine begets Machir. Recollection
therefore is a concubine, an inferior and secondary
quality.[1] This ingenious trifling has a certain charm
in spite of its extravagance, but in less dexterous
hands the method becomes clumsy as well as extravagant. It has, however, the advantage of readily
adapting itself to all tastes and opinions, so that we
are not surprised when an eighteenth-century author
discovers in Old Testament etymology a compendium
of Trinitarian theology.[2] *Ahiah*[3] is derived from *'ehad,*
one, and *yah,* Jehovah, and is thus an assertion of the
Divine unity ; *Reuel*[4] is resolved into a plural verb with
a singular Divine name for its subject : this is an indication of trinity in unity ; *Ahilud*[5] is derived from *'ehad,*
one, and *galud,* begotten, and signifies that the Son is
only-begotten.

Modern scholarship is more rational in its methods, but
attaches no less importance to these ancient names, and
finds in them weighty evidence on problems of criticism
and theology ; and before proceeding to more serious
matters, we may note a few somewhat exceptional names.
As pointed in the present Hebrew text, *Hazarmaveth*[6]
and *Azmaveth*[7] have a certain grim suggestiveness.
Hazarmaveth, court of death, is given as the name of
a descendant of Shem. It is, however, probably the
name of a place transferred to an eponymous ancestor,

---

[1] Philo, *De Cong. Quær. Erud. Grat.,* **8.**
[2] Hiller's *Onomasticon ap.,* Nestle **11.**
[3] vii. 8.
[4] i. 35.
[5] xviii. 15.
[6] i. 20.
[7] viii. 36.

and has been identified with *Hadramawt*, a district in
the south of Arabia. As, however, *Hadramawt*, is a
fertile district of Arabia Felix, the name does not seem
very appropriate. On the other hand, *Azmaveth*,
" strength of death," would be very suitable for some
strong, death-dealing soldier. *Azubah*,[1] " forsaken,"
the name of Caleb's wife, is capable of a variety of
romantic explanations. *Hazelelponi*[2] is remarkable in
its mere form ; and Ewald's interpretation, " Give shade,
Thou who turnest to me Thy countenance," seems
rather a cumbrous signification for the name of a
daughter of the house of Judah. *Jushab-hesed*,[3] " Mercy
will be renewed," as the name of a son of Zerubbabel,
doubtless expresses the gratitude and hope of the
Jews on their return from Babylon.[4] *Jashubi-lehem*,[5]
however, is curious and perplexing. The name has been
interpreted " giving bread " or " turning back to Bethlehem," but the text is certainly corrupt, and the passage
is one of many into which either the carelessness of
scribes or the obscurity of the chronicler's sources
has introduced hopeless confusion. But the most
remarkable set of names is found in 1 Chron. xxv. 4,
where *Giddalti* and *Romantiezer*, *Joshbekashah*, *Mallothi*,
Hothir, *Mahazioth*, are simply a Hebrew sentence
meaning, " I have magnified and exalted help ; sitting
in distress,[6] I have spoken[6] visions in abundance."
We may at once set aside the cynical suggestion that
the author lacked names to complete a genealogy and,
to save the trouble of inventing them separately, took
the first sentence that came to hand and cut it up into
suitable lengths, nor is it likely that a father would

---

[1] ii. 18.   [2] iii. 20.   [3] iv. 22.
[4] iv. 3.   [5] Bertheau, i.l.
[6] The translation of these words is not quite certain.

spread the same process over several years and adopt it for his family. This remarkable combination of names is probably due to some misunderstanding of his sources on the part of the chronicler. His parchment rolls must often have been torn and fragmentary, the writing blurred and half illegible ; and his attempts to piece together obscure and ragged manuscripts naturally resulted at times in mistakes and confusion.

These examples of interesting etymologies might easily be multiplied ; they serve, at any rate, to indicate a rich mine of suggestive teaching. It must, however, be remembered that a name is not necessarily a personal name because it occurs in a genealogy ; cities, districts, and tribes mingle freely with persons in these lists. In the same connection we note that the female names are few and far between, and that of those which do occur the " sisters " probably stand for allied and related families, and not for individuals.

As regards Old Testament theology, we may first notice the light thrown by personal names on the relation of the religion of Israel to that of other Semitic peoples. Of the names in these chapters and elsewhere, a large proportion are compounded of one or other of the Divine names. *El* is the first element in *Elishama, Eliphelet, Eliada,* etc. ; it is the second in *Othniel, Jehaleleel, Asareel,* etc. Similarly *Jehovah* is represented by the initial *Jeho-* in *Jehoshaphat, Jehoiakim, Jehoram,* etc., by the final *-iah* in *Amaziah, Azariah, Hezekiah,* etc. It has been calculated that there are a hundred and ninety names[1] beginning or ending with the equivalent of Jehovah, including most of the kings of Judah and many of the kings of Israel. Moreover, some names which have not these prefixes

---

[1] Nestle, p. 68.

and affixes in their extant form are contractions of older forms which began or ended with a Divine name. Ahaz, for instance, is mentioned in Assyrian inscriptions as Jahuhazi—*i.e.*, Jehoahaz—and Nathan is probably a contracted form of Nethaniah.

There are also numerous compounds of other Divine names. *Zur*, rock, is found in *Pedahzur*,[1] *Shaddai*, A.V. Almighty, in *Ammishaddai*[2]; the two are combined in *Zurishaddai*.[3] *Melech* is a Divine name in *Malchi-ram* and *Malchi-shua*. *Baal* occurs as a Divine name in *Eshbaal* and *Meribbaal*. *Abi*, father, is a Divine name in *Abiram*, *Abinadab*, etc., and probably also *Ahi* in *Ahiram* and *Ammi* in *Amminadab*.[4] Possibly, too, the apparently simple names *Melech*, *Zur*, *Baal*, are contractions of longer forms in which these Divine names were prefixes or affixes.

This use of Divine names is capable of very varied illustration. Modern languages have Christian and Christopher, Emmanuel, Theodosius, Theodora, etc.; names like Hermogenes and Heliogabalus are found in the classical languages. But the practice is specially characteristic of Semitic languages. Mohammedan princes are still called *Abdurrahman*, servant of the Merciful, and *Abdallah*, servant of God ; ancient Phœnician kings were named *Ethbaal* and *Abdalonim*, where *alonim* is a plural Divine name, and the *bal* in Hannibal and Hasdrubal = *baal*. The Assyrian and Chaldæan kings were named after the gods Sin, Nebo, Assur, Merodach, *e.g.*, *Sin-akki-irib* (Sennacherib); *Nebuchadnezzar* ; *Assur-bani-pal* ; *Merodach-baladan*.

Of these Divine names El and Baal are common to Israel and other Semitic peoples, and it has been held

---

[1] Num. i. 10.   [2] Num. i. 12.   [3] Num. i. 6.   [4] Cf. p. 40.

that the Hebrew personal names preserve **traces** of **po**lytheism. In any case, however, the Baal-names are comparatively few, and do not necessarily indicate that Israelites worshipped a Baal distinct from Jehovah ; they may be relics of a time when Baal (Lord) was a title or equivalent of Jehovah, like the later Adonai. Other possible traces of polytheism are few and doubtful. In Baanah and Resheph we may perhaps find the obscure [1] Phœnician deities Anath and Reshaph. On the whole, Hebrew names as compared, for instance, with Assyrian afford little or no evidence of the prevalence of polytheism.

Another question concerns the origin and use of the name Jehovah. Our lists conclusively prove its free use during the monarchy and its existence under the judges. On the other hand, its apparent presence in Jochebed, the name of the mother of Moses, seems to carry it back beyond Moses. Possibly it was a Divine name peculiar to his family or clan. Its occurrence in *Yahubidi*, a king of Hamath, in the time of Sargon may be due to direct Israelite influence. Hamath had frequent relations with Israel and Judah.

Turning to matters of practical religion, how far do these names help us to understand the spiritual life of ancient Israel ? The Israelites made constant use of El and Jehovah in their names, and we have no parallel practice. Were they then so much more religious than we are ? Probably in a sense they were. It is true that the etymology and even the original significance of a name in common use are for all practical purposes quickly and entirely forgotten. A man may go through a life-time bearing the name of Christopher and never know its etymological meaning. At Cambridge and

---

[1] xi. 30; vii. 25 (Nestle).

Oxford sacred names like "Jesus" and "Trinity" are used constantly and familiarly without suggesting anything beyond the colleges so called. The edifying phrase, "God encompasseth us," is altogether lost in the grotesque tavern sign "The Goat and Compasses." Nor can we suppose that the Israelite or the Assyrian often dwelt on the religious significance of the *Jeho-* or *-iah*, the *Nebo*, *Sin*, or *Merodach*, of current proper names. As we have seen, the sense of *-iah*, *-el*, or *Jeho-* was often so little present to men's minds that contractions were formed by omitting them. Possibly because these prefixes and affixes were so common, they came to be taken for granted; it was scarcely necessary to write them, because in any case they would be understood. Probably in historic times *Abi-*, *Ahi-*, and *Ammi-* were no longer recognised as Divine names or titles; and yet the names which could still be recognised as compounded of El and Jehovah must have had their influence on popular feeling. They were part of the religiousness, so to speak, of the ancient East; they symbolised the constant intertwining of religious acts, and words, and thoughts with all the concerns of life. The quality of this ancient religion was very inferior to that of a devout and intelligent modern Christian; it was perhaps inferior to that of Russian peasants belonging to the Greek Church: but ancient religion pervaded life and society more consciously than modern Christianity does; it touched all classes and occasions more directly, if also more mechanically. And, again, these names were not the fossil relics of obsolete habits of thought and feeling, like the names of our churches and colleges; they were the memorials of comparatively recent acts of faith. The name "Elijah" commemorated the

solemn occasion on which a father professed his own
faith and consecrated a new-born child to the true
God by naming his boy "Jehovah is my God." This
name-giving was also a prayer: the child was placed
under the protection of the deity whose name it bore.
The practice might be tainted with superstition; the
name would often be regarded as a kind of amulet;
and yet we may believe that it could also serve to
express a parent's earnest and simple-minded faith.
Modern Englishmen have developed a habit of almost
complete reticence and reserve on religious matters,
and this habit is illustrated by our choice of proper
names. Mary, and Thomas, and James are so familiar
that their Scriptural origin is forgotten, and therefore
they are tolerated; but the use of distinctively Scriptural Christian names is virtually regarded as bad
taste. This reticence is not merely due to increased
delicacy of spiritual feeling: it is partly the result of
the growth of science and of literary and historical
criticism. We have become absorbed in the wonderful
revelations of methods and processes; we are fascinated
by the ingenious mechanism of nature and society.
We have no leisure to detach our thoughts from the
machinery and carry them further on to its Maker and
Director. Indeed, because there is so much mechanism
and because it is so wonderful, we are sometimes asked
to believe that the machine made itself. But this is
a mere phase in the religious growth of mankind:
humanity will tire of some of its new toys, and will
become familiar with the rest; deeper needs and
instincts will reassert themselves; and men will find
themselves nearer in sentiment than they supposed
to the ancient people who named their children after
their God. In this and other matters the East to-day

is the same as of old ; the permanence of its custom is
no inapt symbol of the permanence of Divine truth,
which revolution and conquest are powerless to
change.

> "The East bowed low before the blast
> In patient, deep disdain ;
> She let the legions thunder past,
> And plunged in thought again."

But the Christian Church is mistress of a more compelling magic than even Eastern patience and tenacity :
out of the storms that threaten her, she draws new
energies for service, and learns a more expressive
language in which to declare the glory of God.

Let us glance for a moment at the meanings of the
group of Divine names given above. We have said
that, in addition to *Melech* in *Malchi-*, *Abi*, *Ahi*, and
Ammi are to be regarded as Divine names. One
reason for this is that their use as prefixes is strictly
analogous to that of *El* and *Jeho-*. We have *Abijah*
and *Ahijah* as well as *Elijah*, *Abiel* and *Ammiel* as
well as *Eliel*, *Abiram* and *Ahiram* as well as *Jehoram* ;
Ammishaddai compares with *Zurishaddai*, and *Ammi-
zabad* with *Jehozabad*, nor would it be difficult to add
many other examples. If this view be correct, *Ammi*
will have nothing to do with the Hebrew word for
" people," but will rather be connected with the corresponding Arabic word for " uncle."[1] As the use of
such terms as " brother " and " uncle " for Divine names
is not consonant with Hebrew theology in its historic
period, the names which contain these prefixes must
have come down from earlier ages, and were used in
later times without any consciousness of their original
sense. Probably they were explained by new etymo-

---

[1] Nestle.

logies more in harmony with the spirit of the times; compare the etymology "father of a multitude of nations" given to Abraham. Even *Abi-*, father, in the early times to which its use as a prefix must be referred, cannot have had the full spiritual meaning which now attaches to it as a Divine title. It probably only signified the ultimate source of life. The disappearance of these religious terms from the common vocabulary and their use in names long after their significance had been forgotten are ordinary phenomena in the development of language and religion. How many of the millions who use our English names for the days of the week ever give a thought to Thor or Freya? Such phenomena have more than an antiquarian interest. They remind us that religious terms, and phrases, and formulæ derive their influence and value from their adaptation to the age which accepts them; and therefore many of them will become unintelligible or even misleading to later generations. Language varies continuously, circumstances change, experience widens, and every age has a right to demand that Divine truth shall be presented in the words and metaphors that give it the clearest and most forcible expression. Many of the simple truths that are most essential to salvation admit of being stated once for all; but dogmatic theology fossilises fast, and the bread of one generation may become a stone to the next.

The history of these names illustrates yet another phenomenon. In some narrow and imperfect sense the early Semitic peoples seem to have called God "Father" and "Brother." Because the terms were limited to a narrow sense, the Israelites grew to a level of religious truth at which they could no longer use them; but as they made yet further progress they came to know more

of what was meant by fatherhood and brotherhood,
and gained also a deeper knowledge of God. At length
the Church resumed these ancient Semitic terms ; and
Christians call God " Abba, Father," and speak of the
Eternal Son as their elder Brother. And thus sometimes, but not always, an antique phrase may for a time
seem unsuitable and misleading, and then again may
prove to be the best expression for the newest and
fullest truth. Our criticism of a religious formula may
simply reveal our failure to grasp the wealth of meaning
which its words and symbols can contain.

Turning from these obsolete names to those in
common use—*El; Jehovah; Shaddai; Zur; Melech*—
probably the prevailing idea popularly associated with
them all was that of strength: *El*, strength in the
abstract; *Jehovah*, strength shown in permanence and
independence ; *Shaddai*, the strength that causes terror,
the Almighty from whom cometh destruction[1]; *Zur*,
rock, the material symbol of strength; *Melech*, king,
the possessor of authority. In early times the first
and most essential attribute of Deity is power, but
with this idea of strength a certain attribute of benefi-
cence is soon associated. The strong God is the Ally
of His people ; His permanence is the guarantee of their
national existence ; He destroys their enemies. The
rock is a place of refuge ; and, again, Jehovah's people
may rejoice in the shadow of a great rock in a weary
land. The King leads them to battle, and gives them
their enemies for a spoil.

---

[1] Joel i. 15; Isa. xiii. 6. It is not necessary here to discuss either
the etymological or the theological history of these words in their
earliest usage, nor need we do more than recall the fact that Jehovah
was the term in common use as the personal name of the God of
Israel, while El was rare and sometimes generic.

We must not, however, suppose that pious Israelites would consciously and systematically discriminate between these names, any more than ordinary Christians do between God, Lord, Father, Christ, Saviour, Jesus. Their usage would be governed by changing currents of sentiment very difficult to understand and explain after the lapse of thousands of years. In the year A.D. 3000, for instance, it will be difficult for the historian of dogmatics to explain accurately why some nineteenth-century Christians preferred to speak of "dear Jesus" and others of "the Christ."

But the simple Divine names reveal comparatively little; much more may be learnt from the numerous compounds they help to form. Some of the more curious have already been noticed, but the real significance of this nomenclature is to be looked for in the more ordinary and natural names. Here, as before, we can only select from the long and varied list. Let us take some of the favourite names and some of the roots most often used, almost always, be it remembered, in combination with Divine names. The different varieties of these sacred names rendered it possible to construct various personal names embodying the same idea. Also the same Divine name might be used either as prefix or affix. For instance, the idea that "God knows" is equally well expressed in the names *Eliada* (El-yada'), *Jediael* (Yada'-el), *Jehoiada* (Jeho-yada'), and *Jedaiah* (Yada'-yah). "God remembers" is expressed alike by *Zachariah* and *Jozachar*; "God hears" by *Elishama* (El-shama'), *Samuel* (if for Shama'-el), *Ishmael* (also from Shama'-el), *Shemaiah*, and *Ishmaiah* (*both from* Shama' *and* Yah); "God gives" by *Elnathan, Nethaneel, Jonathan,* and *Nethaniah*; "God helps" by *Eliezer, Azareel, Joezer,* and *Azariah*;

"God is gracious" by *Elhanan, Hananeel, Johanan, Hananiah, Baal-hanan,* and, for a Carthaginian, *Hannibal,* giving us a curious connection between the Apostle of love, John (Johanan), and the deadly enemy of Rome.

The way in which the changes are rung upon these ideas shows how the ancient Israelites loved to dwell upon them. Nestle reckons that in the Old Testament sixty-one persons have names formed from the root *nathan,* to give; fifty-seven from *shama,* to hear; fifty-six from *'azar,* to help; forty-five from *hanan,* to be gracious; forty-four from *zakhar,* to remember. Many persons, too, bear names from the root *yada',* to know. The favourite name is *Zechariah,* which is borne by twenty-five different persons.

Hence, according to the testimony of names, the Israelites' favourite ideas about God were that He heard, and knew, and remembered; that He was gracious, and helped men, and gave them gifts: but they loved best to think of Him as God the Giver. Their nomenclature recognises many other attributes, but these take the first place. The value of this testimony is enhanced by its utter unconsciousness and naturalness; it brings us nearer to the average man in his religious moments than any psalm or prophetic utterance. Men's chief interest in God was as the Giver. The idea has proved very permanent; St. James amplifies it: God is the Giver of every good and perfect gift. It lies latent in names: Theodosius, Theodore, Theodora, and Dorothea. The other favourite ideas are all related to this. God hears men's prayers, and knows their needs, and remembers them; He is gracious, and helps them by His gifts. Could anything be more pathetic than this artless self-revelation? Men's minds have

little leisure for sin and salvation; they are kept down
by the constant necessity of preserving and providing
for a bare existence. Their cry to God is like the
prayer of Jacob, "If Thou wilt give me bread to eat
and raiment to put on!" The very confidence and
gratitude that the names express imply periods of doubt
and fear, when they said, "Can God prepare a table
in the wilderness?" times when it seemed to them
impossible that God could have heard their prayer or
that He knew their misery, else why was there no
deliverance? Had God forgotten to be gracious? Did
He indeed remember? The names come to us as
answers of faith to these suggestions of despair.

Possibly these old-world saints were not more preoccupied with their material needs than most modern
Christians. Perhaps it is necessary to believe in a
God who rules on earth before we can understand the
Father who is in heaven. Does a man really trust in God
for eternal life if he cannot trust Him for daily bread?
But in any case these names provide us with very
comprehensive formulæ, which we are at liberty to
apply as freely as we please : the God who knows,
and hears, and remembers, who is gracious, and helps
men, and gives them gifts. To begin with, note how
in a great array of Old Testament names God is the
Subject, Actor, and Worker; the supreme facts of life
are God and God's doings, not man and man's doings,
what God is to man, not what man is to God. This is
a foreshadowing of the Christian doctrines of grace and
of the Divine sovereignty. And again we are left to
fill in the objects of the sentences for ourselves : God
hears, and remembers, and gives—what? All that we
have to say to Him and all that we are capable of
receiving from Him.

CHAPTER II

HEREDITY

IT has been said that Religion is the great discoverer
of truth, while Science follows her slowly and after
a long interval. Heredity, so much discussed just now,
is sometimes treated as if its principles were a great
discovery of the present century. Popular science is
apt to ignore history and to mistake a fresh nomenclature for an entirely new system of truth, and yet
the immense and far-reaching importance of heredity
has been one of the commonplaces of thought ever
since history began. Science has been anticipated, not
merely by religious feeling, but by a universal instinct.
In the old world political and social systems have been
based upon the recognition of the principle of heredity,
and religion has sanctioned such recognition. Caste
in India is a religious even more than a social institution ; and we use the term figuratively in reference to
ancient and modern life, even when the institution has
not formally existed. Without the aid of definite civil
or religious law the force of sentiment and circumstances suffices to establish an informal system of caste.
Thus the feudal aristocracy and guilds of the Middle
Ages were not without their rough counterparts in the
Old Testament. Moreover, the local divisions of the
Hebrew kingdoms corresponded in theory, at any rate,

to blood relationships; and the tribe, the clan, and the
family had even more fixity and importance than now
belong to the parish or the municipality. A man's
family history or genealogy was the ruling factor in
determining his home, his occupation, and his social
position. In the chronicler's time this was especially
the case with the official ministers of religion, the
Temple establishment to which he himself belonged.
The priests, the Levites, the singers, and doorkeepers
formed castes in the strict sense of the word. A man's
birth definitely assigned him to one of these classes, to
which none but the members of certain families could
belong.

But the genealogies had a deeper significance.
Israel was Jehovah's chosen people, His son, to whom
special privileges were guaranteed by solemn covenant.
A man's claim to share in this covenant depended on
his genuine Israelite descent, and the proof of such
descent was an authentic genealogy. In these chapters
the chronicler has taken infinite pains to collect
pedigrees from all available sources and to construct
a complete set of genealogies exhibiting the lines of
descent of the families of Israel. His interest in this
research was not merely antiquarian: he was investi-
gating matters of the greatest social and religious importance to all the members of the Jewish community, and
especially to his colleagues and friends in the Temple
service. These chapters, which seem to us so dry and
useless, were probably regarded by the chronicler's
contemporaries as the most important part of his work.
The preservation or discovery of a genealogy was
almost a matter of life and death. Witness the episode
in Ezra and Nehemiah[1]: "And of the priests: the

---

[1] Ezra ii. 61–63; Neh. vii. 63–65.

children of Hobaiah, the children of Hakkoz, the
children of Barzillai, which took a wife of the daughters
of Barzillai the Gileadite, and was called after their
name. These sought their register among those that
were reckoned by genealogy, but it was not found; therefore they were deemed polluted and put from the priesthood. And the governor said unto them that they
should not eat of the most holy things, till there stood
up a priest with Urim and Thummim." Cases like
these would stimulate our author's enthusiasm. As
he turned over dusty receptacles, and unrolled frayed
parchments, and painfully deciphered crabbed and
faded script, he would be excited by the hope of discovering some mislaid genealogy that would restore
outcasts to their full status and privileges as Israelites
and priests. Doubtless he had already acquired in
some measure the subtle exegesis and minute casuistry
that were the glory of later Rabbinism. Ingenious
interpretation of obscure writing or the happy emenda-
tion of half-obliterated words might lend opportune
aid in the recovery of a genealogy. On the other hand,
there were vested interests ready to protest against the
too easy acceptance of new claims. The priestly
families of undoubted descent from Aaron would not
thank a chronicler for reviving lapsed rights to a share
in the offices and revenues of the Temple. This
part of our author's task was as delicate as it was
important.

We will now briefly consider the genealogies in
these chapters in the order in which they are given.
Chap. i. contains genealogies of the patriarchal period
selected from Genesis. The existing races of the
world are all traced back through Shem, Ham, and
Japheth to Noah, and through him to Adam. The

chronicler thus accepts and repeats the doctrine of
Genesis that God made of one every nation of men for
to dwell on all the face of the earth.[1] All mankind,
"Greek and Jew, circumcision and uncircumcision,
barbarian, Scythian, bondman, freeman,"[2] were alike
descended from Noah, who was saved from the Flood
by the special care of God; from Enoch, who walked
with God; from Adam, who was created by God in His
own image and likeness. The Israelites did not claim,
like certain Greek clans, to be the descendants of a
special god of their own, or, like the Athenians, to have
sprung miraculously from sacred soil. Their genealogies
testified that not merely Israelite nature, but human
nature, is moulded on a Divine pattern. These apparently barren lists of names enshrine the great principles of the universal brotherhood of men and the
universal Fatherhood of God. The chronicler wrote
when the broad universalism of the prophets was being
replaced by the hard exclusiveness of Judaism; and yet,
perhaps unconsciously, he reproduces the genealogies
which were to be one weapon of St. Paul in his struggle
with that exclusiveness. The opening chapters of
Genesis and Chronicles are among the foundations of
the catholicity of the Church of Christ.

For the antediluvian period only the Sethite genealogy is given. The chronicler's object was simply to
give the origin of existing races; and the descendants of
Cain were omitted, as entirely destroyed by the Flood.

Following the example of Genesis, the chronicler
gives the genealogies of other races at the points at
which they diverged from the ancestral line of Israel,
and then continues the family history of the chosen
race. In this way the descendants of Japheth and

---

[1] Acts xvii. 26.   [2] Col. iii. 11.

Ham, the non-Abrahamic Semites, the Ishmaelites, the sons of Keturah, and the Edomites are successively mentioned.

The relations of Israel with Edom were always close and mostly hostile. The Edomites had taken advantage of the overthrow of the southern kingdom to appropriate the south of Judah, and still continued to occupy it. The keen interest felt by the chronicler in Edom is shown by the large space devoted to the Edomites. The close contiguity of the Jews and Idumæans tended to promote mutual intercourse between them, and even threatened an eventual fusion of the two peoples. As a matter of fact, the Idumæan Herods became rulers of Judæa. To guard against such dangers to the separateness of the Jewish people, the chronicler emphasises the historical distinction of race between them and the Edomites.

From the beginning of the second chapter onwards the genealogies are wholly occupied with Israelites. The author's special interest in Judah is at once manifested. After giving the list of the twelve Patriarchs he devotes two and a half chapters to the families of Judah. Here again the materials have been mostly obtained from the earlier historical books. They are, however, combined with more recent traditions, so that in this chapter matter from different sources is pieced together in a very confusing fashion. One source of this confusion was the principle that the Jewish community could only consist of families of genuine Israelite descent. Now a large number of the returned exiles traced their descent to two brothers, Caleb and Jerahmeel; but in the older narratives Caleb and Jerahmeel are not Israelites. Caleb is a Kenizzite,[1] and his de-

---

[1] Josh. xiv. 6,

scendants and those of Jerahmeel appear in close
connection with the Kenites.[1] Even in this chapter
certain of the Calebites are called Kenites and connected
in some strange way with the Rechabites.[2] Though
at the close of the monarchy the Calebites and Jerahmeelites had become an integral part of the tribe of
Judah, their separate origin had not been forgotten,
and Caleb and Jerahmeel had not been included in the
Israelite genealogies. But after the Exile men came
to feel more and more strongly that a common faith
implied unity of race. Moreover, the practical unity
of the Jews with these Kenizzites overbore the dim
and fading memory of ancient tribal distinctions. Jews
and Kenizzites had shared the Captivity, the Exile, and
the Return; they worked, and fought, and worshipped
side by side; and they were to all intents and purposes
one nation, alike the people of Jehovah. This obvious
and important practical truth was expressed as such
truths were then wont to be expressed. The children
of Caleb and Jerahmeel were finally and formally
adopted into the chosen race. Caleb and Jerahmeel
are no longer the sons of Jephunneh the Kenizzite;
they are the sons of Hezron, the son of Perez, the son
of Judah.[3] A new genealogy was formed as a recognition rather than an explanation of accomplished facts.

Of the section containing the genealogies of Judah,
the lion's share is naturally given to the house of
David, to which a part of the second chapter and the
whole of the third are devoted.

---

[1] 1 Sam. xxvii. 10.

[2] Ver. 55.

[3] The occurrence of Caleb the son of Jephunneh in iv. 15, vi. 56,
in no way militates against this view: the chronicler, like other
redactors, is simply inserting borrowed material without correcting it.
Chelubai in ii. 9 stands for *Caleb*; cf. ii. 18.

Next follow genealogies of the remaining tribes, those of Levi and Benjamin being by far the most complete. Chap. vi., which is devoted to Levi, affords evidence of the use by the chronicler of independent and sometimes inconsistent sources, and also illustrates his special interest in the priesthood and the Temple choir. A list of high-priests from Aaron to Ahimaaz is given twice over (vv. 4–8 and 49–53), but only one line of high-priests is recognised, the house of Zadok, whom Josiah's reforms had made the one priestly family in Israel. Their ancient rivals the high-priests of the house of Eli are as entirely ignored as the antediluvian Cainites. The existing high-priestly dynasty had been so long established that these other priests of Saul and David seemed no longer to have any significance for the religion of Israel.

The pedigree of the three Levitical families of Gershom, Kohath, and Merari is also given twice over: in vv. 16–30 and 31–49. The former pedigree begins with the sons of Levi, and proceeds to their descendants; the latter begins with the founders of the guilds of singers, Heman, Asaph, and Ethan, and traces back their genealogies to Kohath, Gershom, and Merari respectively. But the pedigrees do not agree; compare, for instance, the lists of the Kohathites :—

22–24.	36–38.
Kohath	Kohath
Amminadab	*Izhar*
Korah	Korah
Assir	
Elkanah	
Ebiasaph	Ebiasaph
Assir	Assir

22–24.	36–38
Tahath	Tahath
Uriel	*Zephaniah*
Uzziah	*Azariah*
Shaul	etc.

We have here one of many illustrations of the fact that the chronicler used materials of very different value. To attempt to prove the absolute consistency of all his genealogies would be mere waste of time. It is by no means certain that he himself supposed them to be consistent. The frank juxtaposition of varying lists of ancestors rather suggests that he was prompted by a scholarly desire to preserve for his readers all available evidence of every kind.

In reading the genealogies of the tribe of Benjamin, it is specially interesting to find that in the Jewish community of the Restoration there were families tracing their descent through Mephibosheth and Jonathan to Saul.[1] Apparently the chronicler and his contemporaries shared this special interest in the fortunes of a fallen dynasty, for the genealogy is given twice over. These circumstances are the more striking because in the actual history of Chronicles Saul is all but ignored.

The rest of the ninth chapter deals with the inhabitants of Jerusalem and the ministry of the Temple after the return from the Captivity, and is partly identical with sections of Ezra and Nehemiah. It closes the family history, as it were, of Israel, and its position indicates the standpoint and ruling interests of the chronicler.

---

[1] viii. 33–40; ix. 35–44. We have used Mephibosheth as more familiar, but Chronicles reads Meribbaal, which is more correct.

Thus the nine opening chapters of genealogies and kindred matter strike the key-notes of the whole book. Some are personal and professional ; some are religious. On the one hand, we have the origin of existing families and institutions ; on the other hand, we have the election of the tribe of Judah and the house of David, of the tribe of Levi and the house of Aaron.

Let us consider first the hereditary character of the Jewish religion and priesthood. Here, as elsewhere, the formal doctrine only recognised and accepted actual facts. The conditions which received the sanction of religion were first imposed by the force of circumstances. In primitive times, if there was to be any religion at all, it had to be national; if God was to be worshipped at all, His worship was necessarily national, and He became in some measure a national God. Sympathies are limited by knowledge and by common interest. The ordinary Israelite knew very little of any other people than his own. There was little international comity in primitive times, and nations were slow to recognise that they had common interests. It was difficult for an Israelite to believe that his beloved Jehovah, in whom he had been taught to trust, was also the God of the Arabs and Syrians, who periodically raided his crops, and cattle, and slaves, and sometimes carried off his children, or of the Chaldæans, who made deliberate and complete arrangements for plundering the whole country, rasing its cities to the ground, and carrying away the population into distant exile. By a supreme act of faith, the prophets claimed the enemies and oppressors of Israel as instruments of the will of Jehovah, and the chronicler's genealogies show that he shared this faith ; but it was still inevitable that the Jews should look out upon the world at

large from the standpoint of their own national interests
and experience.   Jehovah was God of heaven and
earth ; but Israelites knew Him through the deliverance
He had wrought for Israel, the punishments He had
inflicted on her sins, and the messages He had entrusted
to her prophets.   As far as their knowledge and
practical experience went, they knew Him as the God
of Israel. The course of events since the fall of
Samaria narrowed still further the local associations
of Hebrew worship.

> " God was wroth,
>   And greatly abhorred Israel,
>   So that He forsook the tabernacle of Shiloh,
>   The tent which He placed among men ;
>
>   *   *   *   *   *
>
>   He refused the tent of Joseph,
>   And chose not the tribe of Ephraim,
>   But chose the tribe of Judah,
>   The Mount Zion which He loved :
>   And He built His sanctuary like the heights,
>   Like the earth, which He hath established for ever." [1]

We are doubtless right in criticising those Jews whose
limitations led them to regard Jehovah as a kind of personal possession, the inheritance of their own nation, and
not of other peoples.   But even here we can only blame
their negations.   Jehovah *was* their inheritance and
personal possession ; but then He was also the inheritance of other nations.   This Jewish heresy is by no
means extinct : white men do not always believe that
their God is equally the God of the negro ; Englishmen
are inclined to think that God is the God of England in
a more especial way than He is the God of France.
When we discourse concerning God in history, we

---

[1] Psalm lxxviii. 59, 60, 67-69.

mostly mean our own history. We can see the hand
of Providence in the wreck of the Armada and the
overthrow of Napoleon ; but we are not so ready to
recognise in the same Napoleon the Divine instrument
that created a new Europe by relieving her peoples
from cruel and degrading tyranny. We scarcely realise
that God cares as much for the Continent as He does
for our island.

We have great and perhaps sufficient excuses, but
we must let the Jews have the benefit of them. God is
as much the God of one nation as of another ; but He
fulfils Himself to different nations in different ways, by
a various providential discipline. Each people is bound
to believe that God has specially adapted His dealings
to its needs, nor can we be surprised if men forget or
fail to observe that God has done no less for their
neighbours. Each nation rightly regards its religious
ideas, and life, and literature as a precious inheritance
peculiarly its own ; and it should not be too severely
blamed for being ignorant that other nations have their
inheritance also. Such considerations largely justify
the interest in heredity shown by the chronicler's
genealogies. On the positive, practical side, religion
is largely a matter of heredity, and ought to be. The
Christian sacrament of baptism is a continual profession
of this truth : our children are " clean " ; they are within
the covenant of grace ; we claim for them the privileges
of the Church to which we belong. That was also part
of the meaning of the genealogies.

In the broad field of social and religious life the
problems of heredity are in some ways less complicated
than in the more exact discussions of physical science.
Practical effects can be considered without attempting
an accurate analysis of causes. Family history not

only determines physical constitution, mental gifts, and moral character, but also fixes for the most part country, home, education, circumstances, and social position. All these were a man's inheritance more peculiarly in Israel than with us; and in many cases in Israel a man was often trained to inherit a family profession. Apart from the ministry of the Temple, we read of a family of craftsmen, of other families that were potters, of others who dwelt with the king for his work, and of the families of the house of them that wrought fine linen.[1] Religion is largely involved in the manifold inheritance which a man receives from his fathers. His birth determines his religious education, the examples of religious life set before him, the forms of worship in which as a child he takes part. Most men live and die in the religion of their childhood; they worship the God of their fathers; Romanist remains Romanist: Protestant remains Protestant. They may fail to grasp any living faith, or may lose all interest in religion; but such religion as most men have is part of their inheritance. In the Israel of the chronicler faith and devotion to God were almost always and entirely inherited. They were part of the great debt which a man owed to his fathers.

The recognition of these facts should tend to foster our humility and reverence, to encourage patriotism and philanthropy. We are the creatures and debtors of the past, though we are slow to own our obligations. We have nothing that we have not received; but we are apt to consider ourselves self-made men, the architects and builders of our own fortunes, who have the right to be self-satisfied, self-assertive, and selfish. The heir of all the ages, in the full vigour of youth, takes his place

---

[1] iv. 14, 21-23.

in the foremost ranks of time, and marches on in the happy consciousness of profound and multifarious wisdom, immense resources, and magnificent opportunity. He forgets or even despises the generations of labour and anguish that have built up for him his great inheritance. The genealogies are a silent protest against such insolent ingratitude. They remind us that in bygone days a man derived his gifts and received his opportunities from his ancestors ; they show us men as the links in a chain, tenants for life, as it were, of our estate, called upon to pay back with interest to the future the debt which they have incurred to the past. We see that the chain is a long one, with many links ; and the slight estimate we are inclined to put upon the work of individuals in each generation recoils upon our own pride. We also are but individuals of a generation that is only one of the thousands needed to work out the Divine purpose for mankind. We are taught the humility that springs from a sense of obligation and responsibility.

We learn reverence for the workers and achievements of the past, and most of all for God. We are reminded of the scale of the Divine working :—

> "A thousand years in Thy sight
> Are but as yesterday when it is past
> And as a watch in the night."

A genealogy is a brief and pointed reminder that God has been working through all the countless generations behind us. The bare series of names is an expressive diagram of His mighty process. Each name in the earlier lists stands for a generation or even for several generations. The genealogies go back into dim, prehistoric periods ; they suggest a past too remote for our imagining. And yet they take us back to Adam, to the very beginning of human life. From that beginning, however many thousands or tens of thousands of years ago, the life of man has been sacred, the object of the Divine care and love, the instrument of the Divine purpose.

Later on we see the pedigree of our race dividing into countless branches, all of which are represented in this sacred diagram of humanity. The Divine working not only extends over all time, but also embraces all the complicated circumstances and relationships of the families of mankind. These genealogies suggest a lesson probably not intended by the chronicler. We recognise the unique character of the history of Israel, but in some measure we discern in this one full and detailed narrative of the chosen people a type of the history of every race. Others had not the election of Israel, but each had its own vocation. God's power, and wisdom, and love are manifested in the history of one chosen people on a scale commensurate with our limited faculties, so that we may gain some faint idea of the marvellous providence in *all* history of the Father from whom *every* family in heaven and on earth is named.

Another principle closely allied to heredity and also discussed in modern times is the solidarity of the race. Humanity is supposed to possess something akin to a common consciousness, personality, or individuality. Such a quality evidently becomes more intense as we narrow its scope from the race to the nation, the clan, and the family ; it has its roots in family relationships. Tribal, national, humanitarian feelings indicate that the larger societies have taken upon themselves something of the character of the

family.   Thus the common feelings and mutual
sympathies of mankind are due ultimately to blood
relationship.   The genealogies that set forth family
histories are the symbols of this brotherhood or
solidarity of our race.   The chart of converging lines
of ancestors in Israel carried men's minds back from
the separate families to their common ancestor ; again,
the ancestry of ancestors led back to a still earlier
common origin, and the process continued till all the
lines met in Noah.   Each stage of the process enlarged
the range of every man's kinship, and broadened
the natural area of mutual help and affection.   It is
true that the Jews failed to learn this larger lesson
from their genealogies, but within their own community they felt intensely the bond of kinship and
brotherhood.   Modern patriotism reproduces the strong
Jewish national feeling, and our humanitarianism is
beginning to extend it to the whole world.   By this
time the facts of heredity have been more carefully
studied and are better understood.   If we drew up
typical genealogies now, they would more fully and
accurately represent the mutual relationships of our
people.   As far as they go, the chronicler's genealogies
form a clear and instructive diagram of the mutual
dependence of man on man and family on family.
The value of the diagram does not require the accuracy
of the actual names any more than the validity
of Euclid requires the actual existence of triangles
called A B C, D E F.   These genealogies are in any
case a true symbol of the facts of family relations ;
but they are drawn, so to speak, in one dimension only,
backwards and forwards in time.   Yet the real family
life exists in three dimensions.   There are numerous
cross-relations, cousinship of all degrees, as well as

sonship and brotherhood. A man has not merely his male ancestors in the directly ascending line—father, grandfather, great-grandfather, etc.—but he has female ancestors as well. By going back three or four generations a man is connected with an immense number of cousins ; and if the complete network of ten or fifteen generations could be worked out, it would probably show some blood bond throughout a whole nation. Thus the ancestral roots of a man's life and character have wide ramifications in the former generations of his people. The further we go back the larger is the element of ancestry common to the different individuals of the same community. The chronicler's genealogies only show us individuals as links in a set of chains. The more complete genealogical scheme would be better illustrated by the ganglia of the nervous system, each of which is connected by numerous nerve fibres with the other ganglia. The Church has been compared to the body, "which is one, and hath many members, and all the members of the body, being many, are one body." Humanity, by its natural kinship, is also such a body ; the nation is still more truly " one body."   Patriotism and humanity are instincts as natural and as binding as those of the family ; and the genealogies express or symbolise the wider family ties, that they may commend the virtues and enforce the duties that arise out of these ties.

Before closing this chapter something may be said on one or two special points. Women are virtually ignored in these genealogies, a fact that rather indicates a failure to recognise their influence than the absence of such influence. Here and there a woman is mentioned for some special reason. For instance, the names of Zeruiah and Abigail are inserted in order to show that Joab, Abishai, and Asahel, together with Amasa, were all cousins of David. The same keen interest in David leads the chronicler to record the names of his wives. It is noteworthy that of the four women who are mentioned in St. Matthew's genealogy of our Lord only two—Tamar and Bath-shua (*i.e.*, Bathsheba)—are mentioned here. Probably St. Matthew was careful to complete the list because Rahab and Ruth, like Tamar and possibly Bath-sheba, were foreigners, and their names in the genealogy indicated a connection between Christ and the Gentiles, and served to emphasise His mission to be the Saviour of the world.

Again, much caution is necessary in applying any principle ·of heredity. A genealogy, as we have seen, suggests our dependence in many ways upon our ancestry. But a man's relations to his kindred are many and complicated ; a quality, for instance, may be latent for one or more generations and then reappear, so that to all appearance a man inherits from his grandfather or from a more remote ancestor rather than from his father or mother. Conversely the presence of certain traits of character in a child does not show that any corresponding tendency has necessarily been active in the life of either parent. Neither must the influence of circumstances be confounded with that of heredity. Moreover, very large allowance must be made for our ignorance of the laws that govern the human will, an ignorance that will often baffle our attempts to find in heredity any simple explanation of men's characters and actions. Thomas Fuller has a quaint " Scripture observation " that gives an important practical application of these principles :—

" Lord, I find the genealogy of my Saviour strangely

chequered with four remarkable changes in four immediate generations :

"1. 'Rehoboam begat Abiam'; that is, a bad father begat a bad son.

"2. 'Abiam begat Asa'; that is, a bad father a good son.

"3. 'Asa begat Jehosaphat'; that is, a good father a good son.

"4. 'Jehosaphat begat Joram'; that is, a good father a bad son.

"I see, Lord, from hence that my father's piety cannot be entailed ; that is bad news for me. But I see also that actual impiety is not always hereditary ; that is good news for my son."

CHAPTER III

STATISTICS

STATISTICS play an important part in Chronicles and in the Old Testament generally. To begin with, there are the genealogies and other lists of names, such as the lists of David's counsellors and the roll of honour of his mighty men. The chronicler specially delights in lists of names, and most of all in lists of Levitical choristers. He gives us lists of the orchestras and choirs who performed when the Ark was brought to Zion[1] and at Hezekiah's passover,[2] also a list of Levites whom Jehoshaphat sent out to teach in Judah.[3] No doubt family pride was gratified when the chronicler's contemporaries and friends read the names of their ancestors in connection with great events in the history of their religion. Possibly they supplied him with the information from which these lists were compiled. An incidental result of the celibacy of the Romanist clergy has been to render ancient ecclesiastical genealogies impossible; modern clergymen cannot trace their descent to the monks who landed with Augustine. Our genealogies might enable a historian to construct lists of the combatants at Agincourt and Hastings; but the Crusades are the only wars of the

---

[1] 1 Chron. xv.   [2] 2 Chron. xvii. 8.
[3] Cf. 2 Chron. xxix. 12 and xxx. 22.

Church militant for which modern pedigrees could furnish a muster-roll.

We find also in the Old Testament the specifications and subscription-lists for the Tabernacle and for Solomon's temple.[1] These statistics, however, are not furnished for the second Temple, probably for the same reason that in modern subscription-lists the donors of shillings and half-crowns are to be indicated by initials, or described as " friends " and " sympathisers," or massed together under the heading " smaller sums."

The Old Testament is also rich in census returns and statements as to the numbers of armies and of the divisions of which they were composed. There are the returns of the census taken twice in the wilderness and accounts of the numbers of the different families who came from Babylon with Zerubbabel and later on with Ezra; there is a census of the Levites in David's time according to their several families[2]; there are the numbers of the tribal contingents that came to Hebron to make David king,[3] and much similar information.

Statistics therefore occupy a conspicuous position in the inspired record of Divine revelation, and yet we often hesitate to connect such terms as " inspiration " and " revelation " with numbers, and names, and details of civil and ecclesiastical organisation. We are afraid lest any stress laid on purely accidental details should distract men's attention from the eternal essence of the Gospel, lest any suggestion that the certainty of Christian truth is dependent on the accuracy of these statistics should become a stumbling-block and destroy

---

[1] Exod. xxv–xxxix. ; 1 Kings vi. ; 1 Chron. xxix. ; 2 Chron. iii., v.
[2] 1 Chron. xv. 4–10.
[3] 1 Chron. xii. 23–37.

the faith of some. Concerning such matters there have been many foolish questions of genealogies, profane and vain babblings, which have increased unto more ungodliness. Quite apart from these, even in the Old Testament a sanctity attaches to the number seven, but there is no warrant for any considerable expenditure of time and thought upon mystical arithmetic. A symbolism runs through the details of the building, furniture, and ritual alike of the Tabernacle and the Temple, and this symbolism possesses a legitimate religious significance ; but its exposition is not specially suggested by the book of Chronicles. The exposition of such symbolism is not always sufficiently governed by a sense of proportion. Ingenuity in supplying subtle interpretations of minute details often conceals the great truths which the symbols are really intended to enforce. Moreover, the sacred writers did not give statistics merely to furnish materials for Cabbala and Gematria or even to serve as theological types and symbols. Sometimes their purpose was more simple and practical. If we knew all the history of the Tabernacle and Temple subscription-lists, we should doubtless find that they had been used to stimulate generous gifts towards the erection of the second Temple. Preachers for building funds can find abundance of suitable texts in Exodus, Kings, and Chronicles.

But Biblical statistics are also examples in accuracy and thoroughness of information, and recognitions of the more obscure and prosaic manifestations of the higher life. Indeed, in these and other ways the Bible gives an anticipatory sanction to the exact sciences.

The mention of accuracy in connection with Chronicles may be received by some readers with a contemptuous smile. But we are indebted to the chronicler for exact and full information about the Jews who returned from Babylon ; and in spite of the extremely severe judgment passed upon Chronicles by many critics, we may still venture to believe that the chronicler's statistics are as accurate as his knowledge and critical training rendered possible. He may sometimes give figures obtained by calculation from uncertain data, but such a practice is quite consistent with honesty and a desire to supply the best available information. Modern scholars are quite ready to present us with figures as to the membership of the Christian Church under Antoninus Pius or Constantine ; and some of these figures are not much more probable than the most doubtful in Chronicles. All that is necessary to make the chronicler's statistics an example to us is that they should be the monument of a conscientious attempt to tell the truth, and this they undoubtedly are.

This Biblical example is the more useful because statistics are often evil spoken of, and they have no outward attractiveness to shield them from popular prejudice. We are told that " nothing is so false as statistics," and that " figures will prove anything "; and the polemic is sustained by works like *Hard Times* and the awful example of Mr. Gradgrind. Properly understood, these proverbs illustrate the very general impatience of any demand for exact thought and expression. If " figures " will prove anything, so will texts.

Though this popular prejudice cannot be altogether ignored, yet it need not be taken too seriously. The opposite principle, when stated, will at once be seen to be a truism. For it amounts to this : exact and comprehensive knowledge is the basis of a right understanding of history, and is a necessary condition of right action This principle is often neglected because it is obvious. Yet, to illustrate it from our author, a knowledge of the size and plan of the Temple greatly adds to the vividness of our pictures of Hebrew religion. We apprehend later Jewish life much more clearly with the aid of the statistics as to the numbers, families, and settlements of the returning exiles; and similarly the account-books of the bailiff of an English estate in the fourteenth century are worth several hundred pages of contemporary theology. These considerations may encourage those who perform the thankless task of compiling the statistics, subscription-lists, and balance-sheets of missionary and philanthropic societies. The zealous and intelligent historian of Christian life and service will need these dry records to enable him to understand his subject, and the highest literary gifts may be employed in the eloquent exposition of these apparently uninteresting facts and figures. Moreover, upon the accuracy of these records depends the possi-bility of determining a true course for the future. Neither societies nor individuals, for instance, can afford to live beyond their income without knowing it.

Statistics, too, are the only form in which many acts of service can be recognised and recorded. Literature can only deal with typical instances, and naturally it selects the more dramatic. The missionary report can only tell the story of a few striking conversions; it may give the history of the exceptional self-denial involved in one or two of its subscriptions; for the rest we must be content with tables and subscription-lists. But these dry statistics represent an infinitude of patience and self-denial, of work and prayer, of Divine grace and blessing. The city missionary may narrate his experiences with a few inquirers and penitents, but the great bulk of his work can only be recorded in the statement of visits paid and services conducted. We are tempted sometimes to disparage these statements, to ask how many of the visits and services had any result; we are impatient sometimes because Christian work is estimated by any such numerical line and measure. No doubt the method has many defects, and must not be used too mechanically; but we cannot give it up without ignoring altogether much earnest and successful labour.

Our chronicler's interest in statistics lays healthy emphasis on the practical character of religion. There is a danger of identifying spiritual force with literary and rhetorical gifts; to recognise the religious value of statistics is the most forcible protest against such identification. The permanent contribution of any age to religious thought will naturally take a literary form, and the higher the literary qualities of religious writing, the more likely it is to survive. Shakespeare, Milton, and Bunyan have probably exercised a more powerful direct religious influence on subsequent generations than all the theologians of the seventeenth century. But the supreme service of the Church in any age is its influence on its own generation, by which it moulds the generation immediately following. That influence can only be estimated by a careful study of all possible information, and especially of statistics. We cannot assign mathematical values to spiritual effects and tabulate them like Board of Trade returns; but real spiritual movements will before long have practical issues, that can be heard, and seen, and felt, and even admit of being put into tables. "The wind bloweth where it listeth, and thou hearest the voice thereof, but knowest not whence it cometh and whither it goeth"[1];

---

[1] John iii. 8.

and yet the boughs and the corn bend before the wind, and the ships are carried across the sea to their desired haven. Tables may be drawn up of the tonnage and the rate of sailing. So is every one that is born of the Spirit. You cannot tell when and how God breathes upon the soul; but if the Divine Spirit be indeed at work in any society, there will be fewer crimes and quarrels, less scandal, and more deeds of charity. We may justly suspect a revival which has no effect upon the statistical records of national life. Subscription-lists are very imperfect tests of enthusiasm, but any wide-spread Christian fervour would be worth little if it did not swell subscription-lists.

Chronicles is not the most important witness to a sympathetic relationship between the Bible and exact science. The first chapter of Genesis is the classic example of the appropriation by an inspired writer of the scientific spirit and method. Some chapters in Job show a distinctly scientific interest in natural phenomena. Moreover, the direct concern of Chronicles is in the religious aspects of social science. And yet there is a patient accumulation of data with no obvious dramatic value : names, dates, numbers, specifications, and ritual which do not improve the literary character of the narrative. This conscientious recording of dry facts, this noting down of anything and everything that connects with the subject, is closely akin to the initial processes of the inductive sciences. True, the chronicler's interests are in some directions narrowed by personal and professional feeling ; but within these limits he is anxious to make a complete record, which, as we have seen, sometimes leads to repetition. Now inductive science is based on unlimited statistics. The astronomer and biologist share the chronicler's appetite for this kind of mental food. The lists in Chronicles are few and meagre compared to the records of Greenwich Observatory or the volumes which contain the data of biology or sociology; but the chronicler becomes in a certain sense the forerunner of Darwin, Spencer, and Galton. The differences are indeed immense. The interval of two thousand odd years between the ancient annalist and the modern scientists has not been thrown away. In estimating the value of evidence and interpreting its significance, the chronicler was a mere child compared with his modern successors. His aims and interests were entirely different from theirs. But yet he was moved by a spirit which they may be said to inherit. His careful collection of facts, even his tendency to read the ideas and institutions of his own time into ancient history, are indications of a reverence for the past and of an anxiety to base ideas and action upon a knowledge of that past. This foreshadows the reverence of modern science for experience, its anxiety to base its laws and theories upon observation of what has actually occurred. The principle that the past determines and interprets the present and the future lies at the root of the theological attitude of the most conservative minds and the scientific work of the most advanced thinkers. The conservative spirit, like the chronicler, is apt to suffer its inherited prepossessions and personal interests to hinder a true observation and understanding of the past. But the chronicler's opportunities and experience were narrow indeed compared with those of theological students to-day; and we have every right to lay stress on the progress which he had achieved and the onward path that it indicated rather than on the yet more advanced stages which still lay beyond his horizon.

CHAPTER IV

FAMILY TRADITIONS

i Chron. i. 10, 19, 46; ii. 3, 7, 34; iv. 9, 10, 18, 22, 27, 34-43; v. 10, 18-22; vii. 21-23; viii. 13.

CHRONICLES is a miniature Old Testament, and may have been meant as a handbook for ordinary people, who had no access to the whole library of sacred writings. It contains nothing corresponding to the books of Wisdom or the apocalyptic literature; but all the other types of Old Testament literature are represented. There are genealogies, statistics, ritual, history, psalms, and prophecies. The interest shown by Chronicles in family traditions harmonises with the stress laid by the Hebrew Scriptures upon family life. The other historical books are largely occupied with the family history of the Patriarchs, of Moses, of Jephthah, Gideon, Samson, Saul, and David. The chronicler intersperses his genealogies with short anecdotes about the different families and tribes. Some of these are borrowed from the older books; but others are peculiar to our author, and were doubtless obtained by him from the family records and traditions of his contemporaries. The statements that " Nimrod began to be mighty upon the earth "[1]; that " the name of one " of Eber's sons " was Peleg, because in his days the

---

[1] i. 10.

earth was divided"[1]; and that Hadad "smote Moab in the field of Midian,"[2] are borrowed from Genesis. As he omits events much more important and more closely connected with the history of Israel, and gives no account of Babel, or of Abraham, or of the conquest of Canaan, these little notes are probably retained by accident, because at times the chronicler copied his authorities somewhat mechanically. It was less trouble to take the genealogies as they stood than to exercise great care in weeding out everything but the bare names.

In one instance,[3] however, the chronicler has erased a curious note to a genealogy in Genesis. A certain Anah is mentioned both in Genesis and Chronicles among the Horites, who inhabited Mount Seir before it was conquered by Edom. Most of us, in reading the Authorised Version, have wondered what historical or religious interest secured a permanent record for the fact that "Anah found the mules in the wilderness, as he fed the asses of Zibeon his father." A possible solution seemed to be that this note was preserved as the earliest reference to the existence of mules, which animals played an important part in the social life of Palestine; but the Revised Version sets aside this explanation by substituting "hot springs" for "mules," and as these hot springs are only mentioned here, the passage becomes a greater puzzle than ever. The chronicler could hardly overlook this curious piece of information, but he naturally felt that this obscure archæological note about the aboriginal Horites did not fall within the scope of his work. On the other

---

[1] i. 19. [2] i. 46.
[3] Cf. Gen. xxxvi. 24 and i Chron. i. 40.

hand, the tragic fates of Er and Achar [1] had a direct genealogical significance. They are referred to in order to explain why the lists contain no descendants of these members of the tribe of Judah. The notes to these names illustrate the more depressing aspects of history. The men who lived happy, honourable lives can be mentioned one after another without any comment; but even the compiler of pedigrees pauses to note the crimes and misfortunes that broke the natural order of life. The annals of old families dwell with melancholy pride on murders, and fatal duels, and suicides. History, like an ancient mansion, is haunted with unhappy ghosts. Yet our interest in tragedy is a testimony to the blessedness of life ; comfort and enjoyment are too monotonously common to be worth recording, but we are attracted and excited by exceptional instances of suffering and sin.

Let us turn to the episodes of family life only found in Chronicles. They may mostly be arranged in little groups of two or three, and some of the groups present us with an interesting contrast.

We learn from ii. 34–41 and iv. 18 that two Jewish families traced their descent from Egyptian ancestors. Sheshan, according to Chronicles, was eighth in descent from Judah and fifth from Jerahmeel, the brother of Caleb. Having daughters, but no son, he gave one of his daughters in marriage to an Egyptian slave named Jarha. The descendants of this union are traced for thirteen generations. Genealogies, however, are not always complete ; and our other data do not suffice to determine even approximately the date of this marriage. But the five generations between Jerahmeel and Sheshan indicate a period long after the

---

[1] *I.e.*, Achan (ii. 3, 7).

Exodus; and as Egypt plays no recorded part in the history of Israel between the Exodus and the reign of Solomon, the marriage may have taken place under the monarchy. The story is a curious parallel to that of Joseph, with the parts of Israelite and Egyptian reversed. God is no respecter of persons; it is not only when the desolate and afflicted in strange lands belong to the chosen people that Jehovah relieves and delivers them. It is true of the Egyptian, as well as of the Israelite, that " the Lord maketh poor and maketh rich."

> " He bringeth low, He also lifteth up;
> He raiseth up the poor out of the dust:
> He lifteth up the needy from the dunghill,
> To make them sit with princes
> And inherit the throne of glory." [1]

This song might have been sung at Jarha's wedding as well as at Joseph's.

Both these marriages throw a sidelight upon the character of Eastern slavery. They show how sharply and deeply it was divided from the hopeless degradation of negro slavery in America. Israelites did not recognise distinctions of race and colour between themselves and their bondsmen so as to treat them as worse than pariahs and regard them with physical loathing. An American considers himself disgraced by a slight taint of negro blood in his ancestry, but a noble Jewish family was proud to trace its descent from an Egyptian slave.

The other story is somewhat different, and rests upon an obscure and corrupt passage in iv. 18. The confusion makes it impossible to arrive at any date,

---

[1] 1 Sam. ii. 7, 8.

even by rough approximation. The genealogical relations of the actors are by no means certain, but
some interesting points are tolerably clear. Some time
after the conquest of Canaan, a descendant of Caleb
married two wives, one a Jewess, the other an
Egyptian. The Egyptian was Bithiah, a daughter of
Pharaoh, *i.e.*, of the contemporary king of Egypt. It
appears probable that the inhabitants of Eshtemoa
traced their descent to this Egyptian princess, while
those of Gedor, Soco, and Zanoah claimed Mered as
their ancestor by his Jewish wife.[1] Here again we
have the bare outline of a romance, which the imagination is at liberty to fill in. It has been suggested that
Bithiah may have been the victim of some Jewish raid
into Egypt, but surely a king of Egypt would have
either ransomed his daughter or recovered her by force
of arms. The story rather suggests that the chiefs
of the clans of Judah were semi-independent and
possessed of considerable wealth and power, so that
the royal family of Egypt could intermarry with them,
as with reigning sovereigns. But if so, the pride of
Egypt must have been greatly broken since the time
when the Pharaohs haughtily refused to give their
daughters in marriage to the kings of Babylon.

Both Egyptian alliances occur among the Kenizzites,
the descendants of the brothers Caleb and Jerahmeel.
In one case a Jewess marries an Egyptian slave; in the
other a Jew marries an Egyptian princess. Doubtless
these marriages did not stand alone, and there were

---

[1] Vv. 17, 18, as they stand, do not make sense. The second
sentence of ver. 18 should be read before "and she bare Miriam" in
ver. 17. Mered and Bithiah formed a tempting subject for the rabbis,
and gave occasion for some of their usual grotesque fancies. Mered
has been identified by them both with Caleb and Moses.

others with foreigners of varying social rank. The stories show that even after the Captivity the tradition survived that the clans in the south of Judah had been closely connected with Egypt, and that Solomon was not the only member of the tribe who had taken an Egyptian wife. Now intermarriage with foreigners is partly forbidden by the Pentateuch; and the prohibition was extended and sternly enforced by Ezra and Nehemiah.[1] In the time of the chronicler there was a growing feeling against such marriages. Hence the traditions we are discussing cannot have originated after the Return, but must be at any rate earlier than the publication of Deuteronomy under Josiah.

Such marriages with Egyptians must have had some influence on the religion of the south of Judah, but probably the foreigners usually followed the example of Ruth, and adopted the faith of the families into which they came. When they said, " Thy people shall be my people," they did not fail to add, "and thy God shall be my God." When the Egyptian princess married the head of a Jewish clan, she became one of Jehovah's people; and her adoption into the family of the God of Israel was symbolised by a new name: " Bithiah," "daughter of Jehovah." Whether later Judaism owed anything to Egyptian influences can only be matter of conjecture; at any rate, they did not pervert the southern clans from their old faith. The Calebites and Jerahmeelites were the backbone of Judah both before and after the Captivity.

The remaining traditions relate to the warfare of the Israelites with their neighbours. The first is a colourless reminiscence, that might have been recorded of

---

[1] Deut. vii. 3; Josh. xxiii. 12; Ezra ix. 1, 2; Neh. xiii. 23.

the effectual prayer of any pious Israelite. The genealogies of chap. iv. are interrupted by a paragraph entirely unconnected with the context. The subject of this fragment is a certain Jabez never mentioned elsewhere, and, so far as any record goes, as entirely "without father, without mother, without genealogy," as Melchizedek himself. As chap. iv. deals with the families of Judah, and in ii. 55 there is a town Jabez also belonging to Judah, we may suppose that the chronicler had reasons for assigning Jabez to that tribe; but he has neither given these reasons, nor indicated how Jabez was connected therewith. The paragraph runs as follows[1]: "And Jabez was honoured above his brethren, and his mother called his name Jabez" (*Ya'bēç*), "saying, In pain" ('*ōçeb*) "I bore him. And Jabez called upon the God of Israel, saying,—

> 'If Thou wilt indeed bless me
> By enlarging my possessions,
> And Thy hand be with me
> To provide pasture,[2] that I be not in distress' ('*ōçeb*).

And God brought about what he asked." The chronicler has evidently inserted here a broken and disconnected fragment from one of his sources; and we are puzzled to understand why he gives so much, and no more. Surely not merely to introduce the etymologies of Jabez; or if Jabez were so important that it was worth while to interrupt the genealogies to furnish two derivations of his name, why are we not told more about him? Who was he, when and where did he live, and at whose expense were his possessions

---

[1] iv. 9, 10.

[2] The reading on which this translation is based is obtained by an alteration of the vowels of the Masoretic text; cf. Bertheau, i.l.

enlarged and pasture provided for him ?   Everything
that could give colour and interest to the narrative is
withheld, and we are merely told that he prayed for
earthly blessing and obtained it.   The spiritual lesson
is obvious, but it is very frequently enforced and
illustrated in the Old Testament.   Why should this
episode about an utterly unknown man be thrust by
main force into an unsuitable context, if it is only one
example of a most familiar truth ?   It has been pointed
out that Jacob vowed a similar vow and built an altar
to El, the God of Israel[1]; but this is one of many
coincidences.   The paragraph certainly tells us something about the chronicler's views on prayer, but
nothing that is not more forcibly stated and exemplified
in many other passages ; it is mainly interesting to us
because of the light it throws on his methods of composition.   Elsewhere he embodies portions of well-
known works and apparently assumes that his readers
are sufficiently versed in them to be able to understand
the point of his extracts.   Probably Jabez was so
familiar to the chronicler's immediate circle that he can
take for granted that a few lines will suffice to recall
all the circumstances to a reader.

We have next a series of much more definite
statements about Israelite prowess and success in wars
against Moab and other enemies.

In iv. 21, 22, we read, " The sons of Shelah the son
of Judah: Er the father of Lecah, and Laadah the
father of Mareshah, and the families of the house of
them that wrought fine linen, of the house of Ashbea;
and Jokim, and the men of Cozeba, and Joash, and
Saraph, who had dominion in Moab and returned to

---

[1] Gen. xxviii. 20; xxxiii. 20,

Bethlehem."[1]   Here again the information is too vague to enable us to fix any date, nor is it quite certain who had dominion in Moab.   The verb "had dominion" is plural in Hebrew, and may refer to all or any of the sons of Shelah.   But, in spite of uncertainties, it is interesting to find chiefs or clans of Judah ruling in Moab.   Possibly this immigration took place when David conquered and partly depopulated the country. The men of Judah may have returned to Bethlehem when Moab passed to the northern kingdom at the disruption, or when Moab regained its independence.

The incident in iv. 34–43 differs from the preceding in having a definite date assigned to it.   In the time of Hezekiah some Simeonite clans had largely increased in number and found themselves straitened for room for their flocks.   They accordingly went in search of new pasturage.   One company went to Gedor, another to Mount Seir.

The situation of Gedor is not clearly known.   It cannot be the Gedor of Josh. xv. 58, which lay in the heart of Judah.   The LXX. has Gerar, a town to the south of Gaza, and this may be the right reading; but whether we read Gedor or Gerar, the scene of the invasion will be in the country south of Judah.   Here the children of Simeon found what they wanted, "fat pasture, and good," and abundant, for "the land was wide."   There was the additional advantage that the inhabitants were harmless and inoffensive and fell an easy prey to their invaders: "The land was quiet and peaceable, for they that dwelt there aforetime were of Ham."   As Ham in the genealogies is the father of Cainan, these peaceable folk would be Cainanites; and

---

[1] This translation is obtained by slightly altering the Masoretic text.

among them were a people called Meunim, probably
not connected with any of the Maons mentioned in
the Old Testament, but with some other town or district of the same name. So "these written by name
came in the days of Hezekiah, king of Judah, and
smote their tents, and the Meunim that were found
there, and devoted them to destruction as accursed,
so that none are left unto this day. And the Simeonites dwelt in their stead."[1]

Then follows in the simplest and most unconscious
way the only justification that is offered for the behaviour of the invaders: "because there was pasture
there for their flocks." The narrative takes for
granted—

> "The good old rule, the simple plan,
>   That they should take who have the power,
>   And they should keep who can."

The expedition to Mount Seir appears to have been
a sequel to the attack on Gedor. Five hundred of the
victors emigrated into Edom, and smote the remnant
of the Amalekites who had survived the massacre
under Saul[2]; "and they also dwelt there unto this
day."

In substance, style, and ideas this passage closely
resembles the books of Joshua and Judges, where the
phrase "unto this day" frequently occurs. Here, of
course, the "day" in question is the time of the
chronicler's authority. When Chronicles was written
the Simeonites in Gedor and Mount Seir had long ago
shared the fate of their victims.

The conquest of Gedor reminds us how in the early
days of the Israelite occupation of Palestine "Judah

---

[1] iv. 41; cf. R.V.   [2] 1 Sam. xv.

went with Simeon his brother into the same southern
lands," and they smote the Canaanites that inhabited
Zephath, and devoted them to destruction as accursed[1];
and how the house of Joseph took Bethel by treachery.[2]
But the closest parallel is the Danite conquest of
Laish.[3] The Danite spies said that the people of Laish
"dwelt in security, after the manner of the Zidonians,
quiet and secure," harmless and inoffensive, like the
Gedorites. Nor were they likely to receive succour
from the powerful city of Zidon or from other allies,
for "they were far from the Zidonians, and had no
dealings with any man." Accordingly, having observed
the prosperous but defenceless position of this peaceable
people, they returned and reported to their brethren,
"Arise, and let us go up against them, for we have
seen the land, and, behold, it is very good ; and are ye
still ? Be not slothful to go and to enter in to possess
the land. When ye go, ye shall come unto a people
secure, and the land," like that of Gedor, "is large,
for God hath given it into your hand, a place where
there is no want of anything that is in the earth."

The moral of these incidents is obvious. When
a prosperous people is peaceable and defenceless, it
is a clear sign that God has delivered them into the
hand of any warlike and enterprising nation that
knows how to use its opportunities. The chronicler,
however, is not responsible for this morality, but he
does not feel compelled to make any protest against
the ethical views of his source. There is a refresh-
ing frankness about these ancient narratives. The wolf
devours the lamb without inventing any flimsy pretext
about troubled waters.

---

[1] Judges i. 17.   [2] Judges i. 22–26.

[3] Judges xviii

But in criticising these Hebrew clans who lived in the dawn of history and religion we condemn ourselves. If we make adequate allowance for the influence of Christ, and the New Testament, and centuries of Christian teaching, Simeon and Dan do not compare unfavourably with modern nations. As we review the wars of Christendom, we shall often be puzzled to find any ground for the outbreak of hostilities other than the defencelessness of the weaker combatant. The Spanish conquest of America and the English conquest of India afford examples of the treatment of weaker races which fairly rank with those of the Old Testament. Even to-day the independence of the smaller European states is mainly guaranteed by the jealousies of the Great Powers. Still there has been progress in international morality; we have got at last to the stage of Æsop's fable. Public opinion condemns wanton aggression against a weak state; and the stronger power employs the resources of civilised diplomacy in showing that not only the absent, but also the helpless, are always wrong. There has also been a substantial advance in humanity towards conquered peoples. Christian warfare even since the Middle Ages has been stained with the horrors of the Thirty Years' War and many other barbarities; the treatment of the American Indians by settlers has often been cruel and unjust; but no civilised nation would now systematically massacre men, women, and children in cold blood. We are thankful for any progress towards better things, but we cannot feel that men have yet realised that Christ has a message for nations as well as for individuals. As His disciples we can only pray more earnestly that the kingdoms of the earth may in deed and truth become the kingdoms of our Lord and of His Christ.

The next incident is more honourable to the Israelites. "The sons of Reuben, and the Gadites, and the half-tribe of Manasseh" did not merely surprise and slaughter quiet and peaceable people : they conquered formidable enemies in fair fight.[1] There are two separate accounts of a war with the Hagrites, one appended to the genealogy of Reuben and one to that of Gad. The former is very brief and general, comprising nothing but a bare statement that there was a successful war and a consequent appropriation of territory. Probably the two paragraphs are different forms of the same narrative, derived by the chronicler from independent sources. We may therefore confine our attention to the more detailed account.

Here, as elsewhere, these Transjordanic tribes are spoken of as "valiant[2] men," "men able to bear buckler and sword and to shoot with the bow, and skilful in war." Their numbers were considerable. While five hundred Simeonites were enough to destroy the Amalekites on Mount Seir, these eastern tribes mustered "forty and four thousand seven hundred and threescore that were able to go forth to war." Their enemies were not "quiet and peaceable people," but the wild Bedouin of the desert, "the Hagrites, with Jetur and Naphish and Nodab." Nodab is mentioned only here ; Jetur and Naphish occur together in the lists of the sons of Ishmael.[3] Ituræa probably derived its name from the tribe of Jetur. The Hagrites or Hagarenes were Arabs closely connected with the Ishmaelites, and they seem to have taken their name from Hagar. In Psalm

---

[1] Vv. 7-10, 18-22.
[2] Deut. xxxiii. 20; 1 Chron. xii. 8, 21.
[3] Gen. xxv. 15.

lxxxiii. 6–8 we find a similar confederacy on a larger scale :—

> "The tents of Edom and the Ishmaelites,
> Moab and the Hagarenes
> Gebal and Ammon and Amalek,
> Philistia with the inhabitants of Tyre,
> Assyria also is joined with them ;
> They have holpen the children of Lot."

There could be no question of unprovoked aggression against these children of Ishmael, that " wild ass of a man, whose hand was against every man, and every man's hand against him."[1] The narrative implies that the Israelites were the aggressors, but to attack the robber tribes of the desert would be as much an act of self-defence as to destroy a hornet's nest. We may be quite sure that when Reuben and Gad marched eastward they had heavy losses to retrieve and bitter wrongs to avenge. We might find a parallel in the campaigns by which robber tribes are punished for their raids within our Indian frontier, only we must remember that Reuben and Gad were not very much more law-abiding or unselfish than their Arab neighbours. They were not engaged in maintaining a *pax Britannica* for the benefit of subject nations ; they were carrying on a struggle for existence with persistent and relentless foes. Another partial parallel would be the border feuds on the Northumbrian marches, when—

> ". . . over border, dale, and fell
> Full wide and far was terror spread;
> For pathless marsh and mountain cell
> The peasant left his lowly shed :
> The frightened flocks and herds were pent
> Beneath the peel's rude battlement,

---

[1] Gen. xvi. 12.

And maids and matrons dropped the tear
While ready warriors seized the spear;
. . . . . . the watchman's eye
Dun wreaths of distant smoke can spy."[1]

But the Israelite expedition was on a larger scale
than any "warden raid," and Eastern passions are
fiercer and shriller than those sung by the Last
Minstrel : the maids and matrons of the desert would
shriek and wail instead of "dropping a tear."

In this great raid of ancient times "the war was of
God," not, as at Laish, because God found for them
helpless and easy victims, but because He helped them
in a desperate struggle. When the fierce Israelite and
Arab borderers joined battle, the issue was at first
doubtful ; and then "they cried to God, and He was
entreated of them, because they put their trust in Him,"
"and they were helped against" their enemies ; "and
the Hagrites were delivered into their hand, and all that
were with them, and there fell many slain, because the
war was of God"; "and they took away their cattle :
of their camels fifty thousand, and of sheep two hundred
and fifty thousand, and of asses two thousand, and of
slaves a hundred thousand." "And they dwelt in
their stead until the captivity."

This "captivity" is the subject of another short
note. The chronicler apparently was anxious to dis-
tribute his historical narratives equally among the
tribes. The genealogies of Reuben and Gad each conclude with a notice of a war, and a similar account
follows that of Eastern Manasseh :—"And they trespassed against the God of their fathers, and went
a-whoring after the gods of the peoples of the land,
whom God destroyed before them. And the God of

---

[1] *Lay of the Last Minstrel*, iv. 3.

Israel stirred up the spirit of Pul, king of Assyria, and
the spirit of Tilgath-pilneser, king of Assyria, and
he carried them away, even the Reubenites, and the
Gadites, and the half-tribe of Manasseh, and brought
them unto Halah, and Habor, and Hara, and to the
river of Gozan, unto this day."[1]   And this war also
was "of God."   Doubtless the descendants of the
surviving Hagrites and Ishmaelites were among the
allies of the Assyrian king, and saw in the ruin of
Eastern Israel a retribution for the sufferings of their
own people; but the later Jews and probably the
exiles in "Halah, Habor, and Hara," and by "the
river of Gozan," far away in North-eastern Mesopotamia,
found the cause of their sufferings in too great an
intimacy with their heathen neighbours: they had
gone a-whoring after their gods.

The last two incidents which we shall deal with in
this chapter serve to illustrate afresh the rough-and-
ready methods by which the chronicler has knotted
together threads of heterogeneous tradition into one
tangled skein.   We shall see further how ready ancient
writers were to represent a tribe by the ancestor from
whom it traced its descent.   We read in vii. 20, 21,
"The sons of Ephraim: Shuthelah, and Bered his son,
and Tahath his son, and Eleadah his son, and Zabad
his son, and Shuthelah his son, and Ezer and Elead,
whom the men of Gath that were born in the land
slew, because they came down to take away their cattle."

Ezer and Elead are apparently brothers of the second
Shuthelah; at any rate, as six generations are mentioned between them and Ephraim, they would seem
to have lived long after the Patriarch.   Moreover, they

---

[1] **Vv. 25, 26.** Note the curious spelling *Tilgath-pilneser* for the
more usual *Tiglath-pileser.*

came down to Gath, so that they must have lived in some hill-country not far off, presumably the hill-country of Ephraim.   But in the next two verses (22 and 23) we read, " And Ephraim their father mourned many days, and his brethren came to comfort him. And he went in to his wife, and she conceived, and bare a son ; and he called his name Beriah, because it went evil with his house."

Taking these words literally, Ezer and Elead were the actual sons of Ephraim ; and as Ephraim and his family were born in Egypt and lived there all their days, these patriarchal cattle-lifters did not come down from any neighbouring highlands, but must have come up from Egypt, all the way from the land of Goshen, across the desert and past several Philistine and Canaanite towns.   This literal sense is simply impossible.   The author from whom the chronicler borrowed this narrative is clearly using a natural and beautiful figure to describe the distress in the tribe of Ephraim when two of its clans were cut off, and the fact that a new clan named Beriah was formed to take their place.   Possibly we are not without information as to how this new clan arose.   In viii. 13 we read of two Benjamites, " *Beriah* and Shema, who were heads of fathers' houses of the inhabitants of Aijalon, who put to flight the inhabitants of Gath."   Beriah and Shema probably, coming to the aid of Ephraim, avenged the defeat of Ezer and Elead ; and in return received the possessions of the clans, who had been cut off, and Beriah was thus reckoned among the children of Ephraim.[1]

The language of ver. 22 is very similar to that of Gen. xxxvii. 34, 35 : "And Jacob mourned for his son

[1] Cf. Bertheau, *ll.*

many days. And all his sons and all his daughters rose up to comfort him"; and the personification of the tribe under the name of its ancestor may be paralleled from Judges xxi. 6: "And the children of Israel repented them for Benjamin their brother."

Let us now reconstruct the story and consider its significance. Two Ephraimite clans, Ezer and Elead, set out to drive the cattle "of the men of Gath, who were born in the land," *i.e.*, of the aboriginal Avvites, who had been dispossessed by the Philistines, but still retained some of the pasture-lands. Falling into an ambush or taken by surprise when encumbered with their plunder, the Ephraimites were cut off, and nearly all the fighting men of the clans perished. The Avvites, reinforced by the Philistines of Gath, pressed their advantage, and invaded the territory of Ephraim, whose border districts, stripped of their defenders, lay at the mercy of the conquerors. From this danger they were rescued by the Benjamite clans Shema and Beriah, then occupying Aijalon[1]; and the men of Gath in their turn were defeated and driven back. The grateful Ephraimites invited their allies to occupy the vacant territory and in all probability to marry the widows and daughters of their slaughtered kinsmen. From that time onwards Beriah was reckoned as one of the clans of Ephraim.

The account of this memorable cattle foray is a necessary note to the genealogies to explain the origin of an important clan and its double connection

---

[1] In Josh. xix. 42, xxi. 24, Aijalon is given to Dan; in Judges i. 34 it is given to Dan, but we are told that Amorites retained possession of it, but became tributary to the house of Joseph; in 2 Chron. xi. 10 it is given to "Judah and Benjamin." As a frontier town, it frequently changed hands.

with Ephraim and Benjamin. Both the chronicler and his authority recorded it because of its genealogical significance, not because they were anxious to perpetuate the memory of the unfortunate raid. In the ancient days to which the episode belonged, a frontier cattle foray seemed as natural and meritorious an enterprise as it did to William of Deloraine. The chronicler does not think it necessary to signify any disapproval—it is by no means certain that he did disapprove—of such spoiling of the uncircumcised; but the fact that he gives the record without comment does not show that he condoned cattle-stealing. Men to-day relate with pride the lawless deeds of noble ancestors, but they would be dismayed if their own sons proposed to adopt the moral code of mediæval barons or Elizabethan buccaneers.

In reviewing the scanty religious ideas involved in this little group of family traditions, we have to remember that they belong to a period of Israelite history much older than that of the chronicler; in estimating their value, we have to make large allowance for the conventional ethics of the times. Religion not only serves to raise the standard of morality, but also to keep the average man up to the conventional standard; it helps and encourages him to do what he believes to be right as well as gives him a better understanding of what right means. Primitive religion is not to be disparaged because it did not at once convert the rough Israelite clansmen into Havelocks and Gordons. In those early days, courage, patriotism, and loyalty to one's tribesmen were the most necessary and approved virtues. They were fostered and stimulated by the current belief in a God of battles, who gave victory to His faithful people. Moreover, the

idea of Deity implied in these traditions, though inade-
quate, is by no means unworthy. God is benevolent ;
He enriches and succours His people ; He answers
prayer, giving to Jabez the land and pasture for which
he asked. He is a righteous God ; He responds to
and justifies His people's faith : " He was entreated of
the Reubenites and Gadites because they put their
trust in Him." On the other hand, He is a jealous
God ; He punishes Israel when " they trespass against
the God of their fathers and go a-whoring after the
gods of the peoples of the land." But the feeling here
attributed to Jehovah is not merely one of personal
jealousy. Loyalty to Him meant a great deal more
than a preference for a god called Jehovah over a god
called Chemosh. It involved a special recognition of
morality and purity, and gave a religious sanction to
patriotism and the sentiment of national unity. Worship of Moabite or Syrian gods weakened a man's
enthusiasm for Israel and his sense of fellowship with
his countrymen, just as allegiance to an Italian prince
and prelate has seemed to Protestants to deprive the
Romanist of his full inheritance in English life and
feeling. He who went astray after other gods did not
merely indulge his individual taste in doctrine and
ritual : he was a traitor to the social order, to the
prosperity and national union, of Israel. Such disloyalty broke up the nation, and sent Israel and Judah
into captivity piecemeal.

CHAPTER V

THE JEWISH COMMUNITY IN THE TIME OF THE CHRONICLER

WE have already referred to the light thrown by Chronicles on this subject. Besides the direct information given in Ezra and Nehemiah, and sometimes in Chronicles itself, the chronicler by describing the past in terms of the present often unconsciously helps us to reconstruct the picture of his own day. We shall have to make occasional reference to the books of Ezra and Nehemiah, but the age of the chronicler is later than the events which they describe, and we shall be traversing different ground from that covered by the volume of the "Expositor's Bible" which deals with them.

Chronicles is full of evidence that the civil and ecclesiastical system of the Pentateuch had become fully established long before the chronicler wrote. Its gradual origin had been forgotten, and it was assumed that the Law in its final and complete form had been known and observed from the time of David onwards. At every stage of the history Levites are introduced, occupying the subordinate position and discharging the menial duties assigned to them by the latest documents of the Pentateuch. In other matters small and

great, especially those concerning the Temple and its
sanctity, the chronicler shows himself so familiar with
the Law that he could not imagine Israel without it.
Picture the life of Judah as we find it in 2 Kings and
the prophecies of the eighth century, put this picture
side by side with another of the Judaism of the New
Testament, and remember that Chronicles is about
a century nearer to the latter than to the former. It
is not difficult to trace the effect of this absorption in
the system of the Pentateuch. The community in and
about Jerusalem had become a Church, and was in
possession of a Bible. But the hardening, despiritual-
ising processes which created later Judaism were
already at work. A building, a system of ritual, and
a set of officials were coming to be regarded as the
essential elements of the Church. The Bible was
important partly because it dealt with these essential
elements, partly because it provided a series of regulations about washings and meats, and thus enabled the
layman to exalt his everyday life into a round of ceremonial observances. The habit of using the Pentateuch
chiefly as a handbook of external and technical ritual
seriously influenced the current interpretation of the
Bible. It naturally led to a hard literalism and a
disingenuous exegesis. This interest in externals is
patent enough in the chronicler, and the tendencies of
Biblical exegesis are illustrated by his use of Samuel
and Kings. On the other hand, we must allow for
great development of this process in the interval
between Chronicles and the New Testament. The
evils of later Judaism were yet far from mature, and
religious life and thought in Palestine were still much
more elastic than they became later on.

We have also to remember that at this period the

zealous observers of the Law can only have formed a portion of the community, corresponding roughly to the regular attendants at public worship in a Christian country. Beyond and beneath the pious legalists were " the people of the land," those who were too careless or too busy to attend to ceremonial ; but for both classes the popular and prominent ideal of religion was made up of a magnificent building, a dignified and wealthy clergy, and an elaborate ritual, alike for great public functions and for the minutiæ of daily life.

Besides all these the Jewish community had its sacred writings. As one of the ministers of the Temple, and, moreover, both a student of the national literature and himself an author, the chronicler represents the best literary knowledge of contemporary Palestinian Judaism ; and his somewhat mechanical methods of composition make it easy for us to discern his indebtedness to older writers. We turn his pages with interest to learn what books were known and read by the most cultured Jews of his time. First and foremost, and overshadowing all the rest, there appears the Pentateuch. Then there is the whole array of earlier Historical Books : Joshua, Ruth, Samuel, and Kings. The plan of Chronicles excludes a direct use of Judges, but it must have been well known to our author. His appreciation of the Psalms is shown by his inserting in his history of David a cento of passages from Psalms xcvi., cv., and cvi. ; on the other hand, Psalm xviii. and other lyrics given in the books of Samuel are omitted by the chronicler. The later Exilic Psalms were more to his taste than ancient hymns, and he unconsciously carries back into the history of the monarchy the poetry as well as the ritual of later times. Both omissi ns and insertions indicate that in

this period the Jews possessed and prized a large
collection of psalms.

There are also traces of the Prophets. Hanani the
seer in his address to Asa[1] quotes Zech. iv. 10: "The
eyes of the Lord, which run to and fro through the
whole earth." Jehoshaphat's exhortation to his people,
"Believe in the Lord your God; so shall ye be established,"[2] is based on Isa. vii. 9: "If ye will not believe,
surely ye shall not be established." Hezekiah's words
to the Levites, "Our fathers . . . have turned away
their faces from the habitation of the Lord, and turned
their backs,"[3] are a significant variation of Jer. ii.
27: "They have turned their back unto Me, and not
their face." The Temple is substituted for Jehovah.

There are of course references to Isaiah and Jeremiah and traces of other prophets; but when account
is taken of them all, it is seen that the chronicler makes
scanty use, on the whole, of the Prophetical Books. It
is true that the idea of illustrating and supplementing
information derived from annals by means of contemporary literature not in narrative form had not yet
dawned upon historians; but if the chronicler had taken
a tithe of the interest in the Prophets that he took in
the Pentateuch and the Psalms, his work would show
many more distinct marks of their influence.

An apocalypse like Daniel and works like Job,
Proverbs, and the other books of Wisdom lay so far
outside the plan and subject of Chronicles that we can
scarcely consider the absence of any clear trace of them
a proof that the chronicler did not either know them or
care for them.

Our brief review suggests that the literary concern

---

[2] Chron. xvi. 9.   [1] 2 Chron. xx. 20.
[3] 2 Chron. xxix. 6.

of the chronicler and his circle was chiefly in the books most closely conn:cted with the Temple; viz., the Historical Books, which contained its history, the Pentateuch, which prescribed its ritual, and the Psalms, which served as its liturgy. The Prophets occupy a secondary place, and Chronicles furnishes no clear evidence as to other Old Testament books.

We also find in Chronicles that the Hebrew language had degenerated from its ancient classical purity, and that Jewish writers had already come very much under the influence of Aramaic.

We may next consider the evidence supplied by the chronicler as to the elements and distribution of the Jewish community in his time. In Ezra and Nehemiah we find the returning exiles divided into the men of Judah, the men of Benjamin, and the priests, Levites, etc. In Ezra ii. we are told that in all there returned 42,360, with 7,337 slaves and 200 "singing men and singing women." The priests numbered 4,289; there were 74 Levites, 128 singers of the children of Asaph, 139 porters, and 392 Nethinim and children of Solomon's servants. The singers, porters, Nethinim, and children of Solomon's servants are not reckoned among the Levites, and there is only one guild of singers: "the children of Asaph." The Nethinim are still distinguished from the Levites in the list of those who returned with Ezra, and in various lists which occur in Nehemiah. We see from the Levitical genealogies and the Levites in I Chron. vi., ix., etc., that in the time of the chronicler these arrangements had been altered. There were now three guilds of singers, tracing their descent to Heman, Asaph, and Ethan [1] or Jeduthun, and reckoned by descent among the Levites

---

[1] I Chron. vi. 31-48, xv. 16-20; cf. psalm titles.

The guild of Heman seems to have been also known as "the sons of Korah."[1] The porters and probably eventually the Nethinim were also reckoned among the Levites.[2]

We see therefore that in the interval between Nehemiah and the chronicler the inferior ranks of the Temple ministry had been reorganised, the musical staff had been enlarged and doubtless otherwise improved, and the singers, porters, Nethinim, and other Temple servants had been promoted to the position of Levites. Under the monarchy many of the Temple servants had been slaves of foreign birth; but now a sacred character was given to the humblest menial who shared in the work of the house of God. In after-times Herod the Great had a number of priests trained as masons, in order that no profane hand might take part in the building of his temple.

Some details have been preserved of the organisation of the Levites. We read how the porters were distributed among the different gates, and of Levites who were over the chambers and the treasuries, and of other Levites how—

"They lodged round about the house of God, because the charge was upon them, and to them pertained the opening thereof morning by morning.

"And certain of them had charge of the vessels of service; for by tale were they brought in, and by tale were they taken out.

"Some of them also were appointed over the furniture, and over all the vessels of the sanctuary, and over the fine flour, and the wine, and the oil, and the frankincense, and the spices.

---

[1] I Chron. vi. 33, 37; cf. Psalm lxxxviii. (title).
[2] I Chron. xvi. 38, 42.

"And some of the sons of the priests prepared the confection of the spices.

"And Mattithiah, one of the Levites who was the first-born of Shallum the Korahite, had the set office over the things that were baked in pans.

"And some of their brethren, of the sons of the Kohathites, were over the shewbread to prepare it every sabbath." [1]

This account is found in a chapter partly identical with Neh. xi., and apparently refers to the period of Nehemiah; but the picture in the latter part of the chapter was probably drawn by the chronicler from his own knowledge of Temple routine. So, too, in his graphic accounts of the sacrifices by Hezekiah and Josiah,[2] we seem to have an eyewitness describing familiar scenes. Doubtless the chronicler himself had often been one of the Temple choir "when the burnt-offering began, and the song of Jehovah began also, together with the instruments of David, king of Israel; and all the congregation worshipped, and the singers sang, and the trumpeters sounded; and all this continued till the burnt-offering was finished." [3] Still the scale of these sacrifices, the hundreds of oxen and thousands of sheep, may have been fixed to accord with the splendour of the ancient kings. Such profusion of victims probably represented rather the dreams than the realities of the chronicler's Temple.

Our author's strong feeling for his own Levitical order shows itself in his narrative of Hezekiah's great sacrifices. The victims were so numerous that there

[1] 1 Chron. ix. 26-32; cf. 1 Chron. xxiii. 24-32.
[2] 2 Chron. xxix.-xxxi.; xxxiv.; xxxv.
[3] 2 Chron. xxix. 27, 28.

were not priests enough to flay them; to meet the
emergency the Levites were allowed on this one
occasion to discharge a priestly function and to take
an unusually conspicuous part in the national festival.
In zeal they were even superior to the priests : " The
Levites were more upright in heart to sanctify themselves than the priests." Possibly here the chronicler
is describing an incident which he could have paralleled
from his own experience. The priests of his time may
often have yielded to a natural temptation to shirk the
laborious and disagreeable parts of their duty; they
would catch at any plausible pretext to transfer their
burdens to the Levites, which the latter would be eager
to accept for the sake of a temporary accession of
dignity. Learned Jews were always experts in the
art of evading the most rigid and minute regulations
of the Law. For instance, the period of service
appointed for the Levites in the Pentateuch was from
the age of thirty to that of fifty.[1] But we gather from
Ezra and Nehemiah that comparatively few Levites
could be induced to throw in their lot with the returning exiles; there were not enough to perform the
necessary duties. To make up for paucity of numbers,
this period of service was increased; and they were
required to serve from twenty years old and upward.[2]
As the former arrangement had formed part of
the law attributed to Moses, in course of time the
later innovation was supposed to have originated with
David.

There were, too, other reasons for increasing the
efficiency of the Levitical order by lengthening their

---

[1] Num. iv. 3, 23, 35.

[2] 1 Chron. xxiii. 24, 27. Probably "twenty" should be read for
"thirty" in ver. 3.

term of service and adding to their numbers. The
establishment of the Pentateuch as the sacred code of
Judaism imposed new duties on priests and Levites
alike. The people needed teachers and interpreters of
the numerous minute and complicated rules by which
they were to govern their daily life. Judges were
needed to apply the laws in civil and criminal cases.
The Temple ministers were the natural authorities on
the Torah ; they had a chief interest in expounding and
enforcing it. But in these matters also the priests
seem to have left the new duties to the Levites. Apparently the first "scribes," or professional students of
the Law, were mainly Levites. There were priests
among them, notably the great father of the order,
"Ezra the priest the scribe," but the priestly families
took little share in this new work. The origin of the
educational and judicial functions of the Levites had
also come to be ascribed to the great kings of Judah.
A Levitical scribe is mentioned in the time of David.[1]
In the account of Josiah's reign we are expressly told
that "of the Levites there were scribes, and officers,
and porters"; and they are described as "the Levites
that taught all Israel."[2] In the same context we have
the traditional authority and justification for this new
departure. One of the chief duties imposed upon the
Levites by the Law was the care and carriage of the
Tabernacle and its furniture during the wanderings in
the wilderness. Josiah, however, bids the Levites "put
the holy ark in the house which Solomon the son of
David, king of Israel, did build ; there shall no more
be a burden upon your shoulders ; now serve the Lord
your God and His people Israel."[3] In other words,

---

[1] 1 Chron. xxiv. 6.   [2] 2 Chron. xxxiv. 13; xxxv. 3.
[3] 2 Chron. xxxv. 3 ; cf. 1 Chron. xxiii. 26.

"You are relieved of a large part of your old duties, and therefore have time to undertake new ones." The immediate application of this principle seems to be that a section of the Levites should do all the menial work of the sacrifices, and so leave the priests, and singers, and porters free for their own special service; but the same argument would be found convenient and conclusive whenever the priests desired to impose any new functions on the Levites.

Still the task of expounding and enforcing the Law brought with it compensations in the shape of dignity, influence, and emolument; and the Levites would soon be reconciled to their work as scribes, and would discover with regret that they could not retain the exposition of the Law in their own hands. Traditions were cherished in certain Levitical families that their ancestors had been " officers and judges " under David[1]; and it was believed that Jehoshaphat had organised a commission largely composed of Levites to expound and administer the Law in country districts.[2] This commission consisted of five princes, nine Levites, and two priests; "and they taught in Judah, having the book of the law of the Lord with them; and they went about throughout all the cities of Judah and taught among the people." As the subject of their teaching was the Pentateuch, their mission must have been rather judicial than religious. With regard to a later passage, it has been suggested that "probably it is the organisation of justice as existing in his own day that he" (the chronicler) "here carries back to Jehoshaphat, so that here most likely we have the oldest testimony to the synedrium of Jerusalem as a

---

[1] 1 Chron. xxvi. 29.   [2] 2 Chron. xvii. 7, 9.

court of highest instance over the provincial synedria, as also to its composition and presidency."[1] We can scarcely doubt that the form the chronicler has given to the tradition is derived from the institutions of his own age, and that his friends the Levites were prominent among the doctors of the Law, and not only taught and judged in Jerusalem, but also visited the country districts.

It will appear from this brief survey that the Levites were very completely organised. There were not only the great classes, the scribes, officers, porters, singers, and the Levites proper, so to speak, who assisted the priests, but special families had been made responsible for details of service : " Mattithiah had the set office over the things that were baked in pans ; and some of their brethren, of the sons of the Kohathites, were over the shewbread, to prepare it every sabbath."[2]

The priests were organised quite differently. The small number of Levites necessitated careful arrangements for using them to the best advantage ; of priests there were enough and to spare. The four thousand two hundred and eighty-nine priests who returned with Zerubbabel were an extravagant and impossible allowance for a single temple, and we are told that the numbers increased largely as time went on. The problem was to devise some means by which all the priests should have some share in the honours and emoluments of the Temple, and its solution was found in the "courses." The priests who returned with Zerubbabel are registered in four families : "the children of Jedaiah, of the house of Jeshua ; . . . the children of Immer ; . . . the children of Pashhur ; . . . the children

---

[1] **Wellhausen,** *History of Israel,* p. 191 ; cf. 2 Chron. xix. 4–11.
[2] 1 Chron. ix. 31, 32.

of Harim."[1] But the organisation of the chronicler's time is, as usual, to be found among the arrangements ascribed to David, who is said to have divided the priests into their twenty-four courses.[2] Amongst the heads of the courses we find Jedaiah, Jeshua, Harim, and Immer, but not Pashhur. Post-Biblical authorities mention twenty-four courses in connection with the second Temple. Zacharias, the father of John the Baptist, belonged to the course of Abijah[3]; and Josephus mentions a course "Eniakim."[4] Abijah was the head of one of David's courses; and Eniakim is almost certainly a corruption of Eliakim, of which name Jakim in Chronicles is a contraction.

These twenty-four courses discharged the priestly duties each in its turn. One was busy at the Temple while the other twenty-three were at home, some perhaps living on the profits of their office, others at work on their farms. The high-priest, of course, was always at the Temple; and the continuity of the ritual would necessitate the appointment of other priests as a permanent staff. The high-priest and the staff, being always on the spot, would have great opportunities for improving their own position at the expense of the other members of the courses, who were only there occasionally for a short time. Accordingly we are told later on that a few families had appropriated nearly all the priestly emoluments.

Courses of the Levites are sometimes mentioned in connection with those of the priests, as if the Levites had an exactly similar organisation.[5] Indeed, twenty-four courses of the singers are expressly named.[6] But

---

[1] Ezra ii. 36-39.
[2] 1 Chron. xxiv. 1-19.
[3] Luke i. 5.
[4] *Bell. Jud.*, IV. iii. 8.
[5] 1 Chron. xxiv. 20-31; 2 Chron. xxxi. 2.
[6] 1 Chron. xxv.

on examination we find that " course " for the Levites
in all cases where exact information is given [1] does not
mean one of a number of divisions which took work in
turn, but a division to which a definite piece of work
was assigned, *e.g.*, the care of the shewbread or of one
of the gates.   The idea that in ancient times there were
twenty-four alternating courses of Levites was not
derived from the arrangements of the chronicler's
age, but was an inference from the existence of priestly
courses.   According to the current interpretation of the
older history, there must have been under the monarchy
a very great many more Levites than priests, and any
reasons that existed for organising twenty-four priestly
courses would apply with equal force to the Levites.
It is true that the names of twenty-four courses of
singers are given, but in this list occurs the remarkable
and impossible group of names already discussed :—

" *I-have-magnified,   I-have-exalted-help ;   Sitting-in-
distress, I-have-spoken In-abundance Visions,*" [2] which
are in themselves sufficient proof that these twenty-
four courses of singers did not exist in the time of the
chronicler.

Thus the chronicler provides material for a fairly
complete account of the service and ministers of the
Temple ; but his interest in other matters was less close
and personal, so that he gives us comparatively little
information about civil persons and affairs.   The
restored Jewish community was, of course, made up
of descendants of the members of the old kingdom of

---

[1] 1 Chron. xxvi. ; Ezra vi. 18 ; Neh. xi. 36.

[2] Recently a complaint was received at the General Post-office
that some newspapers sent from France had failed to arrive.   It was
stated that the names of the papers were—*Il me manque* ; *Plusieurs* ;
Journaux ; *i.e.*, " I am short of " " Several " " Papers."

Judah.   The new Jewish state, like the old, is often
spoken of as "Judah"; but its claim to fully represent
the chosen people of Jehovah is expressed by the
frequent use of the name "Israel."   Yet within this new
Judah the old tribes of Judah and Benjamin are still
recognised.   It is true that in the register of the first
company of returning exiles the tribes are ignored, and
we are not told which families belonged to Judah or
which to Benjamin ; but we are previously told that
the chiefs of Judah and Benjamin rose up to return
to Jerusalem.   Part of this register arranges the companies according to the towns in which their ancestors
had lived before the Captivity, and of these some belong
to Judah and some to Benjamin.   We also learn that
the Jewish community included certain of the children
of Ephraim and Manasseh.[1]   There may also have been
families from the other tribes ; St. Luke, for instance,
describes Anna as of the tribe of Asher.[2]   But the
mass of genealogical matter relating to Judah and
Benjamin far exceeds what is given as to the other
tribes,[3] and proves that Judah and Benjamin were
co-ordinate members of the restored community, and
that no other tribe contributed any appreciable con-
tingent, except a few families from Ephraim and
Manasseh.   It has been suggested that the chronicler
shows special interest in the tribes which had occupied
Galilee—Asher, Naphtali, Zebulun, and Issachar—and
that this special interest indicates that the settlement
of Jews in Galilee had attained considerable dimensions
at the time when he wrote.   But this special interest
is not very manifest ; and later on, in the time of the

---

[1] I Chron. ix. 3.   [2] Luke ii. 36.
[3] Levi of course excepted.

Maccabees, the Jews in Galilee were so few that Simon took them all away with him, together with their wives and their children and all that they had, and brought them into Judæa.

The genealogies seem to imply that no descendants of the Transjordanic tribes or of Simeon were found in Judah in the age of the chronicler.

Concerning the tribe of Judah, we have already noted that it included two families which traced their descent to Egyptian ancestors, and that the Kenizzite clans of Caleb and Jerahmeel had been entirely incorporated in Judah and formed the most important part of the tribe. A comparison of the parallel genealogies of the house of Caleb gives us important information as to the territory occupied by the Jews. In ii. 42–49 we find the Calebites at Hebron and other towns of the south country, in accordance with the older history; but in ii. 50–55 they occupy Bethlehem and Kirjath-jearim and other towns in the neighbourhood of Jerusalem. The two paragraphs are really giving their territory before and after the Exile; during the Captivity Southern Judah had been occupied by the Edomites. It is indeed stated in Neh. xi. 25–30 that the children of Judah dwelt in a number of towns scattered over the whole territory of the ancient tribe; but the list concludes with the significant sentence, " So they *encamped* from Beer-sheba unto the valley of Hinnom." We are thus given to understand that the occupation was not permanent.

We have already noted that much of the space allotted to the genealogies of Judah is devoted to the house of David.[1] The form of this pedigree for the

---

[1] 1 Chron. iii.

generations after the Captivity indicates that the head of the house of David was no longer the chief of the state. During the monarchy only the kings are given as heads of the family in each generation : "Solomon's son was Rehoboam, Abijah his son, Asa his son," etc., etc.; but after the Captivity the first-born no longer occupied so unique a position. We have all the sons of each successive head of the family.

The genealogies of Judah include one or two references which throw a little light on the social organisation of the times. There were "families of scribes which dwelt at Jabez"[1] as well as the Levitical scribes. In the appendix[2] to the genealogies of chap. iv. we read of a house whose families wrought fine linen, and of other families who were porters to the king and lived on the royal estates. The immediate reference of these statements is clearly to the monarchy, and we are told that "the records are ancient"; but these ancient records were probably obtained by the chronicler from contemporary members of the families, who still pursued their hereditary calling.

As regards the tribe of Benjamin, we have seen that there was a family claiming descent from Saul.

The slight and meagre information given about Judah and Benjamin cannot accurately represent their importance as compared with the priests and Levites, but the general impression conveyed by the chronicler is confirmed by our other authorities. In his time the supreme interests of the Jews were religious. The one great institution was the Temple ; the highest order was the priesthood. All Jews were in a measure servants of the Temple ; Ephesus indeed was proud to be called

---

[1] ii. 55.   [2] iv. 21-23.

the temple-keeper of the great Diana, but Jerusalem was far more truly the temple-keeper of Jehovah. Devotion to the Temple gave to the Jews a unity which neither of the older Hebrew states had ever possessed. The kernel of this later Jewish territory seems to have been a comparatively small district of which Jerusalem was the centre. The inhabitants of this district carefully preserved the records of their family history, and loved to trace their descent to the ancient clans of Judah and Benjamin ; but for practical purposes they were all Jews, without distinction of tribe. Even the ministry of the Temple had become more homogeneous ; the non-Levitical descent of some classes of the Temple servants was first ignored and then forgotten, so that assistants at the sacrifices, singers, musicians, scribes, and porters, were all included in the tribe of Levi. The Temple conferred its own sanctity upon all its ministers.

In a previous chapter the Temple and its ministry were compared to a mediæval monastery or the establishment of a modern cathedral. In the same way Jerusalem might be compared to cities, like Ely or Canterbury, which exist mainly for the sake of their cathedrals, only both the sanctuary and city of the Jews came to be on a larger scale. Or, again, if the Temple be represented by the great abbey of St. Edmundsbury, Bury St. Edmunds itself might stand for Jerusalem, and the wide lands of the abbey for the surrounding districts, from which the Jewish priests derived their free-will offerings, and first-fruits, and tithes. Still in both these English instances there was a vigorous and independent secular life far beyond any that existed in Judæa.

A closer parallel to the temple on Zion is to be

found in the immense establishments of the Egyptian
temples. It is true that these were numerous in Egypt,
and the authority and influence of the priesthood were
checked and controlled by the power of the kings;
yet on the fall of the twentieth dynasty the high-priest
of the great temple of Amen at Thebes succeeded in
making himself king, and Egypt, like Judah, had its
dynasty of priest-kings.

The following is an account of the possessions of
the Theban temple of Amen, supposed to be given by
an Egyptian living about B.C. 1350 [1] :—

" Since the accession of the eighteenth dynasty,
Amen has profited more than any other god, perhaps
even more than Pharaoh himself, by the Egyptian
victories over the peoples of Syria and Ethiopia.   Each
success has brought him a considerable share of the
spoil collected upon the battle-fields, indemnities levied
from the enemy, prisoners carried into slavery.   He
possesses lands and gardens by the hundred in Thebes
and the rest of Egypt, fields and meadows, woods,
hunting-grounds, and fisheries; he has colonies in
Ethiopia or in the oases of the Libyan desert, and at
the extremity of the land of Canaan there are cities
under vassalage to him, for Pharaoh allows him to
receive the tribute from them.   The administration of
these vast properties requires as many officials and
departments as that of a kingdom.   It includes innumerable bailiffs for the agriculture; overseers for
the cattle and poultry; treasurers of twenty kinds for
the gold, silver, and copper, the vases and valuable
stuffs; foremen for the workshops and manufactures;
engineers; architects; boatmen; a fleet and an army

---

[1] Maspero, *Ancient Egypt and Assyria*, p. 60.

which often fight by the side of Pharaoh's fleet and army.   It is really a state within the state."

Many of the details of this picture would not be true for the temple of Zion; but the Jews were even more devoted to Jehovah than the Thebans to Amen, and the administration of the Jewish temple was more than " a state within the state " : it was the state itself.

CHAPTER VI

TEACHING BY ANACHRONISM

I Chron. ix. (cf. xv., xvi., xxiii.–xxvii., etc.).

"And David the king said, . . . Who then offereth willingly ? . . . And they gave for the service of the house of God . . . ten thousand darics."—I Chron. **xxix. 1, 5, 7.**

TEACHING by anachronism is a very common and effective form of religious instruction; and Chronicles, as the best Scriptural example of this method, affords a good opportunity for its discussion and illustration.

All history is more or less guilty of anachronism ; every historian perforce imports some of the ideas and circumstances of his own time into his narratives and pictures of the past : but we may distinguish three degrees of anachronism. Some writers or speakers make little or no attempt at archæological accuracy ; others temper the generally anachronistic character of their compositions by occasional reference to the manners and customs of the period they are describing ; and, again, there are a few trained students who succeed in drawing fairly accurate and consistent pictures of ancient life and history.

We will briefly consider the last two classes before returning to the first, in which we are chiefly interested.

Accurate archæology is, of course, part of the ideal
of the scientific historian. By long and careful study
of literature and monuments and by the exercise of
a lively and well-trained imagination, the student
obtains a vision of ancient societies. Nineveh and
Babylon, Thebes and Memphis, rise from their ashes
and stand before him in all their former splendour ;
he walks their streets and mixes with the crowds in
the market-place and the throng of worshippers at the
temple, each "in his habit as he lived." Rameses
and Sennacherib, Ptolemy and Antiochus, all play their
proper parts in this drama of his fancy. He can not
only recall their costumes and features : he can even
think their thoughts and feel their emotions ; he actually
lives in the past. In *Marius the Epicurean,* in Ebers's
Uarda, in Maspero's *Sketches of Assyrian and Egyptian
Life,* and in other more serious works we have some of
the fruits of this enlightened study of antiquity, and
are enabled to see the visions at second hand and in
some measure to live at once in the present and the
past, to illustrate and interpret the one by the other,
to measure progress and decay, and to understand the
Divine meaning of all history. Our more recent
histories and works on life and manners and even our
historical romances, especially those of Walter Scott,
have rendered a similar service to students of English
history. And yet at its very best such realisation of
the past is imperfect ; the gaps in our information are
unconsciously filled in from our experience, and the
ideas of the present always colour our reproduction of
ancient thought and feeling.   The most accurate history
is only a rough approximation to exact truth ; but, like
many other rough approximations, it is exact enough
for many important practical purposes.

But scholarly familiarity with the past has its draw-backs. The scholar may come to live so much amongst ancient memories that he loses touch with his own present. He may gain large stores of information about ancient Israelite life, and yet not know enough of his own generation to be able to make them sharers of his knowledge. Their living needs and circum-stances lie outside his practical experience; he cannot explain the past to them because he does not sym-pathise with their present; he cannot apply its lessons to difficulties and dangers which he does not understand.

Nor is the usefulness of the archæologist merely limited by his own lack of sympathy and experience. He may have both, and yet find that there are few of his contemporaries who can follow him in his excursions into bygone time. These limitations and drawbacks do not seriously diminish the value of archæology, but they have to be taken into account in discussing teach-ing by anachronism, and they have an important bearing on the practical application of archæological knowledge. We shall return to these points later on.

The second degree of anachronism is very common. We are constantly hearing and reading descriptions of Bible scenes and events in which the centuries before and after Christ are most oddly blended. Here and there will be a costume after an ancient monument, a Biblical description of Jewish customs, a few Scrip-tural phrases; but these are embedded in paragraphs which simply reproduce the social and religious ideas of the nineteenth century. For instance, in a recent work, amidst much display of archæological knowledge, we have the very modern ideas that Joseph and Mary went up to Bethlehem at the census, because Joseph and perhaps Mary also had property in Bethlehem, and

8

that when Joseph died " he left her a small but independent fortune." Many modern books might be
named in which Patriarchs and Apostles hold the language and express the sentiments of the most recent
schools of devotional Christianity; and yet an air of
historical accuracy is assumed by occasional touches
of archæology. Similarly in mediæval miracle-plays
characters from the Bible appeared in the dress of the
period, and uttered a grotesque mixture of Scriptural
phrases and vernacular jargon. Much of such work
as this may for all practical purposes be classed
under the third degree of anachronism. Sometimes,
however, the spiritual significance of a passage or an
incident turns upon a simple explanation of some
ancient custom, so that the archæological detail makes
a clear addition to its interest and instructiveness.
But in other cases a little archæology is a dangerous
thing. Scattered fragments of learned information do
not enable the reader in any way to revive the buried
past; they only remove the whole subject further from
his interest and sympathy. He is not reading about
his own day, nor does he understand that the events
and personages of the narrative ever had anything in
common with himself and his experience. The antique
garb, the strange custom, the unusual phrase, disguise
that real humanity which the reader shares with these
ancient worthies. They are no longer men of like
passions with himself, and he finds neither warning
nor encouragement in their story. He is like a spectator of a drama played by poor actors with a limited
stock of properties. The scenery and dresses show
that the play does not belong to his own time, but they
fail to suggest that it ever belonged to any period.
He has a languid interest in the performance as a

spectacle, but his feelings are not touched, and he is never carried away by the acting.

We have laid so much stress on the drawbacks attaching to a little archæology because they will emphasise what we have to say about the use of pure anachronism. Our last illustration, however, reminds us that these drawbacks detract but little from the influence of earnest men. If the acting be good, we forget the scenery and costumes ; the genius of a great preacher more than atones for poor archæology, because, in spite of dress and custom, he makes his hearers feel that the characters of the Bible were instinct with rich and passionate life. We thus arrive at our third degree of pure anachronism.

Most people read their Bible without any reference to archæology. If they dramatise the stories, they do so in terms of their own experience. The characters are dressed like the men and women they know : Nazareth is like their native village, and Jerusalem is like the county town ; the conversations are carried on in the English of the Authorised Version. This reading of Scripture is well illustrated by the description in a recent writer of a modern prophet in Tennessee [1] :—

"There was nought in the scene to suggest to a mind familiar with the facts an Oriental landscape—nought akin to the hills of Judæa. It was essentially of the New World, essentially of the Great Smoky Mountains. Yet ignorance has its licence. It never occurred to Teck Jepson that his Bible heroes had lived elsewhere. Their history had to him an intimate personal relation, as of the story of an ancestor, in the homestead ways and closely familiar. He brooded

---

[1] Craddock, *Despot of Bromsgrove Edge*. Teck Jepson is, of course, an imaginary character, but none the less representative.

upon these narratives, instinct with dramatic interest, enriched with poetic colour, and localised in his robust imagination, till he could trace Hagar's wild wanderings in the fastnesses, could show where Jacob slept and piled his altar of stones, could distinguish the bush, of all others on the 'bald,' that blazed with fire from heaven when the angel of the Lord stood within it. Somehow, even in their grotesque variation, they lost no dignity in their transmission to the modern conditions of his fancy. Did the facts lack significance because it was along the gullied red clay roads of Piomingo Cove that he saw David, the smiling stripling, running and holding high in his hand the bit of cloth cut from Saul's garments while the king had slept in a cave at the base of Chilhowie Mountain ? And how was the splendid miracle of translation discredited because Jepson believed that the chariot of the Lord had rested in scarlet and purple clouds upon the towering summit of Thunderhead, that Elijah might thence ascend into heaven ? "

Another and more familiar example of "singular alterations in date and circumstances" is the version in *Ivanhoe* of the war between Benjamin and the other tribes :—

" How long since in Palestine a deadly feud arose between the tribe of Benjamin and the rest of the Israelitish nation ; and how they cut to pieces well-nigh all the chivalry of that tribe ; and how they swore by our blessed Lady that they would not permit those who remained to marry in their lineage ; and how they became grieved for their vow, and sent to consult his Holiness the Pope how they might be absolved from it ; and how, by the advice of the Holy Father, the youth of the tribe of Benjamin carried off from a superb tournament all the ladies who were there present, and thus won them wives without the consent either of their brides or their brides' families."

It is needless to say that the chronicler was not thus hopelessly at sea about the circumstances of ancient Hebrew history; but he wrote in the same simple, straightforward, childlike spirit. Israel had always been the Israel of his own experience, and it never occurred to him that its institutions under the kings had been other than those with which he was familiar. He had no more hesitation in filling up the gaps in the book of Kings from what he saw round about him than a painter would have in putting the white clouds and blue waters of to-day into a picture of skies and seas a thousand years ago. He attributes to the pious kings of Judah the observance of the ritual of his own times. Their prophets use phrases taken from post-Exilic writings. David is regarded as the author of the existing ecclesiastical system in almost all matters that do not date back to Moses, and especially as the organiser of the familiar music of the Temple. David's choristers sing the hymns of the second Temple. Amongst the contributions of his nobles towards the building of the Temple, we read of ten thousand darics, the daric being a coin introduced by the Persian king Darius.

But we must be careful to recognise that the chronicler writes in perfect good faith. These views of the monarchy were common to all educated and thoughtful men of his time; they were embodied in current tradition, and were probably already to be met with in writing. To charge him with inventing them is absurd; they already existed, and did not need to be invented. He cannot have coloured his narrative in the interests of the Temple and the priesthood When he **lived,** these interests were guaranteed by ancient custom and by the authoritative sanction of the Pentateuchal Law.   The chronicler does not write with the strong feeling of a man who maintains a doubtful cause ; there is no hint of any alternative view which needs to be disproved and rejected in favour of his own.   He expatiates on his favourite themes with happy, leisurely serenity, and is evidently confident that his treatment of them will meet with general and cordial approval.

And doubtless the author of Chronicles " served his own generation by the will of God," and served them in the way he intended.   He made the history of the monarchy more real and living to them, and enabled them to understand better that the reforming kings of Judah were loyal servants of Jehovah and had been used by Him for the furtherance of true religion.   The pictures drawn by Samuel and Kings of David and the best of his successors would not have enabled the Jews of his time to appreciate these facts.   They had no idea of any piety that was not expressed in the current observances of the Law, and Samuel and Kings did not ascribe such observances to the earlier kings of Judah. But the chronicler and his authorities were able to discern in the ancient Scriptures the genuine piety of David and Hezekiah and other kings, and drew what seemed to them the obvious conclusion that these pious kings observed the Law.   They then proceeded to rewrite the history in order that the true character of the kings and their relation to Jehovah might be made intelligible to the people.   The only piety which the chronicler could conceive was combined with observance of the Law ; naturally therefore it was only thus that he could describe piety.   His work would be read with eager interest, and would play a definite and useful part in the religious education of the people. It would bring home to them, as the older histories could not, the abiding presence of Jehovah with Israel and its leaders. Chronicles interpreted history to its own generation by translating older records into the circumstances and ideas of its own time.

And in this it remains our example. Chronicles may fall very far short of the ideal and yet be superior to more accurate histories which fail to make themselves intelligible to their own generation. The ideal history no doubt would tell the story with archæological precision, and then interpret it by modern parallels; the historian would show us what we should actually have seen and heard if we had lived in the period he is describing; he would also help our weak imagination by pointing us to such modern events or persons as best illustrate those ancient times. No doubt Chronicles fails to bring before our eyes an accurate vision of the history of the monarchy; but, as we have said, all history fails somewhat in this respect. It is simply impossible to fulfil the demand for history that shall have the accuracy of an architect's plans of a house or an astronomer's diagrams of the orbit of a planet. Chronicles, however, fails more seriously than most history, and on the whole rather more than most commentaries and sermons.

But this lack of archæological accuracy is far less serious than a failure to make it clear that the events of ancient history were as real and as interesting as those of modern times, and that its personages were actual men and women, with a full equipment of body, mind, and soul. There have been many teachers and preachers, innocent of archæology, who have yet been able to apply Bible narratives with convincing power to the hearts and consciences of their hearers. They may have missed some points and misunderstood others, but they have brought out clearly the main, practical teaching of their subject; and we must not allow amusement at curious anachronisms to blind us to their great gifts in applying ancient history to modern circumstances. For instance, the little captive maid in the story of Naaman has been described by a local preacher as having illuminated texts hung up in her bedroom, and (perambulators not being then in use) as having constructed a go-cart for the baby out of an old tea-chest and four cotton reels. We feel inclined to smile; but, after all, such a picture would make children feel that the captive maid was a girl whom they could understand and might even imitate. A more correct version of the story, told with less human interest, might leave the impression that she was a mere animated doll in a quaint costume, who made impossibly pious remarks.

Enlightened and well-informed Christian teachers may still learn something from the example of the chronicler. The uncritical character of his age affords no excuse to them for shutting their eyes to the fuller light which God has given to their generation. But we are reminded that permanently significant stories have their parallels in every age. There are always prodigal sons, and foolish virgins, importunate widows, and good Samaritans. The ancient narratives are interesting as quaint and picturesque stories of former times; but it is our duty as teachers to discover the modern parallels of their eternal meaning : their lessons are often best enforced by telling them afresh as they would have been told if their authors had lived in our time, in other words by a frank use of anachronism.

It may be objected that the result in the case of Chronicles is not encouraging. Chronicles is far less interesting than Kings, and far less useful in furnishing materials for the historian. These facts, however, are not inconsistent with the usefulness of the book for its own age. Teaching by anachronism simply seeks to render a service to its own generation; its purpose is didactic, and not historical. How many people read the sermons of eighteenth-century divines? But each generation has a right to this special service. The first duty of the religious teacher is for the men and women that look to him for spiritual help and guidance. He may incidentally produce literary work of permanent value for posterity; but a Church whose ministry sacrificed practical usefulness in the attempt to be learned and literary would be false to its most sacred functions. The noblest self-denial of Christian service may often lie in putting aside all such ambition and devoting the ability which might have made a successful author to making Divine truth intelligible and interesting to the uncultured and the unimaginative. Authors themselves are sometimes led to make a similar sacrifice; they write to help the many to-day when they might have written to delight men of literary taste in all ages. Few things are so ephemeral as popular religious literature; it is as quickly and entirely forgotten as last year's sunsets: but it is as necessary and as useful as the sunshine and the clouds, which are being always spent and always renewed. Chronicles is a specimen of this class of literature, and its presence in the canon testifies to the duty of providing a special application of the sacred truths of ancient history for each succeeding generation.

BOOK III

MESSIANIC AND OTHER TYPES

CHAPTER I

TEACHING BY TYPES

A MORE serious charge has been brought against Chronicles than that dealt with in the last chapter. Besides anachronisms, additions, and alterations, the chronicler has made omissions that give an entirely new complexion to the history. He omits, for instance, almost everything that detracts from the character and achievements of David and Solomon; he almost entirely ignores the reigns of Saul and Ishbosheth, and of all the northern kings. These facts are obvious to the most casual reader, and a moment's reflection shows that David as we should know him if we had only Chronicles is entirely different from the historical David of Samuel and Kings. The latter David has noble qualities, but displays great weakness and falls into grievous sin; the David of Chronicles is almost always an hero and a blameless saint.

All this is unquestionably true, and yet the purpose and spirit of Chronicles are honest and praiseworthy. Our judgment must be governed by the relation which the chronicler intended his work to sustain towards the older history. Did he hope that Samuel and Kings would be altogether superseded by this new version of the history of the monarchy, and so eventually be

suppressed and forgotten? There were precedents
that might have encouraged such a hope. The Pentateuch and the books from Joshua to Kings derived their
material from older works; but the older works were
superseded by these books, and entirely disappeared.
The circumstances, however, were different when the
chronicler wrote: Samuel and Kings had been established for centuries. Moreover, the Jewish community
in Babylon still exercised great influence over the
Palestinian Jews. Copies of Samuel and Kings must
have been preserved at Babylon, and their possessors
could not be eager to destroy them, and then to incur
the expense of replacing them by copies of a history
written at Jerusalem from the point of view of the
priests and Levites. We may therefore put aside
the theory that Chronicles was intended altogether to
supersede Samuel and Kings. Another possible theory
is that the chronicler, after the manner of mediæval
historians, composed an abstract of the history of the
world from the Creation to the Captivity as an introduction to his account in Ezra and Nehemiah of the
more recent post-Exilic period. This theory has some
truth in it, but does not explain the fact that Chronicles
is disproportionately long if it be merely such an introduction. Probably the chronicler's main object was to
compose a text-book, which could safely and usefully be
placed in the hands of the common people. There
were obvious objections to the popular use of Samuel
and Kings. In making a selection from his material,
the chronicler had no intention of falsifying history.
Scholars, he knew, would be acquainted with the older
books, and could supplement his narrative from the
sources which he himself had used. In his own work
he was anxious to confine himself to the portions of the

history which had an obvious religious significance, and could readily be used for purposes of edification. He was only applying more thoroughly a principle that had guided his predecessors. The Pentateuch itself is the result of a similar selection, only there and in the other earlier histories a very human interest in dramatic narrative has sometimes interfered with an exclusive attention to edification.

Indeed, the principles of selection adopted by the chronicler are common to many historians. A school history does not dwell on the domestic vices of kings or on the private failings of statesmen. It requires no great stretch of imagination to conceive of a Royalist history of England, that should entirely ignore the Commonwealth. Indeed, historians of Christian missions sometimes show about the same interest in the work of other Churches than their own that Chronicles takes in the northern kingdom. The work of the chronicler may also be compared to monographs which confine themselves to some special aspect of their subject. We have every reason to be thankful that the Divine providence has preserved for us the richer and fuller narrative of Samuel and Kings, but we cannot blame the chronicler because he has observed some of the ordinary canons for the composition of historical text-books.

The chronicler's selective method, however, is carried so far that the historical value of his work is seriously impaired; yet in this respect also he is kept in countenance by very respectable authorities. We are more concerned, however, to point out the positive results of the method. Instead of historical portraits, we are presented with a gallery of ideals, types of character which we are asked either to admire or to condemn. On he one hand, we have David and Solomon, Jehoshaphat and Hezekiah, and the rest of the reforming kings of Judah; on the other hand, there are Jeroboam, and Ahab, and Ahaz, the kings of Israel, and the bad kings of Judah. All these are very sharply defined in either white or black. The types of Chronicles are ideals, and not studies of ordinary human character, with its mingled motives and subtle gradations of light and shade. The chronicler has nothing in common with the authors of modern realistic novels or anecdotal memoirs. His subject is not human nature as it is so much as human nature as it ought to be. There is obviously much to be learnt from such ideal pictures, and this form of inspired teaching is by no means the least effective; it may be roughly compared with our Lord's method of teaching by parables, without, however, at all putting the two upon the same level.

Before examining these types in detail, we may devote a little space to some general considerations upon teaching by types. For the present we will confine ourselves to a non-theological sense of type, using the word to mean any individual who is representative or typical of a class. But the chronicler's individuals do not represent classes of actual persons, but good men as they seem to their most devoted admirers and bad men as they seem to their worst enemies. They are ideal types. Chronicles is not the only literature in which such ideal types are found. They occur in the funeral sermons and obituary notices of popular favourites, and in the pictures which politicians draw in election speeches of their opponents, only in these there is a note of personal feeling from which the chronicler is free.

In fact, all biography tends to idealise; human nature

as it is has generally to be looked for in the pages of fiction. When we have been blessed with a good and brave man, we wish to think of him at his best; we are not anxious to have thrust upon our notice the weaknesses and sins which he regretted and for the most part controlled. Some one who loved and honoured him is asked to write the biography, with a tacit understanding that he is not to give us a picture of the real man in the *déshabille*, as it were, of his own inner consciousness. He is to paint us a portrait of the man as he strove to fashion himself after his own high ideal. The true man, as God knows him and as his fellows should remember him, was the man in his higher nature and nobler aspirations. The rest, surely, was but the vanishing remnant of a repudiated self. The biographer idealises, because he believes that the ideal best represents the real man. This is what the chronicler, with a large faith and liberal charity, has done for David and Solomon.

Such an ideal picture appeals to us with pathetic emphasis. It seems to say, "In spite of temptation, and sin, and grievous falls, this is what I ever aimed at and desired to be. Do not thou content thyself with any lower ideal. My higher nature had its achievements as well as its aspirations. Remember that in thy weakness thou mayest also achieve."

> "What I aspired to be,
> And was not, comforts me;
>   *   *   *   *
> All I could never be,
> All men ignored in me,
> This I was worth to God. . . ."

But we may take these ideals as types, not only in a general sense, but also in a modification of the

9

dogmatic meaning of the word. We are not concerned here with the type as the mere external symbol of truth yet to be revealed; such types are chiefly found in the ritual of the Pentateuch. The circumstances of a man's life may also serve as a type in the narrower sense, but we venture to apply the theological idea of type to the significance of the higher nature in a good man. It has been said in reference to types in the theological sense that " a type is neither a prophecy, nor a symbol, nor an allegory, yet it has relations with each of these. A prophecy is a prediction in words, a type a prediction in things. A symbol is a sensuous representation of a thing; a type is such a representation having a distinctly predictive aspect: . . . a type is an enacted prophecy, a kind of prophecy by action."[1] We cannot, of course, include in our use of the term type " sensuous representation" and some other ideas connected with " type" in a theological sense. Our type is a prediction in persons rather than in things. But the use of the term is justified as including the most essential point: that "a type is an enacted prophecy, a kind of prophecy by action." These personal types are the most real and significant; they have no mere arbitrary or conventional relation to their antitype. The enacted prophecy is the beginning of its own fulfilment, the first-fruits of the greater harvest that is to be. The better moments of the man who is hungering and thirsting after righteousness are a type, a promise, and prophecy of his future satisfaction. They have also a wider and deeper meaning: they show what is possible for humanity, and give an assurance of the spiritual progress of the world. The elect remnant

---

[1] Cave, *Scripture Doctrine of Sacrifice*, p. 163.

of Israel were the type of the great Christian Church ;
the spiritual aspirations and persistent faith of a few
believers were a prophecy that "the earth should be
full of the knowledge of the Lord, as the waters cover
the sea." "The kingdom of heaven is like unto a
grain of mustard seed, . . . which is less than all seeds ;
but when it is grown, it is greater than the herbs,
and becometh a tree." When therefore the chronicler
ignores the evil in David and Solomon and only records
the good, he treats them as types. He takes what
was best in them and sets it forth as a standard and
prophecy for the future, a pattern in the mount to be
realised hereafter in the structure of God's spiritual
temple upon earth.

But the Holy Spirit guided the hopes and intuitions
of the sacred writers to a special fulfilment. We can
see that their types have one antitype in the growth of
the Church and the progress of mankind ; but the Old
Testament looked for their chief fulfilment in a Divine
Messenger and Deliverer: its ideals are types of the
Messiah. The higher life of a good man was a revelation of God and a promise of His highest and best
manifestation in Christ. We shall endeavour to show
in subsequent chapters how Chronicles served to develop
the idea of the Messiah.

But the chronicler's types are not all prophecies of
future progress or Messianic glory. The brighter portions of his picture are thrown into relief by a dark
background. The good in Jeroboam is as completely
ignored as the evil in David. Apart from any question
of historical accuracy, the type is unfortunately a true
one. There is a leaven of the Pharisees and of Herod,
as well as a leaven of the kingdom. If the base leaven
be left to work by itself, it will leaven the whole mass ;

and in a final estimate of the character of those who do evil " with both hands earnestly," little allowance needs to be made for redeeming features. Even if we are still able to believe that there is a seed of goodness in things evil, we are forced to admit that the seed has remained dead and unfertilised, has had no growth and borne no fruit. But probably most men may sometimes be profitably admonished by considering the typical sinner—the man in whose nature evil has been able to subdue all things to itself.

The strange power of teaching by types has been well expressed by one who was herself a great mistress of the art : " Ideas are often poor ghosts : our sun-filled eyes cannot discern them ; they pass athwart us in thin vapour, and cannot make themselves felt ; they breathe upon us with warm breath, they touch us with soft, responsive hands ; they look at us with sad, sincere eyes, and speak to us in appealing tones ; they are clothed in a living human soul ; . . . their presence is a power." [1]

---

[1] George Eliot, *Janet's Repentance*, chap. xix.

CHAPTER II

DAVID—I. HIS TRIBE AND DYNASTY

KING and kingdom were so bound up in ancient life that an ideal for the one implied an ideal for the other; all distinction and glory possessed by either was shared by both. The tribe and kingdom of Judah were exalted by the fame of David and Solomon; but, on the other hand, a specially exalted position is accorded to David in the Old Testament because he is the representative of the people of Jehovah. David himself had been anointed by Divine command to be king of Israel, and he thus became the founder of the only legitimate dynasty of Hebrew kings. Saul and Ishbosheth had no significance for the later religious history of the nation. Apparently to the chronicler the history of true religion in Israel was a blank between Joshua and David; the revival began when the Ark was brought to Zion, and the first steps were taken to rear the Temple in succession to the Mosaic tabernacle. He therefore omits the history of the Judges and Saul. But the battle of Gilboa is given to introduce the reign of David, and incidental condemnation is passed on Saul: "So Saul died for his trespass which he committed against the Lord, because of the word of the Lord, which he kept not, and also for that he asked counsel of one that had a familiar spirit, to inquire

133

thereby, and inquired not of the Lord; therefore He slew him and turned the kingdom unto David the son of Jesse."

The reign of Saul had been an unsuccessful experiment; its only real value had been to prepare the way for David. At the same time the portrait of Saul is not given at full length, like those of the wicked kings, partly perhaps because the chronicler had little interest for anything before the time of David and the Temple, but partly, we may hope, because the record of David's affection for Saul kept alive a kindly feeling towards the founder of the monarchy.

Inasmuch as Jehovah had "turned the kingdom unto David," the reign of Ishbosheth was evidently the intrusion of an illegitimate pretender; and the chronicler treats it as such. If we had only Chronicles, we should know nothing about the reign of Ishbosheth, and should suppose that, on the death of Saul, David succeeded at once to an undisputed sovereignty over all Israel. The interval of conflict is ignored because, according to the chronicler's views, David was, from the first, king *de jure* over the whole nation. Complete silence as to Ishbosheth was the most effective way of expressing this fact.

The same sentiment of hereditary legitimacy, the same formal and exclusive recognition of a *de jure* sovereign, has been shown in modern times by titles like Louis XVIII. and Napoleon III. For both schools of Legitimists the absence of *de facto* sovereignty did not prevent Louis XVII. and Napoleon II. from having been lawful rulers of France. In Israel, moreover, the Divine right of the one chosen dynasty had religious as well as political importance. We have already seen that Israel claimed a hereditary title to its special privileges; it was therefore natural that a hereditary qualification should be thought necessary for the kings. They represented the nation; they were the Divinely appointed guardians of its religion; they became in time the types of the Messiah, its promised Saviour. In all this Saul and Ishbosheth had neither part nor lot; the promise to Israel had always descended in a direct line, and the special promise that was given to its kings and through them to their people began with David. There was no need to carry the history further back.

We have already noticed that, in spite of this general attitude towards Saul, the genealogy of some of his descendants is given twice over in the earlier chapters. No doubt the chronicler made this concession to gratify friends or to conciliate an influential family. It is interesting to note how personal feeling may interfere with the symmetrical development of a theological theory. At the same time we are enabled to discern a practical reason for rigidly ignoring the kingship oɪ Saul and Ishbosheth. To have recognised Saul as the Lord's anointed, like David, would have complicated contemporary dogmatics, and might possibly have given rise to jealousies between the descendants of Saul and those of David. Within the narrow limits of the Jewish community such quarrels might have been inconvenient and even dangerous.

The reasons for denying the legitimacy of the northern kings were obvious and conclusive. Successful rebels who had destroyed the political and religious unity of Israel could not inherit "the sure mercies of David" or be included in the covenant which secured the permanence of his dynasty.

The exclusive association of Messianic ideas with a

single family emphasises their antiquity, continuity, and development. The hope of Israel had its roots deep in the history of the people ; it had grown with their growth and maintained itself through their changing fortunes. As the hope centred in a single family, men were led to expect an individual personal Messiah ; they were being prepared to see in Christ the fulfilment of all righteousness.

But the choice of the house of David involved the choice of the tribe of Judah and the rejection of the kingdom of Samaria. The ten tribes, as well as the kings of Israel, had cut themselves off both from the Temple and the sacred dynasty, and therefore from the covenant into which Jehovah had entered with " the man after his own heart." Such a limitation of the chosen people was suggested by many precedents. Chronicles, following the Pentateuch, tells how the call came to Abraham, but only some of the descendants of one of his sons inherited the promise. Why should not a selection be made from among the sons of Jacob ? But the twelve tribes had been explicitly and solemnly included in the unity of Israel, largely through David himself. The glory of David and Solomon consisted in their sovereignty over a united people. The national recollection of this golden age loved to dwell on the union of the twelve tribes. The Pentateuch added legal sanction to ancient sentiment. The twelve tribes were associated together in national lyrics, like the " Blessing of Jacob " and the " Blessing of Moses." The song of Deborah told how the northern tribes " came to the help of the Lord against the mighty." It was simply impossible for the chronicler to absolutely repudiate the ten tribes ; and so they are formally included in the genealogies of Israel, and are recognised in the history of David and

Solomon. Then the recognition stops. From the time
of the disruption the northern kingdom is quietly but
persistently ignored. Its prophets and sanctuaries were
as illegitimate as its kings. The great struggle of Elijah
and Elisha for the honour of Jehovah is omitted, with
all the rest of their history. Elijah is only mentioned
as sending a letter to Jehoram, king of Judah; Elisha
is never even named.

On the other hand, it is more than once implied that
Judah, with the Levites, and the remnants of Simeon
and Benjamin, are the true Israel. When Rehoboam
"was strong he forsook the law of the Lord, and all
Israel with him." After Shishak's invasion, "the princes
of Israel and the king humbled themselves."[1] The
annals of Manasseh, king of Judah, are said to be
"written among the acts of the kings of Israel."[2] The
register of the exiles who returned with Zerubbabel is
headed "The number of the men of the people of
Israel."[3] The chronicler tacitly anticipates the position
of St. Paul: "They are not all Israel which are of
Israel"; and the Apostle might have appealed to
Chronicles to show that the majority of Israel might
fail to recognise and accept the Divine purpose for
Israel, and that the true Israel would then be found in
an elect remnant. The Jews of the second Temple
naturally and inevitably came to ignore the ten tribes and
to regard themselves as constituting this true Israel. As
a matter of history, there had been a period during which
the prophets of Samaria were of far more importance to
the religion of Jehovah than the temple at Jerusalem;
but in the chronicler's time the very existence of the
ten tribes was ancient history. Then, at any rate,

---

[1] 2 Chron. xii. 1, 6.   [2] 2 Chron. xxxiii. 18.
[3] Ezra ii. 2.

t was true that God's Israel was to be found in the Jewish community, at and around Jerusalem. They inherited the religious spirit of their fathers, and received from them the sacred writings and traditions, and carried on the sacred ritual. They preserved the truth and transmitted it from generation to generation, till at last it was merged in the mightier stream of Christian revelation.

The attitude of the chronicler towards the prophets of the northern kingdom does not in any way represent the actual importance of these prophets to the religion of Israel; but it is a very striking expression of the fact that after the Captivity the ten tribes had long ceased to exercise any influence upon the spiritual life of their nation.

The chronicler's attitude is also open to criticism on another side. He is dominated by his own surroundings, and in his references to the Judaism of his own time there is no formal recognition of the Jewish community in Babylon; and yet even his own casual allusions confirm what we know from other sources, namely that the wealth and learning of the Jews in Babylon were an important factor in Judaism until a very late date. This point perhaps rather concerns Ezra and Nehemiah than Chronicles, but it is closely connected with our present subject, and is most naturally treated along with it. The chronicler might have justified himself by saying that the true home of Israel must be in Palestine, and that a community in Babylon could only be considered as subsidiary to the nation in its own home and worshipping at the Temple. Such a sentiment, at any rate, would have met with universal approval amongst Palestinian Jews. The chronicler might also have replied that the Jews in

Babylon belonged to Judah and Benjamin and were sufficiently recognised in the general prominence given to these tribes. In all probability some Palestinian Jews would have been willing to class their Babylonian kinsmen with the ten tribes. Voluntary exiles from the Temple, the Holy City, and the Land of Promise had in great measure cut themselves off from the full privileges of the people of Jehovah. If, however, we had a Babylonian book of Chronicles, we should see both Jerusalem and Babylon in another light.

The chronicler was possessed and inspired by the actual living present round about him; he was content to let the dead past bury its dead. He was probably inclined to believe that the absent are mostly wrong, and that the men who worked with him for the Lord and His temple were the true Israel and the Church of God. He was enthusiastic in his own vocation and loyal to his brethren. If his interests were somewhat narrowed by the urgency of present circumstances, most men suffer from the same limitations. Few Englishmen realise that the battle of Agincourt is part of the history of the United States, and that Canterbury Cathedral is a monument of certain stages in the growth of the religion of New England. We are not altogether willing to admit that these voluntary exiles from our Holy Land belong to the true Anglo-Saxon Israel.

Churches are still apt to ignore their obligations to teachers who, like the prophets of Samaria, seem to have been associated with alien or hostile branches of the family of God. A religious movement which fails to secure for itself a permanent monument is usually labelled heresy. If it has neither obtained recognition within the Church nor yet organised a sect for itself, its services are forgotten or denied. Even the orthodoxy of one generation is sometimes contemptuous of the older orthodoxy which made it possible; and yet Gnostics, Arians and Athanasians, Arminians and Calvinists, have all done something to build up the temple of faith.

The nineteenth century prides itself on a more liberal spirit. But Romanist historians are not eager to acknowledge the debt of their Church to the Reformers; and there are Protestant partisans who deny that we are the heirs of the Christian life and thought of the mediæval Church and are anxious to trace the genealogy of pure religion exclusively through a supposed succession of obscure and half-mythical sects. Limitations like those of the chronicler still narrow the sympathies of earnest and devout Christians.

But it is time to return to the more positive aspects of the teaching of Chronicles, and to see how far we have already traced its exposition of the Messianic idea. The plan of the book implies a spiritual claim on behalf of the Jewish community of the Restoration. Because they believed in Jehovah, whose providence had in former times controlled the destinies of Israel, they returned to their ancestral home that they might serve and worship the God of their fathers. Their faith survived the ruin of Judah and their own captivity; they recognised the power, and wisdom, and love of God alike in the prosperity and in the misfortunes of their race. "They believed God, and it was counted unto them for righteousness." The great prophet of the Restoration had regarded this new Israel as itself a Messianic people, perhaps even "a light to the Gentiles" and "salvation unto the ends of the earth."[1] The

---

[1] Isa. xlix. 6.

chronicler's hopes were more modest; the new Jerusalem had been seen by the prophet as an ideal vision;
the historian knew it by experience as an imperfect
human society : but he believed none the less in its high
spiritual vocation and prerogatives. He claimed the
future for those who were able to trace the hand of God
in their past.

Under the monarchy the fortunes of Jerusalem had
been bound up with those of the house of David.
The chronicler brings out all that was best in the
history of the ancient kings of Judah, that this ideal
picture of the state and its rulers might encourage
and inspire to future hope and effort. The character
and achievements of David and his successors were
of permanent significance. The grace and favour
accorded to them symbolised the Divine promise for
the future, and this promise was to be realised through
a Son of David.

CHAPTER III

DAVID—II. HIS PERSONAL HISTORY

IN order to understand why the chronicler entirely recasts the graphic and candid history of David given in the book of Samuel, we have to consider the place that David had come to fill in Jewish religion. It seems probable that among the sources used by the author of the book of Samuel was a history of David, written not long after his death, by some one familiar with the inner life of the court. " No one," says the proverb, "is an hero to his valet"; very much what a valet is to a private gentleman courtiers are to a king: their knowledge of their master approaches to the familiarity which breeds contempt. Not that David was ever a subject for contempt or less than an hero even to his own courtiers; but they knew him as a very human hero, great in his vices as well as in his virtues, daring in battle and wise in counsel, sometimes also reckless in sin, yet capable of unbounded repentance, loving not wisely, but too well. And as they knew him, so they described him; and their picture is an immortal possession for all students of sacred life and literature. But it is not the portrait of a Messiah; when we think of the "Son of David," we do not want to be reminded of Bath-sheba.

During the six or seven centuries that elapsed be-

tween the death of David and the chronicler, the name
of David had come to have a symbolic meaning,
which was largely independent of the personal character
and career of the actual king. His reign had become
idealised by the magic of antiquity; it was a glory of
"the good old times." His own sins and failures were
obscured by the crimes and disasters of later kings.
And yet, in spite of all its shortcomings, the "house of
David" still remained the symbol alike of ancient glory
and of future hopes. We have seen from the genealogies how intimate the connection was between the
family and its founder. Ephraim and Benjamin may
mean either patriarchs or tribes. A Jew was not
always anxious to distinguish between the family and
the founder. "David" and "the house of David"
became almost interchangeable terms.

Even the prophets of the eighth century connect the
future destiny of Israel with David and his house.
The child, of whom Isaiah prophesied, was to sit "upon
the throne of David" and be "over his kingdom, to
establish it and to uphold it with judgment and with
righteousness from henceforth even for ever."[1] And,
again, the king who is to "sit . . . in truth, . . . judging,
and seeking judgment, and swift to do righteousness,"
is to have "his throne . . . established in mercy in the
tent of David."[2] When Sennacherib attacked Jerusalem, the city was defended[3] for Jehovah's own sake
and for His servant David's sake. In the word of the
Lord that came to Isaiah for Hezekiah, David super-
sedes, as it were, the sacred fathers of the Hebrew
race; Jehovah is not spoken of as "the God of
Abraham, Isaac, and Jacob," but "the God of David."[4]

---

[1] Isa. ix. 7.
[2] Isa. xvi. 5.
[3] Isa. xxxvii. 35.
[4] Isa. xxxviii. 5.

As founder of the dynasty, he takes rank with the founders of the race and religion of Israel: he is "the patriarch David."[1] The northern prophet Hosea looks forward to the time when "the children of Israel shall return, and seek the Lord their God and David their king"[2]; when Amos wishes to set forth the future prosperity of Israel, he says that the Lord "will raise up the tabernacle of David"[3]; in Micah "the ruler in Israel" is to come forth from Bethlehem Ephrathah, the birthplace of David[4]; in Jeremiah such references to David are frequent, the most characteristic being those relating to the "righteous branch, whom the Lord will raise up unto David," who "shall reign as king and deal wisely, and shall execute judgment and justice in the land, in whose days Judah shall be saved, and Israel shall dwell safely"[5]; in Ezekiel "My servant David" is to be the shepherd and prince of Jehovah's restored and reunited people[6]; Zechariah, writing at what we may consider the beginning of the chronicler's own period, follows the language of his predecessors: he applies Jeremiah's prophecy of "the righteous branch" to Zerubbabel, the prince of the house of David[7]: similarly in Haggai Zerubbabel is the chosen of Jehovah[8]; in the appendix to Zechariah it is said that when "the Lord defends the inhabitants of Jerusalem" "the house of David shall be as God, as the angel of the Lord before them."[9] In the later

---

[1] Acts ii. 29.
[2] Hos. iii. 5.
[3] Amos ix. 11.
[4] Micah v. 2.
[5] Jer. xxiii. 5, 6; cf. xxxiii. 15 and Isa. iv. 2, xi. 1. The Hebrew word used in the last passage is different from that in the preceding.
[6] Ezek. xxxiv. 23, 24; xxxvii. 24, 25.
[7] Zech. iii. 8; the text in vi. 12 is probably corrupt.
Hag. ii. 23.
[9] Zech. xii. 8.

literature, Biblical and apocryphal, the Davidic origin of the Messiah is not conspicuous till it reappears in the Psalms of Solomon [1] and the New Testament, but the idea had not necessarily been dormant meanwhile. The chronicler and his school studied and meditated on the sacred writings, and must have been familiar with this doctrine of the prophets. The interest in such a subject would not be confined to scholars. Doubtless the downtrodden people cherished with ever-growing ardour the glorious picture of the Davidic king. In the synagogues it was not only Moses, but the Prophets, that were read; and they could never allow the picture of the Messianic king to grow faint and pale. [2]

David's name was also familiar as the author of many psalms. The inhabitants of Jerusalem would often hear them sung at the Temple, and they were probably used for private devotion. In this way especially the name of David had become associated with the deepest and purest spiritual experiences.

This brief survey shows how utterly impossible it was for the chronicler to transfer the older narrative bodily from the book of Samuel to his own pages. Large omissions were absolutely necessary. He could not sit down in cold blood to tell his readers that the man whose name they associated with the most sacred memories and the noblest hopes of Israel had been guilty of treacherous murder, and had offered himself to the Philistines as an ally against the people of Jehovah.

From this point of view let us consider the chronicler's omissions somewhat more in detail. In the first place,

---

[1] Written after the death of Pompey.
[2] Schultz, *Old Testament Theology*, ii. **444.**

with one or two slight exceptions, he omits the whole of David's life before his accession to the throne, for two reasons: partly because he is anxious that his readers should think of David as king, the anointed of Jehovah, the Messiah; partly that they may not be reminded of his career as an outlaw and a freebooter and of his alliance with the Philistines.[1] It is probably only an unintentional result of this omission that it enables the chronicler to ignore the important services rendered to David by Abiathar, whose family were rivals of the house of Zadok in the priesthood.

We have already seen that the events of David's reign at Hebron and his struggle with Ishbosheth are omitted because the chronicler does not recognise Ishbosheth as a legitimate king. The omission would also commend itself because this section contains the account of Joab's murder of Abner and David's inability to do more than protest against the crime. "I am this day weak, though anointed king; and these men the sons of Zeruiah are too hard for me,"[2] are scarcely words that become an ideal king.

The next point to notice is one of those significant alterations that mark the chronicler's industry as a redactor. In 2 Sam. v. 21 we read that after the Philistines had been defeated at Baal-perazim they left their images there, and David and his men took them away. Why did they take them away? What did David and his men want with images? Missionaries bring home images as trophies, and exhibit them triumphantly, like soldiers who have captured the enemy's standards. No one, not even an unconverted native, supposes that they have been brought away to be used

---

[1] An incidental reference is made to these facts in 1 Chron. xii. 19.

[2] 2 Sam. iii. 39.

in worship. But the worship of images was no improbable apostacy on the part of an Israelite king. The chronicler felt that these ambiguous words were open to misconstruction ; so he tells us what he assumes to have been their ultimate fate : " And they left their gods there ; and David gave commandment, and they were burnt with fire." [1]

The next omission was obviously a necessary one; it is the incident of Uriah and Bath-sheba. The name Bath-sheba never occurs in Chronicles. When it is necessary to mention the mother of Solomon, she is called Bath-shua, possibly in order that the disgraceful incident might not be suggested even by the use of the name. The New Testament genealogies differ in this matter in somewhat the same way as Samuel and Chronicles. St. Matthew expressly mentions Uriah's wife as an ancestress of our Lord, but St. Luke does not mention her or any other ancestress.

The next omission is equally extensive and important. It includes the whole series of events connected with the revolt of Absalom, from the incident of Tamar to the suppression of the rebellion of Sheba the son of Bichri. Various motives may have contributed to this omission. The narrative contains unedifying incidents, which are passed over as lightly as possible by modern writers like Stanley. It was probably a relief to the chronicler to be able to omit them altogether. There is no heinous sin like the murder of Uriah, but the story leaves a general impression of great weakness on David's part. Joab murders Amasa as he had murdered Abner, and this time there is no record of any protest even on the part of David. But probably the main

---

[1] 2 Sam. v. 21 ; 1 Chron. xiv. 12.

reason for the omission of this narrative is that it mars the ideal picture of David's power and dignity and the success and prosperity of his reign.

The touching story of Rizpah is omitted; the hanging of her sons does not exhibit David in a very amiable light. The Gibeonites propose that "they shall hang them up unto the Lord in Gibeah of Saul, the chosen of the Lord," and David accepts the proposal. This punishment of the children for the sin of their father was expressly against the Law[1]; and the whole incident was perilously akin to human sacrifice. How could they be hung up before Jehovah in Gibeah unless there was a sanctuary of Jehovah in Gibeah? And why should Saul at such a time and in such a connection be called emphatically "the chosen of Jehovah"? On many grounds, it was a passage which the chronicler would be glad to omit.

In 2 Sam. xxi. 15–17 we are told that David waxed faint and had to be rescued by Abishai. This is omitted by Chronicles probably because it detracts from the character of David as the ideal hero. The next paragraph in Samuel also tended to depreciate David's prowess. It stated that Goliath was slain by Elhanan. The chronicler introduces a correction. It was not Goliath whom Elhanan slew, but Lahmi, the brother of Goliath. However, the text in Samuel is evidently corrupt; and possibly this is one of the cases in which Chronicles has preserved the correct text.[2]

Then follow two omissions that are not easily accounted for. 2 Sam. xxii., xxiii., contain two psalms, Psalm xviii. and "the Last Words of David," the latter not included in the Psalter. These psalms are generally

---

considered a late addition to the book of Samuel, and it is barely possible that they were not in the copy used by the chronicler; but the late date of Chronicles makes against this supposition. The psalms may be omitted for the sake of brevity, and yet elsewhere a long cento of passages from post-Exilic psalms is added to the material derived from the book of Samuel. Possibly something in the omitted section jarred upon the theological sensibilities of the chronicler, but it is not clear what. He does not as a rule look below the surface for obscure suggestions of undesirable views. The grounds of his alterations and omissions are usually sufficiently obvious; but these particular omissions are not at present susceptible of any obvious explanation. Further research into the theology of Judaism may perhaps provide us with one hereafter.

Finally, the chronicler omits the attempt of Adonijah to seize the throne, and David's dying commands to Solomon. The opening chapters of the book of Kings present a graphic and pathetic picture of the closing scenes of David's life. The king is exhausted with old age. His authoritative sanction to the coronation of Solomon is only obtained when he has been roused and directed by the promptings and suggestions of the women of his harem. The scene is partly a parallel and partly a contrast to the last days of Queen Elizabeth; for when *her* bodily strength failed, the obstinate Tudor spirit refused to be guided by the suggestions of her courtiers. The chronicler was depicting a person of almost Divine dignity, in whom incidents of human weakness would have been out of keeping; and therefore they are omitted.

David's charge to Solomon is equally human. Solomon is to make up for David's weakness and

undue generosity by putting Joab and Shimei to death ;
on the other hand, he is to pay David's debt of gratitude
to the son of Barzillai.   But the chronicler felt that
David's mind in those last days must surely have been
occupied with the temple which Solomon was to build,
and the less edifying charge is omitted.

Constantine is reported to have said that, for the
honour of the Church, he would conceal the sin of a
bishop with his own imperial purple.   David was more
to the chronicler than the whole Christian episcopate
to Constantine.   His life of David is compiled in the
spirit and upon the principles of lives of saints generally, and his omissions are made in perfect good
faith.

Let us now consider the positive picture of David as
it is drawn for us in Chronicles.   Chronicles would be
published separately, each copy written out on a roll
of its own.   There may have been Jews who had
Chronicles, but not Samuel and Kings, and who knew
nothing about David except what they learned from
Chronicles.   Possibly the chronicler and his friends
would recommend the work as suitable for the education
of children and the instruction of the common people.
It would save its readers from being perplexed by the
religious difficulties suggested by Samuel and Kings.
There were many obstacles, however, to the success of
such a scheme ; the persecutions of Antiochus and the
wars of the Maccabees took the leadership out of the
hands of scholars and gave it to soldiers and statesmen.
The latter perhaps felt more drawn to the real David
than to the ideal, and the new priestly dynasty would
not be anxious to emphasise the Messianic hopes of the
house of David.   But let us put ourselves for a moment
in the position of a student of Hebrew history who

reads of David for the first time in Chronicles and has
no other source of information.

Our first impression as we read the book is that
David comes into the history as abruptly as Elijah or
Melchizedek. Jehovah slew Saul "and turned the
kingdom unto David the son of Jesse."[1] Apparently
the Divine appointment is promptly and enthusiastically
accepted by the nation ; all the twelve tribes come at
once in their tens and hundreds of thousands to Hebron
to make David king. They then march straight to
Jerusalem and take it by storm, and forthwith attempt
to bring up the Ark to Zion. An unfortunate accident
necessitates a delay of three months, but at the end
of that time the Ark is solemnly installed in a tent at
Jerusalem.[2]

We are not told who David the son of Jesse was,
or why the Divine choice fell upon him, or how he
had been prepared for his responsible position, or
how he had so commended himself to Israel as to be
accepted with universal acclaim. He must, however,
have been of noble family and high character; and it
is hinted that he had had a distinguished career as a
soldier.[3] We should expect to find his name in the
introductory genealogies ; and if we have read these
lists of names with conscientious attention, we shall
remember that there are sundry incidental references
to David, and that he was the seventh son of Jesse,[4]
who was descended from the Patriarch Judah, through
Boaz, the husband of Ruth.

As we read further we come to other references
which throw some light on David's early career, and
at the same time somewhat mar the symmetry of the

---

[1] 1 Chron. x. 14.
[2] Cf. xi. 1–9; xii. 23–xiii. 14; xv.
[3] 1 Chron. xi. 2.
[4] 1 Chron. ii. 15.

opening narrative. The wide discrepancy between the chronicler's idea of David and the account given by his authorities prevents him from composing his work on an entirely consecutive and consistent plan. We gather that there was a time when David was in rebellion against his predecessor, and maintained himself at Ziklag and elsewhere, keeping "himself close, because of Saul the son of Kish," and even that he came with the Philistines against Saul to battle, but was prevented by the jealousy of the Philistine chiefs from actually fighting against Saul. There is nothing to indicate the occasion or circumstances of these events.[1] But it appears that even at this period, when David was in arms against the king of Israel and an ally of the Philistines, he was the chosen leader of Israel. Men flocked to him from Judah and Benjamin, Manasseh and Gad, and doubtless from the other tribes as well : " From day to day there came to David to help him, until it was a great host like the host of God."[2]

This chapter partly explains David's popularity after Saul's death ; but it only carries the mystery a stage further back. How did this outlaw and apparently unpatriotic rebel get so strong a hold on the affections of Israel ?

Chap. xii. also provides material for plausible explanations of another difficulty. In chap. x. the army of Israel is routed, the inhabitants of the land take to flight, and the Philistines occupy their cities ; in

---

[1] 1 Chron. xii. 1, 19. There is no certain indication of the date of the events in xi. 10–25. The fact that a " hold " is mentioned in xi. 16, as in xii. 8, 16, is not conclusive proof that they refer to the same period.

[2] xii. 20.

xi. and xii. 23–40 all Israel come straightway to Hebron in the most peaceful and unconcerned fashion to make David king. Are we to understand that his Philistine allies, mindful of that "great host, like the host of God," all at once changed their minds and entirely relinquished the fruits of their victory?

Elsewhere, however, we find a statement that renders other explanations possible. David reigned seven years in Hebron,[1] so that our first impression as to the rapid sequence of events at the beginning of his reign is apparently not correct, and there was time in these seven years for a more gradual expulsion of the Philistines. It is doubtful, however, whether the chronicler intended his original narrative to be thus modified and interpreted.

The main thread of the history is interrupted here and later on[2] to insert incidents which illustrate the personal courage and prowess of David and his warriors. We are also told how busily occupied David was during the three months' sojourn of the Ark in the house of Obed-edom the Gittite. He accepted an alliance with Hiram, king of Tyre; he added to his harem; he successfully repelled two inroads of the Philistines, and made him houses in the city of David.[3]

The narrative returns to its main subject: the history of the sanctuary at Jerusalem. As soon as the Ark was duly installed in its tent, and David was established in his new palace, he was struck by the contrast between the tent and the palace: "Lo, I dwell in a house of cedar, but the ark of the covenant of the Lord dwelleth under curtains." He proposed to substitute a temple for the tent, but was forbidden by his prophet Nathan,

---

[1] 1 Chron. xxix. 27.   [2] xi. 10–47; xx. 4–8.   [3] xiii. 14–xvi.

through whom God promised him that his son should build the Temple, and that his house should be established for ever.[1]

Then we read of the wars, victories, and conquests of David. He is no longer absorbed in the defence of Israel against the Philistines. He takes the aggressive and conquers Gath; he conquers Edom, Moab, Ammon, and Amalek; he and his armies defeat the Syrians in several battles, the Syrians become tributary, and David occupies Damascus with a garrison. " And the Lord gave victory to David whithersoever he went." The conquered were treated after the manner of those barbarous times. David and his generals carried off much spoil, especially brass, and silver, and gold; and when he conquered Rabbah, the capital of Ammon, " he brought forth the people that were therein, and cut them with saws, and with harrows of iron, and with axes. And thus did David unto all the cities of the children of Ammon." Meanwhile his home administration was as honourable as his foreign wars were glorious: " He executed judgment and justice unto all his people "; and the government was duly organised with commanders of the host and the bodyguard, with priests and scribes.[2]

Then follows a mysterious and painful dispensation of Providence, which the historian would gladly have omitted, if his respect for the memory of his hero had not been overruled by his sense of the supreme importance of the Temple. David, like Job, was given over for a season to Satan, and while possessed by this evil spirit displeased God by numbering Israel. His punishment took the form of a great pestilence, which decimated

---

[1] xvii.   [2] xviii.; xx. 3.

his people, until, by Divine command, David erected an altar in the threshing-floor of Ornan the Jebusite and offered sacrifices upon it, whereupon the plague was stayed. David at once perceived the significance of this incident: Jehovah had indicated the site of the future Temple. "This is the house of Jehovah Elohim,[1] and this is the altar of burnt offering for Israel."[2]

This revelation of the Divine will as to the position of the Temple led David to proceed at once with preparations for its erection by Solomon, which occupied all his energies for the remainder of his life.[3] He gathered funds and materials, and gave his son full instructions about the building; he organised the priests and Levites, the Temple orchestra and choir, the doorkeepers, treasurers, officers, and judges; he also organised the army, the tribes, and the royal exchequer on the model of the corresponding arrangements for the Temple.

Then follows the closing scene of David's life. The sun of Israel sets amid the flaming glories of the western sky. No clouds or mists rob him of accustomed splendour. David calls a great assembly of princes and warriors; he addresses a solemn exhortation to them and to Solomon; he delivers to his son instructions for "all the works" which "I have been made to understand in writing from the hand of Jehovah." It is almost as though the plans of the Temple had shared with the first tables of stone the honour of being written with the very finger of God Himself, and David were even greater than Moses. He reminds Solomon of all the preparations he had made, and

---

[1] *I.e.*, virtually Jehovah our God and the only true God.
[2] For a more detailed treatment of this incident see chap. ix.
[3] xxi.–xxix.

appeals to the princes and the people for further gifts;
and they render willingly—thousands of talents of
gold, and silver, and brass, and iron. David offers
prayer and thanksgiving to the Lord: "And David
said to all the congregation, Now bless Jehovah our
God. And all the congregation blessed Jehovah, the
God of their fathers, and bowed down their heads,
and worshipped Jehovah *and the king*. And they
sacrificed sacrifices unto Jehovah, and offered burnt
offerings unto Jehovah, on the morrow after that day,
even a thousand bullocks, a thousand rams, and a
thousand lambs, with their drink offerings and sacrifices
in abundance for all Israel, and did eat and drink
before Jehovah on that day with great gladness. And
they made Solomon king; . . . and David died in a
good old age, full of days, riches, and honour, and
Solomon his son reigned in his stead." [1]

The Roman expressed his idea of a becoming death
more simply: "An emperor should die standing." The
chronicler has given us the same view at greater length;
this is how the chronicler would have wished to die if
he had been David, and how, therefore, he conceives
that God honoured the last hours of the man after His
own heart.

It is a strange contrast to the companion picture in
the book of Kings. There the king is bedridden,
dying slowly of old age; the life-blood creeps coldly
through his veins. The quiet of the sick-room is
invaded by the shrill outcry of an aggrieved woman,
and the dying king is roused to hear that once more
eager hands are clutching at his crown. If the
chronicler has done nothing else, he has helped us

---

[1] xxix. 20–22, 28.

to appreciate better the gloom and bitterness of the
tragedy that was enacted in the last days of David.

What idea does Chronicles give us of the man and
his character? He is first and foremost a man of
earnest piety and deep spiritual feeling. Like the
great religious leaders of the chronicler's own time,
his piety found its chief expression in ritual. The
main business of his life was to provide for the sanctuary
and its services; that is, for the highest fellowship of
God and man, according to the ideas then current.
But David is no mere formalist; the psalm of thanksgiving for the return of the Ark to Jerusalem is a worthy
tribute to the power and faithfulness of Jehovah.[1] His
prayer after God had promised to establish his dynasty
is instinct with devout confidence and gratitude.[2] But
the most gracious and appropriate of these Davidic
utterances is his last prayer and thanksgiving for the
liberal gifts of the people for the Temple.[3]

Next to David's enthusiasm for the Temple, his most
conspicuous qualities are those of a general and soldier:
he has great personal strength and courage, and is
uniformly successful in wars against numerous and
powerful enemies; his government is both able and
upright; his great powers as an organiser and adminis-
trator are exercised both in secular and ecclesiastical
matters; in a word, he is in more senses than one
an ideal king.

Moreover, like Alexander, Marlborough, Napoleon,
and other epoch-making conquerors, he had a great
charm of personal attractiveness; he inspired his
officers and soldiers with enthusiasm and devotion to

---

[1] xvi. 8–36.
[2] xvii. 16–27.
[3] For a short exposition of this passage see Book. IV., Chap. i.

himself.   The pictures of all Israel flocking to him in the
first days of his reign and even earlier, when he was an
outlaw, are forcible illustrations of this wonderful gift ;
and the same feature of his character is at once illustrated and partly explained by the romantic episode at
Adullam.   What greater proof of affection could outlaws
give to their captain than to risk their lives to get him
a draught of water from the well of Bethlehem ?   How
better could David have accepted and ratified their
devotion than by pouring out this water as a most
precious libation to God ?[1]   But the chronicler gives
most striking expression to the idea of David's popularity when he finally tells us in the same breath that
the people worshipped Jehovah and the king.[2]

In drawing an ideal picture, our author has naturally
omitted incidents that might have revealed the defects
of his hero.   Such omissions deceive no one, and are
not meant to deceive any one.   Yet David's failings
are not altogether absent from this history.   He has
those vices which were characteristic alike of his own
age and of the chronicler's, and which indeed are not
yet wholly extinct.   He could treat his prisoners with
barbarous cruelty.   His pride led him to number
Israel, but his repentance was prompt and thorough ;
and the incident brings out alike both his faith in God
and his care for his people.   When the whole episode
is before us, it does not lessen our love and respect for
David.   The reference to his alliance with the Philistines is vague and incidental.   If this were our only
account of the matter, we should interpret it by the
rest of his life, and conclude that if all the facts were
known, they would justify his conduct.

---

[1] 1 Chron. xi. 15-19.   [2] xxix. 20.

In forming a general estimate of David according to Chronicles, we may fairly neglect these less satisfactory episodes. Briefly David is perfect saint and perfect king, beloved of God and man.

A portrait reveals the artist as well as the model, and the chronicler in depicting David gives indications of the morality of his own times. We may deduce from his omissions a certain progress in moral sensitiveness. The book of Samuel emphatically condemns David's treachery towards Uriah, and is conscious of the discreditable nature of many incidents connected with the revolts of Absalom and Adonijah; but the silence of Chronicles implies an even severer condemnation. In other matters, however, the chronicler "judges himself in that which he approveth."[1] Of course the first business of an ancient king was to protect his people from their enemies and to enrich them at the expense of their neighbours. The urgency of these duties may excuse, but not justify, the neglect of the more peaceful departments of the administration. The modern reader is struck by the little stress laid by the narrative upon good government at home; it is just mentioned, and that is about all. As the sentiment of international morality is even now only in its infancy, we cannot wonder at its absence from Chronicles; but we are a little surprised to find that cruelty towards prisoners is included without comment in the character of the ideal king.[2] It is curious that the account in the book of Samuel is slightly ambiguous and might possibly admit of a comparatively mild interpretation; but Chronicles, according to the ordinary translation, says definitely, "He *cut* them with saws." The mere

---

[1] Rom. xiv. 22.

[2] 2 Sam. xii. 31 ; 1 Chron. xx. 3.

reproduction of this passage need not imply full and deliberate approval of its contents ; but it would not have been allowed to remain in the picture of the ideal king, if the chronicler had felt any strong conviction as to the duty of humanity towards one's enemies. Unfortunately we know from the book of Esther and elsewhere that later Judaism had not attained to any wide enthusiasm of humanity.

CHAPTER IV

DAVID—III. HIS OFFICIAL DIGNITY

IN estimating the personal character of David, we have seen that one element of it was his ideal kingship.   Apart from his personality, his name is significant for Old Testament theology, as that of the typical king.   From the time when the royal title " Messiah " began to be a synonym for the hope of Israel, down to the period when the Anglican Church taught the Divine right of kings, and Calvinists insisted on the Divine sovereignty or royal authority of God, the dignity and power of the King of kings have always been illustrated by, and sometimes associated with, the state of an earthly monarch—whereof David is the most striking example.

The times of the chronicler were favourable to the development of the idea of the perfect king of Israel, the prince of the house of David.   There was no king in Israel ; and, as far as we can gather, the living representatives of the house of David held no very prominent position in the community.   It is much easier to draw a satisfactory picture of the ideal monarch when the imagination is not checked and hampered by the faults and failings of an actual Ahaz or Hezekiah.   In earlier times the prophetic hopes for the house of David had often been rudely disappointed, but there had been

ample space to forget the past and to revive the old
hopes in fresh splendour and magnificence. Lack of
experience helped to commend the idea of the Davidic
king to the chronicler. Enthusiasm for a benevolent
despot is mostly confined to those who have not enjoyed
the privilege of living under such autocratic government.

On the other hand, there was no temptation to flatter
any living Davidic king, so that the semi-Divine character of the kingship of David is not set forth after the
gross and almost blasphemous style of Roman emperors
or Turkish sultans. It is indeed said that the people
worshipped Jehovah and the king ; but the essential
character of Jewish thought made it impossible that
the ideal king should sit " in the temple of God, setting
himself forth as God." David and Solomon could not
share with the pagan emperors the honours of Divine
worship in their life-time and apotheosis after their
death. Nothing addressed to any Hebrew king parallels
the panegyric to the Christian emperor Theodosius, in
which allusion is made to his " sacred mind," and he is
told that " as the Fates are said to assist with their
tablets *that God who is the partner in your majesty,* so
does some Divine power serve your bidding, which
writes down and in due time suggests to your memory
the promises which you have made."[1] Nor does
Chronicles adorn the kings of Judah with extravagant
Oriental titles, such as " King of kings of kings of
kings." Devotion to the house of David never over-
steps the bounds of a due reverence, but the Hebrew
idea of monarchy loses nothing by this salutary reserve.

Indeed, the title of the royal house of Judah rested
upon Divine appointment. " Jehovah . . . turned the

---

[1] Hodgkin, *Italy and her Invaders*, i. 205.

kingdom unto David; . . . and they anointed David king over Israel, according to the word of Jehovah by the hand of Samuel."[1] But the Divine choice was confirmed by the cordial consent of the nation; the sovereigns of Judah, like those of England, ruled by the grace of God and the will of the people. Even before David's accession the Israelites had flocked to his standard; and after the death of Saul a great array of the twelve tribes came to Hebron to make David king, " and all the rest also of Israel were of one heart to make David king."[2] Similarly Solomon is the king " whom God hath chosen," and all the congregation make him king and anoint him to be prince.[3] The double election of David by Jehovah and by the nation is clearly set forth in the book of Samuel, and in Chronicles the omission of David's early career empha- sises this election. In the book of Samuel we are shown the natural process that brought about the change of dynasty; we see how the Divine choice took effect through the wars between Saul and the Philistines and through David's own ability and energy. Chroni- cles is mostly silent as to secondary causes, and fixes our attention on the Divine choice as the ultimate ground for David's elevation.

The authority derived from God and the people con- tinued to rest on the same basis. David sought Divine direction alike for the building of the Temple and for his campaigns against the Philistines. At the same time, when he wished to bring up the Ark to Jerusalem, he " consulted with the captains of thousands and of hundreds, even with every leader; and David said unto all the assembly of Israel, If it seem good unto you,

---

[1] x. 14; xi. 3.   [2] xii. 38.   [3] xxix. 1, 22.

and if it be of Jehovah our God, . . . let us bring again
the ark of our God to us : . . . and all the assembly
said that they would do so, for the thing was right in
the eyes of all the people."[1]   Of course the chronicler
does not intend to describe a constitutional monarchy,
in which an assembly of the people had any legal
status.   Apparently in his own time the Jews exercised
their measure of local self-government through an
informal oligarchy, headed by the high-priest; and
these authorities occasionally appealed to an assembly
of the people.   The administration under the monarchy
was carried on in a somewhat similar fashion, only the
king had greater authority than the high-priest, and
the oligarchy of notables were not so influential as the
colleagues of the latter.   But apart from any formal
constitution the chronicler's description of these incidents involves a recognition of the principle of popular
consent in government as well as the doctrine that civil
order rests upon a Divine sanction.

It is interesting to see how a member of a great
ecclesiastical community, imbued, as we should suppose,
with all the spirit of priestcraft, yet insists upon the
royal supremacy both in state and Church.   But to
have done otherwise would have been to go in the
teeth of all history ; even in the Pentateuch the "king
in Jeshurun" is greater than the priest.   Moreover, the
chronicler was not a priest, but a Levite ; and there are
indications that the Levites' ancient jealousy of the
priests had by no means died out.   In Chronicles, at
any rate, there is no question of priests interfering
with the king's secular administration.   They are not
even mentioned as obtaining oracles for David as

---

[1] xiii. 2–4.

Abiathar did before his accession.[1] This was doubtless implied in the original account of the Philistine raids in chap. xiv., but the chronicler may not have understood that "inquiring of God" meant obtaining an oracle from the priests.

The king is equally supreme also in ecclesiastical affairs; we might even say that the civil authorities generally shared this supremacy. Somewhat after the fashion of Cromwell and his major-generals, David utilised "the captains of the host" as a kind of ministry of public worship; they joined with him in organising the orchestra and choir for the services of the sanctuary[2]: probably Napoleon and his marshals would have had no hesitation in selecting anthems for Notre Dame if the idea had occurred to them. David also consulted his captains,[3] and not the priests, about bringing the Ark to Jerusalem. When he gathered the great assembly to make his final arrangements for the building of the Temple, the princes and captains, the rulers and mighty men, are mentioned, but no priests.[4] And, last, all the congregation apparently anoint[5] Zadok to be priest. The chronicler was evidently a pronounced Erastian.[6] David is no mere nominal head of the Church; he takes the initiative in all important matters, and receives the Divine commands either directly or through his prophets Nathan and Gad. Now these prophets are not ecclesiastical authorities; they have nothing to do with the priesthood, and do not correspond to the officials of an organised Church. They are rather the domestic chaplains or confessors of the king, differing from modern chaplains and confessors in having no ecclesiastical superiors. They were

---

[1] I Sam. xxiii. 9–13; xxx. 7, 8.   [3] xiii. I.   [5] xxix. 22.
[2] xxv. 1, 2.   [4] xxviii. I.   [6] But cf. 2 Chr. xxvi.

not responsible to the bishop of any diocese or the general of any order ; they did not manipulate the royal conscience in the interests of any party in the Church ; they served God and the king, and had no other masters. They did not beard David before his people, as Ambrose confronted Theodosius or as Chrysostom rated Eudoxia ; they delivered their message to David in private, and on occasion he communicated it to the people.[1] The king's spiritual dignity is rather enhanced than otherwise by this reception of prophetic messages specially delivered to himself. There is another aspect of the royal supremacy in religion. In this particular instance its object is largely the exaltation of David ; to arrange for public worship is the most honourable function of the ideal king. At the same time the care of the sanctuary is his most sacred duty, and is assigned to him that it may be punctually and worthily discharged. State establishment of the Church is combined with a very thorough control of the Church by the state.

We see then that the monarchy rested on Divine and national election, and was guided by the will of God and of the people. Indeed, in bringing up the Ark[2] the consent of the people is the only recorded indication of the will of God. "Vox populi vox Dei." The king and his government are supreme alike over the state and the sanctuary, and are entrusted with the charge of providing for public worship. Let us try to express the modern equivalents of these principles. Civil government is of Divine origin, and should obtain the consent of the people ; it should be carried on according to the will of God, freely accepted by the

---

[1] Cf. xvii. 4-15 and xxviii. 2-10.   [2] xiii. 1-14.

nation. The civil authority is supreme both in Church and state, and is responsible for the maintenance of public worship.

One at least of these principles is so widely accepted that it is quite independent of any Scriptural sanction from Chronicles. The consent of the people has long been accepted as an essential condition of any stable government. The sanctity of civil government and the sacredness of its responsibilities are coming to be recognised, at present perhaps rather in theory than in practice. We have not yet fully realised how the truth underlying the doctrine of the Divine right of kings applies to modern conditions. Formerly the king was the representative of the state, or even the state itself; that is to say, the king directly or indirectly maintained social order, and provided for the security of life and property. The Divine appointment and authority of the king expressed the sanctity of law and order as the essential conditions of moral and spiritual progress. The king is no longer the state. His Divine right, however, belongs to him, not as a person or as a member of a family, but as the embodiment of the state, the champion of social order against anarchy. The "Divinity that doth hedge a king" is now shared by the sovereign with all the various departments of government. The state—that is to say, the community organised for the common good and for mutual help—is now to be recognised as of Divine appointment and as wielding a Divine authority. "The Lord has turned the kingdom to" the people.

This revolution is so tremendous that it would not be safe to apply to the modern state the remaining principles of the chronicler. Before we could do so we should need to enter into a discussion which would be out of place here, even if we had space for it.

In one point the new democracies agree with the chronicler: they are not inclined to submit secular affairs to the domination of ecclesiastical officials.

The questions of the supremacy of the state over the Church and of the state establishment of the Church involve larger and more complicated issues than existed in the mind or experience of the chronicler. But his picture of the ideal king suggests one idea that is in harmony with some modern aspirations. In Chronicles the king, as the representative of the state, is the special agent in providing for the highest spiritual needs of the people. May we venture to hope that out of the moral consciousness of a nation united in mutual sympathy and service there may arise a new enthusiasm to obey and worship God? Human cruelty is the greatest stumbling-block to belief and fellowship; when the state has somewhat mitigated the misery of "man's inhumanity to man," faith in God will be easier.

CHAPTER V

SOLOMON

THE chronicler's history of Solomon is constructed on the same principles as that of David, and for similar reasons. The builder of the first Temple commanded the grateful reverence of a community whose national and religious life centred in the second Temple. While the Davidic king became the symbol of the hope of Israel, the Jews could not forget that this symbol derived much of its significance from the widespread dominion and royal magnificence of Solomon. The chronicler, indeed, attributes great splendour to the court of David, and ascribes to him a lion's share in the Temple itself. He provided his successor with treasure and materials and even the complete plans, so that on the principle, " Qui facit per alium, facit per se," David might have been credited with the actual building. Solomon was almost in the position of a modern engineer who puts together a steamer that has been built in sections. But, with all these limitations, the clear and obvious fact remained that Solomon actually built and dedicated the Temple. Moreover, the memory of his wealth and grandeur kept a firm hold on the popular imagination ; and these conspicuous blessings were received as certain tokens of the favour of Jehovah.

Solomon's fame, however, was threefold : he was not only the Divinely appointed builder of the Temple and, by the same Divine grace, the richest and most powerful king of Israel : he had also received from Jehovah the gift of " wisdom and knowledge." In his royal splendour and his sacred buildings he only differed in degree from other kings ; but in his wisdom he stood alone, not only without equal, but almost without competitor. Herein he was under no obligation to his father, and the glory of Solomon could not be diminished by representing that he had been anticipated by David. Hence the name of Solomon came to symbolise Hebrew learning and philosophy.

In religious significance, however, Solomon cannot rank with David. The dynasty of Judah could have only one representative, and the founder and eponym of the royal house was the most important figure for the subsequent theology. The interest that later generations felt in Solomon lay apart from the main line of Jewish orthodoxy, and he is never mentioned by the prophets.[1]

Moreover, the darker aspects of Solomon's reign made more impression upon succeeding generations than even David's sins and misfortunes. Occasional lapses into vice and cruelty might be forgiven or even forgotten ; but the systematic oppression of Solomon rankled for long generations in the hearts of the people, and the prophets always remembered his wanton idolatry. His memory was further discredited by the disasters which marked the close of his own reign and the beginning of Rehoboam's. Centuries later these

---

[1] The casual reference in Jer. lii. 20 is only an apparent exception. The passage is really historical, and not prophetic.

feelings still prevailed. The prophets who adapted
the Mosaic law for the closing period of the monarchy
exhort the king to take warning by Solomon, and to
multiply neither horses, nor wives, nor gold and silver.[1]

But as time went on Judah fell into growing poverty
and distress, which came to a head in the Captivity,
and were renewed with the Restoration. The Jews
were willing to forget Solomon's faults in order that
they might indulge in fond recollections of the material
prosperity of his reign. Their experience of the culture
of Babylon led them to feel greater interest and pride
in his wisdom, and the figure of Solomon began to
assume a mysterious grandeur, which has since become
the nucleus for Jewish and Mohammedan legends.
The chief monument of his fame in Jewish literature is
the book of Proverbs, but his growing reputation is
shown by the numerous Biblical and apocryphal works
ascribed to him. His name was no doubt attached to
Canticles because of a feature in his character which
the chronicler ignores. His supposed authorship of
Ecclesiastes and of the Wisdom of Solomon testifies to
the fame of his wisdom, while the titles of the " Psalms
of Solomon " and even of some canonical psalms credit
him with spiritual feeling and poetic power.[2]

When the Wisdom of Jesus the Son of Sirach pro-
poses to " praise famous men," it dwells upon Solomon's
temple and his wealth, and especially upon his wisdom ;
but it does not forget his failings.[3] Josephus celebrates
his glory at great length. The New Testament has
comparatively few notices of Solomon ; but these include

---

[1] Deut. xvii. 16, 17 ; cf. 2 Chron. i. 14–17 and 1 Kings xi. 3–8.
[2] Psalms lxxii. and cxxvii. are attributed to him, the latter, however, only in the Hebrew Bible.
[3] Ecclus. xlvii. 12–21.

references to his wisdom,[1] his splendour,[2] and his temple.[3] The Koran, however, far surpasses the New Testament in its interest in Solomon; and his name and his seal play a leading part in Jewish and Arabian magic. The bulk of this literature is later than the chronicler, but the renewed interest in the glory of Solomon must have begun before his time. Perhaps, by connecting the building of the Temple as far as possible with David, the chronicler marks his sense of Solomon's unworthiness. On the other hand, there were many reasons why he should welcome the aid of popular sentiment to enable him to include Solomon among the ideal Hebrew kings. After all, Solomon had built and dedicated the Temple; he was the "pious founder," and the beneficiaries of the foundation would wish to make the most of his piety. "Jehovah" had "magnified Solomon exceedingly in the sight of all Israel, and bestowed upon him such royal majesty as had not been on any king before him in Israel."[4] King Solomon exceeded all the kings of the earth in riches and wisdom; and all the kings of the earth sought the presence of Solomon, to hear his wisdom, which God had put in his heart."[5] The chronicler would naturally wish to set forth the better side of Solomon's character as an ideal of royal wisdom and splendour, devoted to the service of the sanctuary. Let us briefly compare Chronicles and Kings to see how he accomplished his purpose.

The structure of the narrative in Kings rendered the task comparatively easy: it could be accomplished by removing the opening and closing sections and making

---

[1] Matt. xii. 42.   [2] Acts vii. 47.
[2] Matt. vi. 29.   [4] 1 Chron. xxix. 25.
          [5] 2 Chron. ix. 22, 23.

a few minor changes in the intermediate portion. The opening section is the sequel to the conclusion of David's reign; the chronicler omitted this conclusion, and therefore also its sequel. But the contents of this section were objectionable in themselves. Solomon's admirers willingly forget that his reign was inaugurated by the execution of Shimei, of his brother Adonijah, and of his father's faithful minister Joab, and by the deposition of the high-priest Abiathar. The chronicler narrates with evident approval the strong measures of Ezra and Nehemiah against foreign marriages, and he is therefore not anxious to remind his readers that Solomon married Pharaoh's daughter. He does not, however, carry out his plan consistently. Elsewhere he wishes to emphasise the sanctity of the Ark and tells us that " Solomon brought up the daughter of Pharaoh out of the city of David unto the house that he had built for her, for he said, My wife shall not dwell in the house of David, king of Israel, because the places are holy whereunto the ark of the Lord hath come." [1]

In Kings the history of Solomon closes with a long account of his numerous wives and concubines, his idolatry and consequent misfortunes. All this is omitted by the chronicler; but later on, with his usual inconsistency, he allows Nehemiah to point the moral of a tale he has left untold : " Did not Solomon, king of Israel, sin by these things ? . . . Even him did strange women cause to sin." [2] In the intervening section he omits the famous judgment of Solomon, probably on account of the character of the women concerned. He introduces sundry changes which naturally follow from his belief that the Levitical law was then

---

[1] 2 Chron. viii. 11.   [2] Neh. xiii. 26.

in force.[1] His feeling for the dignity of the chosen
people and their king comes out rather curiously in
two minor alterations. Both authorities agree in telling
us that Solomon had recourse to forced labour for his
building operations; in fact, after the usual Eastern
fashion from the Pyramids down to the Suez Canal,
Solomon's temple and palaces were built by the *corvée*.
According to the oldest narrative, he " raised a levy out
of all Israel."[2] This suggests that forced labour was
exacted from the Israelites themselves, and it would help
to account for Jeroboam's successful rebellion. The
chronicler omits this statement as open to an interpretation derogatory to the dignity of the chosen people, and
not only inserts a later explanation which he found in
the book of Kings, but also another express statement
that Solomon raised his levy of the " strangers that
were in the land of Israel."[3] These statements may
have been partly suggested by the existence of a class
of Temple slaves called Solomon's servants.

The other instance relates to Solomon's alliance with
Hiram, king of Tyre. In the book of Kings we are
told that " Solomon gave Hiram twenty cities in the land
of Galilee."[4] There were indeed redeeming features
connected with the transaction ; the cities were not a
very valuable possession for Hiram : " they pleased him
not "; yet he " sent to the king six score talents of
gold." However, it seemed incredible to the chronicler
that the most powerful and wealthy of the kings of

---

[1] Such changes occur throughout, and need not be further noticed
unless some special interest attaches to them.

[2] 1 Kings v. 13; ix. 22, which seems to contradict this, is an
editorial note.

[3] 2 Chron. ii. 2, 17, 18; viii. 7-10.

[4] 1 Kings ix. 11, 12.

Israel should either cede or sell any portion of
Jehovah's inheritance. He emends the text of his
authority so as to convert it into a casual reference to
certain cities which Hiram had given to Solomon.[1]

We will now reproduce the story of Solomon as
given by the chronicler. Solomon was the youngest
of four sons born to David at Jerusalem by Bath-shua,
the daughter of Ammiel. Besides these three brothers,
he had at least six other elder brothers. As in the cases
of Isaac, Jacob, Judah, and David himself, the birthright fell to a younger son. In the prophetic utterance
which foretold his birth, he was designated to succeed
to his father's throne and to build the Temple. At the
great assembly which closed his father's reign he received instructions as to the plans and services of the
Temple,[2] and was exhorted to discharge his duties
faithfully. He was declared king according to the
Divine choice, freely accepted by David and ratified by
popular acclamation. At David's death no one disputed
his succession to the throne: " All Israel obeyed him;
and all the princes and the mighty men and all the
sons likewise of King David submitted themselves unto
Solomon the king."[3]

His first act after his accession was to sacrifice before
the brazen altar of the ancient Tabernacle at Gibeon.
That night God appeared unto him " and said unto him,
Ask what I shall give thee." Solomon chose wisdom
and knowledge to qualify him for the arduous task of
government. Having thus " sought first the kingdom of
God and His righteousness," all other things—" riches,
wealth, and honour "—were added unto him.[4]

He returned to Jerusalem, gathered a great array of

---

[1] 2 Chron. viii. 1, 2, R.V.   [3] 1 Chron. xxix. 23, 24.
[2] 1 Chron. xxii. 9.   [4] 2 Chron. i. 7–13.

chariots and horses by means of traffic with Egypt, and accumulated great wealth, so that silver, and gold, and cedars became abundant at Jerusalem.[1]

He next proceeded with the building of the Temple, collected workmen, obtained timber from Lebanon and an artificer from Tyre. The Temple was duly erected and dedicated, the king taking the chief and most conspicuous part in all the proceedings. Special reference, however, is made to the presence of the priests and Levites at the dedication. On this occasion the ministry of the sanctuary was not confined to the course whose turn it was to officiate, but "all the priests that were present had sanctified themselves and did not keep their courses ; also the Levites, which were the singers, all of them, even Asaph, Heman, Jeduthun, and their sons and their brethren, arrayed in fine linen, with cymbals, and psalteries, and harps, stood at the east end of the altar, and with them a hundred and twenty priests sounding with trumpets."[2]

Solomon's dedication prayer concludes with special petitions for the priests, the saints, and the king : " Now therefore arise, O Jehovah Elohim, into Thy resting-place, Thou and the ark of Thy strength ; let Thy priests, O Jehovah Elohim, be clothed with salvation, and let Thy saints rejoice in goodness. O Jehovah Elohim, turn not away the face of Thine anointed ; remember the mercies of David Thy servant."[3]

When David sacrificed at the threshing-floor of Ornan the Jebusite, the place had been indicated as the site of the future Temple by the descent of fire from heaven ; and now, in token that the mercy shown to

---

[1] 2 Chron. i. 14–17.   [2] v. 11, 12, peculiar to Chronicles.
[3] vi. 41, 42, peculiar to Chronicles, apparently based on Psalm cxxxii. 8–10.

David should be continued to Solomon, the fire again fell from heaven, and consumed the burnt offering and the sacrifices; and the glory of Jehovah "filled the house of Jehovah,"[1] as it had done earlier in the day, when the Ark was brought into the Temple. Solomon concluded the opening ceremonies by a great festival: for eight days the Feast of Tabernacles was observed according to the Levitical law, and seven days more were specially devoted to a dedication feast.[2]

Afterwards Jehovah appeared again to Solomon, as He had before at Gibeon, and told him that this prayer was accepted. Taking up the several petitions that the king had offered, He promised, "If I shut up heaven that there be no rain, or if I send pestilence among My people; if My people, which are called by My name, shall humble themselves, and pray, and seek My face, and turn from their wicked ways; then will I hear from heaven, and will forgive their sin, and will heal their land. Now Mine eyes shall be open, and Mine ears attent, unto the prayer that is made in this place." Thus Jehovah, in His gracious condescension, adopts Solomon's own words[3] to express His answer to the prayer. He allows Solomon to dictate the terms of the agreement, and merely appends His signature and seal.

Besides the Temple, Solomon built palaces for himself and his wife, and fortified many cities, among the rest Hamath-zobah, formerly allied to David.[4] He also organised the people for civil and military purposes.

---

[1] 1 Chron. xxi. 26; 2 Chron. vii. 1–3, both peculiar to Chronicles.
[2] vii. 8–10, mostly peculiar to Chronicles. The text in 1 Kings viii. 65 has been interpolated from Chronicles.
[3] vii. 13–15, peculiar to Chronicles.
[4] viii. 3, 4, peculiar to Chronicles. Hamath is apparently referred to as a possession of Judah in 2 Kings xiv. 28.

As far as the account of his reign is concerned, the
Solomon of Chronicles appears as "the husband of one
wife"; and that wife is the daughter of Pharaoh. A
second, however, is mentioned later on as the mother
of Rehoboam; she too was a "strange woman," an
Ammonitess, Naamah by name.

Meanwhile Solomon was careful to maintain all the
sacrifices and festivals ordained in the Levitical law,
and all the musical and other arrangements for the
sanctuary commanded by David, the man of God.[1]

We read next of his commerce by sea and land, his
great wealth and wisdom, and the romantic visit of the
queen of Sheba.[2]

And so the story of Solomon closes with this picture
of royal state,—

> "The wealth of Ormus and of Ind,
> Or where the gorgeous East with richest hand
> Showers on her kings barbaric pearl and gold."

Wealth was combined with imperial power and
Divine wisdom. Here, as in the case of Plato's own
pupils Dionysius and Dion of Syracuse, Plato's dream
came true; the prince was a philosopher, and the
philosopher a prince.

At first sight it seems as if this marriage of authority
and wisdom had happier issue at Jerusalem than at
Syracuse. Solomon's history closes as brilliantly as
David's, and Solomon was subject to no Satanic possession and brought no pestilence upon Israel. But
testimonials are chiefly significant in what they omit;
and when we compare the conclusions of the histories
of David and Solomon, we note suggestive differences.

---

[1] viii. 12–16, peculiar in this form to Chronicles, but based upon
1 Kings ix. 25.

[2] ix., as in 1 Kings x. 1–13.

Solomon's life does not close with any scene in which his people and his heir assemble to do him honour and to receive his last injunctions. There are no "last words" of the wise king; and it is not said of him that "he died in a good old age, full of days, riches, and honour." "Solomon slept with his fathers, and he was buried in the city of David his father; and Rehoboam his son reigned in his stead"[1]: that is all. When the chronicler, the professed panegyrist of the house of David, brings his narrative of this great reign to so lame and impotent a conclusion, he really implies as severe a condemnation upon Solomon as the book of Kings does by its narrative of his sins.

Thus the Solomon of Chronicles shows the same piety and devotion to the Temple and its ritual which were shown by his father. His prayer at the dedication of the Temple is parallel to similar utterances of David. Instead of being a general and a soldier, he is a scholar and a philosopher. He succeeded to the administrative abilities of his father; and his prayer displays a deep interest in the welfare of his subjects. His record— in Chronicles—is even more faultless than that of David. And yet the careful student with nothing but Chronicles, even without Ezra and Nehemiah, might somehow get the impression that the story of Solomon, like that of Cambuscan, had been "left half told." In addition to the points suggested by a comparison with the history of David, there is a certain abruptness about its conclusion. The last fact noted of Solomon, before the formal statistics about "the rest of his acts" and the years of his reign, is that horses were brought for him "out of Egypt and out of all lands." Else-

---

[1] ix. 31.

where the chronicler's use of his materials shows a feeling for dramatic effect. We should not have expected him to close the history of a great reign by a reference to the king's trade in horses.[1]

Perhaps we are apt to read into Chronicles what we know from the book of Kings; yet surely this abrupt conclusion would have raised a suspicion that there were omissions, that facts had been suppressed because they could not bear the light. Upon the splendid figure of the great king, with his wealth and wisdom, his piety and devotion, rests the vague shadow of unnamed sins and unrecorded misfortunes. A suggestion of unhallowed mystery attaches itself to the name of the builder of the Temple, and Solomon is already on the way to become the Master of the Genii and the chief of magicians.[2]

---

[1] ix. 28.
[2] It is not suggested that the chronicler intended to convey this impression, or that it would be felt by most of his readers.

CHAPTER VI

SOLOMON (*continued*)

WHEN we turn to consider the spiritual significance of this ideal picture of the history and
character of Solomon, we are confronted by a difficulty
that attends the exposition of any ideal history. An
author's ideal of kingship in the early stages of literature is usually as much one and indivisible as his ideal
of priesthood, of the office of the prophet, and of the
wicked king. His authorities may record different
incidents in connection with each individual; but he
emphasises those which correspond with his ideal, or
even anticipates the higher criticism by constructing
incidents which seem required by the character and
circumstances of his heroes. On the other hand,
where the priest, or the prophet, or the king departs
from the ideal, the incidents are minimised or passed
over in silence. There will still be a certain variety
because different individuals may present different
elements of the ideal, and the chronicler does not
insist on each of his good kings possessing all the
characteristics of royal perfection. Still the tendency
of the process is to make all the good kings alike.
It would be monotonous to take each of them
separately and deduce the lessons taught by their
virtues, because the chronicler's intention is that

they shall all teach the same lessons by the same
kind of behaviour described from the same point of
view. David has a unique position, and has to be
taken by himself; but in considering the features
that must be added to the picture of David in order
to complete the picture of the good king, it is convenient to group Solomon with the reforming kings
of Judah. We shall therefore defer for more consecutive treatment the chronicler's account of their general
characters and careers. Here we shall merely gather
up the suggestions of the different narratives as to the
chronicler's ideal Hebrew king.

The leading points have already been indicated from
the chronicler's history of David. The first and most
indispensable feature is devotion to the temple at
Jerusalem and the ritual of the Pentateuch. This has
been abundantly illustrated from the account of Solomon.
Taking the reforming kings in their order :—

Asa removed the high places which were rivals of
the Temple,[1] renewed the altar of Jehovah, gathered
the people together for a great sacrifice,[2] and made
munificent donations to the Temple treasury.[3]

Similarly Jehoshaphat took away the high places,[4]
and sent out a commission to teach the Law.[5]

Joash repaired the Temple[6]; but, curiously enough,
though Jehoram had restored the high places[7] and
Joash was acting under the direction of the high-priest

---

[1] xiv. 3, 5, contradicting 1 Kings xv. 14 and apparently 2 Chron.
xv. 17.
[2] xv. 8–14, peculiar to Chronicles.
[3] xv. 18, 19.
[4] xvii. 6 contradicts 1 Kings xxii. 43 and 2 Chron. xx. 33.
[5] xvii. 7–9, peculiar to Chronicles.
[6] xxiv. 1–14.
[7] xxi. 11, peculiar to Chronicles.

Jehoiada, it is not stated that the high places were done away with. This is one of the chronicler's rather numerous oversights. Perhaps, however, he expected that so obvious a reform would be taken for granted.

Amaziah was careful to observe "the law in the book of Moses" that "the children should not die for the fathers,"[1] but Amaziah soon turned away from following Jehovah. This is perhaps the reason why in his case also nothing is said about doing away with the high places.

Hezekiah had a special opportunity of showing his devotion to the Temple and the Law. The Temple had been polluted and closed by Ahaz, and its services discontinued. Hezekiah purified the Temple, reinstated the priests and Levites, and renewed the services; he made arrangements for the payment of the Temple revenues according to the provisions of the Levitical law, and took away the high places. He also held a reopening festival and a passover with numerous sacrifices.[2]

Manasseh's repentance is indicated by the restoration of the Temple ritual.[3]

Josiah took away the high places, repaired tne Temple, made the people enter into a covenant to observe the rediscovered Law, and, like Hezekiah, held a great passover.[4]

The reforming kings, like David and Solomon, are specially interested in the music of the Temple and in

---

[1] xxv. 4.

[2] 2 Chron. xxviii. 24–xxxi., mostly peculiar to Chronicles; but compare 2 Kings xviii. 4–7, which mentions the taking away of the high places.

[3] xxxiii. 16.

[4] xxxiv.; xxxv.

all the arrangements that have to do with the porters and doorkeepers and other classes of Levites. Their enthusiasm for the exclusive rights of the one Temple symbolises their loyalty to the one God, Jehovah, and their hatred of idolatry.

Zeal for Jehovah and His temple is still combined with uncompromising assertion of the royal supremacy in matters of religion. The king, and not the priest, is the highest spiritual authority in the nation. Solomon, Hezekiah, and Josiah control the arrangements for public worship as completely as Moses or David. Solomon receives Divine communications without the intervention of either priest or prophet ; he himself offers the great dedication prayer, and when he makes an end of praying, fire comes down from heaven. Under Hezekiah the civil authorities decide when the passover shall be observed : "For the king had taken counsel, and his princes, and all the congregation in Jerusalem, to keep the passover in the second month."[1] The great reforms of Josiah are throughout initiated and controlled by the king. He himself goes up to the Temple and reads in the ears of the people all the words of the book of the covenant that was found in the house of Jehovah. The chronicler still adheres to the primitive idea of the theocracy, according to which the chief, or judge, or king is the representative of Jehovah.

The title to the crown rests throughout on the grace of God and the will of the people. In Judah, however, the principle of hereditary succession prevails throughout. Athaliah is not really an exception : she reigned as the widow of a Davidic king. The double election

---

[1] **XXX. 2.**

of David by Jehovah and by Israel carried with it the election of his dynasty. The permanent rule of the house of David was secured by the Divine promise to its founder. Yet the title is not allowed to rest on mere hereditary right. Divine choice and popular recognition are recorded in the case of Solomon and other kings. "All Israel came to Shechem to make Rehoboam king," and yet revolted from him when he refused to accept their conditions ; but the obstinacy which caused the disruption "was brought about of God, that Jehovah might establish His word which He spake by the hand of Ahijah the Shilonite."

Ahaziah, Joash, Uzziah, Josiah, Jehoahaz, were all set upon the throne by the inhabitants of Judah and Jerusalem.[1] After Solomon the Divine appointment of kings is not expressly mentioned ; Jehovah's control over the tenure of the throne is chiefly shown by the removal of unworthy occupants.

It is interesting to note that the chronicler does not hesitate to record that of the last three sovereigns of Judah two were appointed by foreign kings : Jehoiakim was the nominee of Pharaoh Neco, king of Egypt ; and the last king of all, Zedekiah, was appointed by Nebuchadnezzar, king of Babylon. In like manner, the Herods, the last rulers of the restored kingdom of Judah, were the nominees of the Roman emperors. Such nominations forcibly illustrate the degradations and ruin of the theocratic monarchy. But yet, according to the teaching of the prophets, Pharaoh and Nebuchadnezzar were tools in the hand of Jehovah ; and their nomination was still an indirect Divine appointment. In the chronicler's time, however, Judah was

---

xxii. 1; xxiii. 1–15; xxvi. 1; xxxiii. 25; xxxvi. 1.

thoroughly accustomed to receive her governors from a
Persian or Greek king; and Jewish readers would not
be scandalised by a similar state of affairs in the closing
years of the earlier kingdom.

Thus the reforming kings illustrate the ideal kingship
set forth in the history of David and Solomon : the
royal authority originates in, and is controlled by, the
will of God and the consent of the people ; the king's
highest duty is the maintenance of the worship of
Jehovah; but the king and people are supreme both
in Church and state.

The personal character of the good kings is also very
similar to that of David and Solomon. Jehoshaphat,
Hezekiah, and Josiah are men of spiritual feeling as
well as careful observers of correct ritual.   None of the
good kings, with the exception of Joash and Josiah,
are unsuccessful in war ; and good reasons are given
for the exceptions.   They all display administrative
ability by their buildings, the organisation of the
Temple services and the army, and the arrangements
for the collection of the revenue, especially the dues
of the priests and Levites.

There is nothing, however, to indicate that the
personal charm of David's character was inherited by
his descendants ; but when biography is made merely
a means of edification, it often loses those touches of
nature which make the whole world kin, and are
capable of exciting either admiration or disgust.

The later narrative affords another illustration of the
absence of any sentiment of humanity towards enemies.
As in the case of David, the chronicler records the
cruelty of a good king as if it were quite consistent
with loyalty to Jehovah.   Before he turned away from
following Jehovah, Amariah defeated the Edomites and

smote ten thousand of them. Others were treated like
some of the Malagasy martyrs: "And other ten
thousand did the children of Judah carry away alive,
and brought them unto the top of the rock, and
cast them down from the top of the rock, that they
all were broken in pieces."[1] In this case, however,
the chronicler is not simply reproducing Kings : he has
taken the trouble to supplement his main authority
from some other source, probably local tradition. His
insertion of this verse is another testimony to the
undying hatred of Israel for Edom.

But in one respect the reforming kings are sharply
distinguished from David and Solomon. The record
of their lives is by no means blameless, and their sins
are visited by condign chastisement. They all, with
the single exception of Jotham, come to a bad end.
Asa consulted physicians, and was punished by being
allowed to die of a painful disease.[2] The last event of
Jehoshaphat's life was the ruin of the navy, which he
had built in unholy alliance with Ahaziah, king of
Israel, who did very wickedly.[3] Joash murdered the
prophet Zechariah, the son of the high-priest Jehoiada ;
his great host was routed by a small company of
Syrians, and Joash himself was assassinated by his
servants.[4] Amaziah turned away from following Jehovah, and "brought the gods of the children of Seir, and
set them up to be his gods, and bowed down himself
before them, and burned incense unto them." He was
accordingly defeated by Joash, king of Israel, and
assassinated by his own people.[5] Uzziah insisted on
exercising the priestly function of burning incense to
Jehovah, and so died a leper.[6] "Even Hezekiah ren-

---

[1] xxv. 11. [3] xx. 37. [5] xxv. 14–27.
[2] xvi. 12. [4] xxiv 20–27. [6] xxvi. 16–23.

dered not again according to the benefit done unto
him, for his heart was lifted up in the business of
ambassadors of the princes of Babylon; therefore there
was wrath upon him and upon Judah and Jerusalem.
Notwithstanding Hezekiah humbled himself for the
pride of his heart, both he and the inhabitants of
Jerusalem, so that the wrath of Jehovah came not upon
them in the days of Hezekiah." But yet the last days
of Hezekiah were clouded by the thought that he was
leaving the punishment of his sin as a legacy to Judah
and the house of David.[1] Josiah refused to heed the
warning sent to him by God through the king of
Egypt: "He hearkened not unto the words of Neco
from the mouth of God, and came to fight in the valley
of Megiddo"; and so Josiah died like Ahab: he was
wounded by the archers, carried out of the battle in his
chariot, and died at Jerusalem.[2]

The melancholy record of the misfortunes of the
good kings in their closing years is also found in the
book of Kings. There too Asa in his old age was
diseased in his feet, Jehoshaphat's ships were wrecked,
Joash and Amaziah were assassinated, Uzziah became
a leper, Hezekiah was rebuked for his pride, and
Josiah slain at Megiddo. But, except in the case of
Hezekiah, the book of Kings says nothing about
the sins which, according to Chronicles, occasioned
these sufferings and catastrophes. The narrative in
the book of Kings carries upon the face of it the lesson
that piety is not usually rewarded with unbroken prosperity, and that a pious career does not necessarily
ensure a happy deathbed. The significance of the
chronicler's additions will be considered elsewhere;

---

[1] xxxii. 25-33. [2] xxxv. 20-27.

what concerns us here is his departure from the principles he observed in dealing with the lives of David
and Solomon. They also sinned and suffered ; but the
chronicler omits their sins and sufferings, especially
in the case of Solomon. Why does he pursue an
opposite course with other good kings and blacken
their characters by perpetuating the memory of sins
not mentioned in the book of Kings, instead of confining his record to the happier incidents of their
career ? Many considerations may have influenced
him. The violent deaths of Joash, Amaziah, and
Josiah could neither be ignored nor explained away.
Hezekiah's sin and repentance are closely parallel to
David's in the matter of the census. Although Asa's
disease, Jehoshaphat's alliance with Israel, and Uzziah's
leprosy might easily have been omitted, yet, if some
reformers must be allowed to remain imperfect, there
was no imperative necessity to ignore the infirmities of
the rest. The great advantage of the course pursued
by the chronicler consisted in bringing out a clearly
defined contrast between David and Solomon on the
one hand and the reforming kings on the other. The
piety of the latter is conformed to the chronicler's
ideal ; but the glory and devotion of the former are
enhanced by the crimes and humiliation of the best of
their successors. Hezekiah, doubtless, is not more
culpable than David, but David's pride was the first of
a series of events which terminated in the building of
the Temple ; while the uplifting of Hezekiah's heart
was a precursor of its destruction. Besides, Hezekiah
ought to have profited by David's experience.

By developing this contrast, the chronicler renders
the position of David and Solomon even more unique,
illustrious, and full of religious significance.

Thus as illustrations of ideal kingship the accounts
of the good kings of Judah are altogether subordinate
to the history of David and Solomon. While these
kings of Judah remain loyal to Jehovah, they further
illustrate the virtues of their great predecessors by
showing how these virtues might have been exercised
under different circumstances : how David would have
dealt with an Ethiopian invasion and what Solomon
would have done if he had found the Temple desecrated
and its services stopped. But no essential feature is
added to the earlier pictures.

The lapses of kings who began to walk in the law
of the Lord and then fell away serve as foils to the
undimmed glory of David and Solomon. Abrupt
transitions within the limits of the individual lives of
Asa, Joash, and Amaziah bring out the contrast
between piety and apostacy with startling, dramatic
effect.

We return from this brief survey to consider the
significance of the life of Solomon according to Chronicles. Its relation to the life of David is summed up
in the name Solomon, the Prince of peace. David
is the ideal king, winning by force of arms for Israel
empire and victory, security at home and tribute from
abroad. Utterly subdued by his prowess, the natural
enemies of Israel no longer venture to disturb her
tranquillity. His successor inherits wide dominion,
immense wealth, and assured peace. Solomon, the
Prince of peace, is the ideal king, administering a
great inheritance for the glory of Jehovah and His
temple. His history in Chronicles is one of unbroken
calm. He has a great army and many strong fortresses,
but he never has occasion to use them. He implores
Jehovah to be merciful to Israel when they suffer from

the horrors of war; but he is interceding, not for his
own subjects, but for future generations.   In his
time—

> "No war or battle's sound
> Was heard the world around:
>   The idle spear and shield were high uphung
> The hooked chariot stood
> Unstained with hostile blood;
>   The trumpet spake not to the armèd throng."

Perhaps, to use a paradox, the greatest proof of
Solomon's wisdom was that he asked for wisdom. He
realised at the outset of his career that a wide dominion
is more easily won than governed, that to use great
wealth honourably requires more skill and character
than are needed to amass it.   To-day the world can
boast half a dozen empires surpassing not merely
Israel, but even Rome, in extent of dominion; the
aggregate wealth of the world is far beyond the wildest
dreams of the chronicler: but still the people perish
for lack of knowledge.   The physical and moral foul-
ness of modern cities taints all the culture and tarnishes
all the splendour of our civilisation; classes and
trades, employers and employed, maim and crush one
another in blind struggles to work out a selfish
salvation; newly devised organisations move their un-
wieldy masses—

> ". . . like dragons of the prime
> That tare each other."

iney have a giant's strength, and use it like a giant.
Knowledge comes, but wisdom lingers; and the world
waits for the reign of the Prince of peace who is not
only the wise king, but the incarnate wisdom of God.
   Thus one striking suggestion of the chronicler's

---

[1] Milton,. Hymn to the Nativity.

history of Solomon is the special need of wisdom and Divine guidance for the administration of a great and prosperous empire.

Too much stress, however, must not be laid on the twofold personality of the ideal king. This feature is adopted from the history, and does not express any opinion of the chronicler that the characteristic gifts of David and Solomon could not be combined in a single individual. Many great generals have also been successful administrators. Before Julius Cæsar was assassinated he had already shown his capacity to restore order and tranquillity to the Roman world; Alexander's plans for the civil government of his conquests were as far-reaching as his warlike ambition; Diocletian reorganised the empire which his sword had re-established; Cromwell's schemes of reform showed an almost prophetic insight into the future needs of the English people; the glory of Napoleon's victories is a doubtful legacy to France compared with the solid benefits of his internal reforms.

But even these instances, which illustrate the union of military genius and administrative ability, remind us that the assignment of success in war to one king and a reign of peace to the next is, after all, typical. The limits of human life narrow its possibilities. Cæsar's work had to be completed by Augustus; the great schemes of Alexander and Cromwell fell to the ground because no one arose to play Solomon to their David.

The chronicler has specially emphasised the indebtedness of Solomon to David. According to his narrative, the great achievement of Solomon's reign, the building of the Temple, has been rendered possible by David's preparations. Quite apart from plans and

materials, the chronicler's view of the credit due to
David in this matter is only a reasonable recognition
of service rendered to the religion of Israel.   Whoever
provided the timber and stone, the silver and gold,
for the Temple, David won for Jehovah the land and
the city that were the outer courts of the sanctuary,
and roused the national spirit that gave to Zion its
most solemn consecration.   Solomon's temple was
alike the symbol of David's achievements and the
coping-stone of his work.

By compelling our attention to the dependence of
the Prince of Peace upon the man who "had shed
much blood," the chronicler admonishes us against
forgetting the price that has been paid for liberty and
culture.   The splendid courtiers whose "apparel"
specially pleased the feminine tastes of the queen of
Sheba might feel all the contempt of the superior
person for David's war-worn veterans.   The latter
probably were more at home in the "store cities" than
at Jerusalem.   But without the blood and toil of these
rough soldiers Solomon would have had no opportunity
to exchange riddles with his fair visitor and to dazzle her
admiring eyes with the glories of his temple and palaces.

The blessings of peace are not likely to be preserved
unless men still appreciate and cherish the stern virtues
that flourish in troubled times.   If our own times become
troubled, and their serenity be invaded by fierce conflict,
it will be ours to remember that the rugged life of "the
hold in the wilderness" and the struggles with the
Philistines may enable a later generation to build its
temple to the Lord and to learn the answers to "hard
questions." [1]   Moses and Joshua, David and Solomon,

---

[1] 2 Chron. ix. 1.

remind us again how the Divine work is handed on
from generation to generation: Moses leads Israel
through the wilderness, but Joshua brings them into
the Land of Promise; David collects the materials,
but Solomon builds the Temple. The settlement in
Palestine and the building of the Temple were only
episodes in the working out of the "one increasing
purpose," but one leader and one life-time did not suffice
for either episode. We grow impatient of the scale
upon which God works: we want it reduced to the
limits of our human faculties and of our earthly lives;
yet all history preaches patience. In our demand for
Divine interventions whereby—

> "... sudden in a minute
> All is accomplished, and the work is done,"

we are very Esaus, eager to sell the birthright of the
future for a mess of pottage to-day.

And the continuity of the Divine purpose is only
realised through the continuity of human effort. We
must indeed serve our own generation; but part of
that service consists in providing that the next generation shall be trained to carry on the work, and that
after David shall come Solomon—the Solomon of
Chronicles, and not the Solomon of Kings—and that, if
possible, Solomon shall not be succeeded by Rehoboam.
As we attain this larger outlook, we shall be less
tempted to employ doubtful means, which are supposed
to be justified by their end; we shall be less enthusiastic for processes that bring "quick returns," but give
very "small profits" in the long run. Christian
workers are a little too fond of spiritual jerry-building,
as if sites in the kingdom of heaven were let out on

ninety-nine-year leases; but God builds for eternity, and we are fellow-workers together with Him.

To complete the chronicler's picture of the ideal king, we have to add David's warlike prowess and Solomon's wisdom and splendour to the piety and graces common to both. The result is unique among the many pictures that have been drawn by historians, philosophers, and poets. It has a value of its own, because the chronicler's gifts in the way of history, philosophy, and poetry were entirely subordinated to his interest in theology; and most theologians have only been interested in the doctrine of the king when they could use it to gratify the vanity of a royal patron.

The full-length portrait in Chronicles contrasts curiously with the little vignette preserved in the book which bears the name of Solomon. There, in the oracle which King Lemuel's mother taught him, the king is simply admonished to avoid strange women and strong drink, to "judge righteously, and minister judgment to the poor and needy."[1]

To pass to more modern theology, the theory of the king that is implied in Chronicles has much in common with Wyclif's doctrine of dominion: they both recognise the sanctity of the royal power and its temporal supremacy, and they both hold that obedience to God is the condition of the continued exercise of legitimate rule. But the priest of Lutterworth was less ecclesiastical and more democratic than our Levite.

A more orthodox authority on the Protestant doctrine of the king would be the Thirty-nine Articles. These, however, deal with the subject somewhat slightly. As

---

[1] Prov. xxxi. 1–9.

far as they go, they are in harmony with the chronicler. They assert the unqualified supremacy of the king, both ecclesiastical and civil. Even " general councils may not be gathered together without the commandment and will of princes."[1] On the other hand, princes are not to imitate Uzziah in presuming to exercise the priestly function of offering incense : they are not to minister God's word or sacraments.

Outside theology the ideal of the king has been stated with greater fulness and freedom, but not many of the pictures drawn have much in common with the chronicler's David and Solomon. Machiavelli's prince and Bolingbroke's patriot king belong to a different world ; moreover, their method is philosophical, and not historical : they state a theory rather than draw a picture. Tennyson's Arthur is, what he himself calls him, an " ideal knight " rather than an ideal king. Perhaps the best parallels to David are to be found in the Cyrus of the Greek historians and philosophers and the Alfred of English story. Alfred indeed combines many of the features both of David and Solomon : he secured English unity, and was the founder of English culture and literature ; he had a keen interest in ecclesiastical affairs, great gifts of administration, and much personal attractiveness. Cyrus, again, specially illustrates what we may call the posthumous fortunes of David : his name stood for the ideal of kingship with both Greeks and Persians, and in the *Cyropædia* his life and character are made the basis of a picture of the ideal king.

Many points are of course common to almost all

---

[1] Articles XXI. and XXXVII.

such pictures ; they portray the king as a capable and
benevolent ruler and a man of high personal character.
The distinctive characteristic of Chronicles is the stress
laid on the piety of the king, his care for the honour of
God and the spiritual welfare of his subjects. If the
practical influence of this teaching has not been
altogether beneficent, it is because men have too
invariably connected spiritual profit with organisation,
and ceremonies, and forms of words, sound or
otherwise.

But to-day the doctrine of the state takes the place
of the doctrine of the king. Instead of Cyropædias we
have Utopias. We are asked sometimes to look back,
not to an ideal king, but to an ideal commonwealth, to
the age of the Antonines or to some happy century of
English history when we are told that the human race
or the English people were " most happy and prosperous "; oftener we are invited to contemplate an
imaginary future. We may add to those already made
one or two further applications of the chronicler's
principles to the modern state. His method suggests
that the perfect society will have the virtues of our
actual life without its vices, and that the possibilities
of the future are best divined from a careful study of
the past. The devotion of his kings to the Temple
symbolises the truth that the ideal state is impossible
without recognition of a Divine presence and obedience
to a Divine will.

CHAPTER VII

THE WICKED KINGS

2 CHRON. xxviii., etc.

THE type of the wicked king is not worked out with any fulness in Chronicles. There are wicked kings, but no one is raised to the "bad eminence" of an evil counterpart to David; there is no anti-David, so to speak, no prototype of antichrist. The story of Ahaz, for instance, is not given at the same length and with the same wealth of detail as that of David. The subject was not so congenial to the kindly heart of the chronicler. He was not imbued with the unhappy spirit of modern realism, which loves to dwell on all that is foul and ghastly in life and character; he lingered affectionately over his heroes, and contented himself with brief notices of his villains. In so doing he was largely following his main authority: the books of Samuel and Kings. There too the stories of David and Solomon, of Elijah and Elisha, are told much more fully than those of Jeroboam and Ahab.

But the mention of these names reminds us that the chronicler's limitation of his subject to the history of Judah excludes much of the material that might have been drawn from the earlier history for a picture of the wicked king. If it had been part of the chronicler's plan to tell the story of Ahab, he might

have been led to develop his material and moralise
upon the king's career till the narrative assumed
proportions that would have rivalled the history of
David. Over against the great scene that closed
David's life might have been set another summing
up in one dramatic moment the guilt and ruin of Ahab.
But these schismatic kings were "alienated from the
commonwealth of Israel and strangers from the
covenants of the promise, having no hope and without
God in the world."[1] The disobedient sons of the
house of David were still children within the home,
who might be rebuked and punished ; but the Samaritan
kings, as the chronicler might style them, were outcasts,
left to the tender mercies of the dogs, and sorcerers, and
murderers that were without the Holy City, Cains without any protecting mark upon their forehead.

Hence the wicked kings in Chronicles are of the
house of David. Therefore the chronicler has a
certain tenderness for them, partly for the sake of
their great ancestor, partly because they are kings
of Judah, partly because of the sanctity and religious
significance of the Messianic dynasty. These kings
are not Esaus, for whom there is no place of repentance. The chronicler is happy in being able to discover and record the conversion, as we should term it,
of some kings whose reigns began in rebellion and
apostacy. By a curious compensation, the kings who
begin well end badly, and those who begin badly end
well ; they all tend to about the same average. We
read of Rehoboam[2] that "when he humbled himself
the wrath of the Lord turned from him, that he would
not destroy him altogether ; and, moreover, in Judah

---

[1] Eph. ii. 12.

[2] 2 Chron. xii. 12, peculiar to Chronicles,

there were good things found"; the wickedness of Abijah, which is plainly set forth in the book of Kings,[1] is ignored in Chronicles; Manasseh "humbled himself greatly before the God of his fathers," and turned altogether from the error of his ways[2]; the unfavourable judgment on Jehoahaz recorded in the book of Kings, "And he did that which was evil in the sight of the Lord, according to all that his fathers had done,"[3] is omitted in Chronicles.

There remain seven wicked kings of whom nothing but evil is recorded: Jehoram, Ahaziah, Ahaz, Amon, Jehoiakim, Jehoiachin, and Zedekiah. Of these we may take Ahaz as the most typical instance. As in the cases of David and Solomon, we will first see how the chronicler has dealt with the material derived from the book of Kings; then we will give his account of the career of Ahaz; and finally, by a brief comparison of what is told of Ahaz with the history of the other wicked kings, we will try to construct the chronicler's idea of the wicked king and to deduce its lessons.

The importance of the additions made by the chronicler to the history in the book of Kings will appear later on. In his account of the attack made upon Ahaz by Rezin, king of Damascus, and Pekah, king of Israel, he emphasises the incidents most discreditable to Ahaz. The book of Kings simply states that the two allies "came up to Jerusalem to war; and they besieged Ahaz, but could not overcome him"[4]; Chronicles dwells upon the sufferings and losses inflicted on Judah by this invasion. The book of Kings might have conveyed the impression that the wicked king had been allowed to triumph over his enemies;

---

[1] 1 Kings xv. 3.　　　　　　　　[3] 2 Kings xxiii. 32.
[2] 2 Chron. xxxiii. 11-20, peculiar to Chronicles.　　[4] 2 Kings xvi. 5.

Chronicles guards against this dangerous error by detailing the disasters that Ahaz brought upon his country.

The book of Kings also contains an interesting account of alterations made by Ahaz in the Temple and its furniture. By his orders the high-priest Urijah made a new brazen altar for the Temple after the pattern of an altar that Ahaz had seen in Damascus. As Chronicles narrates the closing of the Temple by Ahaz, it naturally omits these previous alterations. Moreover, Urijah appears in the book of Isaiah as a friend of the prophet; and is referred to by him as a " faithful witness." [1] The chronicler would not wish to perplex his readers with the problem, How could the high-priest, whom Isaiah trusted as a faithful witness, become the agent of a wicked king, and construct an altar for Jehovah after a heathen pattern ?

The chronicler's story of Ahaz runs thus. This wicked king had been preceded by three good kings : Amaziah, Uzziah, and Jotham. Amaziah indeed had turned away from following Jehovah at the end of his reign, but Uzziah had been zealous for Jehovah throughout, not wisely, but too well ; and Jotham shares with Solomon the honour of a blameless record. Without counting Amaziah's reign, king and people had been loyal to Jehovah for sixty or seventy years. The court of the good kings would be the centre of piety and devotion. Ahaz, no doubt, had been carefully trained in obedience to the law of Jehovah, and had grown up in the atmosphere of true religion. Possibly he had known his grandfather Uzziah in the days of his power and glory ; but at any rate, while Ahaz was

---

[1] Isa. viii. 2.

a child, Uzziah was living as a leper in his " several house," and Ahaz must have been familiar with this melancholy warning against presumptuous interference with the Divine ordinances of worship.

Ahaz was twenty years old when he came to the throne, so that he had time to profit by a complete education, and should scarcely have found opportunity to break away from its influence.　His mother's name is not mentioned, so that we cannot say whether, as may have been the case with Rehoboam, some Ammonite woman led him astray from the God of his fathers. As far as we can learn from our author, Ahaz sinned against light and knowledge; with every opportunity and incentive to keep in the right path, he yet went astray.

This is a common feature in the careers of the wicked kings.　It has often been remarked that the first great specialist on education failed utterly in the application of his theories to his own son.　Jehoshaphat, Hezekiah, and Josiah were the most distinguished and the most virtuous of the reforming kings, yet Jehoshaphat was succeeded by Jehoram, who was almost as wicked as Ahaz; Hezekiah's son " Manasseh made Judah and the inhabitants of Jerusalem to err, so that they did evil more than did the nations whom the Lord destroyed before the children of Israel ";[1] Josiah's son and grandsons " did evil in the sight of the Lord."[2]

Many reasons may be suggested for this too familiar spectacle: the impious son of a godly father, the bad successor of a good king.　Heirs-apparent have always been inclined to head an opposition to their fathers' policy, and sometimes on their accession they have

---

[1] 2 Chron. xxxiii. 9.　　[2] 2 Chron. xxxvi. 5, 8, 11.

reversed that policy. When the father himself has been a zealous reformer, the interests that have been harassed by reform are eager to encourage his successor in a retrograde policy; and reforming zeal is often tinged with an inconsiderate harshness that provokes the opposition of younger and brighter spirits. But, after all, this atavism in kings is chiefly an illustration of the slow growth of the higher nature in man. Practically each generation starts afresh with an unregenerate nature of its own, and often nature is too strong for education.

Moreover, a young king of Judah was subject to the evil influence of his northern neighbour. Judah was often politically subservient to Samaria, and politics and religion have always been very intimately associated. At the accession of Ahaz the throne of Samaria was filled by Pekah, whose twenty years' tenure of authority indicates ability and strength of character. It is not difficult to understand how Ahaz was led " to walk in the ways of the kings of Israel " and " to make molten images for the Baals."

Nothing is told us of the actual circumstances of these innovations. The new reign was probably inaugurated by the dismissal of Jotham's ministers and the appointment of the personal favourites of the new king. The restoration of old idolatrous cults would be a natural advertisement of a new departure in the government. So when the establishment of Christianity was a novelty in the empire, and men were not assured of its permanence, Julian's accession was accompanied by an apostacy to paganism; and later aspirants to the purple promised to follow his example. But the worship of Jehovah was not at once suppressed. He was not deposed from His throne as the

Divine King of Judah; He was only called upon to share His royal authority with the Baals of the neighbouring peoples.

But although the Temple services might still be performed, the king was mainly interested in introducing and observing a variety of heathen rites. The priesthood of the Temple saw their exclusive privileges disregarded and the rival sanctuaries of the high places and the sacred trees taken under royal patronage. But the king's apostacy was not confined to the milder forms of idolatry. His weak mind was irresistibly attracted by the morbid fascination of the cruel rites of Moloch: " He burnt incense in the valley of the son of Hinnom, and burnt his children in the fire, according to the abomination of the heathen, whom the Lord cast out before the children of Israel."

The king's devotions to his new gods were rudely interrupted. The insulted majesty of Jehovah was vindicated by two disastrous invasions. First, Ahaz was defeated by Rezin, king of Syria, who carried away a great multitude of captives to Damascus; the next enemy was one of those kings of Israel in whose idolatrous ways Ahaz had chosen to walk. The delicate flattery implied by Ahaz becoming Pekah's proselyte failed to conciliate that monarch. He too defeated the Jews with great slaughter. Amongst his warriors was a certain Zichri, whose achievements recalled the prowess of David's mighty men: he slew Maaseiah the king's son and Azrikam, the ruler of the house, the Lord High Chamberlain, and Elkanah, that was next unto the king, the Prime Minister. With these notables, there perished in a single day a hundred and twenty thousand Jews, all of them valiant men. Their wives and children, to the number of two hundred thousand, were carried captive to Samaria. All these misfortunes happened to Judah "because they had forsaken Jehovah, the God of their fathers."

And yet Jehovah in wrath remembered mercy. The Israelite army approached Samaria with their endless train of miserable captives, women and children, ragged and barefoot, some even naked, filthy and footsore with forced marches, left hungry and thirsty after prisoners' scanty rations. Multiply a thousandfold the scenes depicted on Egyptian and Assyrian monuments, and you have the picture of this great slave caravan. The captives probably had no reason to fear the barbarities which the Assyrians loved to inflict upon their prisoners, but yet their prospects were sufficiently gloomy. Before them lay a life of drudgery and degradation in Samaria. The more wealthy might hope to be ransomed by their friends; others, again, might be sold to the Phœnician traders, to be carried by them to the great slave marts of Nineveh and Babylon or even oversea to Greece. But in a moment all was changed. "There was a prophet of Jehovah, whose name was Oded, and he went out to meet the army and said unto them, Behold, because Jehovah, the God of your fathers, was wroth with Judah, He hath delivered them into your hand; and ye have slain them in a rage which hath reached up unto heaven. And now ye purpose to keep the children of Judah and of Jerusalem for male and female slaves; but are there not even with you trespasses of your own against Jehovah your God? Now hear me therefore, and send back the captives, for the fierce wrath of Jehovah is upon you."

Meanwhile "the princes and all the congregation of Samaria" were waiting to welcome their victorious

army, possibly in "the void place at the entering in
of the gate of Samaria." Oded's words, at any rate,
had been uttered in their presence. The army did not
at once respond to the appeal; the two hundred thousand slaves were the most valuable part of their spoil,
and they were not eager to make so great a sacrifice.
But the princes made Oded's message their own.
Four heads of the children of Ephraim are mentioned
by name as the spokesmen of the "congregation," the
king being apparently absent on some other warlike
expedition. These four were Azariah the son of
Johanan, Berechiah the son of Meshillemoth, Jehizkiah
the son of Shallum, and Amasa the son of Hadlai.
Possibly among the children of Ephraim who dwelt in
Jerusalem after the Return there were descendants of
these men, from whom the chronicler obtained the
particulars of this incident. The princes "stood up
against them that came from the war," and forbade
their bringing the captives into the city. They repeated
and expanded the words of the prophet: "Ye purpose
that which will bring upon us a trespass against
Jehovah, to add unto our sins and to our trespass, for
our trespass is great, and there is fierce wrath against
Israel." The army were either convinced by the
eloquence or overawed by the authority of the prophet
and the princes: "They left the captives and the spoil
before all the princes and the congregation." And the
four princes "rose up, and took the captives, and with
the spoil clothed all that were naked among them, and
arrayed them, and shod them, and gave them to eat and
to drink, and anointed them, and carried all the feeble
of them upon asses, and brought them to Jericho, the
city of palm trees, unto their brethren; then they
returned to Samaria."

Apart from incidental allusions, this is the last reference in Chronicles to the northern kingdom. The
long history of division and hostility closes with this
humane recognition of the brotherhood of Israel and
Judah. The sun, so to speak, did not go down upon
their wrath. But the king of Israel had no personal
share in this gracious act. At the first it was Jeroboam
that made Israel to sin ; throughout the history the
responsibility for the continued division would specially
rest upon the kings, and at the last there is no sign of
Pekah's repentance and no prospect of his pardon.

The various incidents of the invasions of Rezin and
Pekah were alike a solemn warning and an impressive
appeal to the apostate king of Judah. He had multiplied
to himself gods of the nations round about, and yet had
been left without an ally, at the mercy of a hostile
confederation, against whom his new gods either could
not or would not defend him. The wrath of Jehovah
had brought upon Ahaz one crushing defeat after
another, and yet the only mitigation of the sufferings of
Judah had also been the work of Jehovah. The returning captives would tell Ahaz and his princes how in
schismatic and idolatrous Samaria a prophet of Jehovah
had stood forth to secure their release and obtain for
them permission to return home. The princes and
people of Samaria had hearkened to his message, and
the two hundred thousand captives stood there as the
monument of Jehovah's compassion and of the obedient
piety of Israel. Sin was bound to bring punishment ;
and yet Jehovah waited to be gracious. Wherever there
was room for mercy, He would show mercy. His wrath
and His compassion had alike been displayed before
Ahaz. Other gods could not protect their worshippers
against Him ; He only could deliver and restore His

people. He had not even waited for Ahaz to repent before He had given him proof of His willingness to forgive.[1]

Such Divine goodness was thrown away upon Ahaz; there was no token of repentance, no promise of amendment; and so Jehovah sent further judgments upon the king and his unhappy people. The Edomites came and smote Judah, and carried away captives; the Philistines also invaded the cities of the lowland and of the south of Judah, and took Beth-shemesh, Aijalon, Gederoth, Soco, Timnah, Gimzo, and their dependent villages, and dwelt in them; and Jehovah brought Judah low because of Ahaz. And the king hardened his heart yet more against Jehovah, and cast away all restraint, and trespassed sore against Jehovah. Instead of submitting himself, he sought the aid of the kings of Assyria, only to receive another proof of the vanity of all earthly help so long as he remained unreconciled to Heaven. Tilgath-pilneser, king of Assyria, welcomed this opportunity of interfering in the affairs of Western Asia, and saw attractive prospects of levying blackmail impartially on his ally and his enemies. He came unto Ahaz, "and distressed him, but strengthened him not." These new troubles were the occasion of fresh wickedness on the part of the king: to pay the price of this worse than useless intervention, he took away a portion not only from his own treasury and from the princes, but also from the treasury of the Temple, and gave it to the king of Assyria.

Thus betrayed and plundered by his new ally, he trespassed "yet more against Jehovah, this same king Ahaz." It is almost incredible that one man could be

---

[1] 2 Chron. xxviii. 5–15, peculiar to Chronicles; cf. 2 Kings xvi. 5, 6.

guilty of so much sin; the chronicler is anxious that
his readers should appreciate the extraordinary wickedness of this man, this same king Ahaz. In him the
chastening of the Lord yielded no peaceable fruit of
righteousness; he would not see that his misfortunes
were sent from the offended God of Israel. With
perverse ingenuity, he found in them an incentive to
yet further wickedness. His pantheon was not large
enough. He had omitted to worship the gods of
Damascus. These must be powerful deities, whom it
would be worth while to conciliate, because they had
enabled the kings of Syria to overrun and pillage Judah.
Therefore Ahaz sacrificed to the gods of Syria, that they
might help him. "But," says the chronicler, "they were
the ruin of him and of all Israel." Still Ahaz went on
consistently with his policy of comprehensive eclecticism.
He made Jerusalem a very Athens for altars, which were
set up at every street corner; he discovered yet other
gods whom it might be advisable to adore: "And in
every several city of Judah he made high places to burn
incense unto other gods."

Hitherto Jehovah had still received some share of
the worship of this most religious king, but apparently
Ahaz came to regard Him as the least powerful of his
many supernatural allies. He attributed his misfortunes,
not to the anger, but to the helplessness, of Jehovah.
Jehovah was specially the God of Israel; if disaster
after disaster fell upon His people, He was evidently
less potent than Baal, or Moloch, or Rimmon. It was
a useless expense to maintain the worship of so impotent a deity. Perhaps the apostate king was acting
in the blasphemous spirit of the savage who flogs his
idol when his prayers are not answered. Jehovah, he
thought, should be punished for His neglect of the in-

14

terests of Judah. "Ahaz gathered together the vessels of the house of God, and cut in pieces the vessels of the house of God, and shut up the doors of the house of Jehovah";[1] he had filled up the measure of his iniquities.

And thus it came to pass that in the Holy City, "which Jehovah had chosen to cause His name to dwell there," almost the only deity who was not worshipped was Jehovah. Ahaz did homage to the gods of all the nations before whom he had been humiliated; the royal sacrifices smoked upon a hundred altars, but no sweet savour of burnt offering ascended to Jehovah. The fragrance of the perpetual incense no longer filled the holy place morning and evening; the seven lamps of the golden candlestick were put out, and the Temple was given up to darkness and desolation. Ahaz had contented himself with stripping the sanctuary of its treasures; but the building itself, though closed, suffered no serious injury. A stranger visiting the city, and finding it full of idols, could not fail to notice the great pile of the Temple and to inquire what image, splendid above all others, occupied that magnificent shrine. Like Pompey, he would learn with surprise that it was not the dwelling-place of any image, but the symbol of an almighty and invisible presence. Even if the stranger were some Moabite worshipper of Chemosh, he would feel dismay at the wanton profanity with which Ahaz had abjured the God of his fathers and desecrated the temple built by his great ancestors. The annals of Egypt and Babylon told of the misfortunes which had befallen those monarchs who were unfaithful to their national gods. The pious heathen

---

[1] 2 Chron. xxviii. 16–25, peculiar to Chronicles; cf. 2 Kings xvi. 7–18.

would anticipate disaster as the punishment of Ahaz's apostacy.

Meanwhile the ministers of the Temple shared its ruin and degradation ; but they could feel the assurance that Jehovah would yet recall His people to their allegiance and manifest Himself once more in the Temple. The house of Aaron and the tribe of Levi possessed their souls in patience till the final judgment of Jehovah should fall upon the apostate. They had not long to wait : after a reign of only sixteen years, Ahaz died at the early age of thirty-six. We are not told that he died in battle or by the visitation of God. His health may have been broken by his many misfortunes, or by vicious practices that would naturally accompany his manifold idolatries ; but in any case his early death would be regarded as a Divine judgment. The breath was scarcely out of his body before his religious innovations were swept away by a violent reaction. The people at once passed sentence of condemnation on his memory : " They brought him not into the sepulchres of the kings of Israel." [1] His successor inaugurated his reign by reopening the Temple, and brought back Judah to the obedience of Jehovah. The monuments of the impious worship of the wicked king, his multitudinous idols, and their ritual passed away like an evil dream, like " the track of a ship in the sea or a bird in the air."

The leading features of this career are common to most of the wicked kings and to the evil days of the good kings " Walking in the ways of the kings of Israel " was the great crime of Jehoshaphat and his successors Jehoram and Ahaziah. Other kings, like

---

[1] xxviii. 27, peculiar to Chronicles.

Manasseh, built high places and followed after the
abominations of the heathen whom Jehovah cast out
before the children of Israel. Asa's lapse into wickedness began by plundering the Temple treasury to
purchase an alliance with a heathen king, the king
of Syria, against whose successor Ahaz in his turn
hired the king of Assyria. Amaziah adopted the gods
of Edom, as Ahaz the gods of Syria, but with less
excuse, for Amaziah had conquered Edom. Other
crimes are recorded among the evil doings of the
kings : Asa had recourse to physicians, that is,
probably to magic ; Jehoram slew his brethren ; Joash
murdered the son of his benefactor Jehoiada ; but
the supreme sin was disloyalty to Jehovah and the
Temple, and of this sin the chronicler's brief history
of Ahaz is the most striking illustration. Ahaz is the
typical apostate : he hardens his heart alike against
the mercy of Jehovah and against His repeated judgment. He is a very Pharaoh among the kings of
Judah. The discipline that should have led to repentance is continually perverted to be the occasion of new
sin, and at last the apostate dies in his iniquity. The
effect of the picture is heightened by its insistence on
this one sin of apostacy ; other sins are illustrated and
condemned elsewhere, but here the chronicler would
have us concentrate our attention on the rise, progress,
and ruin of the apostate. Indeed, this one sin implied and involved all others ; the man who suppressed
the worship of Jehovah, and revelled in the obscene
superstitions of heathen cults, was obviously capable
of any enormity. The chronicler is not indifferent
to morality as compared with ritual, and he sees in the
neglect of Divinely appointed ritual an indication of
a character rotten through and through. In his time

neglect of ritual on the part of the average man or
the average king implied neglect of religion, or rather
adherence to an alien and immoral faith.

Thus the supreme sin of the wicked kings naturally
contrasts with the highest virtue of the good kings.
The standing of both is determined by their attitude
towards Jehovah. The character of the good kings
is developed in greater detail than that of their wicked
brethren; but we should not misrepresent the chronicler's
views, if we ascribed to the wicked kings all the vices
antithetic to the virtues of his royal ideal. Nevertheless the picture actually drawn fixes our attention
upon their impious denial of the God of Israel. Much
Church history has been written on the same principle :
Constantine is a saint because he established Christianity; Julian is an incarnation of wickedness because
he became an apostate ; we praise the orthodox Theodosius, and blame the Arian Valens. Protestant historians have canonised Henry VIII. and Elizabeth,
and have prefixed an unholy epithet to the name of
their kinswoman, while Romanist writers interchange
these verdicts. But underlying even such opposite
judgments there is the same valid principle, the
principle that was in the mind of the chronicler : that
the king's relation to the highest and purest truth
accessible to him, whatever that truth may be, is a
just criterion of his whole character. The historian
may err in applying the criterion. but its general
principle is none the less sound.

For the character of the wicked nation we are not
left to the general suggestions that may be derived
from the wicked king. The prophets show us that it
was by no vicarious condemnation that priests and
people shared the ruin of their sovereign. In their

pages the subject is treated from many points of view: Israel and Judah, Edom and Tyre, Egypt, Assyria, and Babylon, serve in their turn as models for the picture of the wicked nation. In the Apocalypse the ancient picture is adapted to new circumstances, and the City of the Seven Hills takes the place of Babylon. Modern prophets have further adapted the treatment of the subject to their own times, and for the most part to their own people. With stern and uncompromising patriotism, Carlyle and Ruskin have sought righteousness for England even at the expense of its reputation ; they have emphasised its sin and selfishness in order to produce repentance and reform. For other teachers the history of foreign peoples has furnished the picture of the wicked nation, and the France of the Revolution or the "unspeakable" Turk has been held up as an example of all that is abominable in national life.

Any detailed treatment of this theme in Scripture would need an exposition, not merely of Chronicles, but of the whole Bible. We may, however, make one general application of the chronicler's principle that the wicked nation is the nation that forgets God. We do not now measure a people's religion by the number and magnificence of its priests and churches, or by the amount of money devoted to the maintenance of public worship. The most fatal symptoms of national depravity are the absence of a healthy public opinion, indifference to character in politics, neglect of education as a means of developing character, and the stifling of the spirit of brotherhood in a desperate struggle for existence. When God is thus forgotten, and the gracious influences of His Spirit are no longer recognised in public and private life, a country may well be degraded into the ranks of the wicked nations.

The perfectly general terms in which the doings and
experiences of Ahaz are described facilitate the application of their warnings to the ordinary individual. His
royal station only appears in the form and scale of his
wickedness, which in its essence is common to him with
the humblest sinner. Every young man enters, like
Ahaz, upon a royal inheritance; character and career
are as all-important to a peasant or a shopgirl as they
are to an emperor or a queen. When a girl of seven
teen or a youth of twenty succeeds to some historic
throne, we are moved to think of the heavy burden of
responsibility laid upon inexperienced shoulders and of
the grave issues that must be determined during the
swiftly passing years of their early manhood and woman-
hood. Alas, this heavy burden and these grave issues
are but the common lot. The young sovereign is happy
in the fierce light that beats upon his throne, for he is
not allowed to forget the dignity and importance of
life. History, with its stories of good and wicked kings,
has obviously been written for his instruction; if the
time be out of joint, as it mostly is, he has been born to
set it right. It is all true, yet it is equally true for
every one of his subjects. His lot is only the common
lot set upon a hill, in the full sunlight, to illustrate,
interpret, and influence lower and obscurer lives.
People take such eager interest in the doings of royal
families, their christenings, weddings, and funerals,
because therein the common experience is, as it were,
glorified into adequate dignity and importance.

" Ahaz was twenty years old when he began to reign,
and he reigned sixteen years in Jerusalem "; but most
men and women begin to reign before they are twenty.
The history of Judah for those sixteen years was really
determined long before Ahaz was invested with crown

and sceptre. Men should all be educated to reign, to respect themselves and appreciate their opportunities. We do in some measure adopt this principle with promising lads. Their energies are stimulated by the prospect of making a fortune or a name, or the more soaring imagination dreams of a seat on the woolsack or on one of the Front Benches. Gifted girls are also encouraged, as becomes their gifts, to achieve a brilliant marriage or a popular novel. We need to apply the principle more consistently and to recognise the royal dignity of the average life and of those whom the superior person is pleased to call commonplace people. It may then be possible to induce the ordinary young man to take a serious interest in his own future. The stress laid on the sanctity and supreme value of the individual soul has always been a vital element of evangelical teaching ; like most other evangelical truths, it is capable of deeper meaning and wider application than are commonly recognised in systematic theology.

We have kept our sovereign waiting too long on the threshold of his kingdom ; his courtiers and his people are impatient to know the character and intentions of their new master. So with every heir who succeeds to his royal inheritance. The fortunes of millions may depend upon the will of some young Czar or Kaiser ; the happiness of a hundred tenants or of a thousand workmen may rest on the disposition of the youthful inheritor of a wide estate or a huge factory ; but none the less in the poorest cottage mother and father and friends wait with trembling anxiety to see how the boy or girl will " turn out " when they take their destinies into their own hands and begin to reign. Already perhaps some tender maiden watches in hope and fear, in mingled pride and misgiving, the rapidly unfolding character of the youth to whom she has promised to commit all the happiness of a life-time.

And to each one in turn there comes the choice of Hercules ; according to the chronicler's phrase, the young king may either " do right in the eyes of Jehovah, like David his father," or he may walk " in the ways of the kings of Israel, and make molten images for the Baals."

The " right doings of David his father" may point to family traditions, which set a high standard of noble conduct for each succeeding generation. The teaching and influence of the pious Jotham are represented by the example of godliness set in many a Christian home, by the wise and loving counsel of parents and friends. And Ahaz has many modern parallels, sons and daughters upon whom every good influence seems spent in vain. They are led astray into the ways of the kings of Israel, and make molten images for the Baals.   There were several dynasties of the kings of Israel, and the Baals were many and various ; there are many tempters who deliberately or unconsciously lay snares for souls, and they serve different powers of evil.   Israel was for the most part more powerful, wealthy, and cultured than Judah.   When Ahaz came to the throne as a mere youth, Pekah was apparently in the prime of life and the zenith of power. He is no inapt symbol of what the modern tempter at any rate desires to appear : the showy, pretentious man of the world, who parades his knowledge of life, and impresses the inexperienced youth with his shrewdness and success, and makes his victim eager to imitate him, to walk in the ways of the kings of Israel.

Moreover, the prospect of making molten images for the Baals is an insidious temptation. Ahaz perhaps found the decorous worship of the one God dull and monotonous. Baals meant new gods and new rites, with all the excitement of novelty and variety. Jotham may not have realised that this youth of twenty was a man : the heir-apparent may have been treated as a child and left too much to the women of the harem. Responsible activity might have saved Ahaz. The Church needs to recognise that healthy, vigorous youth craves interesting occupation and even excitement. If a father wishes to send his son to the devil, he cannot do better than make that son's life, both secular and religious, a routine of monotonous drudgery. Then any pinchbeck king of Israel will seem a marvel of wit and good fellowship, and the making of molten images a most pleasing diversion. A molten image is something solid, permanent, and conspicuous, a standing advertisement of the enterprise and artistic taste of the maker ; he engraves his name on the pedestal, and is proud of the honourable distinction. Many of our modern molten images are duly set forth in popular works, for instance the reputation for impure life, or hard drinking, or reckless gambling, to achieve which some men have spent their time, and money, and toil. Other molten images are dedicated to another class of Baals : Mammon the respectable and Belial the polite.

The next step in the history of Ahaz is also typical of many a rake's progress. The king of Israel, in whose ways he has walked, turns upon him and plunders him ; the experienced man of the world gives his pupil painful proof of his superiority, and calls in his confederates to share the spoil. Now surely the victim's eyes will be opened to the life he is leading and the character of his associates. By no means. Ahaz has been conquered by Syria, and there-

fore he will worship the gods of Syria, and he will
have a confederate of his own in the Assyrian king.
The victim tries to master the arts by which he has
been robbed and ill-treated; he will become as un-
scrupulous as his masters in wickedness. He seeks
the profit and distinction of being the accomplice of
bold and daring sinners, men as pre-eminent in evil
as Tilgath-pilneser in Western Asia; and they, like
the Assyrian king, take his money and accept his
flattery: they use him and then cast him off more
humiliated and desperate than ever. He sinks into
a prey of meaner scoundrels: the Edomites and Philistines of fast life; and then, in his extremity, he builds
new high places and sacrifices to more new gods; he
has recourse to all the shifty expedients and sordid
superstitions of the devotees of luck and chance.

All this while he has still paid some external homage
to religion; he has observed the conventions of honour
and good breeding. There have been services, as it
were, in the temple of Jehovah. Now he begins to
feel that this deference has not met with an adequate
reward; he has been no better treated than the
flagrantly disreputable: indeed, these men have often
got the better of him. "It is vain to serve God; what
profit is there in keeping His charge and in walking
mournfully before the Lord of hosts? The proud are
called happy; they that work wickedness are built up:
they tempt God, and are delivered." His moods vary;
and, with reckless inconsistency, he sometimes derides
religion as worthless and unmeaning, and sometimes
seeks to make God responsible for his sins and misfortunes. At one time he says he knows all about
religion and has seen through it; he was brought up
to pious ways, and his mature judgment has shown

him that piety is a delusion; he will no longer countenance its hypocrisy and cant: at another time he complains that he has been exposed to special temptations and has not been provided with special safeguards; the road that leads to life has been made too steep and narrow, and he has been allowed without warning and remonstrance to tread "the primrose path that leads to the everlasting bonfire"; he will cast off altogether the dull formalities and irksome restraints of religion; he will work wickedness with a proud heart and a high hand. His happiness and success have been hindered by pedantic scruples; now he will be built up and delivered from his troubles. He gets rid of the few surviving relics of the old honourable life. The service of prayer and praise ceases; the lamp of truth is put out; the incense of holy thought no longer perfumes the soul; and the temple of the Spirit is left empty, and dark, and desolate.

At last, in what should be the prime of manhood, the sinner, broken-hearted, worn out in mind and body, sinks into a dishonoured grave.

The career and fate of Ahaz may have other parallels besides this, but it is sufficiently clear that the chronicler's picture of the wicked king is no mere antiquarian study of a vanished past. It lends itself with startling facility to illustrate the fatal downward course of any man who, entering on the royal inheritance of human life, allies himself with the powers of darkness and finally becomes their slave.

CHAPTER VIII

THE PRIESTS

THE Israelite priesthood must be held to include the Levites. Their functions and status differed from those of the house of Aaron in degree, and not in kind. They formed a hereditary caste set apart for the service of the sanctuary, and as such they shared the revenues of the Temple with the sons of Aaron. The priestly character of the Levites is more than once implied in Chronicles. After the disruption, we are told that " the priests and the Levites that were in all Israel resorted to Rehoboam," because " Jeroboam and his sons cast them off, that they should not exercise the priest's office unto Jehovah." On an emergency, as at Hezekiah's great feast at the reopening of the Temple, the Levites might even discharge priestly functions. Moreover, the chronicler seems to recognise the priestly character of the whole tribe of Levi by retaining in a similar connection the old phrase " the priests the Levites." [1]

The relation of the Levites to the priests, the sons of Aaron, was not that of laymen to clergy, but of an inferior clerical order to their superiors. When

---

[1] 2 Chron. xi. 13, 14, xxix. 34, xxx. 27, all peculiar to Chronicles. In xxx. 27 the text is doubtful; many authorities have "the priests and the Levites."

Charlotte Brontë has occasion to devote a chapter to curates, she heads it " Levitical." The Levites, again, like deacons in the Church of England, were forbidden to perform the most sacred ritual of Divine service. Technically their relation to the sons of Aaron might be compared to that of deacons to priests or of priests to bishops. From the point of view of numbers,[1] revenues, and social standing, the sons of Aaron might be compared to the dignitaries of the Church: archbishops, bishops, archdeacons, deans, and incumbents of livings with large incomes and little work ; while the Levites would correspond to the more moderately paid and fully occupied clergy. Thus the nature of the distinction between the priests and the Levites shows that they were essentially only two grades of the same order ; and this corresponds roughly to what has been generally denoted by the term " priesthood." Priest hood, however, had a more limited meaning in Israel than in later times. In some branches of the Christian Church, the priests exercise or claim to exercise functions which in Israel belonged to the prophets or the king.

Before considering the central and essential idea of the priest as a minister of public worship, we will notice some of his minor duties. We have seen that the sanctity of civil government is emphasised by the religious supremacy of the king; the same truth is also illustrated by the fact that the priests and Levites were sometimes the king's officers for civil affairs. Under David, certain Levites of Hebron are spoken of as having the oversight of all Israel, both east and

---

[1] *I.e.*, in the view given us by the chronicler of the period of the monarchy, after the Return the priests were far more numerous than the Levites.

west of Jordan, not only "for all the business of Jehovah," but also "for the service of the king."[1] The business of the law-courts was recognised by Jehoshaphat as the judgment of Jehovah, and accordingly amongst the judges there were priests and Levites.[2] Similarly the mediæval governments often found their most efficient and trustworthy administrators in the bishops and clergy, and were glad to reinforce their secular authority by the sanction of the Church; and even to-day bishops sit in Parliament: incumbents preside over vestries, and sometimes act as county magistrates. But the interest of religion in civil government is most manifest in the moral influence exercised unofficially by earnest and public-spirited ministers of all denominations.

The chronicler refers more than once to the educational work of the priests, and especially of the Levites. The English version probably gives his real meaning when it attributes to him the phrase "teaching priest."[3] Jehoshaphat's educational commission was largely composed of priests and Levites, and Levites are spoken of as scribes. Jewish education was largely religious, and naturally fell into the hands of the priesthood, just as the learning of Egypt and Babylon was chiefly in the hands of priests and magi. The Christian ministry maintained the ancient traditions: the monasteries were the homes of mediæval learning, and till recently England and Scotland mainly owed their schools to the Churches, and almost all schoolmasters of any position were in holy orders—priests and Levites.

---

[1] 1 Chron. xxvi. 30–32.

[2] 2 Chron. xix. 4–11.

[3] 2 Chron. xv. 3. In the older literature the phrase would bear a more special and technical meaning.

Under our new educational system the free choice of the people places many ministers of religion on the school boards.

The next characteristic of the priesthood is not so much in accordance with Christian theory and practice. The house of Aaron and the tribe of Levi were a Church militant in a very literal sense. In the beginning of their history the tribe of Levi earned the blessing of Jehovah by the pious zeal with which they flew to arms in His cause and executed His judgment upon their guilty fellow-countrymen.[1] Later on, when "Israel joined himself unto Baal-peor, and the anger of Jehovah was kindled against Israel,"[2] then stood up Phinehas, "the ancestor of the house of Zadok," and executed judgment.

> "And so the plague was stayed,
> And that was counted unto him for righteousness
> Unto all generations for evermore."[3]

But the militant character of the priesthood was not confined to its early history. Amongst those who "came armed for war to David to Hebron to turn the kingdom of Saul to him, according to the word of Jehovah," were four thousand six hundred of the children of Levi and three thousand seven hundred of the house of Aaron, "and Zadok, a young man mighty of valour, and twenty-two captains of his father's house."[4] "The third captain of David's army for the third month was Benaiah the son of Jehoiada the priest."[5]

David's Hebronite overseers were all "mighty men of valour." When Judah went out to war, the trumpets

---

[1] Exod. xxxii. 26–35.   [3] Psalm cvi. 30, 31.
[2] Num. xxv. 3.   [4] I Chron. xii. 23-28.
[5] I Chron. xxvii. 5; cf., however, R.V. marg.

of the priests gave the signal for battle[1]; when the high-priest Jehoiada recovered the kingdom for Joash, the Levites compassed the king round about, every man with his weapons in his hand[2]; when Nehemiah rebuilt the wall of Jerusalem, "every one with one of his hands wrought in the work, and with the other held his weapon,"[3] and amongst the rest the priests. Later on, when Jehovah delivered Israel from the hand of Antiochus Epiphanes, the priestly family of the Maccabees, in the spirit of their ancestor Phinehas, fought and died for the Law and the Temple. There were priestly soldiers as well as priestly generals, for we read how " at that time certain priests, desirous to show their valour, were slain in battle, for that they went out to fight inadvisedly."[4] In the Jewish war the priest Josephus was Jewish commander in Galilee.

Christianity has aroused a new sentiment with regard to war. We believe that the servant of the Lord must not strive in earthly battles. Arms may be lawful for the Christian citizen, but it is felt to be unseemly that the ministers who are the ambassadors of the Prince of Peace should themselves be men of blood. Even in the Middle Ages fighting prelates like Odo, Bishop of Bayeux, were felt to be exceptional anomalies; and the prince-bishops and electoral archbishops were often ecclesiastics only in name. To-day the Catholic Church in France resents the conscription of its seminarists as an act of vindictive persecution.

And yet the growth of Christian sentiment in favour

---

[1] 2 Chron. xiii. 12.
[2] 2 Chron. xxiii. 7. All the passages referred to in this paragraph are peculiar to Chronicles.
[3] Neh. iv. 17.
[4] 1 Macc. v. 67.

of peace has not prevented the occasional combination of the soldier and the ecclesiastic. If Islam has had its armies of dervishes, Cyril's monks fought for orthodoxy at Alexandria and at Constantinople with all the ferocity of wild beasts. The Crusaders, the Templars, the Knights of St. John, were in varying degrees partly priests and partly soldiers. Cromwell's Ironsides, when they were wielding carnal weapons in their own defence or in any other good cause, were as expert as any Levites at exhortations and psalms and prayers; and in our own day certain generals and admirals are fond of playing the amateur ecclesiastic. In this, as in so much else, while we deny the form of Judaism, we retain its spirit. Havelock and Gordon were no unworthy successors of the Maccabees.

The characteristic function, however, of the Jewish priesthood was their ministry in public worship, in which they represented the people before Jehovah. In this connection public worship does not necessarily imply that the public were present, or that the worship in question was the united act of a great assembly. Such worshipping assemblies were not uncommon, especially at the feasts; but ordinary public worship was worship on behalf of the people, not by the people. The priests and Levites were part of an elaborate system of symbolic ritual. Worshippers might gather in the Temple courts, but the Temple itself was not a place in which public meetings for worship were held, and the people were not admitted into it. The Temple was Jehovah's house, and His presence there was symbolised by the Ark. In this system of ritual the priests and Levites represented Israel; their sacrifices and ministrations were the acceptable offerings of the nation to God. If the sacrifices were duly offered by the priests "according to all that was written in the law of Jehovah, and if the priests with trumpets and the Levites with psalteries, and harps, and cymbals duly ministered before the ark of Jehovah to celebrate, and thank, and praise Jehovah, the God of Israel," then the Divine service of Israel was fully performed. The whole people could not be regularly present at a single sanctuary, nor would they be adequately represented by the inhabitants of Jerusalem and casual visitors from the rest of the country. Three times a year the nation was fully and naturally represented by those who came up to the feasts, but usually the priests and Levites stood in their place.

When an assembly gathered for public worship at a feast or any other time, the priests and Levites expressed the devotion of the people. They performed the sacrificial rites, they blew the trumpets and played upon the psalteries, and harps, and cymbals, and sang the praises of Jehovah. The people were dismissed by the priestly blessing. When an individual offered a sacrifice as an act of private worship, the assistance of the priests and Levites was still necessary. At the same time the king as well as the priesthood might lead the people in praise and prayer, and the Temple psalmody was not confined to the Levitical choir. When the Ark was brought away from Kirjath-jearim, "David and all Israel played before God with all their might, even with songs, and with harps, and with psalteries, and with timbrels, and with cymbals, and with trumpets"; and when at last the Ark had been safely housed in Jerusalem, and the due sacrifices had all been offered, David dismissed the people in priestly fashion by blessing them in the name of Jehovah.[1] At

---

[1] I Chron. xiii. 8; xvi. 2.

the two solemn assemblies which celebrated the beginning and the close of the great enterprise of building the
Temple, public prayer was offered, not by the priests,
but by David[1] and Solomon.[2] Similarly Jehoshaphat
led the prayers of the Jews when they gathered to
seek deliverance from the invading Moabites and
Ammonites. Hezekiah at his great passover both
exhorted the people and interceded for them, and
Jehovah accepted his intercession; but on this occasion,
when the festival was over, it was not the king, but
" the priests the Levites,"[3] who " arose and blessed the
people: and their voice was heard, and their prayer
came up to His holy habitation, even unto heaven."
In the descriptions of Hezekiah's and Josiah's festivals,
the orchestra and choir, of course, are busy with the
music and singing; otherwise the main duty of the
priests and Levites is to sacrifice. In his graphic
account of Josiah's passover, the chronicler no doubt
reproduces on a larger scale the busy scenes in which
he himself had often taken part. The king, the princes,
and the chiefs of the Levites had provided between
them thirty-seven thousand six hundred lambs and
kids and three thousand eight hundred oxen for sacrifices; and the resources of the establishment of the
Temple were taxed to the utmost. " So the service
was prepared, and the priests stood in their place, and
the Levites by the courses, according to the king's
commandment. And they killed the passover, and the
priests sprinkled the blood, which they received of their
hand, and the Levites flayed the sacrifices. And they
removed the burnt offerings, that they might give them

[1] 1 Chron. xxix. 10–19.
[2] 2 Chron. vi.
[3] 2 Chron. xx. 4–13; xxx. 6–9, 18–21, 27.

according to the divisions of the fathers' houses of the children of the people, to offer unto Jehovah, as it is written in the law of Moses ; and so they did with the oxen. And they roasted the passover according to the ordinance ; and they boiled the holy offerings in pots, and caldrons, and pans, and carried them quickly to all the children of the people. And afterward they prepared for themselves and for the priests, because the priests the sons of Aaron were busied in offering the burnt offerings and the fat until night ; therefore the Levites prepared for themselves and for the priests the sons of Aaron. And the singers were in their place, and the porters were at their several gates ; they needed not to depart from their service, for their brethren the Levites prepared for them. So all the service of Jehovah was prepared the same day, to keep the passover, and to offer burnt offerings upon the altar of Jehovah." [1] Thus even in the accounts of great public gatherings for worship the main duty of the priests and Levites is to perform the sacrifices. The music and singing naturally fall into their hands, because the necessary training is only possible to a professional choir. Otherwise the now symbolic portions of the service, prayer, exhortation, and blessing, were not exclusively reserved to ecclesiastics.

The priesthood, like the Ark, the Temple, and the ritual, belonged essentially to the system of religious symbolism. This was their peculiar domain, into which no outsider might intrude. Only the Levites could touch the Ark. When the unhappy Uzzah " put forth his hand to the Ark," " the anger of Jehovah was kindled against him ; and he smote Uzzah so that he

---

[1] 2 Chron. xxxv.

died there before God."[1] The king might offer up public
prayer; but when Uzziah ventured to go into the Temple
to burn incense upon the altar of incense, leprosy broke
forth in his forehead, and the priests thrust him out
quickly from the Temple.[2]

Thus the symbolic and representative character of
the priesthood and ritual gave the sacrifices and other
ceremonies a value in themselves, apart alike from the
presence of worshippers and the feelings or "intention"
of the officiating minister. They were the provision
made by Israel for the expression of its prayer, its
penitence and thanksgiving. When sin had estranged
Jehovah from His people, the sons of Aaron made
atonement for Israel; they performed the Divinely
appointed ritual by which the nation made submission
to its offended King and cast itself upon His mercy.
The Jewish sacrifices had features which have survived
in the sacrifice of the Mass, and the multiplication of
sacrifices arose from motives similar to those that lead
to the offering up of many masses.

One would expect, as has happened in the Christian
Church, that the ministrants of the symbolic ritual
would annex the other acts of public worship, not
only praise, but also prayer and exhortation. Considerations of convenience would suggest such an
amalgamation of functions; and among the priests,
while the more ambitious would see in preaching a
means of extending their authority, the more earnest
would be anxious to use their unique position to promote
the spiritual life of the people. Chronicles, however,
affords few traces of any such tendency; and the great
scene in the book of Nehemiah in which Ezra and the

---

[1] 1 Chron. xiii. 10.   [2] 2 Chron. xxvi. 16–23.

Levites expound the Law had no connection with the
Temple and its ritual. The development of the Temple
service was checked by its exclusive privileges; it was
simply impossible that the single sanctuary should
continue to provide for all the religious wants of the
Jews, and thus supplementary and inferior places
of worship grew up to appropriate the non-ritual elements of service. Probably even in the chronicler's
time the division of religious services between the
Temple and the synagogue had already begun, with
the result that the representative and symbolic character
of the priesthood is almost exclusively emphasised.

The representative character of the priesthood has
another aspect. Strictly the priest represented the
nation before Jehovah; but in doing so it was inevitable
that he should also in some measure represent Jehovah
to the nation. He could not be the channel of worship
offered to God without being also the channel of Divine
grace to man. From the priest the worshipper learnt
the will of God as to correct ritual, and received the
assurance that the atoning sacrifice was duly accepted.
The high-priest entered within the veil to make atonement for Israel; he came forth as the bearer of Divine
forgiveness and renewed grace, and as he blessed the
people he spoke in the name of Jehovah. We have
been able to discern the presence of these ideas in
Chronicles, but they are not very conspicuous. The
chronicler was not a layman; he was too familiar with
priests to feel any profound reverence for them. On
the other hand, he was not himself a priest, but was
specially preoccupied with the musicians, the Levites,
and the doorkeepers; so that probably he does not
give us an adequate idea of the relative dignity of the
priests and the honour in which they were held by the

people. Organists and choirmasters, it is said, seldom take an exalted view of their minister's office.

The chronicler deals more fully with a matter in which priests and Levites were alike interested : the revenues of the Temple. He was doubtless aware of the bountiful provision made by the Law for his order, and loved to hold up this liberality of kings, princes, and people in ancient days for his contemporaries to admire and imitate. He records again and again the tens of thousands of sheep and oxen provided for sacrifice, not altogether unmindful of the rich dues that must have accrued to the priests out of all this abundance ; he tells us how Hezekiah first set the good example of appointing " a portion of his substance for the burnt offerings," and then " commanded the people that dwelt at Jerusalem to give the portion of the priests and the Levites that they might give themselves to the law of the Lord. And as soon as the commandment came abroad the children of Israel gave in abundance the first-fruits of corn, wine, and oil, and honey, and of all the increase of the field ; and the tithe of all things brought they in abundantly."[1] These were the days of old, the ancient years when the offering of Judah and Jerusalem was pleasant to Jehovah ; when the people neither dared nor desired to offer on God's altar a scanty tale of blind, lame, and sick victims ; when the tithes were not kept back, and there was meat in the house of God[2] when, as Hezekiah's high-priest testified, they could eat and have enough and yet leave plenty.[3] The manner in which the chronicler tells the tale of ancient abundance suggests that his days were like the days

---

[1] 2 Chron. xxxi. 3–5.   [2] Mal. i. 8 ; iii. 4, 10.
[3] 2 Chron. xxxi. 10.

of Malachi. He was no pampered ecclesiastic, revelling
in present wealth and luxury, but a man who suffered
hard times, and looked back wistfully to the happier
experiences of his predecessors.

Let us now restore the complete picture of the
chronicler's priest from his scattered references to the
subject. The priest represents the nation before
Jehovah, and in a less degree represents Jehovah to
the nation; he leads their public worship, especially at
the great festal gatherings; he teaches the people the
Law. The high character, culture, and ability of the
priests and Levites occasions their employment as
judges and in other responsible civil offices. If occasion
required, they could show themselves mighty men of
valour in their country's wars. Under pious kings,
they enjoyed ample revenues which gave them independence, added to their importance in the eyes of
the people, and left them at leisure to devote themselves
exclusively to their sacred duties.

In considering the significance of this picture, we
can pass over without special notice the exercise by
priests and Levites of the functions of leadership in
public worship, teaching, and civil government. They
are not essential to the priesthood, but are entirely
consistent with the tenure of the priestly office, and
naturally become associated with it. Warlike prowess
was certainly no part of the priesthood; but, whatever
may be true of Christian ministers, it is difficult to
charge the priests of the Lord of hosts with inconsistency because, like Jehovah Himself, they were
men of war [1] and went forth to battle in the armies of
Israel. When a nation was continually fighting for its

---

[1] Exod. xv. 3.

very existence, it was impossible for one tribe out of the twelve to be non-combatant.

With regard to the representative character of the priests, it would be out of place here to enter upon the burning questions of sacerdotalism; but we may briefly point out the permanent truth underlying the ancient idea of the priesthood. The ideal spiritual life in every Church is one of direct fellowship between God and the believer.

"Speak to Him, thou, for He hears, and spirit with spirit can meet;
Closer is He than breathing, and nearer than hands and feet."

And yet a man may be truly religious and not realise this ideal, or only realise it very imperfectly. The gift of an intense and real spiritual life may belong to the humblest and poorest, to men of little intellect and less learning; but, none the less, it is not within the immediate reach of every believer, or indeed of any believer at every time. The descendants of Mr. Little-faith and Mr. Ready-to-halt are amongst us still, and there is no immediate prospect of their race becoming extinct. Times come when we are all glad to put ourselves under the safe conduct of Mr. Great-heart. There are many whose prayers seem to themselves too feebly winged to rise to the throne of grace; they are encouraged and helped when their petitions are borne upwards on the strong pinions of another's faith. George Eliot has pictured the Florentines as awed spectators of Savonarola's audiences with Heaven. To a congregation sometimes the minister's prayers are a sacred and solemn spectacle; his spiritual feeling is beyond them; he intercedes for blessings they neither desire nor understand; they miss the heavenly vision which stirs his soul. He is not their spokesman, but

their priest; he has entered the holy place, bearing
with him the sins that crave forgiveness, the fears that
beg for deliverance, the hopes that yearn to be fulfilled.
Though the people may remain in the outer court, yet
they are fully assured that he has passed into the
very presence of God. They listen to him as to one
who has had actual speech with the King and received
the assurance of His goodwill towards them. When
the vanguard of the Ten Thousand first sighted the
Euxine, the cry of " Thalassa ! Thalassa ! " (" The sea !
the sea ! ") rolled backward along the line of march ;
the rearguard saw the long-hoped-for sight with the
eyes of the pioneers. Much unnecessary self-reproach
would be avoided if we accepted this as one of God's
methods of spiritual education, and understood that
we all have in a measure to experience this discipline
in humility. The priesthood of the believer is not
merely his right to enter for himself into the immediate
presence of God : it becomes his duty and privilege
to represent others. But times will also come when he
himself will need the support of a priestly intercession
in the Divine presence-chamber, when he will seek out
some one of quick sympathy and strong faith and say,
" Brother, pray for me." Apart from any ecclesiastical
theory of the priesthood, we all recognise that there
are God-ordained priests, men and women, who can
inspire dull souls with a sense of the Divine presence
and bring to the sinful and the struggling the assurance
of Divine forgiveness and help. If one in ten among
the official priests of the historic Churches had possessed
these supreme gifts, the world would have accepted
the most extravagant sacerdotalism without a murmur.
As it is, every minister, every one who leads the
worship of a congregation, assumes for the time being

functions and should possess the corresponding qualifications. In his prayers he speaks for the people; he represents them before God; on their behalf he enters into the Divine presence; they only enter with him, if, as their spokesman and representative, he has grasped their feelings and raised them to the level of Divine fellowship. He may be an untutored labourer in his working garments; but if he can do this, this spiritual gift makes him a priest of God. But this Christian priesthood is not confined to public service; as the priest offered sacrifice for the individual Jew, so the man of spiritual sympathies helps the individual to draw near his Maker. "To pray with people" is a well-known ministry of Christian service, and it involves this priestly function of presenting another's prayers to God. This priesthood for individuals is exercised by many a Christian who has no gifts of public utterance.

The ancient priest held a representative position in a symbolic ritual, a position partly independent of his character and spiritual powers. Where symbolic ritual is best suited for popular needs, there may be room for a similar priesthood to-day. Otherwise the Christian priesthood is required to represent the people not in symbol, but in reality, to carry not the blood of dead victims into a material Holy of holies, but living souls into the heavenly temple.

There remains one feature of the Jewish priestly system upon which the chronicler lays great stress: the endowments and priestly dues. In the case of the high-priest and the Levites, whose whole time was devoted to sacred duties, it was obviously necessary that those who served the altar should live by the altar. The same principle would apply, but with much less force, to the twenty-four courses of priests, each of which in its turn officiated at the Temple. But, apart from the needs of the priesthood, their representative character demanded that they should be able to maintain a certain state. They were the ambassadors of Israel to Jehovah. Nations have always been anxious that the equipment and suite of their representative at a foreign court should be worthy of their power and wealth; moreover, the splendour of an embassy should be in proportion to the rank of the sovereign to whom it is accredited. In former times, when the social symbols were held of more account, a first-rate power would have felt itself insulted if asked to receive an envoy of inferior rank, attended by only a meagre train. Israel, by her lavish endowment of the priesthood, consulted her own dignity and expressed her sense of the homage due to Jehovah. The Jews could not express their devotion in the same way as other nations. They had to be content with a single sanctuary, and might not build a multitude of magnificent temples or adorn their cities with splendid, costly statues in honour of God. There were limits to their expenditure upon the sacrifices and buildings of the Temple; but the priesthood offered a large opportunity for pious generosity. The chronicler felt that loyal enthusiasm to Jehovah would always use this opportunity, and that the priests might consent to accept the distinction of wealth and splendour for the honour alike of Israel and Jehovah. Their dignity was not personal to themselves, but rather the livery of a self-effacing servitude. For the honour of the Church, Thomas a Becket kept up a great establishment, appeared in his robes of office, and entertained a crowd of guests with luxurious fare; while he himself wore a hair shirt next his skin and fasted like an ascetic

monk. When the Jews stinted the ritual or the
ministrants of Jehovah, they were doing what they
could to put Him to open shame before the nations.
Julian's experience in the grove of Daphne at Antioch
was a striking illustration of the collapse of paganism :
the imperial champion of the ancient gods must have
felt his heart sink within him when he was welcomed
to that once splendid sanctuary by one shabby priest
dragging a solitary and reluctant goose to the deserted
altar. Similarly Malachi saw that Israel's devotion to
Jehovah was in danger of dying out when men chose
the refuse of their flocks and herds and offered them
grudgingly at the shrine.

The application of these principles leads directly to
the question of a paid ministry ; but the connection is
not so close as it appears at first sight, nor are we
yet in possession of all the data which the chronicler
furnishes for its discussion. Priestly duties form an
essential, but not predominant, part of the work of most
Christian ministers. Still the loyal believer must
always be anxious that the buildings, the services, and
the men which, for himself and for the world, represent
his devotion to Christ, should be worthy of their high
calling. But his ideas of the symbolism suitable for
spiritual realities are not altogether those of the
chronicler : he is less concerned with number, size,
and weight, with tens of thousands of sheep and oxen,
vast quantities of stone and timber, brass and iron,
and innumerable talents of gold and silver. Moreover,
in this special connection the secondary priestly function of representing God to man has been expressly
transferred by Christ to the least of His brethren.
Those who wish to honour God with their substance
in the person of His earthly representatives are enjoined

to seek for them in hospitals, and workhouses, and prisons, to find these representatives in the hungry, the thirsty, the friendless, the naked, the captives. No doubt Christ is dishonoured when those who dwell in "houses of cedar" are content to worship Him in a mean, dirty church, with a half-starved minister; but the most disgraceful proof of the Church's disloyalty to Christ is to be seen in the squalor and misery of men, and women, and children whose bodies were ordained of God to be the temples of His Holy Spirit.

This is only one among many illustrations of the truth that in Christ the symbolism of religion took a new departure. His Church enjoys the spiritual realities prefigured by the Jewish temple and its ministry. Even where Christian symbols are parallel to those of Judaism, they are less conventional and richer in their direct spiritual suggestiveness.

CHAPTER IX

THE PROPHETS

ONE remarkable feature of Chronicles as compared with the book of Kings is the greater interest shown by the former in the prophets of Judah. The chronicler, by confining his attention to the southern kingdom, was compelled to omit almost all reference to Elijah and Elisha, and thus exclude from his work some of the most thrilling chapters in the history of the prophets of Israel. Nevertheless the prophets as a whole play almost as important a part in Chronicles as in the book of Kings. Compensation is made for the omission of the two great northern prophets by inserting accounts of several prophets whose messages were addressed to the kings of Judah.

The chronicler's interest in the prophets was very different from the interest he took in the priests and Levites. The latter belonged to the institutions of his own time, and formed his own immediate circle. In dealing with their past, he was reconstructing the history of his own order; he was able to illustrate and supplement from observation and experience the information afforded by his sources.

But when the chronicler wrote, prophets had ceased to be a living institution in Judah. The light that had shone so brightly in Isaiah and Jeremiah burned feebly in Haggai, Zechariah, and Malachi, and then went out.

Not long after the chronicler's time the failure of prophecy is expressly recognised. The people whose synagogues have been burnt up complain,—

> " We see not our signs;
> There is no more any prophet." [1]

When Judas Maccabæus appointed certain priests to cleanse the Temple after its pollution by the Syrians, they pulled down the altar of burnt offerings because the heathen had defiled it, and laid up the stones in the mountain of the Temple in a convenient place, until there should come a prophet to show what should be done with them. [2] This failure of prophecy was not merely brief and transient. It marked the disappearance of the ancient order of prophets. A parallel case shows how the Jews had become aware that the high-priest no longer possessed the special gifts connected with the Urim and Thummim. When certain priests could not find their genealogies, they were forbidden " to eat of the most holy things till there stood up a priest with Urim and with Thummim." [3] We have no record of any subsequent appearance of " a priest with Urim and with Thummim " or of any prophet of the old order.

Thus the chronicler had never seen a prophet; his conception of the personality and office of the prophet was entirely based upon ancient literature, and he took no professional interest in the order. At the same time he had no prejudice against them; they had no living successors to compete for influence and endowments

---

[1] Psalm lxxiv. 8, 9. This psalm is commonly regarded as Maccabæan, but may be as early as the chronicler or even earlier.

[2] 1 Macc. iv. 46.

[3] Ezra ii. 63.

with the priests and Levites. Possibly the Levites, as
the chief religious teachers of the people, claimed some
sort of apostolic succession from the prophets; but
there are very slight grounds for any such theory.
The chronicler's information on the whole subject was
that of a scholar with a taste for antiquarian research.

Let us briefly examine the part played by the
prophets in the history of Judah as given by Chronicles.
We have first, as in the book of Kings, the references
to Nathan and Gad: they make known to David the
will of Jehovah as regards the building of the Temple
and the punishment of David's pride in taking the
census of Israel. David unhesitatingly accepts their
messages as the word of Jehovah. It is important to
notice that when Nathan is consulted about building
the Temple he first answers, apparently giving a mere
private opinion, "Do all that is in thine heart, for God
is with thee"; but when "the word of God comes"
to him, he retracts his former judgment and forbids
David to build the Temple. Here again the plan of
the chronicler's work leads to an important omission:
his silence as to the murder of Uriah prevents him
from giving the beautiful and instructive account of
the way in which Nathan rebuked the guilty king.
Later narratives exhibit other prophets in the act of
rebuking most of the kings of Judah, but none of these
incidents are equally striking and pathetic. At the
end of the histories of David and of most of the later
kings we find notes which apparently indicate that, in
the chronicler's time, the prophets were credited with
having written the annals of the kings with whom they
were contemporary. In connection with Hezekiah's
reformation we are incidentally told that Nathan and
Gad were associated with David in making arrange-

ments for the music of the Temple : "He set the Levites in the house of Jehovah, with cymbals, with psalteries, and with harps, according to the commandment of David and of Gad the king's seer and Nathan the prophet, for the commandment was of Jehovah by His prophets." [1]

In the account of Solomon's reign, the chronicler omits the interview of Ahijah the Shilonite with Jeroboam, but refers to it in the history of Rehoboam. From this point, in accordance with his general plan, he omits almost all missions of prophets to the northern kings.

In Rehoboam's reign, we have recorded, as in the book of Kings, a message from Jehovah by Shemaiah forbidding the king and his two tribes of Judah and Benjamin to attempt to compel the northern tribes to return to their allegiance to the house of David. Later on, when Shishak invaded Judah, Shemaiah was commissioned to deliver to the king and princes the message, " Thus saith Jehovah : Ye have forsaken Me ; therefore have I also left you in the hand of Shishak." [2] But when they repented and humbled themselves before Jehovah, Shemaiah announced to them the mitigation of their punishment.

Asa's reformation was due to the inspired exhortations of a prophet called both Oded and Azariah the son of Oded. Later on Hanani the seer rebuked the king for his alliance with Benhadad, king of Syria. " Then Asa was wroth with the seer, and put him in the prison-house ; for he was in a rage with him because of this thing." [3]

---

[1] 2 Chron. xxix. 25, peculiar to Chronicles.
[2] 2 Chron. xii. 5-8, peculiar to Chronicles.
[3] 2 Chron. xv.-xvi. 10, peculiar to Chronicles.

Jehoshaphat's alliance with Ahab and his consequent
visit to Samaria enabled the chronicler to introduce
from the book of Kings the striking narrative of
Micaiah the son of Imlah ; but this alliance with Israel
earned for the king the rebukes of Jehu the son of
Hanani the seer and Eliezar the son of Dodavahu of
Mareshah.   However, on the occasion of the Moabite
and Ammonite invasion Jehoshaphat and his people
received the promise of Divine deliverance from
" Jahaziel the son of Zechariah, the son of Benaiah, the
son of Jeiel, the son of Mattaniah the Levite, of tne
sons of Asaph." [1]

The punishment of the wicked king Jehoram was
announced to him by " a writing from Elijah the
prophet." [2]   His son Ahaziah apparently perished
without any prophetic warning ; but when Joash and
his princes forsook the house of Jehovah and served
the Asherim and the idols, " He sent prophets to them
to bring them again to Jehovah," among the rest
Zechariah the son of Jehoiada the priest.   Joash
turned a deaf ear to the message, and put the prophet
to death. [3]

When Amaziah bowed down before the gods of
Edom and burned incense unto them, Jehovah sent
unto him a prophet whose name is not recorded.   His
mission failed, like that of Zechariah the son of
Jehoiada ; and Amaziah, like Joash, showed no respect
for the person of the messenger of Jehovah.   In this
case the prophet escaped with his life.   He began to
deliver his message, but the king's patience soon failed,
and he said unto the prophet, " Have we made thee of

---

[1] 2 Chron. xix. 2, 3, xx. 14-18, 37, all peculiar to Chronicles.
[2] xxi. 12-15, peculiar to Chronicles.
[3] xxiv. 18-22, peculiar to Chronicles.

the king's counsel? forbear; why shouldest thou be smitten?" The prophet, we are told, "forbare"; but his forbearance did not prevent his adding one brief and bitter sentence: "I know that God hath determined to destroy thee, because thou hast done this and hast not hearkened unto my counsel."[1] Then apparently he departed in peace and was not smitten.

We have now reached the period of the prophets whose writings are extant. We learn from the headings of their works that Isaiah saw his "vision," and that the word of Jehovah came unto Hosea, in the days of Uzziah, Jotham, Ahaz, and Hezekiah; that the word of Jehovah came to Micah in the days of Jotham, Ahaz, and Hezekiah; and that Amos "saw" his "words" in the days of Uzziah. But the chronicler makes no reference to any of these prophets in connection with either Uzziah, Jotham, or Ahaz. Their writings would have afforded the best possible materials for his history, yet he entirely neglected them. In view of his anxiety to introduce into his narrative all missions of prophets of which he found any record, we can only suppose that he was so little interested in the prophetical writings that he neither referred to them nor recollected their dates.

To Ahaz in Chronicles, in spite of all his manifold and persistent idolatry, no prophet was sent. The absence of Divine warning marks his extraordinary wickedness. In the book of Samuel the culmination of Jehovah's displeasure against Saul is shown by His refusal to answer him either by dreams, by Urim, or by prophets. He sends no prophet to Ahaz, because the wicked king of Judah is utterly reprobate. Prophecy,

---

[1] xxv. 15, 16, peculiar to Chronicles.

the token of the Divine presence and favour, has abandoned a nation given over to idolatry, and has even taken a temporary refuge in Samaria. Jerusalem was no longer worthy to receive the Divine messages, and Oded was sent with his words of warning and humane exhortation to the children of Ephraim. There he met with a prompt and full obedience, in striking contrast to the reception accorded by Joash and Amaziah to the prophets of Jehovah.

The chronicler's history of the reign of Hezekiah further illustrates his indifference to the prophets whose writings are extant. In the book of Kings great prominence is given to Isaiah. In the account of Sennacherib's invasion his messages to Hezekiah are given at considerable length.[1] He announces to the king his approaching death and Jehovah's gracious answers to Hezekiah's prayer for a respite and his request for a sign. When Hezekiah, in his pride of wealth, displayed his treasures to the Babylonian ambassadors, Isaiah brought the message of Divine rebuke and judgment. Chronicles characteristically devotes three long chapters to ritual and Levites, and dismisses Isaiah in half a sentence : " And Hezekiah the king and Isaiah the prophet, the son of Amoz, prayed because of this "—*i.e.*, the threatening language of Sennacherib—" and cried to Heaven." [2] In the accounts of Hezekiah's sickness and recovery and of the Babylonian embassy the references to Isaiah are entirely omitted. These omissions may be due to lack of space, so much of which had been devoted to the Levites that there was none to spare for the prophet.

---

[1] 2 Kings xix. 5–7, 20–34.   [2] xxxii. 20.

Indeed, at the very point where prophecy began to exercise a controlling influence over the religion of Judah the chronicler's interest in the subject altogether flags. He tells us that Jehovah spake to Manasseh and to his people, and refers to "the words of the seeis that spake to him in the name of Jehovah, the God of Israel";[1] but he names no prophet and does not record the terms of any Divine message. In the case of Manasseh his sources may have failed him, but we have seen that in Hezekiah's reign he deliberately passes over most of the references to Isaiah.

The chronicler's narrative of Josiah's reign adheres more closely to the book of Kings. He reproduces the mission from the king to the prophetess Huldah and her Divine message of present forbearance and future judgment. The other prophet of this reign is the heathen king Pharaoh Necho, through whose mouth the Divine warning is given to Josiah. Jeremiah is only mentioned as lamenting over the last good king.[2] In the parallel text of this passage in the apocryphal book of Esdras Pharaoh's remonstrance is given in a somewhat expanded form; but the editor of Esdras shrank from making the heathen king the mouthpiece of Jehovah. While Chronicles tells us that Josiah "hearkened not unto the words of Neco from the mouth of God," Esdras, glaringly inconsistent both with the context and the history, tells us that he did not regard "the words of the prophet Jeremiah spoken by the mouth of the Lord."[3] This amended statement is borrowed from the chronicler's account of Zedekiah, who "humbled not himself before Jeremiah

---

[1] xxxiii. 10, 18.

[2] xxxv. 21, 22, 25, peculiar to Chronicles.

[3] I Esdras i. 28.

the prophet, speaking from the mouth of Jehovah."
But this king was not alone in his disobedience. As
the inevitable ruin of Jerusalem drew near, the whole
nation, priests and people alike, sank deeper and deeper
in sin. In these last days, "where sin abounded, grace
did yet more abound." Jehovah exhausted the resources
of His mercy: "Jehovah, the God of their fathers, sent
to them by His messengers, rising up early and sending,
because He had compassion on His people and on His
dwelling-place." It was all in vain: "They mocked
the messengers of God, and despised His words and
scoffed at His prophets, until the wrath of Jehovah
arose against His people, till there was no remedy."
There are two other references in the concluding paragraphs of Chronicles to the prophecies of Jeremiah;
but the history of prophecy in Judah closes with this
last great unavailing manifestation of prophetic activity.

Before considering the general idea of the prophet
that may be collected from the various notices in
Chronicles, we may devote a little space to the chronicler's curious attitude towards our canonical prophets.
For the most part he simply follows the book of Kings
in making no reference to them; but his almost entire
silence as to Isaiah suggests that his imitation of his
authority in other cases is deliberate and intentional,
especially as we find him inserting one or two references
to Jeremiah not taken from the book of Kings. The
chronicler had much more opportunity of using the
canonical prophets than the author or authors of the
book of Kings. The latter wrote before Hebrew
literature had been collected and edited; but the
chronicler had access to all the literature of the
monarchy, Captivity, and even later times. His numerous
extracts from almost the entire range of the Historical

Books, together with the Pentateuch and Psalms, show
that his plan included the use of various sources, and
that he had both the means and ability to work out his
plan. He makes two references to Haggai and Zechariah,[1] so that if he ignores Amos, Hosea, and Micah,
and all but ignores Isaiah, we can only conclude that he
does so of set purpose. Hosea and Amos might be
excluded on account of their connection with the
northern kingdom; possibly the strictures of Isaiah
and Micah on the priesthood and ritual made the
chronicler unwilling to give them special prominence.
Such an attitude on the part of a typical representative
of the prevailing school of religious thought has an
important bearing on the textual and other criticism
of the early prophets. If they were neglected by the
authorities of the Temple in the interval between Ezra
and the Maccabees, the possibility of late additions and
alterations is considerably increased.

Let us now turn to the picture of the prophets
drawn for us by the chronicler. Both prophet and
priest are religious personages, otherwise they differ
widely in almost every particular; we cannot even
speak of them as both holding religious offices. The
term "office" has to be almost unjustifiably strained
in order to apply it to the prophet, and to use it thus
without explanation would be misleading. The qualifications, status, duties, and rewards of the priests are
all fully prescribed by rigid and elaborate rules; but
the prophets were the children of the Spirit: "The
wind bloweth where it listeth, and thou hearest the
voice thereof, but knowest not whence it cometh and
whither it goeth; so is every one that is born of the

---

[1] Ezra v. 1; vi. 14.

Spirit." The priest was bound to be a physically perfect male of the house of Aaron; the prophet might be of any tribe and of either sex. The warlike Deborah found a more peaceful successor in Josiah's counsellor Huldah, and among the degenerate prophets of Nehemiah's time a prophetess Noadiah[1] is specially mentioned. The priestly or Levitical office did not exclude its holder from the prophetic vocation. The Levite Jahaziel delivered the message of Jehovah to Jehoshaphat; and the prophet Zechariah, whom Joash put to death, was the son of the high-priest Jehoiada, and therefore himself a priest. Indeed, upon occasion the prophetic gift was exercised by those whom we should scarcely call prophets at all. Pharaoh Necho's warning to Jehoshaphat is exactly parallel to the prophetic exhortations addressed to other kings. In the crisis of David's fortunes at Ziklag, when Judah and Benjamin came out to meet him with apparently doubtful intentions, their adhesion to the future king was decided by a prophetic word given to the mighty warrior Amasai: "Then the Spirit came upon Amasai, who was one of the thirty, and he said, Thine are we, David, and on thy side, thou son of Jesse: peace, peace, be unto thee, and peace be to thine helpers; for thy God helpeth thee."[2] In view of this wide distribution of the prophetic gift, we are not surprised to find it frequently exercised by the pious kings. They receive and communicate to the nation direct intimations of the Divine will. David gives to Solomon and the people the instructions which God has given him with regard to the Temple; God's promises are personally addressed to Solomon, without the intervention of either

---

[1] Neh. vi. 14.   [2] 1 Chron. xii. 18, peculiar to Chronicles.

prophet or priest; Abijah rebukes and exhorts Jeroboam and the Israelites very much as other prophets address the wicked kings; the speeches of Hezekiah and Josiah might equally well have been delivered by one of the prophets. David indeed is expressly called a prophet by St. Peter[1]; and though the immediate reference is to the Psalms, the chronicler's history both of David and of other kings gives them a valid claim to rank as prophets.

The authority and status of the prophets rested on no official or material conditions, such as hedged in the priestly office on every side. Accordingly their ancestry, previous history, and social standing are matters with which the historian has no concern. If the prophet happens also to be a priest or Levite, the chronicler, of course, knows and records his genealogy. It was essential that the genealogy of a priest should be known, but there are no genealogies of the prophets; their order was like that of Melchizedek, standing on the page of history " without father, without mother, without genealogy "; they appear abruptly, with no personal introduction, they deliver their message, and then disappear with equal abruptness. Sometimes not even their names are given. They had the one qualification compared with which birth and sex, rank and reputation, were trivial and meaningless things. The living word of Jehovah was on their lips; the power of His Spirit controlled their hearers; messenger and message were alike their own credentials. The supreme religious authority of the prophet testified to the subordinate and accidental character of all rites and symbols. On the other hand, the combination of

---

[1] Acts ii. 30.

priest and prophet in the same system proved the
loftiest spirituality, the most emphatic recognition of
the direct communion of the soul with God, to be consistent with an elaborate and rigid system of ritual.
The services and ministry of the Temple were like
lamps whose flame showed pale and dim when earth
and heaven were lit up by the lightnings of prophetic
inspiration.

The gifts and functions of the prophets did not lend
themselves to any regular discipline or organisation ;
but we can roughly distinguish between two classes of
prophets.   One class seem to have exercised their gifts
more systematically and continuously than others.   Gad
and Nathan, Isaiah and Jeremiah, became practically
the domestic chaplains and spiritual advisers of David,
Hezekiah, and the last kings of Judah.   Others are only
mentioned as delivering a single message ; their ministry
seems to have been occasional, perhaps confined to a
single period of their lives.   The Divine Spirit was
free to take the whole life or to take a part only ; He
was not to be conditioned even by gifts of His own
bestowal.

Human organisation naturally attempted to classify
the possessors of the prophetic gift, to set them apart
as a regular order, perhaps even to provide them with
a suitable training, and, still more impossible task, to
select the proper recipients of the gift and to produce
and foster the prophetic inspiration.   We read elsewhere of " schools of the prophets " and " sons of the
prophets."   The chronicler omits all reference to such
institutions or societies ; he declines to assign them any
place in the prophetic succession in Israel.   The gift
of prophecy was absolutely dependent on the Divine
will. and could not be claimed as a necessary appur-

tenance of the royal court at Jerusalem or a regular
order in the kingdom of Judah. The priests are included
in the list of David's ministers, but not the prophets
Gad and Nathan. Abijah mentions among the special
privileges of Judah " priests ministering unto Jehovah,
even the sons of Aaron and the Levites in their work " ;
it does not occur to him to name prophets among the
regular and permanent ministers of Jehovah.

The chronicler, in fact, does not recognise the professional prophet. The fifty sons of the prophets that
watched Elisha divide the waters in the name of the
God of Elijah were no more prophets for him than the
four hundred and fifty prophets of Baal and the four
hundred prophets of the Asherah that ate at Jezebel's
table. The true prophet, like Amos, need not be either
a prophet or the son of a prophet in the professional
sense. Long before the chronicler's time the history
and teaching of the great prophets had clearly established the distinction between the professional prophet,
who was appointed by man or by himself, and the
inspired messenger, who received a direct commission
from Jehovah.

In describing the prophet's sole qualification we have
also stated his function. He was the messenger of
Jehovah, and declared His will. The priest in his
ministrations represented Israel before God, and in
a measure represented God to Israel. The rites and
ceremonies over which he presided symbolised the
permanent and unchanging features of man's religious
experience and the eternal righteousness and mercy
of Him who is the same yesterday, to-day, and for ever.
From generation to generation men received the good
gifts of God, and brought the offerings of their gratitude ; they sinned against God and came to seek

forgiveness; and the house of Aaron met them generation after generation in the same priestly robes, with
the same rites, in the one Temple, in token of the
unchanging willingness of Jehovah to accept and forgive His children.

The prophet, too, represented God to man; his words
were the words of God; through him the Divine presence and the Divine Spirit exerted their influence over
the hearts and consciences of his hearers. But while
the priestly ministrations symbolised the fixity and
permanence of God's eternal majesty, the prophets
expressed the infinite variety of His Divine nature and
its continual adaptation to all the changes of human
life. They came to the individual and to the nation in
each crisis of history with the Divine message that
enabled them to suit themselves to altered circumstances, to grapple with new difficulties, and to solve
new problems. The priest and the prophet together
set forth the great paradox that the unchanging God is
the source of all change.

> "Lord God, by whom all change is wrought,
> By whom new things to birth are brought,
>   In whom no change is known,
>
> *   *   *   *   *   *
>
> To Thee we rise, in Thee we rest;
> We stay at home, we go in quest,
>   Still Thou art our abode:
> The rapture swells, the wonder grows,
> As full on us new life still flows
>   From our unchanging God."

The prophetic utterances recorded by the chronicler
illustrate the work of the prophets in delivering the
message that met the present needs of the people.
There is nothing in Chronicles to encourage the
unspiritual notion that the main object of prophecy

was to give exact and detailed information as to the
remote future. There is prediction necessarily : it was
impossible to declare the will of God without stating
the punishment of sin and the victory of righteousness ;
but prediction is only part of the declaration of God's
will. In Gad and Nathan prophecy appears as a means
of communication between the inquiring soul and God ;
it does not, indeed, gratify curiosity, but rather gives
guidance in perplexity and distress. The later prophets
constantly intervene to initiate reform or to hinder the
carrying out of an evil policy. Gad and Nathan lent
their authority to David's organisation of the Temple
music; Asa's reform originated in the exhortation of
Oded the prophet; Jehoshaphat went out to meet the
Moabite and Ammonite invaders in response to the
inspiriting utterance of Jahaziel the Levite ; Josiah
consulted the prophetess Huldah before carrying out
his reformation ; the chiefs of Ephraim sent back the
Jewish captives in obedience to another Oded. On the
other hand, Shemaiah prevented Rehoboam from fighting against Israel ; Micaiah warned Ahab and Jehoshaphat not to go up against Ramoth-gilead.

Often, however, the prophetic message gives the
interpretation of history, the Divine judgment upon
conduct, with its sentence of punishment or reward.
Hanani the seer, for instance, comes to Asa to show
him the real value of his apparently satisfactory alliance
with Benhadad, king of Syria : " Because thou hast
relied on the king of Syria, and hast not relied on
Jehovah thy God, therefore is the host of the king of
Syria escaped out of thine hand. . . . Herein thou
hast done foolishly ; for from henceforth thou shalt
have wars." Jehoshaphat is told why his ships were
broken : " Because thou hast joined thyself with

Ahaziah, Jehovah hath destroyed thy works." Thus
the prophetic declaration of Divine judgment came to
mean almost exclusively rebuke and condemnation.
The witness of a good conscience may be left to speak
for itself; God does not often need to send a prophet
to His obedient servants in order to signify His
approval of their righteous acts. But the censures of
conscience need both the stimulus of external suggestion and the support of external authority. Upon the
prophets was constantly laid the unwelcome task of
rousing and bracing the conscience for its stern duty.
They became the heralds of Divine wrath, the precur-
sors of national misfortune. Often, too, the warnings
that should have saved the people were neglected or
resented, and thus became the occasion of new sin and
severer punishment. We must not, however, lay too
much stress on this aspect of the prophets' work.
They were no mere Cassandras, announcing inevitable
ruin at the hands of a blind destiny; they were not
always, or even chiefly, the messengers of coming doom.
If they declared the wrath of God, they also vindicated
His justice; in the day of the Lord which they so often
foretold, mercy and grace tempered and at last over-
came judgment. They taught, even in their sternest
utterances, the moral government of the world and the
benevolent purpose of its Ruler. These are man's only
hope, even in his sin and suffering, the only ground
for effort, and the only comfort in misfortune.

There are, however, one or two elements in the
chronicler's notices of the prophets that scarcely harmonise with this general picture. The scanty references
of the books of Samuel and Kings to the "schools"
and sons of the prophets have suggested the theory
that the prophets were the guardians of national educa-

tion, culture, and literature. The chronicler expressly assigns the function to the Levites, and does not recognise that the " schools of the prophets" had any permanent significance for the religion of Israel, possibly because they chiefly appear in connection with the northern kingdom. At the same time, we find this idea of the literary character of the prophets in Chronicles in a new form. The authorities referred to in the subscriptions to each reign bear the names of the prophets who flourished during the reign. The primary significance of the tradition followed by the chronicler is the supreme importance of the prophet for his period; he, and not the king, gives it a distinctive character. Therefore the prophet gives his name to his period, as the consuls at Rome, the Archon Basileus at Athens, and the Assyrian priests gave their own names to their year of office. Probably by the time Chronicles was written the view had been adopted which we know prevailed later on, and it was supposed that the prophets wrote the Historical Books which bore their names. The ancient prophets had given the Divine interpretation of the course of events and pronounced the Divine judgment on history. The Historical Books were written for religious edification; they contained a similar interpretation and judgment. The religious instincts of later Judaism rightly classed them with the prophetic Scriptures.

The striking contrast we have been able to trace between the priests and the prophets in their qualifications and duties extends also to their rewards. The book of Kings gives us glimpses of the way in which the reverent gratitude of the people made some provision for the maintenance of the prophets. We are all familiar with the hospitality of the Shunammite, and we read how "a man from Baal-shalishah" brought first-fruits to Elisha.[1] But the chronicler omits all such references as being connected with the northern kingdom, and does not give us any similar information as to the prophets of Judah. He is not usually indifferent as to ways and means. He devotes some space to the revenues of the kings of Judah, and delights to dwell on the sources of priestly income. But it never seems to occur to him that the prophets have any wants to be provided for. To use George Macdonald's phrase, he is quite content to leave them "on the lily and sparrow footing." The priesthood and the Levites must be richly endowed ; the honour of Israel and of Jehovah is concerned in their having cities, tithes, first-fruits, and offerings. Prophets are sent to reproach the people when the priestly dues are withheld ; but for themselves the prophets might have said with St. Paul, " We seek not yours, but you." No one supposed that the authority and dignity of the prophets needed to be supported by ecclesiastical status, splendid robes, and great incomes. Spiritual force so manifestly resided in them that they could afford to dispense with the most impressive symbols of power and authority. On the other hand, they received an honour that was never accorded to the priesthood : they suffered persecution for the cause of Jehovah. Zechariah the son of Jehoiada was put to death, and Micaiah the son of Imlah was imprisoned. We are never told that the priest as priest suffered persecution. Ahaz closed the Temple, Manasseh set up an idol in the house of God, but we do not read of either Ahaz or Manasseh that they slew the priests of Jehovah. The teaching

---

[1] 2 Kings iv. 42.

of the prophets was direct and personal, and thus eminently calculated to excite resentment and provoke persecution; the priestly services, however, did not at all interfere with concurrent idolatry, and the priests were accustomed to receive and execute the orders of the kings. There is nothing to suggest that they sought to obtrude the worship of Jehovah upon unwilling converts; and it is not improbable that some, at any rate, of the priests allowed themselves to be made the tools of the wicked kings. On the eve of the Captivity we read that " the chiefs of the priests and the people trespassed very greatly after all the abominations of the heathen, and they polluted the house of Jehovah." No such disloyalty is recorded of the prophets in Chronicles. The most splendid incomes cannot purchase loyalty. It is still true that " the hireling fleeth because he is a hireling "; men's most passionate devotion is for the cause in which they have suffered.

We have seen that the modern ministry presents certain parallels to the ancient priesthood. Where are we to look for an analogue to the prophet? If the minister be, in a sense, a priest when he leads the worship of the people, is he also a prophet when he preaches to them? Preaching is intended to be— perhaps we may venture to say that it mostly is—a declaration of the will of God. Moreover, it is not the exposition of a fixed and unchangeable ritual or even of a set of rigid theological formulæ. The preacher, like the prophet, seeks to meet the demands for new light that are made by constantly changing circumstances; he seeks to adapt the eternal truth to the varying needs of individual lives. So far he is a prophet, but the essential qualifications of the prophet are still to be sought after.   Isaiah and Jeremiah did not declare the word of Jehovah as they had learnt it from a Bible or any other book, nor yet according to the traditions of a school or the teaching of great authorities; such declaration might be made by the scribes and rabbis in later times.   But the prophets of Chronicles received their message from Jehovah Himself; while they mused upon the needs of the people, the fire of inspiration burned within them; then they spoke.   Moreover, like their great antitype, they spoke with authority, and not as the scribes; their words carried with them conviction even when they did not produce obedience. The reality of men's conviction of their Divine authority was shown by the persecution to which they were subjected.   Are these tokens of the prophet also the notes of the Christian ministry of preaching?   Prophets were found among the house of Aaron and from the tribe of Levi, but not every Levite or priest was a prophet.   Every branch of the Christian Church has numbered among its official ministers men who delivered their message with an inspired conviction of its truth; in them the power and presence of the Spirit have compelled a belief in their authority to speak for God: this belief has received the twofold attestation of hearts and consciences submitted to the Divine will on the one hand or of bitter and rancorous hostility on the other.   In every Church we find the record of men who have spoken, " not in words which man's wisdom teacheth, but which the Spirit teacheth." Such were Wyclif and Latimer, Calvin and Luther, George Whitefield and the Wesleys; such, too, were Moffat and Livingstone.   Nor need we suppose that in the modern Christian Church the gift of prophecy has been confined to men of brilliant genius who have

been conspicuously successful. In the sacred canon
Haggai and Obadiah stand side by side with Isaiah,
Jeremiah, and Ezekiel. The chronicler recognises the
prophetic calling of men too obscure to be mentioned
by name. He whom God hath sent speaketh the
words of God, not necessarily the orator whom men
crowd to hear and whose name is recorded in history ;
and God giveth not the Spirit by measure. Many of
the least distinguished of His servants are truly His
prophets, speaking, by the conviction He has given
them, a message which comes home with power to
some hearts at any rate, and is a savour of life unto
life and of death unto death. The seals of their
ministry are to be found in redeemed and purified
lives, and also only too often in the bitter and
vindictive ill-will of those whom their faithfulness has
offended.

We naturally expect to find that the official ministry
affords the most suitable sphere for the exercise of the
gift of prophecy. Those who are conscious of a Divine
message will often seek the special opportunities which
the ministry affords. But our study of Chronicles
reminds us that the vocation of the prophet cannot
be limited to any external organisation; it was not
confined to the official ministry of Israel ; it cannot
be conditioned by recognition by bishops, presby-
teries, conferences, or Churches; it will often find its
only external credential in a gracious influence over individual lives. Nay, the prophet may have his Divine
vocation and be entirely rejected of men. In Chronicles
we find prophets, like Zechariah the son of Jehoiada,
whose one Divine message is received with scorn and
defiance.

In practice, if not in theory, the Churches have long

since recognised that the prophetic gift is found outside any official ministry, and that they may be taught the will of God by men and women of all ranks and callings. They have provided opportunities for the free exercise of such gifts in lay preaching, missions, Sunday-schools, meetings of all kinds.

We have here stumbled upon another modern controversy: the desirability of women preaching. Chronicles mentions prophetesses as well as prophets; on the other hand, there were no Jewish priestesses. The modern minister combines some priestly duties with the opportunity, at least, of exercising the gift of prophecy. The mention of only two or three prophetesses in the Old Testament shows that the possession of the gift by women was exceptional. These few instances, however, are sufficient to prove that God did not in old times limit the gift to men; they suggest at any rate the possibility of its being possessed by women now, and when women have a Divine message the Church will not venture to quench the Spirit. Of course the application of these broad principles would have to be adapted to the circumstances of individual Churches. Huldah, for instance, is not described as delivering any public address to the people; the king sent his ministers to consult her in her own house. Whatever hesitation may be felt about the public ministry of women, no one will question their Divine commission to carry the messages of God to the bedsides of the sick and the homes of the poor. Most of us have known women to whom men have gone, as Josiah's ministers went to Huldah, to " inquire of the Lord."

Another practical question, the payment of the ministers of religion, has already been raised by the chronicler's account of the revenues of the priests. What more do we learn on the subject from his silence as to the maintenance of the prophets? The silence is, of course, eloquent as to the extent to which even a pious Levite may be preoccupied with his own worldly interests and quite indifferent to other people's; but it would not have been possible if the idea of revenues and endowments for the prophets had ever been very familiar to men's minds. It has been said that to-day the prophet sells his inspiration, but the gift of God can no more be bought and sold with money now than in ancient Israel. The purely spiritual character of true prophecy, its entire dependence on Divine inspiration, makes it impossible to hire a prophet at a fixed salary regulated by the quality and extent of his gifts. By the grace of God, there is an intimate practical connection between the work of the official ministry and the inspired declaration of the Divine will; and this connection has its bearing upon the payment of ministers. Men's gratitude is stirred when they have received comfort and help through the spiritual gifts of their minister, but in principle there is no connection between the gift of prophecy and the payment of the ministry. A Church can purchase the enjoyment of eloquence, learning, intellect, and industry; a high character has a pecuniary value for ecclesiastical as well as for commercial purposes The prophet may be provided with leisure, society, and literature so that the Divine message may be delivered in its most attractive form; he may be installed in a large and well-appointed building, so that he may have the best possible opportunity of delivering his message; he will naturally receive a larger income when he surrenders obscure and limited opportunities to minister in some more suitable sphere. But when we have said all, it is still only the accessories that have to do with payment, not the Divine gift of prophecy itself. When the prophet's message is not comforting, when his words grate upon the theological and social prejudices of his hearers, especially when he is invited to curse and is Divinely compelled to bless, there is no question of payment for such ministry. It has been said of Christ, "For the minor details necessary to secure respect, and obedience, and the enthusiasm of the vulgar, for the tact, the finesse, the compromising faculty, the judicious ostentation of successful politicians —for these arts He was not prepared." [1] Those who imitate their Master often share His reward.

The slight and accidental connection of the payment of ministers with their prophetic gifts is further illustrated by the free exercise of such gifts by men and women who have no ecclesiastical status and do not seek any material reward. Here again any exact adoption of ancient methods is impossible; we may accept from the chronicler the great principle that loyal believers will make all adequate provision for the service and work of Jehovah, and that they will be prepared to honour Him in the persons of those whom they choose to represent them before Him, and also of those whom they recognise as delivering to them His messages. On the other hand, the prophet—and for our present purpose we may extend the term to the humblest and least gifted Christian who in any way seeks to speak for Christ—the prophet speaks by the impulse of the Spirit and from no meaner motive.

With regard to the functions of the prophet, the

---

[1] Abbott, *Through Nature to Christ*, p. 295.

Spirit is as entirely free to dictate His own message as He is to choose His own messenger. The chronicler's prophets were concerned with foreign politics— alliances with Syria and Assyria, wars with Egypt and Samaria—as well as with the ritual of the Temple and the worship of Jehovah. They discerned a religious significance in the purely secular matter of a census. Jehovah had His purposes for the civil government and international policy of Israel as well as for its creed and services. If we lay down the principle that politics, whether local or national, are to be kept out of the pulpit, we must either exclude from the official ministry all who possess any measure of the prophetic gift, or else carefully stipulate that, if they be conscious of any obligation to declare the Lord's will in matters of public righteousness, they shall find some more suitable place than the Lord's house and some more suitable time than the Lord's day. When we suggest that the prophet should mind his own business by confining himself to questions of doctrine, worship, and the religious experiences of the individual, we are in danger of denying God's right to a voice in social and national affairs.

Turning, however, to more directly ecclesiastical affairs, we have noted that Asa's reformation received its first impulse from the utterances of the prophet Azariah or Oded, and also that one feature of the prophet's work is to provide for the fresh needs developed by changing circumstances. A priesthood or any other official ministry is often wanting in elasticity; it is necessarily attached to an established organisation and trammelled by custom and tradition. The Holy Spirit in all ages has commissioned prophets as the free agents in new movements in the Divine government of the world

They may be ecclesiastics, like many of the Reformers and like the Wesleys; but they are not dominated by the official spirit. The initial impulse that moves such men is partly one of recoil from their environment; and the environment in return casts them out. Again, prophets may become ecclesiastics, like the tinker to whom English-speaking Christians owe one of their great religious classics and the cobbler who stirred up the Churches to missionary enthusiasm. Or they may remain from beginning to end without official status in any Church, like the apostle of the anti-slavery movement. In any case the impulse to a larger, purer, and nobler standard of life than that consecrated by long usage and ancient tradition does not come from the ecclesiastical official because of his official training and experience; the living waters that go out of Jerusalem in the day of the Lord are too wide, and deep, and strong to flow in the narrow rock-hewn aqueducts of tradition : they make new channels for themselves; and these channels are the men who do not demand that the Spirit shall speak according to familiar formulæ and stereotyped ideas, but are willing to be the prophets of strange and even uncongenial truth. Or, to use the great metaphor of St. John's Gospel, with such men, both for themselves and for others, the water that the Lord gives them becomes a well of water springing up unto eternal life.

But the chronicler's picture of the work of the prophets has its darker side. Few were privileged to give the signal for an immediate and happy refor-mation. Most of the prophets were charged with messages of rebuke and condemnation, so that they were ready to cry out with Jeremiah, " Woe is me, my mother, that thou hast borne me, a man of strife and a man of contention to the whole earth! I have not lent on usury, neither have men lent to me on usury, yet every one of them doth curse me."[1]

Perhaps even to-day the prophetic spirit often charges its possessors with equally unwelcome duties. We trust that the Christian conscience is more sensitive than that of ancient Israel, and that the Church is more ready to profit by the warnings addressed to it; but the response to the sterner teaching of the Spirit is not always accompanied by a kindly feeling towards the teacher, and even where there is progress, the progress is slow compared to the eager longing of the prophet for the spiritual growth of his hearers. And yet the sequel of the chronicler's history suggests some relief to the gloomier side of the picture. Prophet after prophet utters his unavailing and seemingly useless rebuke, and delivers his announcement of coming ruin, and at last the ruin falls upon the nation. But that is not the end. Before the chronicler wrote there had arisen a restored Israel, purified from idolatry and delivered from many of its former troubles. The Restoration was only rendered possible through the continued testimony of the prophets to the Lord and His righteousness. However barren of immediate results such testimony may seem to-day, it is still the word of the Lord that cannot return unto Him void, but shall accomplish that which He pleaseth and shall prosper in the thing whereto He sent it.

The chronicler's conception of the prophetic character of the historian, whereby his narrative sets forth God's will and interprets His purposes, is not altogether popular at present. The teleological view of history is

[1] Jer. xv. 10

somewhat at a discount.   Yet the prophetic method, so
to speak, of Carlyle and Ruskin is largely historical;
and even in so unlikely a quarter as the works of
George Eliot we can find an example of didactic history.
Romola is largely taken up with the story of Savonarola, told so as to bring out its religious significance.
But teleological history is sometimes a failure even
from the standpoint of the Christian student, because it
defeats its own ends.   He who is bent on deducing
lessons from history may lay undue stress on part of
its significance and obscure the rest.   The historian is
perhaps most a prophet when he leaves history to
speak for itself.   In this sense, we may venture to
attribute a prophetic character to purely scientific
history; accurate and unbiassed narrative is the best
starting-point for the study of the religious significance
of the course of events.

In concluding our inquiry as to how far modern
Church life is illustrated by the work of the prophets,
one is tempted to dwell for a moment on the methods
they did not use and the subjects not dealt with in
their utterances.   This theme, however, scarcely belongs
to the exposition of Chronicles; it would be more
appropriate to a complete examination of the history
and writings of the prophets.   One point, however,
may be noticed.   Their utterances in Chronicles lay
less direct stress on moral considerations than the
writings of the canonical prophets, not because of any
indifference to morality, but because, seen in the
distance of a remote past, all other sins seemed to be
summed up in faithlessness to Jehovah.   Perhaps we
may see in this a suggestion of a final judgment of
history, which should be equally instructive to the
religious man who has any inclination to disparage

morality and to the moral man who wishes to ignore religion.

Our review and discussion of the varied references of Chronicles to the prophets brings home to us with fresh force the keen interest felt in them by the chronicler and the supreme importance he attached to their work. The reverent homage of a Levite of the second Temple centuries after the golden age of prophecy is an eloquent testimony to the unique position of the prophets in Israel. His treatment of the subject shows that the lofty ideal of their office and mission had lost nothing in the course of the development of Judaism; his selection from the older material emphasises the independence of the true prophet of any professional status or consideration of material reward; his sense of the importance of the prophets to the State and Church in Judah is an encouragement to those "who look for redemption in Jerusalem," and who trust the eternal promise of God that in all times of His people's need He "will raise up a prophet from among their brethren, . . . and I will put My words in his mouth, and he shall speak unto them all that I shall command them."[1] "The memorial of the prophets was blessed, . . . for they comforted Jacob, and delivered them by assured hope."[2] Many prophets of the Church have also left a blessed memorial of comfort and deliverance, and God ever renews this more than apostolic succession.

---

[1] Deut. xviii. 18.   [2] Ecclus. xlix. 10.

CHAPTER X

SATAN

1 Chron. xxi.-xxii. 1.

"And again the anger of Jehovah was kindled against Israel, and He moved David against them saying, Go, number Israel and Judah."
—2 Sam. xxiv. 1.

"And Satan stood up against Israel, and moved David to number Israel."—1 Chron. xxi. 1.

"Let no man say when he is tempted, I am tempted of God; for God cannot be tempted with evil, and He Himself tempteth no man: but each man is tempted when he is drawn away by his own lust and enticed."—James i. 13, 14.

THE census of David is found both in the book of Samuel and in Chronicles, in very much the same form; but the chronicler has made a number of small but important alterations and additions. Taken together, these changes involve a new interpretation of the history, and bring out lessons that cannot so easily be deduced from the narrative in the book of Samuel. Hence it is necessary to give a separate exposition of the narrative in Chronicles.

As before, we will first review the alterations made by the chronicler and then expound the narrative in the form in which it left his hand, or rather in the form in which it stands in the Masoretic text. Any attempt to deal with the peculiarly complicated problem of the textual criticism of Chronicles would be out of

270

place here. Probably there are no corruptions of the
text that would appreciably affect the general exposition
of this chapter.

At the very outset the chronicler substitutes Satan
for Jehovah, and thus changes the whole significance of
the narrative. This point is too important to be dealt
with casually, and must be reserved for special consideration later on. In ver. 2 there is a slight change
that marks the different points of the views of the
Chronicler and the author of the narrative in the
book of Samuel. The latter had written that Joab
numbered the people from Dan to Beersheba, a merely
conventional phrase indicating the extent of the census.
It might possibly, however, have been taken to denote
that the census began in the north and was concluded
in the south. To the chronicler, whose interests all
centred in Judah, such an arrangement seemed absurd ;
and he carefully guarded against any mistake by altering
"Dan to Beersheba" into "Beersheba to Dan." In
ver. 3 the substance of Joab's words is not altered,
but various slight touches are added to bring out more
clearly and forcibly what is implied in the book of
Samuel. Joab had spoken of the census as being the
king's pleasure.[1] It was scarcely appropriate to speak
of David "taking pleasure in" a suggestion of Satan.
In Chronicles Joab's words are less forcible, "Why doth
my lord require this thing ?" Again, in the book of
Samuel Joab protests against the census without
assigning any reason. The context, it is true, readily
supplies one ; but in Chronicles all is made clear by the
addition, "Why will he" (David) "be a cause of guilt
unto Israel ?" Further on the chronicler's special

---

[1] R.V. "delight in" is somewhat too strong.

interest in Judah again betrays itself.   The book of
Samuel described, with some detail, the progress of the
enumerators through Eastern and Northern Palestine
by way of Beersheba to Jerusalem.   Chronicles having
already made them start from Beersheba, omits these
details.

In ver. 5 the numbers in Chronicles differ not only
from those of the older narrative, but also from the
chronicler's own statistics in chap. xxvii.   In this
last account the men of war are divided into twelve
courses of twenty-four thousand each, making a total
of two hundred and eighty-eight thousand ; in the
book of Samuel Israel numbers eight hundred thousand,
and Judah five hundred thousand; but in our
passage Israel is increased to eleven hundred thousand,
and Judah is reduced to four hundred and seventy
thousand.   Possibly the statistics in chap. xxvii.
are not intended to include all the fighting men,
otherwise the figures cannot be harmonised.   The
discrepancy between our passage and the book of
Samuel is perhaps partly explained by the following
verse, which is an addition of the chronicler.   In the
book of Samuel the census is completed, but our
additional verse states that Levi and Benjamin were
not included in the census.   The chronicler understood
that the five hundred thousand assigned to Judah in
the older narrative were the joint total of Judah and
Benjamin ; he accordingly reduced the total by thirty
thousand, because, according to his view, Benjamin was
omitted from the census.   The increase in the number
of the Israelites is unexpected.   The chronicler does
not usually overrate the northern tribes.   Later on
Jeroboam, eighteen years after the disruption, takes the
field against Abijah with " eight hundred thousand

chosen men," a phrase that implies a still larger number of fighting men, if all had been mustered. Obviously the rebel king would not be expected to be able to bring into the field as large a force as the entire strength of Israel in the most flourishing days of David. The chronicler's figures in these two passages are consistent, but the comparison is not an adequate reason for the alteration in the present chapter. Textual corruption is always a possibility in the case of numbers, but on the whole this particular change does not admit of a satisfactory explanation.

In ver. 7 we have a very striking alteration. According to the book of Samuel, David's repentance was entirely spontaneous : " David's heart smote him after that he had numbered the people "[1]; but here God smites Israel, and then David's conscience awakes. In ver. 12 the chronicler makes a slight addition, apparently to gratify his literary taste. In the original narrative the third alternative offered to David had been described simply as " the pestilence," but in Chronicles the words " the sword of Jehovah " are added in antithesis to " the sword of Thine enemies " in the previous verse.

Ver. 16, which describes David's vision of the angel with the drawn sword, is an expansion of the simple statement of the book of Samuel that David saw the angel. In ver. 18 we are not merely told that Gad spake to David, but that he spake by the command of the angel of Jehovah. Ver. 20, which tells us how Ornan saw the angel, is an addition of the chronicler's. All these changes lay stress upon the intervention of the angel, and illustrate the interest

---

[1] It is, however, possible that the text in Samuel is a corruption of text more closely parallel to that of Chronicles.

taken by Judaism in the ministry of angels. Zechariah, the prophet of the Restoration, received his messages by the dispensation of angels; and the title of the last canonical prophet, Malachi, probably means "the Angel." The change from Araunah to Ornan is a mere question of spelling. Possibly Ornan is a somewhat Hebraised form of the older Jebusite name Araunah.

In ver. 22 the reference to "a full price" and other changes in the form of David's words are probably due to the influence of Gen. xxiii. 9. In ver. 23 the chronicler's familiarity with the ritual of sacrifice has led him to insert a reference to a meal offering, to accompany the burnt offering. Later on the chronicler omits the somewhat ambiguous words which seem to speak of Araunah as a king. He would naturally avoid anything like a recognition of the royal status of a Jebusite prince.

In ver. 25 David pays much more dearly for Ornan's threshing-floor than in the book of Samuel. In the latter the price is fifty shekels of silver, in the former six hundred shekels of gold. Most ingenious attempts have been made to harmonise the two statements. It has been suggested that fifty shekels of silver means silver to the value of fifty shekels of gold and paid in gold, and that six hundred shekels of gold means the value of six hundred shekels of silver paid in gold. A more lucid but equally impossible explanation is that David paid fifty shekels for every tribe, six hundred in all.[1] The real reason for the change is that when the Temple became supremely important to the Jews the small price of fifty shekels for the site seemed derogatory to the dignity of the sanctuary; six

---

[1] Noldius and R. Salom. *apud* Bertheau l. l.

hundred shekels of gold was a more appropriate sum.
Abraham had paid four hundred shekels for a burying-
place; and a site for the Temple, where Jehovah had
chosen to put His name, must surely have cost more.
The chronicler followed the tradition which had grown
up under the influence of this feeling.

Chaps. xxi. 27–xxii. 1 are an addition. According to
the Levitical law, David was falling into grievous sin
in sacrificing anywhere except before the Mosaic altar
of burnt offering. The chronicler therefore states the
special circumstances that palliated this offence against
the exclusive privileges of the one sanctuary of Jehovah.
He also reminds us that this threshing-floor became
the site of the altar of burnt offering for Solomon's
temple. Here he probably follows an ancient and
historical tradition; the prominence given to the
threshing-floor in the book of Samuel indicates the
special sanctity of the site. The Temple is the only
sanctuary whose site could be thus connected with the
last days of David. When the book of Samuel was
written, the facts were too familiar to need any explanation; every one knew that the Temple stood on the
site of Araunah's threshing-floor. The chronicler,
writing centuries later, felt it necessary to make an
explicit statement on the subject.

Having thus attempted to understand how our
narrative assumed its present form, we will now tell
the chronicler's story of these incidents. The long
reign of David was drawing to a close. Hitherto he
had been blessed with uninterrupted prosperity and
success. His armies had been victorious over all the
enemies of Israel, the borders of the land of Jehovah
had been extended, David himself was lodged with
princely splendour, and the services of the Ark were

conducted with imposing ritual by a numerous array
of priests and Levites.   King and people alike were
at the zenith of their glory.   In worldly prosperity
and careful attention to religious observances David
and his people were not surpassed by Job himself.
Apparently their prosperity provoked the envious
malice of an evil and mysterious being, who appears
only here in Chronicles : Satan, the persecutor of Job.
The trial to which he subjected the loyalty of David
was more subtle and suggestive than his assault upon
Job.   He harassed Job as the wind dealt with the
traveller in the fable, and Job only wrapped the cloak
of his faith closer about him ; Satan allowed David to
remain in the full sunshine of prosperity, and seduced
him into sin by fostering his pride in being the
powerful and victorious prince of a mighty people.
He suggested a census.   David's pride would be
gratified by obtaining accurate information as to the
myriads of his subjects.   Such statistics would be
useful for the civil organisation of Israel ; the king
would learn where and how to recruit his army or
to find an opportunity to impose additional taxation.
The temptation appealed alike to the king, the soldier,
and the statesman, and did not appeal in vain.   David
at once instructed Joab and the princes to proceed
with the enumeration ; Joab demurred and protested :
the census would be a cause of guilt unto Israel.
But not even the great influence of the commander-
in-chief could turn the king from his purpose.   His
word prevailed against Joab, wherefore Joab departed,
and went throughout all Israel, and came to Jerusalem.
This brief general statement indicates a long and
laborious task, simplified and facilitated in some
measure by the primitive organisation of society and

by rough and ready methods adopted to secure the
very moderate degree of accuracy with which an
ancient Eastern sovereign would be contented. When
Xerxes wished to ascertain the number of the vast
army with which he set out to invade Greece, his
officers packed ten thousand men into as small a space
as possible and built a wall round them; then they
turned them out, and packed the space again and
again; and so in time they ascertained how many
tens of thousands of men there were in the army.
Joab's methods would be different, but perhaps not
much more exact. He would probably learn from
the "heads of fathers' houses" the number of fighting
men in each family. Where the hereditary chiefs of
a district were indifferent, he might make some rough
estimate of his own. We may be sure that both Joab
and the local authorities would be careful to err on the
safe side. The king was anxious to learn that he
possessed a large number of subjects. Probably as
the officers of Xerxes went on with their counting
they omitted to pack the measured area as closely
as they did at first; they might allow eight or nine
thousand to pass for ten thousand. Similarly David's
servants would, to say the least, be anxious not to
underestimate the number of his subjects. The work
apparently went on smoothly; nothing is said that
indicates any popular objection or resistance to the
census; the process of enumeration was not interrupted
by any token of Divine displeasure against the "cause
of guilt unto Israel." Nevertheless Joab's misgivings
were not set at rest; he did what he could to limit
the range of the census and to withdraw at least two
of the tribes from the impending outbreak of Divine
wrath. The tribe of Levi would be exempt from

taxation and the obligation of military service ; Joab
could omit them without rendering his statistics less
useful for military and financial purposes. In not
including the Levites in the general census of Israel,
Joab was following the precedent set by the numbering
in the wilderness.

Benjamin was probably omitted in order to protect
the Holy City, the chronicler following that form of the
ancient tradition which assigned Jerusalem to Benjamin.[1]
Later on,[2] however, the chronicler seems to imply that
these two tribes left to the last were not numbered
because of the growing dissatisfaction of Joab with his
task : " Joab the son of Zeruiah began to number, but
finished not." But these different reasons for the
omission of Levi and Benjamin do not mutually exclude
each other. Another limitation is also stated in the
later reference : " David took not the number of them
twenty years old and under, because Jehovah had
said that He would increase Israel like to the stars of
heaven." This statement and explanation seems a
little superfluous ; the census was specially concerned
with the fighting men, and in the book of Numbers only
those over twenty are numbered. But we have seen
elsewhere that the chronicler has no great confidence
in the intelligence of his readers, and feels bound to
state definitely matters that have only been implied and
might be overlooked. Here, therefore, he calls our
attention to the fact that the numbers previously given
do not comprise the whole male population, but only
the adults.

---

[1] Josh. xviii. 28 ; Judges i. 21, as against Josh. xv. 63 ; Judges i. 8,
which assign the city to Judah.

[2] 1 Chron. xxvii. 23, 24.

At last the census, so far as it was carried out at all, was finished, and the results were presented to the king. They are meagre and bald compared to the volumes of tables which form the report of a modern census. Only two divisions of the country are recognised : " Judah" and " Israel," or the ten tribes. The total is given for each : eleven hundred thousand for Israel, four hundred and seventy thousand for Judah, in all fifteen hundred and seventy thousand. Whatever details may have been given to the king, he would be chiefly interested in the grand total. Its figures would be the most striking symbol of the extent of his authority and the glory of his kingdom.

Perhaps during the months occupied in taking the census David had forgotten the ineffectual protests of Joab, and was able to receive his report without any presentiment of coming evil. Even if his mind were not altogether at ease, all misgivings would for the time be forgotten. He probably made or had made for him some rough calculation as to the total of men, women, and children that would correspond to the vast array of fighting men. His servants would not reckon the entire population at less than nine or ten millions. His heart would be uplifted with pride as he contemplated the statement of the multitudes that were the subjects of his crown and prepared to fight at his bidding. The numbers are moderate compared with the vast populations and enormous armies of the great powers of modern Europe ; they were far surpassed by the Roman empire and the teeming populations of the valleys of the Nile, the Euphrates, and the Tigris ; but during the Middle Ages it was not often possible to find in Western Europe so large a population under one government or so numerous an army under one banner. The resources of Cyrus may not have been greater when he started on his career of conquest; and when Xerxes gathered into one motley horde the warriors of half the known world, their total was only about double the number of David's robust and warlike Israelites. There was no enterprise that was likely to present itself to his imagination that he might not have undertaken with a reasonable probability of success. He must have regretted that his days of warfare were past, and that the unwarlike Solomon, occupied with more peaceful tasks, would allow this magnificent instrument of possible conquests to rust unused.

But the king was not long left in undisturbed enjoyment of his greatness. In the very moment of his exaltation, some sense of the Divine displeasure fell upon him.[1] Mankind has learnt by a long and sad experience to distrust its own happiness. The brightest hours have come to possess a suggestion of possible catastrophe, and classic story loved to tell of the unavailing efforts of fortunate princes to avoid their inevitable downfall. Polycrates and Crœsus, however, had not tempted the Divine anger by ostentatious pride; David's power and glory had made him neglectful of the reverent homage due to Jehovah, and he had sinned in spite of the express warnings of his most trusted minister.

When the revulsion of feeling came, it was complete. The king at once humbled himself under the mighty hand of God, and made full acknowledgment of his sin and folly: "I have sinned greatly in that I have done this thing: but now put away, I beseech Thee, the iniquity of Thy servant, for I have done very foolishly."

---

[1] Ver. 7 is apparently a general anticipation of the narrative in vv. 9-15.

The narrative continues as in the book of Samuel. Repentance could not avert punishment, and the punishment struck directly at David's pride of power and glory. The great population was to be decimated either by famine, war, or pestilence. The king chose to suffer from the pestilence, "the sword of Jehovah": "Let me fall now into the hand of Jehovah, for very great are His mercies; and let me not fall into the hand of man. So Jehovah sent a pestilence upon Israel, and there fell of Israel seventy thousand men." Not three days since Joab handed in his report, and already a deduction of seventy thousand would have to be made from its total; and still the pestilence was not checked, for "God sent an angel unto Jerusalem to destroy it." If, as we have supposed, Joab had withheld Jerusalem from the census, his pious caution was now rewarded: "Jehovah repented Him of the evil, and said to the destroying angel, It is enough; now stay thine hand." At the very last moment the crowning catastrophe was averted. In the Divine counsels Jerusalem was already delivered, but to human eyes its fate still trembled in the balance: "And David lifted up his eyes, and saw the angel of Jehovah stand between the earth and the heaven, having a drawn sword in his hand stretched out over Jerusalem." So another great Israelite soldier lifted up his eyes beside Jericho and beheld the captain of the host of Jehovah standing over against him with his sword drawn in his hand.[1] Then the sword was drawn to smite the enemies of Israel, but now it was turned to smite Israel itself. David and his elders fell upon their faces as Joshua had done before them: "And David said unto

---

[1] Josh. v. 13.

God, Is it not I that commanded the people to be
numbered? even I it is that have sinned and done very
wickedly; but these sheep, what have they done? Let
Thine hand, I pray Thee, O Jehovah my God, be
against me and against my father's house, but not
against Thy people, that they should be plagued."

The awful presence returned no answer to the guilty
king, but addressed itself to the prophet Gad, and
commanded *him* to bid David go up and build an altar
to Jehovah in the threshing-floor of Ornan the Jebusite.
The command was a message of mercy. Jehovah permitted David to build Him an altar; He was prepared
to accept an offering at his hands. The king's prayers
were heard, and Jerusalem was saved from the pestilence. But still the angel stretched out his drawn
sword over Jerusalem; he waited till the reconciliation
of Jehovah with His people should have been duly
ratified by solemn sacrifices. At the bidding of the
prophet, David went up to the threshing-floor of Ornan
the Jebusite. Sorrow and reassurance, hope and fear,
contended for the mastery. No sacrifice could call back
to life the seventy thousand victims whom the pestilence
had already destroyed, and yet the horror of its ravages
was almost forgotten in relief at the deliverance of
Jerusalem from the calamity that had all but overtaken
it. Even now the uplifted sword might be only held
back for a time; Satan might yet bring about some
heedless and sinful act, and the respite might end not
in pardon, but in the execution of God's purpose of
vengeance. Saul had been condemned because he
sacrificed too soon; now perhaps delay would be fatal.
Uzzah had been smitten because he touched the Ark;
till the sacrifice was actually offered who could tell
whether some thoughtless blunder would not again

provoke the wrath of Jehovah ? Under ordinary circumstances David would not have dared to sacrifice
anywhere except upon the altar of burnt offering before
the tabernacle at Gibeon ; he would have used the
ministry of priests and Levites. But ritual is helpless
in great emergencies. The angel of Jehovah with the
drawn sword seemed to bar the way to Gibeon, as once
before he had barred Balaam's progress when he came
to curse Israel. In his supreme need David builds his
own altar and offers his own sacrifices ; he receives the
Divine answer without the intervention this time of
either priest or prophet. By God's most merciful and
mysterious grace, David's guilt and punishment, his
repentance and pardon, broke down all barriers between
himself and God.

But, as he went up to the threshing-floor, he was
still troubled and anxious. The burden was partly lifted
from his heart, but he still craved full assurance of
pardon. The menacing attitude of the destroying angel
seemed to hold out little promise of mercy and forgiveness, and yet the command to sacrifice would be cruel
mockery if Jehovah did not intend to be gracious to
His people and His anointed

At the threshing-floor Ornan and his four sons were
threshing wheat, apparently unmoved by the prospect
of the threatened pestilence. In Egypt the Israelites
were protected from the plagues with which their
oppressors were punished. Possibly now the situation
was reversed, and the remnant of the Canaanites in
Palestine were not afflicted by the pestilence that fell
upon Israel. But Ornan turned back and saw the
angel ; he may not have known the grim mission with
which the Lord's messenger had been entrusted, but
the aspect of the destroyer, his threatening attitude, and

the lurid radiance of his unsheathed and outstretched sword must have seemed unmistakable tokens of coming calamity. Whatever might be threatened for the future, the actual appearance of this supernatural visitant was enough to unnerve the stoutest heart; and Ornan's four sons hid themselves.

Before long, however, Ornan's terrors were somewhat relieved by the approach of less formidable visitors. The king and his followers had ventured to show themselves openly, in spite of the destroying angel; and they had ventured with impunity. Ornan went forth and bowed himself to David with his face to the ground. In ancient days the father of the faithful, oppressed by the burden of his bereavement, went to the Hittites to purchase a burying-place for his wife. Now the last of the Patriarchs, mourning for the sufferings of his people, came by Divine command to the Jebusite to purchase the ground on which to offer sacrifices, that the plague might be stayed from the people. The form of bargaining was somewhat similar in both cases. We are told that bargains are concluded in much the same fashion to-day. Abraham had paid four hundred shekels of silver for the field of Ephron in Machpelah, "with the cave which was therein, and all the trees that were in the field." The price of Ornan's threshing-floor was in proportion to the dignity and wealth of the royal purchaser and the sacred purpose for which it was designed. The fortunate Jebusite received no less than six hundred shekels of gold.

David built his altar, and offered up his sacrifices and prayers to Jehovah. Then, in answer to David's prayers, as later in answer to Solomon's, fire fell from heaven upon the altar of burnt offering, and all this while the sword of Jehovah flamed across the heavens above Jerusalem, and the destroying angel remained passive, but to all appearances unappeased. But as the fire of God fell from heaven, Jehovah gave yet another final and convincing token that He would no longer execute judgment against His people. In spite of all that had happened to reassure them, the spectators must have been thrilled with alarm when they saw that the angel of Jehovah no longer remained stationary, and that his flaming sword was moving through the heavens. Their renewed terror was only for a moment : " the angel put up his sword again into the sheath thereof," and the people breathed more freely when they saw the instrument of Jehovah's wrath vanish out of their sight.

The use of Machpelah as a patriarchal burying-place led to the establishment of a sanctuary at Hebron, which continued to be the seat of a debased and degenerate worship even after the coming of Christ. It is even now a Mohammedan holy place. But on the threshing-floor of Ornan the Jebusite there was to arise a more worthy memorial of the mercy and judgment of Jehovah. Without the aid of priestly oracle or prophetic utterance, David was led by the Spirit of the Lord to discern the significance of the command to perform an irregular sacrifice in a hitherto unconsecrated place. When the sword of the destroying angel interposed between David and the Mosaic tabernacle and altar of Gibeon, the way was not merely barred against the king and his court on one exceptional occasion. The incidents of this crisis symbolised the cutting off for ever of the worship of Israel from its ancient shrine and the transference of the Divinely appointed centre of the worship of Jehovah to the threshing-floor of Ornan the Jebusite, that is

to say to Jerusalem, the city of David and the capital
of Judah.

The lessons of this incident, so far as the chronicler
has simply borrowed from his authority, belong to the
exposition of the book of Samuel. The main features
peculiar to Chronicles are the introduction of the evil
angel Satan, together with the greater prominence
given to the angel of Jehovah, and the express statement that the scene of David's sacrifice became the site
of Solomon's altar of burnt offering.

The stress laid upon angelic agency is characteristic
of later Jewish literature, and is especially marked in
Zechariah and Daniel. It was no doubt partly due to
the influence of the Persian religion, but it was also a
development from the primitive faith of Israel, and the
development was favoured by the course of Jewish
history. The Captivity and the Restoration, with the
events that preceded and accompanied these revolutions,
enlarged the Jewish experience of nature and man.
The captives in Babylon and the fugitives in Egypt
saw that the world was larger than they had imagined.
In Josiah's reign the Scythians from the far North
swept over Western Asia, and the Medes and Persians
broke in upon Assyria and Chaldæa from the remote
East. The prophets claimed Scythians, Medes, and
Persians as the instruments of Jehovah. The Jewish
appreciation of the majesty of Jehovah, the Maker and
Ruler of the world, increased as they learnt more of
the world He had made and ruled; but the invasion
of a remote and unknown people impressed them with
the idea of infinite dominion and unlimited resources,
beyond all knowledge and experience. The course of
Israelite history between David and Ezra involved as
great a widening of man's ideas of the universe as

the discovery of America or the establishment of
Copernican astronomy. A Scythian invasion was
scarcely less portentous to the Jews than the descent of
an irresistible army from the planet Jupiter would be
to the civilised nations of the nineteenth century. The
Jew began to shrink from intimate and familiar fellowship with so mighty and mysterious a Deity. He felt
the need of a mediator, some less exalted being, to
stand between himself and God. For the ordinary
purposes of everyday life the Temple, with its ritual
and priesthood, provided a mediation ; but for unforeseen contingencies and exceptional crises the Jews
welcomed the belief that a ministry of angels provided
a safe means of intercourse between himself and the
Almighty. Many men have come to feel to-day that
the discoveries of science have made the universe so
infinite and marvellous that its Maker and Governor is
exalted beyond human approach. The infinite spaces
of the constellations seem to intervene between the
earth and the presence-chamber of God ; its doors are
guarded against prayer and faith by inexorable laws ;
the awful Being, who dwells within, has become
" unmeasured in height, undistinguished into form."
Intellect and imagination alike fail to combine the
manifold and terrible attributes of the Author of nature
into the picture of a loving Father. It is no new
experience, and the present century faces the situation
very much as did the chronicler's contemporaries.
Some are happy enough to rest in the mediation of
ritual priests ; others are content to recognise, as of
old, powers and forces, not now, however, personal
messenger of Jehovah, but the physical agencies of
" that which makes for righteousness." Christ came
to supersede the Mosaic ritual and the ministry of

angels; He will come again to bring those who are far
off into renewed fellowship with His Father and theirs.

On the other hand, the recognition of Satan, the evil
angel, marks an equally great change from the theology of the book of Samuel.   The primitive Israelite
religion had not yet reached the stage at which the
origin and existence of moral evil became an urgent
problem of religious thought; men had not yet
realised the logical consequences of the doctrine of
Divine unity and omnipotence. Not only was material
evil traced to Jehovah as the expression of His just
wrath against sin, but " morally pernicious acts were
quite frankly ascribed to the direct agency of God." [1]
God hardens the heart of Pharaoh and the Canaanites;
Saul is instigated by an evil spirit from Jehovah to
make an attempt upon the life of David; Jehovah
moves David to number Israel; He sends forth a
lying spirit that Ahab's prophets may prophesy falsely
and entice him to his ruin.[2] The Divine origin of
moral evil implied in these passages is definitely stated
in the book of Proverbs: " Jehovah hath made everything for its own end, yea even the wicked for the day
of evil"; in Lamentations, " Out of the mouth of the
Most High cometh there not evil and good?" and in
the book of Isaiah, " I form the light, and create
darkness; I make peace, and create evil; I am Jehovah,
that doeth all these things." [3]

The ultra-Calvinism, so to speak, of earlier Israelite
religion was only possible so long as its full significance
was not understood. An emphatic assertion of the

---

[1] Schultz, *Old Testament Theology*, ii. 270.
[2] Exod. iv. 21; Josh. xi. 20; 1 Sam. xix. 9, 10; 2 Sam. xxiv. 1
1 Kings xxii. 20-23.
[3] Prov. xvi. 4; Lam. iii. 38; Isa. xlv. 7.

absolute sovereignty of the one God was necessary as a protest against polytheism, and later on against dualism as well. For practical purposes men's faith needed to be protected by the assurance that God worked out His purposes in and through human wickedness. The earlier attitude of the Old Testament towards moral evil had a distinct practical and theological value.

But the conscience of Israel could not always rest in this view of the origin of evil. As the standard of morality was raised, and its obligations were more fully insisted on, as men shrank from causing evil themselves and from the use of deceit and violence, they hesitated more and more to ascribe to Jehovah what they sought to avoid themselves. And yet no easy way of escape presented itself. The facts remained ; the temptation to do evil was part of the punishment of the sinner and of the discipline of the saint. It was impossible to deny that sin had its place in God's government of the world ; and in view of men's growing reverence and moral sensitiveness, it was becoming almost equally impossible to admit without qualification or explanation that God was Himself the Author of evil. Jewish thought found itself face to face with the dilemma against which the human intellect vainly beats its wings, like a bird against the bars of its cage.

However, even in the older literature there were suggestions, not indeed of a solution of the problem, but of a less objectionable way of stating facts. In Eden the temptation to evil comes from the serpent ; and, as the story is told, the serpent is quite independent of God ; and the question of any Divine authority or permission for its action is not in any way dealt

19

with.   It is true that the serpent was one of the beasts
of the field which the Lord God had made, but the narrator
probably did not consider the question of any Divine
responsibility for its wickedness.   Again, when Ahab
is enticed to his ruin, Jehovah does not act directly, but
through the twofold agency first of the lying spirit
and then of the deluded prophets.   This tendency to
dissociate God from any direct agency of evil is further
illustrated in Job and Zechariah.   When Job is to be
tried and tempted, the actual agent is the malevolent
Satan; and the same evil spirit stands forth to accuse
the high-priest Joshua[1] as the representative of Israel.
The development of the idea of angelic agency afforded
new resources for the reverent exposition of the facts
connected with the origin and existence of moral evil.
If a sense of Divine majesty led to a recognition of the
angel of Jehovah as the Mediator of revelation, the
reverence for Divine holiness imperatively demanded
that the immediate causation of evil should also be
associated with angelic agency.   This agent of evil
receives the name of Satan, the adversary of man, the
advocatus diaboli who seeks to discredit man before God,
the impeacher of Job's loyalty and of Joshua's purity.
Yet Jehovah does not resign any of His omnipotence.
In Job Satan cannot act without God's permission; he
is strictly limited by Divine control: all that he does
only illustrates Divine wisdom and effects the Divine
purpose.   In Zechariah there is no refutation of the
charge brought by Satan; its truth is virtually admitted:
nevertheless Satan is rebuked for his attempt to hinder
God's gracious purposes towards His people.   Thus
later Jewish thought left the ultimate Divine sovereignty

---

[1] Zech. iii. 1.

untouched, but attributed the actual and direct **causation** of moral evil to malign spiritual agency.

Trained in this school, the chronicler must **have read** with something of a shock that Jehovah moved David to commit the sin of numbering Israel. He was familiar with the idea that in such matters Jehovah used or permitted the activity of Satan. Accordingly he **carefully** avoids reproducing any words from the book of Samuel that imply a direct Divine temptation of David, **and** ascribes it to the well-known and crafty animosity of Satan against Israel. In so doing, he has gone somewhat further than his predecessors : he is not careful to emphasise any Divine permission given to **Satan** or Divine control exercised over him. The **subsequent** narrative implies an overruling for good, **and the** chronicler may have expected his readers **to understand** that Satan here stood in the same **relation to** God as in Job and Zechariah ; but the abrupt and isolated introduction of Satan to bring about the **fall of** David invests the arch-enemy with a new and **more** independent dignity.

The progress of the Jews in moral and spiritual **life** had given them a keener appreciation both of good and evil, and of the contrast and opposition between them. Over against the pictures of the good kings, and of the angel of the Lord, the generation of the chronicler set the complementary pictures of the wicked kings and the evil angel. They had a higher ideal to strive after, a clearer vision of the kingdom of God ; they also saw more vividly the depths of Satan and recoiled with horror from the abyss revealed to them.

Our text affords a striking illustration **of the** **tendency to** emphasise the recognition of Satan **as** the instrument of evil and to ignore the question of the relation of God to the origin of evil. Possibly no more practical attitude can be assumed towards this difficult question. The absolute relation of evil to the Divine sovereignty is one of the problems of the ultimate nature of God and man. Its discussion may throw many sidelights upon other subjects, and will always serve the edifying and necessary purpose of teaching men the limitations of their intellectual powers. Otherwise theologians have found such controversies barren, and the average Christian has not been able to derive from them any suitable nourishment for his spiritual life. Higher intelligences than our own, we have been told,—

> "......... reasoned high
> Of providence, foreknowledge, will, and fate,
> Fixed fate, free-will, foreknowledge absolute,
> And found no end, in wandering mazes lost."

On the other hand, it is supremely important that the believer should clearly understand the reality of temptation as an evil spiritual force opposed to Divine grace. Sometimes this power of Satan will show itself as " the alien law in his members, warring against the law of his mind and bringing him into captivity under the law of sin, which is in his members." He will be conscious that " he is drawn away by his own lust and enticed." But sometimes temptation will rather come from the outside. A man will find his " adversary" in circumstances, in evil companions, in " the sight of means to do ill deeds "; the serpent whispers in his ear, and Satan moves him to wrong-doing. Let him not imagine for a moment that he is delivered over to the powers of evil ; let him realise clearly that with every temptation God provides a way of escape. Every

man knows in his own conscience that speculative difficulties can neither destroy the sanctity of moral obligation nor hinder the operation of the grace of God.

Indeed, the chronicler is at one with the books of
Job and Zechariah in showing us the malice of Satan
overruled for man's good and God's glory. In Job the
affliction of the Patriarch only serves to bring out his
faith and devotion, and is eventually rewarded by
renewed and increased prosperity; in Zechariah the
protest of Satan against God's gracious purposes for
Israel is made the occasion of a singular display of
God's favour towards His people and their priest. In
Chronicles the malicious intervention of Satan leads up
to the building of the Temple.

Long ago Jehovah had promised to choose a place
in Israel wherein to set His name; but, as the chronicler
read in the history of his nation, the Israelites dwelt
for centuries in Palestine, and Jehovah made no
sign: the ark of God still dwelt in curtains. Those
who still looked for the fulfilment of this ancient
promise must often have wondered by what prophetic
utterance or vision Jehovah would make known His
choice. Bethel had been consecrated by the vision of
Jacob, when he was a solitary fugitive from Esau, paying
the penalty of his selfish craft; but the lessons of past
history are not often applied practically, and probably no
one ever expected that Jehovah's choice of the site for
His one temple would be made known to His chosen
king, the first true Messiah of Israel, in a moment of
even deeper humiliation than Jacob's, or that the Divine
announcement would be the climax of a series of events
initiated by the successful machinations of Satan.

Yet herein lies one of the main lessons of the incident. Satan's machinations are not really successful;

he often attains his immediate object, but is always defeated in the end.   He estranges David from Jehovah for a moment, but eventually Jehovah and His people are drawn into closer union, and their reconciliation is sealed by the long-expected choice of a site for the Temple.   Jehovah is like a great general, who will sometimes allow the enemy to obtain a temporary advantage, in order to overwhelm him in some crushing defeat.   The eternal purpose of God moves onward, unresting and unhasting ; its quiet and irresistible persistence finds special opportunity in the hindrances that seem sometimes to check its progress.   In David's case a few months showed the whole process complete : the malice of the Enemy ; the sin and punishment of his unhappy victim ; the Divine relenting and its solemn symbol in the newly consecrated altar.   But with the Lord one day is as a thousand years, and a thousand years as one day ; and this brief episode in the history of a small people is a symbol alike of the eternal dealings of God in His government of the universe and of His personal care for the individual soul.   How short-lived has been the victory of sin in many souls !   Sin is triumphant ; the tempter seems to have it all his own way, but his first successes only lead to his final rout ; the devil is cast out by the Divine exorcism of chastisement and forgiveness ; and he learns that his efforts have been made to subserve the training in the Christian warfare of such warriors as Augustine and John Bunyan.   Or, to take a case more parallel to that of David, Satan catches the saint unawares, and entraps him into sin ; and, behold, while the evil one is in the first flush of triumph, his victim is back again at the throne of grace in an agony of contrition, and before long the repentant sinner is bowed down into a new humility at the undeserved graciousness of the Divine pardon : the chains of love are riveted with a fuller constraint about his soul, and he is tenfold more the child of God than before.

And in the larger life of the Church and the world Satan's triumphs are still the heralds of his utter defeat. He prompted the Jews to slay Stephen; and the Church were scattered abroad, and went about preaching the word; and the young man at whose feet the witnesses laid down their garments became the Apostle of the Gentiles. He tricked the reluctant Diocletian into ordering the greatest of the persecutions, and in a few years Christianity was an established religion in the empire. In more secular matters the apparent triumph of an evil principle is usually the signal for its downfall. In America the slave-holders of the Southern States rode rough-shod over the Northerners for more than a generation, and then came the Civil War.

These are not isolated instances, and they serve to warn us against undue depression and despondency when for a season God seems to refrain from any intervention with some of the evils of the world. We are apt to ask in our impatience,—

> "Is there not wrong too bitter for atoning?
> What are these desperate and hideous years?
> Hast Thou not heard Thy whole creation groaning,
> Sighs of the bondsman, and a woman's tears?"

The works of Satan are as earthly as they are devilish; they belong to the world, which passeth away, with the lust thereof : but the gracious providence of God has all infinity and all eternity to work in. Where to-day we can see nothing but the destroying angel with his flaming sword, future generations shall behold the temple of the Lord.

David's sin, and penitence, and pardon were no inappropriate preludes to this consecration of Mount Moriah. The Temple was not built for the use of blameless saints, but the worship of ordinary men and women. Israel through countless generations was to bring the burden of its sins to the altar of Jehovah. The sacred splendour of Solomon's dedication festival duly represented the national dignity of Israel and the majesty of the God of Jacob; but the self-abandonment of David's repentance, the deliverance of Jerusalem from impending pestilence, the Divine pardon of presumptuous sin, constituted a still more solemn inauguration of the place where Jehovah had chosen to set His name. The sinner, seeking the assurance of pardon in atoning sacrifice, would remember how David had then received pardon for his sin, and how the acceptance of his offerings had been the signal for the disappearance of the destroying angel. So in the Middle Ages penitents founded churches to expiate their sins. Such sanctuaries would symbolise to sinners in after-times the possibility of forgiveness; they were monuments of God's mercy as well as of the founders' penitence. To-day churches, both in fabric and fellowship, have been made sacred for individual worshippers because in them the Spirit of God has moved them to repentance and bestowed upon them the assurance of pardon. Moreover, this solemn experience consecrates for God His most acceptable temples in the souls of those that love Him.

One other lesson is suggested by the happy issues of Satan's malign interference in the history of Israel as understood by the chronicler. The inauguration of the

new altar was a direct breach of the Levitical law, and
involved the superseding of the altar and tabernacle that
had hitherto been the only legitimate sanctuary for the
worship of Jehovah.   Thus the new order had its origin
in the violation of existing ordinances and the neglect
of an ancient sanctuary.   Its early history constituted
a declaration of the transient character of sanctuaries
and systems of ritual.   God would not eternally limit
Himself to any building, or His grace to the observance
of any forms of external ritual.   Long before the
chronicler's time Jeremiah had proclaimed this lesson
in the ears of Judah: "Go ye now unto My place
which was in Shiloh, where I caused My name to dwell
at the first, and see what I did to it for the wickedness
of My people Israel. . . . I will do unto the house
which is called by My name, wherein ye trust, and unto
the place which I gave to you and your fathers, as I
have done to Shiloh. . . .   I will make this house like
Shiloh, and will make this city a curse to all the nations
of the earth." [1]   In the Tabernacle all things were made
according to the pattern that was showed to Moses in
the mount ; for the Temple David was made to understand the pattern of all things "in writing from the
hand of Jehovah." [2]   If the Tabernacle could be set
aside for the Temple, the Temple might in its turn give
place to the universal Church.   If God allowed David
in his great need to ignore the one legitimate altar of
the Tabernacle and to sacrifice without its officials, the
faithful Israelite might be encouraged to believe that
in extreme emergency Jehovah would accept his offering
without regard to place or priest.

The principles here involved are of very wide applica-

---

[1] Jer. vii. 12-14; xxvi. 6.   [2] ı Chron. xxviii. 19.

tion. Every ecclesiastical system was at first a new departure. Even if its highest claims be admitted, they simply assert that within historic times God set aside some other system previously enjoying the sanction of His authority, and substituted for it a more excellent way. The Temple succeeded the Tabernacle ; the synagogue appropriated in a sense part of the authority of the Temple ; the Church superseded both synagogue and Temple. God's action in authorising each new departure warrants the expectation that He may yet sanction new ecclesiastical systems ; the authority which is sufficient to establish is also adequate to supersede. When the Anglican Church broke away from the unity of Western Christendom by denying the supremacy of the Pope and refusing to recognise the orders of other Protestant Churches, she set an example of dissidence that was naturally followed by the Presbyterians and Independents. The revolt of the Reformers against the theology of their day in a measure justifies those who have repudiated the dogmatic systems of the Reformed Churches. In these and in other ways to claim freedom from authority, even in order to set up a new authority of one's own, involves in principle at least the concession to others of a similar liberty of revolt against one's self.

CHAPTER XI

CONCLUSION

IN dealing with the various subjects of this book, we have reserved for separate treatment their relation to the Messianic hopes of the Jews and to the realisation of these hopes in Christ. The Messianic teaching of Chronicles is only complete when we collect and combine the noblest traits in its pictures of David and Solomon, of prophets, priests, and kings. We cannot ascribe to Chronicles any great influence on the subsequent development of the Jewish idea of the Messiah. In the first place, the chronicler does not point out the bearing which his treatment of history has upon the expectation of a future deliverer. He has no formal intention of describing the character and office of the Messiah ; he merely wishes to write a history so as to emphasise the facts which most forcibly illustrated the sacred mission of Israel. And, in the second place, Chronicles never exercised any great influence over Jewish thought, and never attained to anything like the popularity of the books of Samuel and Kings. Many circumstances conspired to prevent the Temple ministry from obtaining an undivided authority over later Judaism. The growth of their power was broken in upon by the persecutions of Antiochus and the wars of the Maccabees. The ministry of the Temple under the Maccabæan high-priests must have been very different from that to which the chronicler belonged. Even if the priests and Levites still exercised any influence upon theology, they were overshadowed by the growing importance of the rabbinical schools of Babylon and Palestine. Moreover, the rise of Hellenistic Judaism and the translation of the Scriptures into Greek introduced another new and potent factor into the development of the Jewish religion. Of all the varied forces that were at work few or none tended to assign any special authority to Chronicles, nor has it left any very marked traces on later literature. Josephus indeed uses it for his history, but the New Testament is under very slight obligation to our author.

But Chronicles reveals to us the position and tendencies of Jewish thought in the interval between Ezra and the Maccabees. The Messiah was expected to renew the ancient glories of the chosen people, " to restore the kingdom to Israel"; we learn from Chronicles what sort of a kingdom He was to restore. We see the features of the ancient monarchy that were dear to the memories of the Jews, the characters of the prophets, priests, and kings whom they delighted to honour. As their ideas of the past shaped and coloured their hopes for the future, their conception of what was noblest and best in the history of the monarchy was at the same time the measure of what they expected in the Messiah. However little influence Chronicles may have exerted as a piece of literature, the tendencies of which it is a monument continued to leaven the thought of Israel, and are everywhere manifest in the New Testament.

We have to bear in mind that Messiah, ".Anointed," was the familiar title of the Israelite kings; its use for the priests was late and secondary. The use of a royal title to denote the future Saviour of the nation shows us that He was primarily conceived of as an ideal king; and apart from any formal enunciation of this conception, the title itself would exercise a controlling influence upon the development of the Messianic idea. Accordingly in the New Testament we find that the Jews were looking for a king; and Jesus calls His new society the Kingdom of Heaven.

But for the chronicler the Messiah, the Anointed of Jehovah, is no mere secular prince. We have seen how the chronicler tends to include religious duties and prerogatives among the functions of the king. David and Solomon and their pious successors are supreme alike in Church and state as the earthly representatives of Jehovah. The actual titles of priest and prophet are not bestowed upon the kings, but they are virtually priests in their care for and control over the buildings and ritual of the Temple, and they are prophets when, like David and Solomon, they hold direct fellowship with Jehovah and announce His will to the people. Moreover, David, as " the Psalmist of Israel," had become the inspired interpreter of the religious experience of the Jews. The ancient idea of the king as the victorious conqueror was gradually giving place to a more spiritual conception of his office; the Messiah was becoming more and more a definitely religious personage. Thus Chronicles prepared the way for the acceptance of Christ as a spiritual Deliverer, who was not only King, but also Priest and Prophet. In fact, we may claim the chronicler's own implied authority for including in the picture of the coming King the characteristics he ascribes to the priest and the prophet. Thus the Messiah of Chronicles is

distinctly more spiritual and less secular than the
Messiah of popular Jewish enthusiasm in our Lord's
own time. Whereas in the chronicler's time the
tendency was to spiritualise the idea of the king, the
tenure of the office of high-priest by the Maccabæan
princes tended rather to secularise the priesthood and
to restore older and cruder conceptions of the Messianic
King.

Let us see how the chronicler's history of the house
of David illustrates the person and work of the Son
of David, who came to restore the ancient monarchy
in the spiritual kingdom of which it was the symbol.
The Gospels introduce our Lord very much as the
chronicler introduces David : they give us His genealogy, and pass almost immediately to His public ministry.
Of His training and preparation for that ministry, of
the chain of earthly circumstances that determined the
time and method of His entry upon the career of a
public Teacher, they tell us next to nothing. We are
only allowed one brief glimpse of the life of the holy
Child; our attention is mainly directed to the royal
Saviour when He has entered upon His kingdom ;
and His Divine nature finds expression in mature
manhood, when none of the limitations of childhood
detract from the fulness of His redeeming service and
sacrifice.

The authority of Christ rests on the same basis as
that of the ancient kings : it is at once human and
Divine. In Christ indeed this twofold authority is in
one sense peculiar to Himself ; but in the practical
application of His authority to the hearts and consciences of men He treads in the footsteps of His
ancestors. His kingdom rests on His own Divine
commission and on the consent of His subjects. God

has given Him the right to rule, but He will not reign in any heart till He receives its free submission. And still, as of old, Christ, thus chosen and well beloved of God and man, is King over the whole life of His people, and claims to rule over them in their homes, their business, their recreation, their social and political life, as well as in their public and private worship. If David and his pious successors were devoted to Jehovah and His temple, if they protected their people from foreign foes and wisely administered the affairs of Israel, Christ sets us the example of perfect obedience to the Father; He gives us deliverance and victory in our warfare against principalities and powers, against the world rulers of this darkness, and against the spiritual hosts of wickedness in heavenly places; He administers in peace and holiness the inner kingdom of the believing heart. All that was foreshadowed both by David and Solomon is realised in Christ. The warlike David is a symbol of the holy warfare of Christ and the Church militant, of Him who came not to send peace on earth, but a sword; Solomon is the symbol of Christ, the Prince of peace in the Church triumphant. The tranquillity and splendour of the reign of the first son of David are types of the serene glory of Christ's kingdom as it is partly realised in the hearts of His children and as it will be fully realised in heaven; the God-given wisdom of Solomon prefigures the perfect knowledge and understanding of Him who is Himself the Word and Wisdom of God.

The shadows that darken the history of the kings of Judah and even the life of David himself remind us that the Messiah moved upon a far higher moral and spiritual level than the monarchs whose royal dignity was a type of His own. Like David, He was exposed to the machinations of Satan; but, unlike David, He successfully resisted the tempter. He was in "all points tempted like as we are, yet without sin."

The great priestly work of David and Solomon was the building of the Temple and the organisation of its ritual and ministry. By this work the kings made splendid provision for fellowship between Jehovah and His people, and for the system of sacrifices, whereby a sinful nation expressed their penitence and received the assurance of forgiveness. This has been the supreme work of Christ: through Him we have access to God; we enter into the holy place, into the Divine presence, by a new and living way, that is to say His flesh; He has brought us into the perpetual fellowship of the Spirit. And whereas Solomon could only build one temple, to which the believer paid occasional visits and obtained the sense of Divine fellowship through the ministry of the priests, Christ makes every faithful heart the temple of sacred service, and He has offered for us the one sacrifice, and provides a universal atonement.

In His priesthood, as in His sacrifice, He represents us before God, and this representation is not merely technical and symbolic: in Him we find ourselves brought near to God, and our desires and aspirations are presented as petitions at the throne of the heavenly grace. But, on the other hand, in His love and righteousness He represents God to us, and brings the assurance of our acceptance.

Other minor features of the office and rights of the priests and Levites find a parallel in Christ. He also is our Teacher and our Judge; to Him and to His service all worldly wealth may be consecrated. Christ is in all things the spiritual Heir of the house of Aaron as well as of the house of David; because He is a Priest for ever after the order of Melchizedek, He, like Melchizedek, is also King of Salem; of His kingdom and of His priesthood there shall be no end. But while Christ is to the Kingdom of Heaven what David was to the Israelite monarchy, while in the different aspects of His work He is at once Temple, Priest, and Sacrifice, yet in the ministry of His earthly life He is above all a Prophet, the supreme successor of Elijah and Isaiah. It was only in a figure that He sat upon David's throne; it formed no part of His plan to exercise earthly dominion : His kingdom was not of this world. He did not belong to the priestly tribe, and performed none of the external acts of priestly ritual; He did not base His authority upon any genealogy with regard to priesthood, as the Epistle to the Hebrews says, "It is evident that our Lord hath sprung out of Judah, as to which tribe Moses spake nothing concerning priests." [1] His royal birth had its symbolic value, but He never asked men to believe in Him because of His human descent from David. He relied as little on the authority of office as on that of birth. Officially He was neither scribe nor rabbi. Like the prophets, His only authority was His Divine commission and the witness of the Spirit in the hearts of His hearers. The people recognised Him as a prophet; they took Him for Elijah or one of the prophets; He spoke of Himself as a prophet : "Not without honour, save in his own country." We have seen that, while the priests ministered to the regular and recurring needs of the people, the Divine

---

[1] Heb. vii. 14.

20

guidance in special emergencies and the Divine
authority for new departures were given by the
prophets. By a prophet Jehovah brought Israel out
of Egypt,[1] and Christ as a Prophet led His people out
of the bondage of the Law into the liberty of the
Gospel. By Him the Divine authority was given for
the greatest religious revolution that the world has
ever seen. And still He is the Prophet of the Church.
He does not merely provide for the religious wants
that are common to every race and to every generation :
as the circumstances of His Church alter, and the
believer is confronted with fresh difficulties and called
upon to undertake new tasks, Christ reveals to His
people the purpose and counsel of God. Even the
record of His earthly teaching is constantly found to
have anticipated the needs of our own time ; His Spirit
enables us to discover fresh applications of the truths
He taught: and through Him special light is sought
and granted for the guidance of individuals and of the
Church in their need.

But in Chronicles special stress is laid on the darker
aspects of the work of the prophets. They constantly
appear to administer rebukes and announce coming
punishment. Both Christ and His apostles were
compelled to assume the same attitude towards Israel.
Like Jeremiah, their hearts sank under the burden
of so stern a duty. Christ denounced the Pharisees,
and wept over the city that knew not the things
belonging to its peace ; He declared the impending
ruin of the Temple and the Holy City. Even so His
Spirit still rebukes sin, and warns the impenitent of
inevitable punishment.

---

[1] Hos. xii. 13.

We have seen also in Chronicles that no stress was laid on any material rewards for the prophets, and that their fidelity was sometimes recompensed with persecution and death. Like Christ Himself, they had nothing to do with priestly wealth and splendour. The silence of the chronicler to the income of these prophets makes them fitting types of Him who had not where to lay His head. A discussion of the income of Christ would almost savour of blasphemy; we should shrink from inquiring how far "those who derived spiritual profit from His teaching gave Him substantial proofs of their appreciation of His ministry." Christ's recompense at the hands of the world and of the Jewish Church was that which former prophets had received. Like Zechariah the son of Jehoiada, He was persecuted and slain; He delivered a prophet's message, and died a prophet's death.

But, besides the chronicler's treatment of the offices of prophet, priest, and king, there was another feature of his teaching which would prepare the way for a clear comprehension of the person and work of Christ. We have noticed how the growing sense of the power and majesty of Jehovah seemed to set Him at a distance from man, and how the Jews welcomed the idea of the mediation of an angelic ministry. And yet the angels were too vague and unfamiliar, too little known, and too imperfectly understood to satisfy men's longing for some means of fellowship between themselves and the remote majesty of an almighty God; while still their ministry served to maintain faith in the possibility of mediation, and to quicken the yearning after some better way of access to Jehovah. When Christ came He found this faith and yearning waiting to be satisfied; they opened a door through which Christ found

His way into hearts prepared to receive Him. In Him
the familiar human figures of priest and prophet were
exalted into the supernatural dignity of the Angel of
Jehovah. Men had long strained their eyes in vain to
a far-off heaven ; and, behold, a human voice recalled
their gaze to the earth ; and they turned and found God
beside them, kindly and accessible, a Man with men.
They realised the promise that a modern poet puts into
David's mouth :—

" . . . O Saul, it shall be
A face like my face that receives thee; a Man like to me
Thou shalt love and be loved by for ever; a Hand like this hand
Shall throw open the gates of new life to thee ! See the Christ
stand ! "

We have thus seen how the figures of the chronicler's
history—prophet, priest, king, and angel—were types
and foreshadowings of Christ. We may sum up this
aspect of his teaching by a quotation from a modern
exponent of Old Testament theology :—

" Moses the prophet is the first type of the Mediator.
By his side stands Aaron the priest, who connects the
people with God, and consecrates it. . . . But from
the time of David both these figures pale in the
imagination of the people before the picture of the
Davidic king. His is the figure which appears the
most indispensable condition of all true happiness for
Israel. David is the third and by far the most perfect
type of the Consummator." [1]

This recurrence to the king as the most perfect type
of the Redeemer suggests a last application of the
Messianic teaching of the chronicler. In discussing his

---

[1] Schultz, *Old Testament Theology*, ii. 353.

pictures of the kings, we have ventured to give them a
meaning adapted to modern political life. In Israel the
king stood for the state. When a community combined
for common action to erect a temple or repel an invader,
the united force was controlled and directed by the
king; he was the symbol of national union and
co-operation. To-day, when a community acts as a
whole, its agent and instrument is the civil government;
the state is the people organised for the common good,
subordinating individual ends to the welfare of the
whole nation. Where the Old Testament has "king,"
its modern equivalent may read the state or the civil
government,—nay, even for special purposes the municipality, the county council, or the school board. Shall
we obtain any helpful or even intelligible result if we
apply this method of translation to the doctrine of
the Messiah? Externally at any rate the translation
bears a startling likeness to what has been regarded
as a specially modern development. "Israel looked
for salvation from the king," would read, "Modern
society should seek salvation from the state." As-
suredly there are many prophets who have taken up
this burden without any idea that their new heresy
was only a reproduction of old and forgotten orthodoxy.
But the history of the growth of the Messianic idea
supplies a correction to the primitive baldness of this
principle of salvation by the state. In time the picture
of the Messianic king came to include the attributes of
the prophet and the priest. If we care to complete our
modern application, we must affirm that the state can
never be a saviour till it becomes sensitive to Divine
influences and conscious of a Divine presence.

When we see how the Messianic hope of Israel was
purified and ennobled to receive a fulfilment glorious

beyond its wildest dreams, we are encouraged to believe that the fantastic visions of the Socialist may be divinely guided to some reasonable ideal and may prepare the way for some further manifestation of the grace of God. But the Messianic state, like the Messiah, may be called upon to suffer and die for the salvation of the world, that it may receive a better resurrection.

BOOK IV

THE INTERPRETATION OF HISTORY

CHAPTER I

THE LAST PRAYER OF DAVID

I Chron. xxix. 10-19.

IN order to do justice to the chronicler's method of
presenting us with a number of very similar
illustrations of the same principle, we have in the
previous book grouped much of his material under a
few leading subjects. There remains the general
thread of the history, which is, of course, very much
the same in Chronicles as in the book of Kings, and
need not be dwelt on at any length. At the same time
some brief survey is necessary for the sake of com-
pleteness and in order to bring out the different
complexion given to the history by the chronicler's
alterations and omissions. Moreover, there are a
number of minor points that are most conveniently
dealt with in the course of a running exposition.

The special importance attached by the chronicler
to David and Solomon has enabled us to treat their
reigns at length in discussing his picture of the ideal
king; and similarly the reign of Ahaz has served as an
illustration of the character and fortunes of the wicked
kings. We therefore take up the history at the
accession of Rehoboam, and shall simply indicate very
briefly the connection of the reign of Ahaz with what

precedes and follows. But before passing on to
Rehoboam we must consider "The Last Prayer of
David," a devotional paragraph peculiar to Chronicles.
The detailed exposition of this passage would have
been out of proportion in a brief sketch of the
chronicler's account of the character and reign of
David, and would have had no special bearing on the
subject of the ideal king. On the other hand, the
"Prayer" states some of the leading principles which
govern the chronicler in his interpretation of the
history of Israel; and its exposition forms a suitable
introduction to the present division of our subject.

The occasion of this prayer was the great closing
scene of David's life, which we have already described.
The prayer is a thanksgiving for the assurance David
had received that the accomplishment of the great
purpose of his life, the erection of a temple to Jehovah,
was virtually secured. He had been permitted to
collect the materials for the building, he had received
the plans of the Temple from Jehovah, and had placed
them in the willing hands of his successor. The
princes and the people had caught his own enthusiasm
and lavishly supplemented the bountiful provision
already made for the future work. Solomon had been
accepted as king by popular acclamation. Every
possible preparation had been made that could be made,
and the aged king poured out his heart in praise to God
for His grace and favour.

The prayer falls naturally into four subdivisions:
vv. 10-13 are a kind of doxology in honour of Jehovah;
in vv. 14-16 David acknowledges that Israel is entirely
dependent upon Jehovah for the means of rendering
Him acceptable service; in ver. 17 he claims that he
and his people have offered willingly unto Jehovah; and

in vv. 18 and 19 he prays that Solomon and the
people may build the Temple and abide in the Law.

In the doxology God is addressed as "Jehovah, the
God of Israel, our Father," and similarly in ver. 18
as "Jehovah, the God of Abraham, of Isaac, and of
Israel." For the chronicler the accession of David is
the starting-point of Israelite history and religion, but
here, as in the genealogies, he links his narrative to
that of the Pentateuch, and reminds his readers that
the crowning dispensation of the worship of Jehovah
in the Temple rested on the earlier revelations to
Abraham, Isaac, and Israel.

We are at once struck by the divergence from the
usual formula : "Abraham, Isaac, and Jacob." Moreover,
when God is referred to as the God of the Patriarch
personally, the usual phrase is "the God of Jacob."
The formula, "God of Abraham, Isaac, and Israel,"
occurs again in Chronicles in the account of Hezekiah's
reformation ; it only occurs elsewhere in the history of
Elijah in the book of Kings.[1] The chronicler avoids
the use of the name "Jacob," and for the most part calls
the Patriarch "Israel." "Jacob" only occurs in two
poetic quotations, where its omission was almost impossible, because in each case "Israel" is used in the
parallel clause.[2] This choice of names is an application of
the same principle that led to the omission of the discreditable incidents in the history of David and Solomon.
Jacob was the supplanter. The name suggested the
unbrotherly craft of the Patriarch. It was not desirable
that the Jews should be encouraged to think of Jehovah
as the God of a grasping and deceitful man. Jehovah
was the God of the Patriarch's nobler nature and

---

[1] 2 Chron. xxx. 6; 1 Kings xviii. 36.
[2] 1 Chron. xvi. 13, 17 ; Gen. xxxii. 28.

higher life, the God of Israel, who strove with God
and prevailed.

In the doxology that follows the resources of language are almost exhausted in the attempt to set forth
adequately "the greatness, and the power, and the
glory, and the victory, and the majesty, . . . the riches
and honour, . . . the power and might," of Jehovah.
These verses read like an expansion of the simple
Christian doxology, "Thine is the kingdom, the power,
and the glory," but in all probability the latter is an
abbreviation from our text.   In both there is the same
recognition of the ruling omnipotence of God ; but the
chronicler, having in mind the glory and power of
David and his magnificent offerings for the building
of the Temple, is specially careful to intimate that
Jehovah is the source of all worldly greatness : " Both
riches and honour come of Thee, . . . and in Thy hand
it is to make great and to give strength unto all."

The complementary truth, the entire dependence of
Israel on Jehovah, is dealt with in the next verses.
David has learnt humility from the tragic consequences
of his fatal census ; his heart is no longer uplifted with
pride at the wealth and glory of his kingdom ; he claims
no credit for the spontaneous impulse of generosity
that prompted his munificence.   Everything is traced
back to Jehovah : "All things come of Thee, and of
Thine own have we given Thee."   Before, when David
contemplated the vast population of Israel and the great
array of his warriors, the sense of God's displeasure
fell upon him ; now, when the riches and honour of
his kingdom were displayed before him, he may have
felt the chastening influence of his former experience.
A touch of melancholy darkened his spirit for a moment ;
standing upon the brink of the dim, mysterious Sheol,

he found small comfort in barbaric abundance of timber
and stone, jewels, talents, and darics ; he saw the empti-
ness of all earthly splendour.   Like Abraham before
the children of Heth, he stood before Jehovah a
stranger and a sojourner.[1]   Bildad the Shuhite had
urged Job to submit himself to the teaching of a venerable orthodoxy, because "we are of yesterday and
know nothing, because our days upon earth are a
shadow."[2]   The same thought made David feel his
insignificance, in spite of his wealth and royal dominion :
"Our days on the earth are as a shadow, and there
is no abiding."

He turns from these sombre thoughts to the con-
soling reflection that in all his preparations he has
been the instrument of a Divine purpose, and has
served Jehovah willingly.   To-day he can approach
God with a clear conscience : "I know also, my God,
that Thou triest the heart and hast pleasure in uprightness.   As for me, in the uprightness of my heart I
have willingly offered all these things."   He rejoiced,
moreover, that the people had offered willingly.   The
chronicler anticipates the teaching of St. Paul that
"the Lord loveth a cheerful giver."   David gives of
his abundance in the same spirit in which the widow
gave her mite.   The two narratives are mutually supplementary.   It is possible to apply the story of the
widow's mite so as to suggest that God values our
offerings in inverse proportion to their amount.   We
are reminded by the willing munificence of David that
the rich may give of his abundance as simply and
humbly and as acceptably as the poor man gives of
his poverty.

---

[1] Gen. xxiii. 4 ; cf. Psalms xxxix. 13, cxix. 19.
[2] Job viii. 9.

But however grateful David might be for the pious and generous spirit by which his people were now possessed, he did not forget that they could only abide in that spirit by the continued enjoyment of Divine help and grace. His thanksgiving concludes with prayer. Spiritual depression is apt to follow very speedily in the train of spiritual exaltation; days of joy and light are granted to us that we may make provision for future necessity.

David does not merely ask that Israel may be kept in external obedience and devotion : his prayer goes deeper. He knows that out of the heart are the issues of life, and he prays that the heart of Solomon and the thoughts of the heart of the people may be kept right with God. Unless the fountain of life were pure, it would be useless to cleanse the stream. David's special desire is that the Temple may be built, but this desire is only the expression of his loyalty to the Law. Without the Temple the commandments, and testimonies, and statutes of the Law could not be rightly observed. But he does not ask that the people may be constrained to build the Temple and keeping the Law in order that their hearts may be made perfect; their hearts are to be made perfect that they may keep the Law.

Henceforward throughout his history the chronicler's criterion of a perfect heart, a righteous life, in king and people, is their attitude towards the Law and the Temple. Because their ordinances and worship formed the accepted standard of religion and morality, through which men's goodness would naturally express themselves. Similarly only under a supreme sense of duty to God and man may the Christian willingly violate the established canons of religious and social life.

We may conclude by noticing a curious feature in the wording of David's prayer. In the nineteenth, as in the first, verse of this chapter the Temple, according to our English versions, is referred to as "the palace." The original word *bîrâ* is probably Persian, though a parallel form is quoted from the Assyrian. As a Hebrew word it belongs to the latest and most corrupt stage of the language as found in the Old Testament ; and only occurs in Chronicles, Nehemiah, Esther, and Daniel. In putting this word into the mouth of David, the chronicler is guilty of an anachronism, parallel to his use of the word "darics." The word *bîrâ* appears to have first become familiar to the Jews as the name of a Persian palace or fortress in Susa; it is used in Nehemiah of the castle attached to the Temple, and in later times the derivative Greek name *Baris* had the same meaning. It is curious to find the chronicler, in his effort to find a sufficiently dignified title for the temple of Jehovah, driven to borrow a word which belonged originally to the royal magnificence of a heathen empire, and which was used later on to denote the fortress whence a Roman garrison controlled the fanaticism of Jewish worship.[1] The chronicler's intention, no doubt, was to intimate that the dignity of the Temple surpassed that of any royal palace. He could not suppose that it was greater in extent or constructed of more costly materials; the living presence of Jehovah was its one supreme and unique distinction. The King gave honour to His dwelling-place.

---

[1] Called, however, at that time Antonia.

CHAPTER II

REHOBOAM AND ABIJAH: THE IMPORTANCE OF RITUAL

2 CHRON. x.–xiii.

THE transition from Solomon to Rehoboam brings to light a serious drawback of the chronicler's principle of selection. In the history of Solomon we read of nothing but wealth, splendour, unchallenged dominion, and superhuman wisdom; and yet the breath is hardly out of the body of the wisest and greatest king of Israel before his empire falls to pieces. We are told, as in the book of Kings, that the people met Rehoboam with a demand for release from "the grievous service of thy father," and yet we were expressly told only two chapters before that "of the children of Israel did Solomon make no servants for his work; but they were men of war, and chief of his captains, and rulers of his chariots and of his horsemen." [1] Rehoboam apparently had been left by the wisdom of his father to the companionship of headstrong and featherbrained youths; he followed their advice rather than that of Solomon's grey-headed counsellors, with the result that the ten tribes successfully revolted and chose Jeroboam for their king. Rehoboam assembled an army to reconquer his

---

[1] viii. 9.

lost territory, but Jehovah through the prophet
Shemaiah forbade him to make war against Jeroboam.

The chronicler here and elsewhere shows his
anxiety not to perplex simple minds with unnecessary
difficulties. They might be harassed and disturbed
by the discovery that the king, who built the Temple
and was specially endowed with Divine wisdom, had
fallen into grievous sin and been visited with condign
punishment. Accordingly everything that discredits
Solomon and detracts from his glory is omitted. The
general principle is sound; an earnest teacher, alive to
his responsibility, will not wantonly obtrude difficulties
upon his hearers; when silence does not involve
disloyalty to truth, he will be willing that they should
remain in ignorance of some of the more mysterious
dealings of God in nature and history. But silence
was more possible and less dangerous in the chronicler's time than in the nineteenth century. He could
count upon a docile and submissive spirit in his
readers ; they would not inquire beyond what they were
told : they would not discover the difficulties for themselves. Jewish youths were not exposed to the attacks
of eager and militant sceptics, who would force these
difficulties upon their notice in an exaggerated form,
and at once demand that they should cease to believe
in anything human or Divine.

And yet, though the chronicler had great advantages
in this matter, his own narrative illustrates the narrow
limits within which the principle of the suppression of
difficulties can be safely applied. His silence as to
Solomon's sins and misfortunes makes the revolt
of the ten tribes utterly inexplicable. After the
account of the perfect wisdom, peace, and prosperity of
Solomon's reign, the revolt comes upon an intelligent

reader with a shock of surprise and almost of incredu-
lity.   If he could not test the chronicler's narrative
by that of the book of Kings—and it was no part of
the chronicler's purpose that his history should be
thus tested—the violent transition from Solomon's
unbroken prosperity to the catastrophe of the disruption would leave the reader quite uncertain as to
the general credibility of Chronicles.   In avoiding
Scylla, our author has fallen into Charybdis; he has
suppressed one set of difficulties only to create others.
If we wish to help intelligent inquirers and to aid
them to form an independent judgment, our safest plan
will often be to tell them all we know ourselves and to
believe that difficulties, which in no way mar our
spiritual life, will not destroy their faith.

In the next section[1] the chronicler tells how for
three years Rehoboam administered his diminished
kingdom with wisdom and success; he and his people
walked in the way of David and Solomon, and his
kingdom was established, and he was strong.   He
fortified fifteen cities in Judah and Benjamin, and put
captains in them, and store of victuals, and oil and
wine, and shields and spears, and made them exceeding strong.   Rehoboam was further strengthened by
deserters from the northern kingdom.   Though the
Pentateuch and the book of Joshua assigned to the
priests and Levites cities in the territory held by
Jeroboam, yet their intimate association with the
Temple rendered it impossible for them to remain
citizens of a state hostile to Jerusalem.   The chronicler
indeed tells us that " Jeroboam and his sons cast them
off, that they should not execute the priest's office unto

---

[1] xi. 5-xii. 1, peculiar to Chronicles.

Jehovah, and appointed others to be priests for the
high places and the he-goats and for the calves which
he had." It is difficult to understand what the chronicler means by this statement. On the face of it, we
should suppose that Jeroboam refused to employ the
house of Aaron and the tribe of Levi for the worship
of his he-goats and calves, but the chronicler could not
describe such action as casting "them off that they
should not execute the priest's office unto Jehovah."
The passage has been explained to mean that Jeroboam
sought to hinder them from exercising their functions
at the Temple by preventing them from visiting Judah ;
but to confine the priests and Levites to his own
kingdom would have been a strange way of casting
them off. However, whether driven out by Jeroboam
or escaping from him, they came to Jerusalem and
brought with them from among the ten tribes other
pious Israelites, who were attached to the worship of
the Temple. Judah and Jerusalem became the home
of all true worshippers of Jehovah ; and those who
remained in the northern kingdom were given up to
idolatry or the degenerate and corrupt worship of the
high places. The chronicler then gives us some account
of Rehoboam's harem and children, and tells that he
dealt wisely, and dispersed his twenty-eight sons
"throughout all the lands of Judah and Benjamin, unto
every fenced city." He gave them the means of maintaining a luxurious table, and provided them with
numerous wives, and trusted that, being thus happily
circumstanced, they would lack leisure, energy, and
ambition to imitate Absalom and Adonijah.

Prosperity and security turned the head of Rehoboam
as they had done that of David : " He forsook the law of
Jehovah, and all Israel with him." "All Israel" means

all the subjects of Rehoboam ; the chronicler treats the
ten tribes as cut off from Israel.   The faithful worshippers of Jehovah in Judah had been reinforced by
the priests, Levites, and all other pious Israelites from
the northern kingdom ; and yet in three years they
forsook the cause for which they had left their country
and their father's house.   Punishment was not long
delayed, for Shishak, king of Egypt, invaded Judah with
an immense host and took away the treasures of the
house of Jehovah and of the king's house.

The chronicler explains why Rehoboam was not
more severely punished.[1]   Shishak appeared before
Jerusalem with his immense host : Ethiopians, Lubim
or Lybians, and Sukiim, a mysterious people only mentioned here.   The LXX. and Vulgate translate Sukiim
" Troglodytes," apparently identifying them with the
cave-dwellers on the western or Ethiopian coast of the
Red Sea.   In order to find safety from these strange
and barbarous enemies, Rehoboam and his princes were
gathered together in Jerusalem.   Shemaiah the prophet
appeared before them, and declared that the invasion
was Jehovah's punishment for their sin, whereupon
they humbled themselves, and Jehovah accepted their
penitent submission.   He would not destroy Jerusalem,
but the Jews should serve Shishak, " that they may
know My service and the service of the kingdoms of
the countries."   When they threw off the yoke of
Jehovah, they sold themselves into a worse bondage.
There is no freedom to be gained by repudiating the
restraints of morality and religion.   If we do not choose
to be the servants of obedience unto righteousness,
our only alternative is to become the slaves " of sin

---

[1] xii. 2-8, 12, peculiar to Chronicles.

unto death." The repentant sinner may return to his true allegiance, and yet he may still be allowed to taste something of the bitterness and humiliation of the bondage of sin. His Shishak may be some evil habit or propensity or special liability to temptation, that is permitted to harass him without destroying his spiritual life. In time the chastening of the Lord works out the peaceable fruits of righteousness, and the Christian is weaned for ever from the unprofitable service of sin.

Unhappily the repentance inspired by trouble and distress is not always real and permanent. Many will humble themselves before the Lord in order to avert imminent ruin, and will forsake Him when the danger has passed away. Apparently Rehoboam soon fell away again into sin, for the final judgment upon him is, " He did that which was evil, because he set not his heart to seek Jehovah."[1] David in his last prayer had asked for a " perfect heart" for Solomon, but he had not been able to secure this blessing for his grandson, and Rehoboam was " the foolishness of the people, one that had no understanding, who turned away the people through his counsel."[2]

Rehoboam was succeeded by his son Abijah, concerning whom we are told in the book of Kings that " he walked in all the sins of his father, which he had done before him ; and his heart was not perfect with Jehovah his God, as the heart of David his father." The chronicler omits this unfavourable verdict ; he does not indeed classify Abijah among the good kings by the usual formal statement that " he did that which was good and right in the eyes of Jehovah," but Abijah delivers a hortatory speech and by Divine assistance

---

[1] xii. 14, peculiar to Chronicles.
[2] Ecclus. xlvii. 23.

obtains a great victory over Jeroboam.   There is not a
suggestion of any evil-doing on the part of Abijah ; and
yet we gather from the history of Asa that in Abijah's
reign the cities of Judah were given up to idolatry, with
all its paraphernalia of " strange altars, high places,
Asherim, and sun-images."   As in the case of Solomon,
so here, the chronicler has sacrificed even the consistency of his own narrative to his care for the reputation
of the house of David.   How the verdict of ancient
history upon Abijah came to be set aside we do not
know.   The charitable work of whitewashing the bad
characters of history has always had an attraction for
enterprising annalists; and Abijah was a more promising
subject than Nero, Tiberius, or Henry VIII.   The
chronicler would rejoice to discover one more good
king of Judah ; but yet why should the record of Abijah's
sins be expunged, while Ahaziah and Amon were still
held up to the execration of posterity ?   Probably the
chronicler was anxious that nothing should mar the
effect of his narrative of Abijah's victory.   If his later
sources had recorded anything equally creditable of
Ahaziah and Amon, he might have ignored the judgment of the book of Kings in their case also.

The section [1] to which the chronicler attaches so
much importance describes a striking episode in the
chronic warfare between Judah and Israel.   Here
Israel is used, as in the older history, to mean the
northern kingdom, and does not denote the spiritual
Israel—*i.e.*, Judah—as in the previous chapter.   This
perplexing variation in the use of the term " Israel "
shows how far Chronicles has departed from the religious
ideas of the book of Kings, and reminds us that the

----

[1] xiii. 3-22, peculiar to Chronicles.

chronicler has only partially and imperfectly assimilated his older material.

Abijah and Jeroboam had each gathered an immense army, but the army of Israel was twice as large as that of Judah : Jeroboam had eight hundred thousand to Abijah's four hundred thousand. Jeroboam advanced, confident in his overwhelming superiority and happy in the belief that Providence sides with the strongest battalions. Abijah, however, was nothing dismayed by the odds against him ; his confidence was in Jehovah. The two armies met in the neighbourhood of Mount Zemaraim, upon which Abijah fixed his camp. Mount Zemaraim was in the hill-country of Ephraim, but its position cannot be determined with certainty ; it was probably near the border of the two kingdoms. Possibly it was the site of the Benjamite city of the same name mentioned in the book of Joshua in close connection with Bethel.[1] If so, we should look for it in the neighbourhood of Bethel, a position which would suit the few indications of place given by the narrative.

Before the battle, Abijah made an effort to induce his enemies to depart in peace. From the vantage-ground of his mountain camp he addressed Jeroboam and his army as Jotham had addressed the men of Shechem from Mount Gerizim.[2] Abijah reminded the rebels—for as such he regarded them—that Jehovah, the God of Israel, had given the kingdom over Israel to David for ever, even to him and to his sons, by a covenant of salt, by a charter as solemn and unalterable as that by which the heave-offerings had been given to the sons of Aaron.[3] The obligation of an Arab host to the guest who had sat at meat with him

---

[1] Josh. xviii. 22.   [2] Judges ix. 8.   [3] Num. xviii. 19.

and eaten of his salt was not more binding than the
Divine decree which had given the throne of Israel to
the house of David. And yet Jeroboam the son of
Nebat had dared to infringe the sacred rights of the
elect dynasty. He, the slave of Solomon, had risen
up and rebelled against his master.

The indignant prince of the house of David not
unnaturally forgets that the disruption was Jehovah's
own work, and that Jeroboam rose up against his
master, not at the instigation of Satan, but by the
command of the prophet Ahijah.[1] The advocates of
sacred causes even in inspired moments are apt to be
one-sided in their statements of fact.

While Abijah is severe upon Jeroboam and his
accomplices and calls them "vain men, sons of Belial,"
he shows a filial tenderness for the memory of Rehoboam. That unfortunate king had been taken at a
disadvantage, when he was young and tender-hearted
and unable to deal sternly with rebels. The tenderness which could threaten to chastise his people with
scorpions must have been of the kind—

"That dared to look on torture and could not look on war";

it only appears in the history in Rehoboam's headlong
flight to Jerusalem. No one, however, will censure
Abijah for taking an unduly favourable view of his
father's character.

But whatever advantage Jeroboam may have found
in his first revolt, Abijah warns him that now he need
not think to withstand the kingdom of Jehovah in the
hands of the sons of David. He is no longer opposed
to an unseasoned youth, but to men who know their
overwhelming advantage. Jeroboam need not think to

---

[1] 2 Chron. x. 15.

supplement and complete his former achievements by adding Judah and Benjamin to his kingdom. Against his superiority of four hundred thousand soldiers Abijah can set a Divine alliance, attested by the presence of priests and Levites and the regular performance of the pentateuchal ritual, whilst the alienation of Israel from Jehovah is clearly shown by the irregular orders of their priests. But let Abijah speak for himself: "Ye be a great multitude, and there are with you the golden calves which Jeroboam made you for gods." Possibly Abijah was able to point to Bethel, where the royal sanctuary of the golden calf was visible to both armies : " Have ye not driven out the priests of Jehovah, the sons of Aaron and the Levites, and made for yourselves priests in heathen fashion ? When any one comes to consecrate himself with a young bullock and seven rams, ye make him a priest of them that are no gods. But as for us, Jehovah is our God, and we have not forsaken Him ; and we have priests, the sons of Aaron, ministering unto Jehovah, and the Levites, doing their appointed work : and they burn unto Jehovah morning and evening burnt offerings and sweet incense : the shewbread also they set in order upon the table that is kept free from all uncleanness ; and we have the candlestick of gold, with its lamps, to burn every evening ; for we observe the ordinances of Jehovah our God ; but ye have forsaken Him. And, behold, God is with us at our head, and His priests, with the trumpets of alarm, to sound an alarm against you. O children of Israel, fight ye not against Jehovah, the God of your fathers ; for ye shall not prosper."

This speech, we are told, "has been much admired. It was well suited to its object, and exhibits correct notions of the theocratical institutions." But, like much other admirable eloquence, in the House of Commons and elsewhere, Abijah's speech had no effect upon those to whom it was addressed.   Jeroboam apparently utilised the interval to plant an ambush in the rear of the Jewish army.

Abijah's speech is unique.   There have been other instances in which commanders have tried to make oratory take the place of arms, and, like Abijah, they have mostly been unsuccessful ; but they have usually appealed to lower motives.   Sennacherib's envoys tried ineffectually to seduce the garrison of Jerusalem from their allegiance to Hezekiah, but they relied on threats of destruction and promises of " a land of corn and wine, a land of bread and vineyards, a land of oil olive and honey."   There is, however, a parallel instance of more successful persuasion.   When Octavian was at war with his fellow-triumvir Lepidus, he made a daring attempt to win over his enemy's army.   He did not address them from the safe elevation of a neighbouring mountain, but rode openly into the hostile camp.   He appealed to the soldiers by motives as lofty as those urged by Abijah, and called upon them to save their country from civil war by deserting Lepidus.   At the moment his appeal failed, and he only escaped with a wound in his breast; but after a while his enemy's soldiers came over to him in detachments, and eventually Lepidus was compelled to surrender to his rival.   But the deserters were not altogether influenced by pure patriotism.   Octavian had carefully prepared the way for his dramatic appearance in the camp of Lepidus, and had used grosser means of persuasion than arguments addressed to patriotic feeling.

Another instance of a successful appeal to a hostile

force is found in the history of the first Napoleon, when he was marching on Paris after his return from Elba.   Near Grenoble he was met by a body of royal troops.   He at once advanced to the front, and exposing his breast, exclaimed to the opposing ranks, "Here is your emperor ; if any one would kill me, let him fire."   The detachment, which had been sent to arrest his progress, at once deserted to their old commander. Abijah's task was less hopeful : the soldiers whom Octavian and Napoleon won over had known these generals as lawful commanders of Roman and French armies respectively, but Abijah could not appeal to any old associations in the minds of Jeroboam's army ; the Israelites were animated by ancient tribal jealousies, and Jeroboam was made of sterner stuff than Lepidus or Louis XVIII.   Abijah's appeal is a monument of his humanity, faith, and devotion ; and if it failed to influence the enemy, doubtless served to inspirit his own army.

At first, however, things went hardly with Judah. They were outgeneralled as well as outnumbered ; Jeroboam's main body attacked them in front, and the ambush assailed their rear.   Like the men of Ai, "when Judah looked back, behold, the battle was before and behind them."   But Jehovah, who fought against Ai, was fighting for Judah, and they cried unto Jehovah ; and then, as at Jericho, "the men of Judah gave a shout, and when they shouted, God smote Jeroboam and all Israel before Abijah and Judah." The rout was complete, and was accompanied by terrible slaughter.   No fewer than five hundred thousand Israelites were slain by the men of Judah.   The latter pressed their advantage, and took the neighbouring city of Bethel and other Israelite towns.   For the time

Israel was " brought under," and did not recover from its tremendous losses during the three years of Abijah's reign. As for Jeroboam, Jehovah smote him, and he died ; but " Abijah waxed mighty, and took unto himself fourteen wives, and begat twenty-and-two sons and sixteen daughters."[1] His history closes with the record of these proofs of Divine favour, and he " slept with his fathers, and they buried him in the city of David, and Asa his son reigned in his stead."

The lesson which the chronicler intends to teach by his narrative is obviously the importance of ritual, not the importance of ritual apart from the worship of the true God ; he emphasises the presence of Jehovah with Judah, in contrast to the Israelite worship of calves and those that are no gods. The chronicler dwells upon the maintenance of the legitimate priesthood and the prescribed ritual as the natural expression and clear proof of the devotion of the men of Judah to their God.

It may help us to realise the significance of Abijah's speech, if we try to construct an appeal in the same spirit for a Catholic general in the Thirty Years' War addressing a hostile Protestant army. Imagine Wallenstein or Tilly, moved by some unwonted spirit of pious oratory, addressing the soldiers of Gustavus Adolphus :—

" We have a pope who sits in Peter's chair, bishops and priests ministering unto the Lord, in the true apostolical succession. The sacrifice of the Mass is daily offered ; matins, laud, vespers, and compline are all duly celebrated ; our churches are fragrant with incense and glorious with stained glass and images ; we have crucifixes, and lamps, and candles ; and

---

[1] This verse must of course be understood to give his whole family history, and not merely that of his three years' reign.

our priests are fitly clothed in ecclesiastical vestments ; for we observe the traditions of the Church, but ye have forsaken the Divine order. Behold, God is with us at our head ; and we have banners blessed by the Pope. O ye Swedes, ye fight against God; ye shall not prosper."

As Protestants we may find it difficult to sympathise with the feelings of a devout Romanist or even with those of a faithful observer of the complicated Mosaic ritual. We could not construct so close a parallel to Abijah's speech in terms of any Protestant order of service, and yet the objections which any modern denomination feels to departures from its own forms of worship rest on the same principles as those of Abijah. In the abstract the speech teaches two main lessons : the importance of an official and duly accredited ministry and of a suitable and authoritative ritual. These principles are perfectly general, and are not confined to what is usually known as sacerdotalism and ritualism. Every Church has in practice some official ministry. even those Churches that profess to owe their separate existence to the necessity for protesting against an official ministry. Men whose chief occupation is to denounce priestcraft may themselves be saturated with the sacerdotal spirit. Every Church, too, has its ritual. The silence of a Friends' meeting is as much a rite as the most elaborate genuflexion before a highly ornamented altar. To regard either the absence or presence of rites as essential is equally ritualistic. The man who leaves his wonted place of worship because "Amen" is sung at the end of a hymn is as bigoted a ritualist as his brother who dare not pass an altar without crossing himself. Let us then consider the chronicler s two principles in this broad sense. The official ministry of Israel consisted of the priests and Levites, and the chronicler counted it a proof of the piety of the Jews that they adhered to this ministry and did not admit to the priesthood any one who could bring a young bullock and seven rams. The alternative was not between a hereditary priesthood and one open to any aspirant with special spiritual qualifications, but between a duly trained and qualified ministry on the one hand and a motley crew of the forerunners of Simon Magus on the other. It is impossible not to sympathise with the chronicler. To begin with, the property qualification was too low. If livings are to be purchased at all, they should bear a price commensurate with the dignity and responsibility of the sacred office. A mere entrance fee, so to speak, of a young bullock and seven rams must have flooded Jeroboam's priesthood with a host of adventurers, to whom the assumption of the office was a matter of social or commercial speculation. The private adventure system of providing for the ministry of the word scarcely tends to either the dignity or the efficiency of the Church. But, in any case, it is not desirable that mere worldly gifts, money, social position, or even intellect should be made the sole passports to Christian service; even the traditions and education of a hereditary priesthood would be more probable channels of spiritual qualifications.

Another point that the chronicler objects to in Jeroboam's priests is the want of any other than a property qualification. Any one who chose could be a priest. Such a system combined what might seem opposite vices. It preserved an official ministry; these self-appointed priests formed a clerical order; and yet it gave no guarantee whatever of either fitness or devotion. The chronicler, on the other hand, by the importance he attaches to the Levitical priesthood, recognises the necessity of an official ministry, but is anxious that it should be guarded with jealous care against the intrusion of unsuitable persons. A conclusive argument for an official ministry is to be found in its formal adoption by most Churches and its uninvited appearance in the rest. We should not now be contented with the safeguards against unsuitable ministers to be found in hereditary succession ; the system of the Pentateuch would be neither acceptable nor possible in the nineteenth century : and yet, if it had been perfectly administered, the Jewish priesthood would have been worthy of its high office, nor were the times ripe for the substitution of any better system. Many of the considerations which justify hereditary succession in a constitutional monarchy might be adduced in defence of a hereditary priesthood. Even now, without any pressure of law or custom, there is a certain tendency towards hereditary succession in the ministerial office. It would be easy to name distinguished ministers who were inspired for the high calling by their fathers' devoted service, and who received an invaluable preparation for their life-work from the Christian enthusiasm of a clerical household. The clerical ancestry of the Wesleys is only one among many illustrations of an inherited genius for the ministry.

But though the best method of obtaining a suitable ministry varies with changing circumstances, the chronicler's main principle is of permanent and universal application. The Church has always felt a just concern that the official representatives of its faith and order should commend themselves to every man's conscience in the sight of God. The prophet needs neither testimonials nor official status : the word of the Lord can have free course without either ; but the appointment or election to ecclesiastical office entrusts the official with the honour of the Church and in a measure of its Master.

The chronicler's other principle is the importance of a suitable and authoritative ritual. We have already noticed that any order of service that is fixed by the constitution or custom of a Church involves the principle of ritual. Abijah's speech does not insist that only the established ritual should be tolerated; such questions had not come within the chronicler's horizon. The merit of Judah lay in possessing and practising a legitimate ritual, that is to say in observing the Pauline injunction to do all things decently and in order. The present generation is not inclined to enforce any very stringent obedience to Paul's teaching, and finds it difficult to sympathise with Abijah's enthusiasm for the symbolism of worship. But men to-day are not radically different from the chronicler's contemporaries, and it is as legitimate to appeal to spiritual sensibility through the eye as through the ear ; architecture and decoration are neither more nor less spiritual than an attractive voice and impressive elocution. Novelty and variety have, or should have, their legitimate place in public worship ; but the Church has its obligations to those who have more regular spiritual wants. Most of us find much of the helpfulness of public worship in the influence of old and familiar spiritual associations, which can only be maintained by a measure of per- manence and fixity in Divine service. The symbolism of the Lord's Supper never loses its freshness, and yet it is restful because familiar and impressive because ancient. On the other hand, the maintenance of this ritual is a constant testimony to the continuity of Christian life and faith. Moreover, in this rite the great bulk of Christendom finds the outward and visible sign of its unity.

Ritual, too, has its negative value. By observing the Levitical ordinances the Jews were protected from the vagaries of any ambitious owner of a young bullock and seven rams. While we grant liberty to all to use the form of worship in which they find most spiritual profit, we need to have Churches whose ritual will be comparatively fixed. Christians who find themselves most helped by the more quiet and regular methods of devotion naturally look to a settled order of service to protect them from undue and distracting excitement.

In spite of the wide interval that separates the modern Church from Judaism, we can still discern a unity of principle, and are glad to confirm the judgment of Christian experience from the lessons of an older and different dispensation. But we should do injustice to the chronicler's teaching if we forgot that for his own times his teaching was capable of much more definite and forcible application. Christianity and Islam have purified religious worship throughout Europe, America, and a large portion of Asia. We are no longer tempted by the cruel and loathsome rites of heathenism. The Jews knew the wild extravagance, gross immorality, and ruthless cruelty of Phœnician and Syrian worship. If we had lived in the chronicler's age and had shared his experience of idolatrous rites, we should have also shared his enthusiasm for the pure and lofty ritual of the Pentateuch. We should have regarded it as a Divine barrier between Israel and the abominations of heathenism, and should have been jealous for its strict observance.

22

CHAPTER III

ASA : DIVINE RETRIBUTION

2 CHRON. xiv.-xvi.

ABIJAH, dying, as far as we can gather from Chronicles, in the odour of sanctity, was succeeded by his son Asa. The chronicler's history of Asa is much fuller than that which is given in the book of Kings. The older narrative is used as a framework into which material from later sources is freely inserted. The beginning of the new reign was singularly promising. Abijah had been a very David, he had fought the battles of Jehovah, and had assured the security and independence of Judah. Asa, like Solomon, entered into the peaceful enjoyment of his predecessor's exertions in the field. "In his days the land was quiet ten years," as in the days when the judges had delivered Israel, and he was able to exhort his people to prudent effort by reminding them that Jehovah had given them rest on every side.[1] This interval of quiet was used for both religious reform and military precautions.[2] The high places and heathen idols and symbols which had somehow survived Abijah's zeal for the Mosaic ritual were swept away, and Judah was commanded to

---

[1] xiv. 1, 7, peculiar to Chronicles.
[2] xiv. 3-9, peculiar to Chronicles.

seek Jehovah and observe the Law; and he built
fortresses with towers, and gates, and bars, and
raised a great army " that bare bucklers and spears,"
—no mere hasty levy of half-armed peasants with
scythes and axes. The mighty array surpassed even
Abijah's great muster of four hundred thousand from
Judah and Benjamin : there were five hundred and
eighty thousand men, three hundred thousand out of
Judah that bare bucklers and spears and two hundred
and eighty thousand out of Benjamin that bare shields
and drew bows. The great muster of Benjamites under
Asa is in striking contrast to the meagre tale of six
hundred warriors that formed the whole strength of
Benjamin after its disastrous defeat in the days of the
judges ; and the splendid equipment of this mighty host
shows the rapid progress of the nation from the
desperate days of Shamgar and Jael or even of Saul's
early reign, when "there was neither shield nor spear
seen among forty thousand in Israel."

These references to buildings, especially fortresses,
to military stores and the vast numbers of Jewish and
Israelite armies, form a distinct class amongst the
additions made by the chronicler to the material
taken from the book of Kings. They are found in
the narratives of the reigns of David, Rehoboam,
Jehoshaphat, Uzziah, Jotham, Manasseh, in fact in
the reigns of nearly all the good kings ; Manasseh's
building was done after he had turned from his evil
ways.[1] Hezekiah and Josiah were too much occupied
with sacred festivals on the one hand and hostile
invaders on the other to have much leisure for building,

---

[1] I Chron. xii., etc. ; 2 Chron. xi. 5 ff., xvii. 12 ff., xxvi. 9 ff. xxvii.
4 ff., xxxiii. 14.

and it would not have been in keeping with Solomon's character as the prince of peace to have laid stress on his arsenals and armies. Otherwise the chronicler, living at a time when the warlike resources of Judah were of the slightest, was naturally interested in these reminiscences of departed glory; and the Jewish provincials would take a pride in relating these pieces of antiquarian information about their native towns, much as the servants of old manor-houses delight to point out the wing which was added by some famous Cavalier or by some Jacobite squire.

Asa's warlike preparations were possibly intended, like those of the Triple Alliance, to enable him to maintain peace; but if so, their sequel did not illustrate the maxim, "Si vis pacem, para bellum." The rumour of his vast armaments reached a powerful monarch: "Zerah the Ethiopian."[1] The vagueness of this description is doubtless due to the remoteness of the chronicler from the times he is describing. Zerah has sometimes been identified with Shishak's successor, Osorkon I., the second king of the twenty-second Egyptian dynasty. Zerah felt that Asa's great army was a standing menace to the surrounding princes, and undertook the task of destroying this new military power: "He came out against them." Numerous as Asa's forces were, they still left him dependent upon Jehovah, for the enemy were even more numerous and better equipped. Zerah led to a battle an army of a million men, supported by three hundred war chariots. With this enormous host he came to Mareshah, at the foot of the Judæan highlands, in a direction south-west of Jerusalem. In spite of the inferiority of his army, Asa came out to

---

[1] xiv. 9-15.

meet him; "and they set the battle in array in the
valley of Zephathah at Mareshah." Like Abijah, Asa
felt that, with his Divine Ally, he need not be afraid
of the odds against him even when they could be
counted by hundreds of thousands. Trusting in
Jehovah, he had taken the field against the enemy ;
and now at the decisive moment he made a confident
appeal for help : " Jehovah, there is none beside Thee
to help between the mighty and him that hath no
strength." Five hundred and eighty thousand men
seemed nothing compared to the host arrayed against
them, and outnumbering them in the proportion of
nearly two to one. " Help us, Jehovah our God ; for
we rely on Thee, and in Thy name are we come against
this multitude. Jehovah, Thou art our God; let not
man prevail against Thee."

Jehovah justified the trust reposed in Him. He smote
the Ethiopians, and they fled towards the south-west
in the direction of Egypt; and Asa and his army
pursued them as far as Gerar, with fearful slaughter,
so that of Zerah's million followers not one remained
alive.[1] Of course this statement is hyperbolical. The
carnage was enormous, and no living enemies remained
in sight. Apparently Gerar and the neighbouring
cities had aided Zerah in his advance and attempted
to shelter the fugitives from Mareshah. Paralysed
with fear of Jehovah, whose avenging wrath had
been so terribly manifested, these cities fell an easy
prey to the victorious Jews. They smote and spoiled
all the cities about Gerar, and reaped a rich harvest,

---

[1] So R.V. marg. ; R.V. text (with which A.V. is in substantial agreement) : "There fell of the Ethiopians so many that they could not
recover themselves"; *i.e.*, the routed army were never able to rally.

"for there was much spoil in them." It seems that the nomad tribes of the southern wilderness had also in some way identified themselves with the invaders; Asa attacked them in their turn. "They smote also the tents of cattle"; and as the wealth of these tribes lay in their flocks and herds, "they carried away sheep in abundance and camels, and returned to Jerusalem."

This victory is closely parallel to that of Abijah over Jeroboam. In both the numbers of the armies are reckoned by hundreds of thousands; and the hostile host outnumbers the army of Judah in the one case by exactly two to one, in the other by nearly that proportion: in both the king of Judah trusts with calm assurance to the assistance of Jehovah, and Jehovah smites the enemy; the Jews then massacre the defeated army and spoil or capture the neighbouring cities.

These victories over superior numbers may easily be paralleled or surpassed by numerous striking examples from secular history. The odds were greater at Agincourt, where at least sixty thousand French were defeated by not more than twenty thousand Englishmen; at Marathon the Greeks routed a Persian army ten times as numerous as their own; in India English generals have defeated innumerable hordes of native warriors, as when Wellesley—

"Against the myriads of Assaye
Clashed with his fiery few and won."

For the most part victorious generals have been ready to acknowledge the succouring arm of the God of battles. Shakespeare's Henry V. after Agincourt speaks altogether in the spirit of Asa's prayer:—

> "... O God, Thy arm was here;
> And not to us, but to Thy arm alone,
> Ascribe we all. . . . . .
> . . . . Take it, God,
> For it is only Thine."

When the small craft that made up Elizabeth's fleet defeated the huge Spanish galleons and galleasses, and the storms of the northern seas finished the work of destruction, the grateful piety of Protestant England felt that its foes had been destroyed by the breath of the Lord; "Afflavit Deus et dissipantur."

The principle that underlies such feelings is quite independent of the exact proportions of opposing armies. The victories of inferior numbers in a righteous cause are the most striking, but not the most significant, illustrations of the superiority of moral to material force. In the wider movements of international politics we may find even more characteristic instances. It is true of nations as well as of individuals that—

> "The Lord killeth and maketh alive;
> He bringeth down to the grave and bringeth up:
> The Lord maketh poor and maketh rich;
> He bringeth low, He also lifteth up:
> He raiseth up the poor out of the dust,
> He lifteth up the needy from the dunghill,
> To make them sit with princes
> And inherit the throne of glory."

Italy in the eighteenth century seemed as hopelessly divided as Israel under the judges, and Greece as completely enslaved to the "unspeakable Turk" as the Jews to Nebuchadnezzar; and yet, destitute as they were of any material resources, these nations had at their disposal great moral forces : the memory of ancient greatness and the sentiment of nationality; and to-day Italy can count hundreds of thousands like the chronicler's Jewish kings, and Greece builds her fortresses by land and her ironclads to command the sea. The Lord has fought for Israel.

But the principle has a wider application. A little examination of the more obscure and complicated movements of social life will show moral forces everywhere overcoming and controlling the apparently irresistible material forces opposed to them. The English and American pioneers of the movements for the abolition of slavery had to face what seemed an impenetrable phalanx of powerful interests and influences; but probably any impartial student of history would have foreseen the ultimate triumph of a handful of earnest men over all the wealth and political power of the slave-owners. The moral forces at the disposal of the abolitionists were obviously irresistible. But the soldier in the midst of smoke and tumult may still be anxious and despondent at the very moment when the spectator sees clearly that the battle is won ; and the most earnest Christian workers sometimes falter when they realise the vast and terrible forces that fight against them. At such times we are both rebuked and encouraged by the simple faith of the chronicler in the overruling power of God.

It may be objected that if victory were to be secured by Divine intervention, there was no need to muster five hundred and eighty thousand men or indeed any army at all. If in any and every case God disposes, what need is there for the devotion to His service of our best strength, and energy, and culture, or of any human effort at all ? A wholesome spiritual instinct leads the chronicler to emphasise the great preparations of Abijah and Asa. We have no right to look for Divine co-operation till we have done our best ; we are not to

sit with folded hands and expect a complete salvation
to be wrought for us, and then to continue as idle
spectators of God's redemption of mankind : we are
to tax our resources to the utmost to gather our
hundreds of thousands of soldiers ; we are to work out
our own salvation with fear and trembling, for it is God
that worketh in us both to will and to do of His good
pleasure.

This principle may be put in another way. Even
to the hundreds of thousands the Divine help is still
necessary. The leaders of great hosts are as dependent
upon Divine help as Jonathan and his armour-bearer
fighting single-handed against a Philistine garrison, or
David arming himself with a sling and stone against
Goliath of Gath. The most competent Christian
worker in the prime of his spiritual strength needs
grace as much as the untried youth making his first
venture in the Lord's service.

At this point we meet with another of the chronicler's
obvious self-contradictions. At the beginning of the
narrative of Asa's reign we are told that the king did
away with the high places and the symbols of idolatrous
worship, and that, because Judah had thus sought
Jehovah, He gave them rest. The deliverance from
Zerah is another mark of Divine favour. And yet in
the fifteenth chapter Asa, in obedience to prophetic
admonition, takes away the abominations from his
dominions, as if there had been no previous reformation,
but we are told that the high places were not taken out
of Israel. The context would naturally suggest that
Israel here means Asa's kingdom, as the true Israel of
God ; but as the verse is borrowed from the book of
Kings, and " out of Israel " is an editorial addition
made by the chronicler, it is probably intended to

harmonise the borrowed verse with the chronicler's previous statement that Asa did away with the high places. If so, we must understand that Israel means the northern kingdom, from which the high places had not been removed, though Judah had been purged from these abominations. But here, as often elsewhere, Chronicles taken alone affords no explanation of its inconsistencies.

Again, in Asa's first reformation he commanded Judah to seek Jehovah and to do the Law and the commandments; and accordingly Judah sought the Lord. Moreover, Abijah, about seventeen years [1] before Asa's second reformation, made it his special boast that Judah had not forsaken Jehovah, but had priests ministering unto Jehovah, "the sons of Aaron and the Levites in their work." During Rehoboam's reign of seventeen years Jehovah was duly honoured for the first three years, and again after Shishak's invasion in the fifth year of Rehoboam. So that for the previous thirty or forty years the due worship of Jehovah had only been interrupted by occasional lapses into disobedience. But now the prophet Oded holds before this faithful people the warning example of the "long seasons" when Israel was without the true God, and without a teaching priest, and without law. And yet previously Chronicles supplies an unbroken list of high-priests from Aaron downwards. In response to Oded's appeal, the king and people set about the work of reformation as if they had tolerated some such neglect of God, the priests, and the Law as the prophet had described.

Another minor discrepancy is found in the statement

---

[1] The second reformation is dated early in Asa's fifteenth year, and Abijah only reigned three years.

that " the heart of Asa was perfect all his days "; this
is reproduced verbatim from the book of Kings.
Immediately afterwards the chronicler relates the evil
doings of Asa in the closing years of his reign.

Such contradictions render it impossible to give a
complete and continuous exposition of Chronicles that
shall be at the same time consistent. Nevertheless
they are not without their value for the Christian
student. They afford evidence of the good faith of the
chronicler. His contradictions are clearly due to his
use of independent and discrepant sources, and not to
any tampering with the statements of his authorities.
They are also an indication that the chronicler attaches
much more importance to spiritual edification than to
historical accuracy. When he seeks to set before his
contemporaries the higher nature and better life of the
great national heroes, and thus to provide them with an
ideal of kingship, he is scrupulously and painfully
careful to remove everything that would weaken the
force of the lesson which he is trying to teach ; but he is
comparatively indifferent to accuracy of historical detail.
When his authorities contradict each other as to the
number or the date of Asa's reformations, or even the
character of his later years, he does not hesitate to
place the two narratives side by side and practically to
draw lessons from both. The work of the chronicler
and its presence with the Pentateuch and the Synoptic
Gospels in the sacred canon imply an emphatic declaration of the judgment of the Spirit and the Church
that detailed historical accuracy is not a necessary
consequence of inspiration. In expounding this second
narrative of a reformation by Asa, we shall make no
attempt at complete harmony with the rest of Chronicles ;
any inconsistency between the exposition here and

elsewhere will simply arise from a faithful adherence to our text.

The occasion then of Asa's second reformation[1] was as follows: Asa was returning in triumph from his great defeat of Zerah, bringing with him substantial fruits of victory in the shape of abundant spoil. Wealth and power had proved a snare to David and Rehoboam, and had involved them in grievous sin. Asa might also have succumbed to the temptations of prosperity; but, by a special Divine grace not vouchsafed to his predecessors, he was guarded against danger by a prophetic warning. At the very moment when Asa might have expected to be greeted by the acclamations of the inhabitants of Jerusalem, when the king would be elate with the sense of Divine favour, military success, and popular applause, the prophet's admonition checked the undue exaltation which might have hurried Asa into presumptuous sin. Asa and his people were not to presume upon their privilege; its continuance was altogether dependent upon their continued obedience: if they fell into sin, the rewards of their former loyalty would vanish like fairy gold. " Hear ye me, Asa, and all Judah and Benjamin: Jehovah is with you while ye be with Him; and if ye seek Him, He will be found of you; but if ye forsake Him, He will forsake you." This lesson was enforced from the earlier history of Israel. The following verses are virtually a summary of the history of the judges :—

" Now for long seasons Israel was without the true God, and without teaching priest, and without law."

---

[1] xv., based upon I Kings xv. 13-15, but the great bulk of the chapter is peculiar to Chronicles; the original passage from Kings is reproduced, with slight changes in vv. 16-18.

Judges tells how again and again Israel fell away from Jehovah. "But when in their distress they turned unto Jehovah, the God of Israel, and sought Him, He was found of them."

Oded's address is very similar to another and somewhat fuller summary of the history of the judges, contained in Samuel's farewell to the people, in which he reminded them how when they forgot Jehovah, their God, He sold them into the hand of their enemies, and when they cried unto Jehovah, He sent Zerubbabel, and Barak, and Jephthah, and Samuel, and delivered them out of the hand of their enemies on every side, and they dwelt in safety.[1] Oded proceeds to other characteristics of the period of the judges : "There was no peace to him that went out, nor to him that came in ; but great vexations were upon all the inhabitants of the lands. And they were broken in pieces, nation against nation and city against city, for God did vex them with all adversity."

Deborah's song records great vexations : the highways were unoccupied, and the travellers walked through by-ways ; the rulers ceased in Israel ; Gideon "threshed wheat by the winepress to hide it from the Midianites." The breaking of nation against nation and city against city will refer to the destruction of Succoth and Penuel by Gideon, the sieges of Shechem and Thebez by Abimelech, the massacre of the Ephraimites by Jephthah, and the civil war between Benjamin and the rest of Israel and the consequent destruction of Jabesh-gilead.[2]

---

[1] 1 Sam. xii. 9-11. "Barak" with LXX. and Peshito ; Masoretic text has "Bedan."

[2] Judges v. 6, 7 ; vi. 11 ; viii. 15-17 ; ix. ; xii. 1-7 ; xx. ; xxi.

"But," said Oded, "be ye strong, and let not your hands be slack, for your work shall be rewarded." Oded implies that abuses were prevalent in Judah which might spread and corrupt the whole people, so as to draw down upon them the wrath of God and plunge them into all the miseries of the times of the judges. These abuses were wide-spread, supported by powerful interests and numerous adherents. The queen-mother, one of the most important personages in an Eastern state, was herself devoted to heathen observ-ances. Their suppression needed courage, energy, and pertinacity; but if they were resolutely grappled with, Jehovah would reward the efforts of His servants with success, and Judah would enjoy prosperity. Accordingly Asa took courage and put away the abominations out of Judah and Benjamin and the cities he held in Ephraim. The abominations were the idols and all the cruel and obscene accompaniments of heathen worship.[1] In the prophet's exhortation to be strong, and not be slack, and in the corresponding state-ment that Asa took courage, we have a hint for all reformers. Neither Oded nor Asa underrated the serious nature of the task before them. They counted the cost, and with open eyes and full knowledge con-fronted the evil they meant to eradicate. The full significance of the chronicler's language is only seen when we remember what preceded the prophet's appeal to Asa. The captain of half a million soldiers, the conqueror of a million Ethiopians with three hundred chariots, has to take courage before he can bring himself to put away the abominations out of his own dominions. Military machinery is more readily created

---

[1] Cf. 1 Kings xv. 12.

than national righteousness; it is easier to slaughter
one's neighbours than to let light into the dark places
that are full of the habitations of cruelty; and vigorous
foreign policy is a poor substitute for good administration. The principle has its application to the individual.
The beam in our own eye seems more difficult to extract
than the mote in our brother's, and a man often needs
more moral courage to reform himself than to denounce
other people's sins or urge them to accept salvation.
Most ministers could confirm from their own experience
Portia's saying, "I can easier teach twenty what were
good to be done than be one of the twenty to follow
mine own teaching."

Asa's reformation was constructive as well as
destructive; the toleration of "abominations" had
diminished the zeal of the people for Jehovah, and
even the altar of Jehovah before the porch of the Temple
had suffered from neglect: it was now renewed, and
Asa assembled the people for a great festival. Under
Rehoboam many pious Israelites had left the northern
kingdom to dwell where they could freely worship at
the Temple; under Asa there was a new migration,
"for they fell to him out of Israel in abundance when
they saw that Jehovah his God was with him." And
so it came about that in the great assembly which Asa
gathered together at Jerusalem not only Judah and
Benjamin, but also Ephraim, Manasseh, and Simeon,
were represented. The chronicler has already told us
that after the return from the Captivity some of the
children of Ephraim and Manasseh dwelt at Jerusalem
with the children of Judah and Benjamin,[1] and he is
always careful to note any settlement of members of

---

1 Chron. ix. 3.

the ten tribes in Judah or any acquisition of northern territory by the kings of Judah. Such facts illustrated his doctrine that Judah was the true spiritual Israel, the real δωδεκάφυλον, or twelve-tribed whole, of the chosen people.

Asa's festival was held in the third month of his fifteenth year, the month Sivan, corresponding roughly to our June. The Feast of Weeks, at which first-fruits were offered, fell in this month; and his festival was probably a special celebration of this feast. The sacrifice of seven hundred oxen and seven thousand sheep out of the spoil taken from the Ethiopians and their allies might be considered a kind of first-fruits. The people pledged themselves most solemnly to permanent obedience to Jehovah; this festival and its offerings were to be first-fruits or earnest of future loyalty. "They entered into a covenant to seek Jehovah, the God of their fathers, with all their heart and with all their soul; . . . they sware unto Jehovah with a loud voice, and with shouting, and with trumpets, and with cornets." The observance of this covenant was not to be left to the uncertainties of individual loyalty; the community were to be on their guard against offenders, Achans who might trouble Israel. According to the stern law of the Pentateuch,[1] "whosoever would not seek Jehovah, the God of Israel, should be put to death, whether small or great, whether man or woman." The seeking of Jehovah, so far as it could be enforced by penalties, must have consisted in external observances; and the usual proof that a man did not seek Jehovah would be found in his seeking other gods and taking part in heathen rites. Such

---

[1] Exod. xxii. 20; Deut. xiii. 5, 9, 15.

apostacy was not merely an ecclesiastical offence : it involved immorality and a falling away from patriotism. The pious Jew could no more tolerate heathenism than we could tolerate in England religions that sanctioned polygamy or suttee.

Having thus entered into covenant with Jehovah, "all Judan rejoiced at their oath because they had sworn with all their heart, and sought Him with their whole desire." At the beginning, no doubt, they, like their king, "took courage"; they addressed themselves with reluctance and apprehension to an unwelcome and hazardous enterprise. They now rejoiced over the Divine grace that had inspired their efforts and been manifested in their courage and devotion, over the happy issue of their enterprise, and over the universal enthusiasm for Jehovah; and He set the seal of His approval upon their gladness, He was found of them, and Jehovah gave them rest round about, so that there was no more war for twenty years : unto the thirty-fifth year of Asa's reign. It is an unsavoury task to put away abominations : many foul nests of unclean birds are disturbed in the process; men would not choose to have this particular cross laid upon them, but only those who take up their cross and follow Christ can hope to enter into the joy of the Lord.

The narrative of this second reformation is completed by the addition of details borrowed from the book of Kings. The chronicler next recounts how in the thirty-sixth year of Asa's reign Baasha began to fortify Ramah as an outpost against Judah, but was forced to abandon his undertaking by the intervention of the Syrian king, Benhadad, whom Asa hired with his own treasures and those of the Temple; whereupon Asa carried off Baasha's stones and timber and built Geba

23

and Mizpah as Jewish outposts against Israel. With
the exception of the date and a few minor changes, the
narrative so far is taken verbatim from the book of
Kings. The chronicler, like the author of the priestly
document of the Pentateuch, was anxious to provide
his readers with an exact and complete system of
chronology; he was the Ussher or Clinton of his
generation. His date of the war against Baasha is
probably based upon an interpretation of the source
used for chap. xv.; the first reformation secured a
rest of ten years, the second and more thorough
reformation a rest exactly twice as long as the first.
In the interest of these chronological references, the
chronicler has sacrificed a statement twice repeated in
the book of Kings: that there was war between Asa
and Baasha all their days. As Baasha came to the
throne in Asa's third year, the statement of the book of
Kings would have seemed to contradict the chronicler's
assertion that there was no war from the fifteenth to
the thirty-fifth year of Asa's reign.[1]

After his victory over Zerah, Asa received a Divine
message[2] which somewhat checked the exuberance of
his triumph; a similar message awaited him after his
successful expedition to Ramah. By Oded Jehovah
had warned Asa, but now He commissioned Hanani
the seer to pronounce a sentence of condemnation.
The ground of the sentence was that Asa had not
relied on Jehovah, but on the king of Syria.

Here the chronicler echoes one of the key-notes of
the great prophets. Isaiah had protested against the
alliance which Ahaz concluded with Assyria in order to
obtain assistance against the united onset of Rezin,

---

[1] I Kings xv. 16, 32, 33.   [2] xvi. 7-10, peculiar to Chronicles.

king of Syria, and Pekah, king of Israel, and had predicted that Jehovah would bring upon **Ahaz,** his people, and his dynasty days that had not come since the disruption, even the king of Assyria.[1] When this prediction was fulfilled, and the thundercloud of Assyrian invasion darkened all the land of Judah, the **Jews,** in their lack of faith, looked to Egypt for deliverance ; and again Isaiah denounced the foreign alliance : "Woe to them that go down to Egypt for help, . . . but they look not unto the Holy One of Israel, neither seek Jehovah ; . . . the strength of Pharaoh shall be your shame, and the trust in the shadow of Egypt your confusion."[2] So Jeremiah in his turn protested against a revival of the Egyptian alliance : " Thou shalt be ashamed of Egypt also, as thou wast ashamed of Assyria."[3]

In their successive calamities the Jews could derive no comfort from a study of previous history ; the pretext upon which each of their oppressors had intervened in the affairs of Palestine had been an invitation from Judah. In their trouble they had sought a remedy worse than the disease ; the consequences of this political quackery had always demanded still more desperate and fatal medicines. Freedom from the border raids of the Ephraimites was secured at the price of the ruthless devastations of Hazael ; deliverance from Rezin only led to the wholesale massacres and spoliation of Sennacherib. Foreign alliance was an opiate that had to be taken in continually increasing doses, till at last it caused the death of the patient.

Nevertheless these are not the lessons which the seer seeks to impress upon Asa. Hanani takes a

---

[1] Isa. vii. 17.   [2] Isa. xxxi. 1 ; xxx. 3.   [3] Jer. ii. 36.

loftier tone. He does not tell him that his unholy alliance with Benhadad was the first of a chain of circumstances that would end in the ruin of Judah. Few generations are greatly disturbed by the prospect of the ruin of their country in the distant future : "After us the Deluge." Even the pious king Hezekiah, when told of the coming captivity of Judah, found much comfort in the thought that there should be peace and truth in his days. After the manner of the prophets, Hanani's message is concerned with his own times. To his large faith the alliance with Syria presented itself chiefly as the loss of a great opportunity. Asa had deprived himself of the privilege of fighting with Syria, whereby Jehovah would have found fresh occasion to manifest His infinite power and His gracious favour towards Judah. Had there been no alliance with Judah, the restless and warlike king of Syria might have joined Baasha to attack Asa ; another million of the heathen and other hundreds of their chariots would have been destroyed by the resistless might of the Lord of Hosts. And yet, in spite of the great object-lesson he had received in the defeat of Zerah, Asa had not thought of Jehovah as his Ally. He had forgotten the all-observing, all-controlling providence of Jehovah, and had thought it necessary to supplement the Divine protection by hiring a heathen king with the treasures of the Temple ; and yet "the eyes of Jehovah run to and fro throughout the whole earth, to show Himself strong in behalf of them whose heart is perfect toward Him." With this thought, that the eyes of Jehovah run to and fro throughout the earth, Zechariah [1] comforted the Jews in the dark days

---

[1] Zech. iv. 10,

between the Return and the rebuilding of the Temple. Possibly during Asa's twenty years of tranquillity his faith had become enfeebled for want of any severe discipline. It is only with a certain reserve that we can venture to pray that the Lord will "take from our lives the strain and stress." The discipline of helplessness and dependence preserves the consciousness of God's loving providence. The resources of Divine grace are not altogether intended for our personal comfort; we are to tax them to the utmost, in the assurance that God will honour all our drafts upon His treasury. The great opportunities of twenty years of peace and prosperity were not given to Asa to lay up funds with which to bribe a heathen king, and then, with this reinforcement of his accumulated resources to accomplish the mighty enterprise of stealing Baasha's stones and timber and building the walls of a couple of frontier fortresses. With such a history and such opportunities behind him, Asa should have felt himself competent, with Jehovah's help, to deal with both Baasha and Benhadad, and should have had courage to confront them both.

Sin like Asa's has been the supreme apostacy of the Church in all her branches and through all her generations : Christ has been denied, not by lack of devotion, but by want of faith. Champions of the truth, reformers and guardians of the Temple, like Asa, have been eager to attach to their holy cause the cruel prejudices of ignorance and folly, the greed and vindictiveness of selfish men. They have feared lest these potent forces should be arrayed amongst the enemies of the Church and her Master. Sects and parties have eagerly contested the privilege of counselling a profligate prince how he should satisfy his thirst for blood and exercise his wanton and brutal insolence ; the Church has countenanced almost every iniquity and striven to quench by persecution every new revelation of the Spirit, in order to conciliate vested interests and established authorities. It has even been suggested that national Churches and great national vices were so intimately allied that their supporters were content that they should stand or fall together. On the other hand, the advocates of reform have not been slow to appeal to popular jealousy and to aggravate the bitterness of social feuds. To Hanani the seer had come the vision of a larger and purer faith, that would rejoice to see the cause of Satan supported by all the evil passions and selfish interests that are his natural allies. He was assured that the greater the host of Satan, the more signal and complete would be Jehovah's triumph. If we had his faith, we should not be anxious to bribe Satan to cast out Satan, but should come to understand that the full muster of hell assailing us in front is less dangerous than a few companies of diabolic mercenaries in our own array. In the former case the overthrow of the powers of darkness is more certain and more complete.

The evil consequences of Asa's policy were not confined to the loss of a great opportunity, nor were his treasures the only price he was to pay for fortifying Geba and Mizpah with Baasha's building materials. Hanani declared to him that from henceforth he should have wars. This purchased alliance was only the beginning, and not the end, of troubles. Instead of the complete and decisive victory which had disposed of the Ethiopians once for all, Asa and his people were harassed and exhausted by continual warfare. The Christian life would have more decisive victories, and

would be less of a perpetual and wearing struggle, if
we had faith to refrain from the use of doubtful means
for high ends.

Oded's message of warning had been accepted and
obeyed, but Asa was now no longer docile to Divine
discipline.   David and Hezekiah submitted themselves
to the censure of Gad and Isaiah; but Asa was wroth
with Hanani and put him in prison, because the
prophet had ventured to rebuke him.   His sin against
God corrupted even his civil administration; and
the ally of a heathen king, the persecutor of God's
prophet, also oppressed the people.   Three years[1] after
the repulse of Baasha a new punishment fell upon
Asa : his feet became grievously diseased.   Still he did
not humble himself, but was guilty of further sin[2]: he
sought not Jehovah, but the physicians.   It is probable
that to seek Jehovah concerning disease was not merely
a matter of worship.   Reuss has suggested that the
legitimate practice of medicine belonged to the schools
of the prophets; but it seems quite as likely that in
Judah, as in Egypt, any existing knowledge of the
art of healing was to be found among the priests.
Conversely physicians who were neither priests nor
prophets of Jehovah were almost certain to be ministers
of idolatrous worship and magicians.   They failed
apparently to relieve their patient : Asa lingered in
pain and weakness for two years, and then died.
Possibly the sufferings of his latter days had protected
his people from further oppression, and had at once
appealed to their sympathy and removed any cause
for resentment.   When he died, they only remembered

---

[1] The date, as before, is peculiar to Chronicles.
[2] xvi. 12 *b*, peculiar to Chronicles.

his virtues and achievements; and buried him with royal magnificence, with sweet odours and divers kinds of spices; and made a very great burning for him, probably of aromatic woods.

In discussing the chronicler's picture of the good kings, we have noticed that, while Chronicles and the book of Kings agree in mentioning the misfortunes which as a rule darkened their closing years, Chronicles in each case records some lapse into sin as preceding these misfortunes. From the theological standpoint of the chronicler's school, these invidious records of the sins of good kings were necessary in order to account for their misfortunes. The devout student of the book of Kings read with surprise that of the pious kings who had been devoted to Jehovah and His temple, whose acceptance by Him had been shown by the victories vouchsafed to them, one had died of a painful disease in his feet, another in a lazar-house, two had been assassinated, and one slain in battle. Why had faith and devotion been so ill rewarded? Was it not vain to serve God? What profit was there in keeping His ordinances? The chronicler felt himself fortunate in discovering amongst his later authorities additional information which explained these mysteries and justified the ways of God to man. Even the good kings had not been without reproach, and their misfortunes had been the righteous judgment on their sins.

The principle which guided the chronicler in this selection of material was that sin was always punished by complete, immediate, and manifest retribution in this life, and that conversely all misfortune was the punishment of sin. There is a simplicity and apparent justice about this theory that has always made it the

leading doctrine of a certain stage of moral development. It was probably the popular religious teaching in
Israel from early days till the time when our Lord found
it necessary to protest against the idea that the Galilæans
whose blood Pilate had mingled with their sacrifices
were sinners above all Galilæans because they had
suffered these things, or that the eighteen upon whom
the tower in Siloam fell, and killed them, were offenders
above all the inhabitants of Jerusalem. This doctrine
of retribution was current among the Greeks. When
terrible calamities fell upon men, their neighbours
supposed these to be the punishment of specially
heinous crimes. When the Spartan king Cleomenes
committed suicide, the public mind in Greece at once
inquired of what particular sin he had thus paid the
penalty. The horrible circumstances of his death were
attributed to the wrath of some offended deity, and the
cause of the offence was sought for in one of his many
acts of sacrilege. Possibly he was thus punished
because he had bribed the priestess of the Delphic
oracle. The Athenians, however, believed that his
sacrilege had consisted in cutting down trees in their
sacred grove at Eleusis ; but the Argives preferred to
hold that he came to an untimely end because he had
set fire to a grove sacred to their eponymous hero
Argos. Similarly, when in the course of the Pelopon-
nesian war the Æginetans were expelled from their
island, this calamity was regarded as a punishment
inflicted upon them because fifty years before they had
dragged away and put to death a suppliant who had
caught hold of the handle of the door of the temple
of Demeter Theomophorus. On the other hand, the
wonderful way in which on four or five occasions the
ravages of pestilence delivered Dionysius of Syracuse

from his Carthaginian enemies was attributed by his admiring friends to the favour of the gods.

Like many other simple and logical doctrines, this Jewish theory of retribution came into collision with obvious facts, and seemed to set the law of God at variance with the enlightened conscience. " Beneath the simplest forms of truth the subtlest error lurks." The prosperity of the wicked and the sufferings of the righteous were a standing religious difficulty to the devout Israelite. . The popular doctrine held its ground tenaciously, supported not only by ancient prescription, but also by the most influential classes in society. All who were young, robust, wealthy, powerful, or successful were interested in maintaining a doctrine that made health, riches, rank, and success the outward and visible signs of righteousness. Accordingly the simplicity of the original doctrine was hedged about with an ingenious and elaborate apologetic. The prosperity of the wicked was held to be only for a season ; before he died the judgment of God would overtake him. It was a mistake to speak of the sufferings of the righteous: these very sufferings showed that his righteousness was only apparent, and that in secret he had been guilty of grievous sin.

Of all the cruelty inflicted in the name of orthodoxy there is little that can surpass the refined torture due to this Jewish apologetic. Its cynical teaching met the sufferer in the anguish of bereavement, in the pain and depression of disease, when he was crushed by sudden and ruinous losses or publicly disgraced by the unjust sentence of a venal law-court. Instead of receiving sympathy and help, he found himself looked upon as a moral outcast and pariah on account of his misfortunes ; when he most needed Divine grace, he was bidden to

regard himself as a special object of the wrath of
Jehovah. If his orthodoxy survived his calamities, he
would review his past life with morbid retrospection,
and persuade himself that he had indeed been guilty
above all other sinners.

The book of Job is an inspired protest against the
current theory of retribution, and the full discussion of
the question belongs to the exposition of that book.
But the narrative of Chronicles, like much Church
history in all ages, is largely controlled by the contro-
versial interests of the school from which it emanated.
In the hands of the chronicler the story of the kings
of Judah is told in such a way that it becomes a polemic
against the book of Job. The tragic and disgraceful
death of good kings presented a crucial difficulty to the
chronicler's theology. A good man's other misfortunes
might be compensated for by prosperity in his latter
days; but in a theory of retribution which required a
complete satisfaction of justice in this life there could
be no compensation for a dishonourable death. Hence
the chronicler's anxiety to record any lapses of good
kings in their latter days.

The criticism and correction of this doctrine belongs,
as we have said, to the exposition of the book of Job.
Here we are rather concerned to discover the permanent
truth of which the theory is at once an imperfect and
exaggerated expression. To begin with, there are sins
which bring upon the transgressor a swift, obvious, and
dramatic punishment. Human law deals thus with some
sins; the laws of health visit others with a similar
severity; at times the Divine judgment strikes down
men and nations before an awe-stricken world. Amongst
such judgments we might reckon the punishments of
royal sins so frequent in the pages of Chronicles.

God's judgments are not usually so immediate and manifest, but these striking instances illustrate and enforce the certain consequences of sin. We are dealing now with cases in which God was set at nought; and, apart from Divine grace, the votaries of sin are bound to become its slaves and victims. Ruskin has said, " Medicine often fails of its effect, but poison never; and while, in summing the observation of past life not unwatchfully spent, I can truly say that I have a thousand times seen Patience disappointed of her hope and Wisdom of her aim, I have never yet seen folly fruitless of mischief, nor vice conclude but in calamity." [1] Now that we have been brought into a fuller light and delivered from the practical dangers of the ancient Israelite doctrine, we can afford to forget the less satisfactory aspects of the chronicler's teaching, and we must feel grateful to him for enforcing the salutary and necessary lesson that sin brings inevitable punishment, and that therefore, whatever present appearances may suggest, " the world was certainly not framed for the lasting convenience of hypocrites, libertines, and oppressors." [2]

Indeed, the consequences of sin are regular and exact; and the judgments upon the kings of Judah in Chronicles accurately symbolise the operations of Divine discipline. But pain, and ruin, and disgrace are only secondary elements in God's judgments; and most often they are not judgments at all. They have their uses as chastisements; but if we dwell upon them with too emphatic an insistence, men suppose that pain is a worse evil than sin, and that sin is only to be avoided because it causes suffering to the sinner. The really serious

---

[1] *Time and Tide*, xii. 67.   [2] George Eliot, *Romola*, xxi.

consequence of evil acts is the formation and confirmation of evil character.　Herbert Spencer says in his *First Principles*[1] "that motion once set up along any line becomes itself a cause of subsequent motion along that line."　This is absolutely true in moral and spiritual dynamics : every wrong thought, feeling, word, or act, every failure to think, feel, speak, or act rightly, at once alters a man's character for the worse.　Henceforth he will find it easier to sin and more difficult to do right ; he has twisted another strand into the cord of habit : and though each may be as fine as the threads of a spider's web, in time there will be cords strong enough to have bound Samson before Delilah shaved off his seven locks.　This is the true punishment of sin : to lose the fine instincts, the generous impulses, and the nobler ambitions of manhood, and become every day more of a beast and a devil.

---

[1] **Part II., Chap. IX.**

CHAPTER IV

JEHOSHAPHAT—THE DOCTRINE OF NON-RESISTANCE

2 CHRON. xvii.–xx.

ASA was succeeded by his son Jehoshaphat, and his reign began even more auspiciously[1] than that of Asa. The new king had apparently taken warning from the misfortunes of Asa's closing years; and as he was thirty-five years old when he came to the throne, he had been trained before Asa fell under the Divine displeasure. He walked in the first ways of his father David, before David was led away by Satan to number Israel. Jehoshaphat's heart was lifted up, not with foolish pride, like Hezekiah's, but "in the ways of Jehovah." He sought the God of his father, and walked in God's commandments, and was not led astray by the evil example and influence of the kings of Israel, neither did he seek the Baals. While Asa had been enfeebled by illness and alienated from Jehovah, the high places and the Asherim had sprung up again like a crop of evil weeds; but Jehoshaphat once more removed them. According to the chronicler, this removing of high places was a very labour of Sisyphus: the stone was no sooner rolled up to the top of the hill

---

[1] xvii., peculiar to Chronicles.

366

than it rolled down again. Jehoshaphat seems to have had an inkling of this ; he felt that the destruction of idolatrous sanctuaries and symbols was like mowing down weeds and leaving the roots in the soil. Accordingly he made an attempt to deal more radically with the evil : he would take away the inclination as well as the opportunity for corrupt rites. A commission of princes, priests, and Levites was sent throughout all the cities of Judah to instruct the people in the law of Jehovah. Vice will always find opportunities ; it is little use to suppress evil institutions unless the people are educated out of evil propensities. If, for instance, every public-house in England were closed to-morrow, and there were still millions of throats craving for drink, drunkenness would still prevail, and a new administration would promptly reopen gin-shops.

Because the new king thus earnestly and consistently sought the God of his fathers, Jehovah was with him, and established the kingdom in his hand. Jehoshaphat received all the marks of Divine favour usually bestowed upon good kings. He waxed great exceedingly ; he had many fortresses, an immense army, and much wealth ; he built castles and cities of store ; he had arsenals for the supply of war material in the cities of Judah. And these cities, together with other defensible positions and the border cities of Ephraim occupied by Judah, were held by strong garrisons. While David had contented himself with two hundred and eighty-eight thousand men from all Israel, and Abijah had led forth four hundred thousand, and Asa five hundred and eighty thousand, there waited on Jehoshaphat, in addition to his numerous garrisons, *eleven hundred and sixty thousand men.* Of these seven hundred and eighty thousand were men of Judah in three divisions, and three hundred and eighty thousand were Benjamites in two divisions. Probably the steady increase of the armies of Abijah, Asa, and Jehoshaphat symbolises a proportionate increase of Divine favour.

The chronicler records the names of the captains of the five divisions. Two of them are singled out for special commendation : Eliada the Benjamite is styled "a mighty man of valour," and of the Jewish captain Amaziah the son of Zichri it is said that he offered either himself or his possessions willingly to Jehovah, as David and his princes had offered, for the building of the Temple. The devout king had devout officers.

He had also devoted subjects. All Judah brought him presents, so that he had great riches and ample means to sustain his royal power and splendour. Moreover, as in the case of Solomon and Asa, his piety was rewarded with freedom from war : "The fear of Jehovah fell upon all the kingdoms round about, so that they made no war against Jehoshaphat." Some of his weaker neighbours were overawed by the spectacle of his great power ; the Philistines brought him presents and tribute money, and the Arabians immense flocks of rams and he-goats, seven thousand seven hundred of each.

Great prosperity had the usual fatal effect upon Jehoshaphat's character. In the beginning of his reign he had strengthened himself against Israel and had refused to walk in their ways ; now power had developed ambition, and he sought and obtained the honour of marrying his son Jehoram to Athaliah the daughter of Ahab, the mighty and magnificent king of Israel, possibly also the daughter of the Phœnician princess Jezebel, the devotee of Baal. This family connection of course implied political alliance. After a time

Jehoshaphat went down to visit his new ally, and was hospitably received.[1]

Then follows the familiar story of Micaiah the son of Imlah, the disastrous expedition of the two kings, and the death of Ahab, almost exactly as in the book of Kings. There is one significant alteration : both narratives tell us how the Syrian captains attacked Jehoshaphat because they took him for the king of Israel and gave up their pursuit when he cried out, and they discovered their mistake ; but the chronicler adds the explanation that Jehovah helped him and God moved them to depart from him. And so the master of more than a million soldiers was happy in being allowed to escape on account of his insignificance, and returned in peace to Jerusalem. Oded and Hanani had met his predecessors on their return from victory ; now Jehu the son of Hanani[2] met Jehoshaphat when he came home defeated. Like his father, the prophet was charged with a message of rebuke. An alliance with the northern kingdom was scarcely less reprehensible than one with Syria : " Shouldest thou help the wicked, and love them that hate Jehovah ? Jehovah is wroth with thee." Asa's previous reforms were not allowed to mitigate the severity of his condemnation, but Jehovah was more merciful to Jehoshaphat. The prophet makes mention of his piety and his destruction of idolatrous symbols, and no further punishment is inflicted upon him.

The chronicler's addition to the account of the king's escape from the Syrian captains reminds us that God still watches over and protects His children even when they are in the very act of sinning against Him.

---

[2] Chron. xviii. 1-3.   [2] xix. 1-3, peculiar to Chronicles.

Jehovah knew that Jehoshaphat's sinful alliance with Ahab did not imply complete revolt and apostacy. Hence doubtless the comparative mildness of the prophet's reproof.

When Jehu's father Hanani rebuked Asa, the king flew into a passion, and cast the prophet into prison; Jehoshaphat received Jehu's reproof in a very different spirit[1]: he repented himself, and found a new zeal in his penitence. Learning from his own experience the proneness of the human heart to go astray, he went out himself amongst his people to bring them back to Jehovah; and just as Asa in his apostacy oppressed his people, Jehoshaphat in his renewed loyalty to Jehovah showed himself anxious for good government. He provided judges in all the walled towns of Judah, with a court of appeal at Jerusalem; he solemnly charged them to remember their responsibility to Jehovah, to avoid bribery, and not to truckle to the rich and powerful. Being themselves faithful to Jehovah, they were to inculcate a like obedience and warn the people not to sin against the God of their fathers. Jehoshaphat's exhortation to his new judges concludes with a sentence whose martial resonance suggests trial by combat rather than the peaceful proceedings of a law-court: " Deal courageously, and Jehovah defend the right!"

The principle that good government must be a necessary consequence of piety in the rulers has not been so uniformly observed in later times as in the pages of Chronicles. The testimony of history on this point is not altogether consistent. In spite of all the faults of the orthodox and devout Greek

---

[1] xix. 4–11, peculiar to Chronicles,

emperors Theodosius the Great and Marcian, their administration rendered important services to the empire. Alfred the Great was a distinguished statesman and warrior as well as zealous for true religion. St. Louis of France exercised a wise control over Church and state. It is true that when a woman reproached him in open court with being a king of friars, of priests, and of clerks, and not a true king of France, he replied with saintly meekness, "You say true! It has pleased the Lord to make me king; it had been well if it had pleased Him to make some one king who had better ruled the realm."[1] But something must be allowed for the modesty of the saint; apart from his unfortunate crusades, it would have been difficult for France or even Europe to have furnished a more beneficent sovereign. On the other hand, Charlemagne's successor, the Emperor Louis the Pious, and our own kings Edward the Confessor and the saintly Henry VI., were alike feeble and inefficient; the zeal of the Spanish kings and their kinswoman Mary Tudor is chiefly remembered for its ghastly cruelty; and in comparatively recent times the misgovernment of the States of the Church was a byword throughout Europe. Many causes combined to produce this mingled record. The one most clearly contrary to the chronicler's teaching was an immoral opinion that the Christian should cease to be a citizen, and that the saint has no duties to society. This view is often considered to be the special vice of monasticism, but it reappears in one form or another in every generation. The failure of the administration of Louis the Pious is partly explained when we read that he was with difficulty prevented

---

[1] Milman, *Latin Christianity*, Book XI., Chap. L.

from entering a monastery. In our own day there are those who think that a newspaper should have no interest for a really earnest Christian. According to their ideas, Jehoshaphat should have divided his time between a private oratory in his palace and the public services of the Temple, and have left his kingdom to the mercy of unjust judges at home and heathen enemies abroad, or else have abdicated in favour of some kinsman whose heart was not so perfect with Jehovah. The chronicler had a clearer insight into Divine methods, and this doctrine of his is not one that has been superseded together with the Mosaic ritual.

Possibly the martial tone of the sentence that concludes the account of Jehoshaphat as the Jewish Justinian is due to the influence upon the chronicler's mind of the incident[1] which he now describes.

Jehoshaphat's next experience was parallel to that of Asa with Zerah. When his new reforms were completed, he was menaced with a formidable invasion. His new enemies were almost as distant and strange as the Ethiopians and Lubim who had followed Zerah. We hear nothing about any king of Israel or Damascus, the usual leaders of assaults upon Judah; we hear instead of a triple alliance against Judah. Two of the allies are Moab and Ammon; but the Jewish kings were not wont to regard these as irresistible foes, so that the extreme dismay which takes possession of king and people must be due to the third ally: the "Meunim."[2] The Meunim we have already met with in connection with the exploits of the children of

---

[1] xx. 1–30, peculiar to Chronicles.

[2] So R.V. marg., with the LXX. The Targum has "Edomites," the A.V. is not justified by the Hebrew, and the R.V. does not make sense.

Simeon in the reign of Hezekiah; they are also
mentioned in the reign of Uzziah,[1] and nowhere else,
unless indeed they are identical with the Maonites, who
are named with the Amalekites in Judges x. 12. They
are thus a people peculiar to Chronicles, and appear
from this narrative to have inhabited Mount Seir, by
which term " Meunim" is replaced as the story proceeds.[2]
Since the chronicler wrote so long after the events he
describes, we cannot attribute to him any very exact
knowledge of political geography. Probably the term
" Meunim" impressed his contemporaries very much as
it does a modern reader, and suggested countless hordes
of Bedouin plunderers; Josephus calls them a great
army of Arabians. This host of invaders came from
Edom,[2] and having marched round the southern end of
the Dead Sea, were now at Engedi, on its western shore.
The Moabites and Ammonites might have crossed the
Jordan by the fords near Jericho; but this route would
not have been convenient for their allies the Meunim,
and would have brought them into collision with the
forces of the northern kingdom.

On this occasion Jehoshaphat does not seek any
foreign alliance. He does not appeal to Syria, like Asa,
nor does he ask Ahab's successor to repay in kind the
assistance given to Ahab at Ramoth-gilead, partly
perhaps because there was no time, but chiefly because
he had learnt the truth which Hanani had sought to
teach his father, and which Hanani's son had taught
him. He does not even trust in his own hundreds of

---

[1] Cf. 1 Chron. iv. 41, R.V.; and 2 Chron. xxvi. 7.

[2] One Hebrew manuscript is quoted as having this reading. A.R.V.,
with the ordinary Masoretic text, have "Syria"; but it is simply absurd
to suppose that a multitude from beyond the sea from Syria would first
make their appearance on the western shore of the Dead Sea.

thousands of soldiers, all of whom cannot have perished at Ramoth-gilead; his confidence is placed solely and absolutely in Jehovah. Jehoshaphat and his people made no military preparations; subsequent events justified their apparent neglect: none were necessary. Jehoshaphat sought Divine help instead, and proclaimed a fast throughout Judah; and all Judah gathered themselves to Jerusalem to ask help of Jehovah. This great national assembly met "before the new court" of the Temple. The chronicler, who is supremely interested in the Temple buildings, has told us nothing about any new court, nor is it mentioned elsewhere; our author is probably giving the title of a corresponding portion of the second Temple : the place where the people assembled to meet Jehoshaphat would be the great court built by Solomon.[1]

Here Jehoshaphat stood up as the spokesman of the nation, and prayed to Jehovah on their behalf and on his own. He recalls the Divine omnipotence; Jehovah is God of earth and heaven, God of Israel and Ruler of the heathen, and therefore able to help even in this great emergency :—

" O Jehovah, God of our fathers, art Thou not God in heaven ? Dost Thou not rule all the kingdoms of the heathen ? And in Thy hand is power and might, so that none is able to withstand Thee."

The land of Israel had been the special gift of Jehovah to His people, in fulfilment of His ancient promise to Abraham :—

"Didst not Thou, O our God, dispossess the inhabitants of this land in favour of Thy people Israel,

---

[1] 2 Chron. iv. 9.

and gavest it to the seed of Abraham Thy friend for
ever ? "

And now long possession had given Israel a pre-
scriptive right to the Land of Promise ; and they had,
so to speak, claimed their rights in the most formal
and solemn fashion by erecting a temple to the God of
Israel. Moreover, the prayer of Solomon at the dedication of the Temple had been accepted by Jehovah as
the basis of His covenant with Israel, and Jehoshaphat
quotes a clause from that prayer or covenant which
had expressly provided for such emergencies as the
present :—

"And they " (Israel) " dwelt in the land, and built
Thee therein a sanctuary for Thy name, saying, If evil
come upon us, the sword, judgment, pestilence, or
famine, we will stand before this house and before
Thee (for Thy name is in this house), and cry unto
Thee in our affliction ; and Thou wilt hear and save." [1]

Moreover, the present invasion was not only an
attempt to set aside Jehovah's disposition of Palestine
and the long-established rights of Israel : it was also
gross ingratitude, a base return for the ancient forbearance of Israel towards her present enemies :—

"And now, behold, the children of Ammon and Moab
and Mount Seir, whom Thou wouldest not let Israel
invade when they came out of the land of Egypt, but
they turned aside from them and destroyed them not—
behold how they reward us by coming to dispossess
us of Thy possession which Thou hast caused us to
possess."

For this nefarious purpose the enemies of Israel had

---

[1] Ver. 9; cf. 2 Chron. vi. 28, and the whole paragraph (vv. 22-30)
of which our verse is a brief abstract.

come up in overwhelming numbers, but Judah was
confident in the justice of its cause and the favour of
Jehovah :—

"O our God, wilt Thou not execute judgment
against them ? for we have no might against this great
company that cometh against us, neither know we
what to do, but our eyes are upon Thee."

Meanwhile the great assemblage stood in the attitude of supplication before Jehovah, not a gathering of
mighty men of valour praying for blessing upon their
strength and courage, but a mixed multitude, men and
women, children and infants, seeking sanctuary, as it
were, at the Temple, and casting themselves in their
extremity upon the protecting care of Jehovah. Possibly when the king finished his prayer the assembly
broke out into loud, wailing cries of dismay and agonised
entreaty; but the silence of the narrative rather
suggests that Jehoshaphat's strong, calm faith communicated itself to the people, and they waited quietly
for Jehovah's answer, for some token or promise of
deliverance. Instead of the confused cries of an excited
crowd, there was a hush of expectancy, such as sometimes falls upon an assembly when a great statesman
has risen to utter words which will be big with the
fate of empires.

And the answer came, not by fire from heaven or
any visible sign, not by voice of thunder accompanied
by angelic trumpets, nor by angel or archangel, but
by a familiar voice hitherto unsuspected of any supernatural gifts, by a prophetic utterance whose only
credentials were given by the influence of the Spirit
upon the speaker and his audience. The chronicler
relates with evident satisfaction how, in the midst of
that great congregation, the Spirit of Jehovah came,

not upon king, or priest, or acknowledged prophet, but
upon a subordinate minister of the Temple, a Levite
and member of the Temple choir like himself. He is
careful to fix the identity of this newly called prophet
and to gratify the family pride of existing Levitical
families by giving the prophet's genealogy for several
generations. He was Jahaziel the son of Zechariah, the
son of Benaiah, the son of Jeiel, the son of Mattaniah, of
the sons of Asaph. The very names were encouraging. What more suitable names could be found for a
messenger of Divine mercy than Jahaziel—" God gives
prophetic vision "—the son of Zechariah—" Jehovah
remembers "?

Jahaziel's message showed that Jehoshaphat's prayer
had been accepted; Jehovah responded without reserve
to the confidence reposed in Him: He would vindicate
His own authority by delivering Judah; Jehoshaphat
should have blessed proof of the immense superiority
of simple trust in Jehovah over an alliance with
Ahab or the king of Damascus. Twice the prophet
exhorts the king and people in the very words that
Jehovah had used to encourage Joshua when the
death of Moses had thrown upon him all the heavy
responsibilities of leadership: " Fear not, nor be
dismayed." They need no longer cling like frightened
suppliants to the sanctuary, but are to go forth at once,
the very next day, against the enemy. That they may
lose no time in looking for them, Jehovah announces
the exact spot where the enemy are to be found:
" Behold, they are coming by the ascent of Hazziz,[1] and
ye shall find them at the end of the ravine before the
wilderness of Jeruel." This topographical description
was doubtless perfectly intelligible to the chronicler's

---

[1] Not Ziz, as A.R.V.

contemporaries, but it is no longer possible to fix exactly the locality of Hazziz or Jeruel. The ascent of Hazziz has been identified with the Wady Husasa, which leads up from the coast of the Dead Sea north of Engedi, in the direction of Tekoa; but the identification is by no means certain.

The general situation, however, is fairly clear: the allied invaders would come up from the coast into the highlands of Judah by one of the wadies leading inland; they were to be met by Jehoshaphat and his people on one of the " wildernesses," or plateaus of pasture-land, in the neighbourhood of Tekoa.

But the Jews went forth, not as an army, but in order to be the passive spectators of a great manifestation of the power of Jehovah. They had no concern with the numbers and prowess of their enemies; Jehovah Himself would lay bare His mighty arm, and Judah should see that no foreign ally, no millions of native warriors, were necessary for their salvation : "Ye shall not need to fight in this battle; take up your position, stand still and see the deliverance of Jehovah with you, O Judah and Jerusalem."

Thus had Moses addressed Israel on the eve of the passage of the Red Sea. Jehoshaphat and his people owned and honoured the Divine message as if Jahaziel were another Moses; they prostrated themselves on the ground before Jehovah. The sons of Asaph had already been privileged to provide Jehovah with His prophet; these Asaphites represented the Levitical clan of Gershom : but now the Kohathites, with their guild of singers, the sons of Korah, " stood up to praise Jehovah, the God of Israel, with an exceeding loud voice," as the Levites sang when the foundations of the second Temple were laid, and when Ezra and

Nehemiah made the people enter into a new covenant with their God.

Accordingly on the morrow the people rose early in the morning and went out to the wilderness of Tekoa, ten or twelve miles south of Jerusalem. In ancient times generals were wont to make a set speech to their armies before they led them into battle, so Jehoshaphat addresses his subjects as they pass out before him. He does not seek to make them confident in their own strength and prowess ; he does not inflame their passions against Moab and Ammon, nor exhort them to be brave and remind them that they fight this day for the ashes of their fathers and the temple of their God. Such an address would have been entirely out of place, because the Jews were not going to fight at all. Jehoshaphat only bids them have faith in Jehovah and His prophets. It is a curious anticipation of Pauline teaching. Judah is to be "saved by faith" from Moab and Ammon, as the Christian is delivered by faith from sin and its penalty. The incident might almost seem to have been recorded in order to illustrate the truth that St. Paul was to teach. It is strange that there is no reference to this chapter in the epistles of St. Paul and St. James, and that the author of the Epistle to the Hebrews does not remind us how " by faith Jehoshaphat was delivered from Moab and Ammon."

There is no question of military order, no reference to the five great divisions into which the armies of Judah and Benjamin are divided in chap. xvii. Here, as at Jericho, the captain of Israel is chiefly concerned to provide musicians to lead his army. When David was arranging for the musical services before the Ark, he took counsel with his captains. In this unique military expedition there is no mention of captains; they were not necessary, and if they were present, there was no opportunity for them to show their skill and prowess in battle. In an even more democratic spirit Jehoshaphat takes counsel with the people—that is, probably makes some proposition, which is accepted with universal acclamation.

The Levitical singers, dressed in the splendid robes [1] in which they officiated at the Temple, were appointed to go before the people, and offer praises unto Jehovah, and sing the anthem, "Give thanks unto Jehovah, for His mercy endureth for ever." These words or their equivalent are the opening words, and the second clause the refrain, of the post-Exilic Psalms: cvi., cvii., cxviii., and cxxxvi. As the chronicler has already ascribed Psalm cvi. to David, he possibly ascribes all four to David, and intends us to understand that one or all of them were sung by the Levites on this occasion. Later Judaism was in the habit of denoting a book or section of a book by its opening words.

And so Judah, a pilgrim caravan rather than an army, went on to its Divinely appointed tryst with its enemies, and at its head the Levitical choir sang the Temple hymns. It was not a campaign, but a sacred function, on a much larger scale a procession such as may be seen winding its way, with chants and incense, banners, images, and crucifixes, through the streets of Catholic cities.

Meanwhile Jehovah was preparing a spectacle to gladden the eyes of His people and reward their implicit faith and exact obedience; He was working for those who were waiting for Him. Though Judah was

---

[1] הדרת קדֶשׁ, literally, as A.R.V., "beauty of holiness"; *i.e.*, sacred robes. Translate with R.V. marg. "praise in the beauty of holiness,' not, as A.R.V., "praise the beauty of holiness."

still far from its enemies, yet, like the trumpet at Jericho, the strain of praise and thanksgiving was the signal for the Divine intervention : " When they began to sing and praise, Jehovah set liers in wait against the children of Ammon, Moab, and Mount Seir." Who were these liers in wait ? They could not be men of Judah : *they* were not to fight, but to be passive spectators of their own deliverance. Did the allies set an ambush for Judah, and was it thus that they were afterwards led to mistake their own people for enemies ? Or does the chronicler intend us to understand that these " liers in wait " were spirits ; that the allied invaders were tricked and bewildered like the shipwrecked sailors in the *Tempest*; or that when they came to the wilderness of Jeruel there fell upon them a spirit of mutual distrust, jealousy, and hatred, that had, as it were, been waiting for them there ? But, from whatever cause, a quarrel broke out amongst them ; and they were smitten. When Ammonite, Moabite, and Edomite met, there were many private and public feuds waiting their opportunity ; and such confederates were as ready to quarrel among themselves as a group of Highland clans engaged in a Lowland foray. " Ammon and Moab stood up against the inhabitants of Mount Seir utterly to slay and destroy them." But even Ammon and Moab soon dissolved their alliance ; and at last, partly maddened by panic, partly intoxicated by a wild thirst for blood, a very Berserker frenzy, all ties of friendship and kindred were forgotten, and every man's hand was against his brother. " When they had made an end of the inhabitants of Seir, every one helped to destroy another."

While this tragedy was enacting, and the air was rent with the cruel yells of that death struggle,

Jehoshaphat and his people moved on in tranquil pilgrimage to the cheerful sound of the songs of Zion. At last they reached an eminence, perhaps the long, low summit of some ridge overlooking the plateau of Jeruel. When they had gained this watchtower of the wilderness, the ghastly scene burst upon their gaze. Jehovah had kept His word : they had found their enemy. They "looked upon the multitude," all those hordes of heathen tribes that had filled them with terror and dismay. They were harmless enough now : the Jews saw nothing but "dead bodies fallen to the earth "; and in that Aceldama lay all the multitude of profane invaders who had dared to violate the sanctity of the Promised Land : " There were none that escaped." So had Israel looked back after crossing the Red Sea and seen the corpses of the Egyptians washed up on the shore.[1] So when the angel of Jehovah smote Sennacherib,—

> "Like the leaves of the forest when autumn hath blown,
> That host on the morrow lay withered and strown."

There is no touch of pity for the wretched victims of their own sins. Greeks of every city and tribe could feel the pathos of the tragic end of the Athenian expedition against Syracuse ; but the Jews had no ruth for the kindred tribes that dwelt along their frontier, and the age of the chronicler had not yet learnt that Jehovah had either tenderness or compassion for the enemies of Israel.

The spectators of this carnage—we cannot call them victors—did not neglect to profit to the utmost by their great opportunity. They spent three days in

---

[1] Exod. xiv. 30.

stripping the dead bodies; and as Orientals delight
in jewelled weapons and costly garments, and their
chiefs take the field with barbaric ostentation of
wealth, the spoil was both valuable and abundant:
"riches, and raiment,[1] and precious jewels, . . . more
than they could carry away."

In collecting the spoil, the Jews had become dispersed
through all the wide area over which the fighting
between the confederates must have extended; but on
the fourth day they gathered together again in a
neighbouring valley and gave solemn thanks for their
deliverance: "There they blessed Jehovah; therefore
the name of that place was called the valley of Berachah
unto this day." West of Tekoa,[2] not too far from the
scene of carnage, a ruin and a wady still bear the name
"Bereikut"; and doubtless in the chronicler's time the
valley was called Berachah, and local tradition furnished
our author with this explanation of the origin of the
name.

When the spoil was all collected, they returned to
Jerusalem as they came, in solemn procession, headed,
no doubt, by the Levites, with psalteries, and harps, and
trumpets. They came back to the scene of their anxious
supplications : to the house of Jehovah. But yesterday,
as it were, they had assembled before Jehovah, terror-
stricken at the report of an irresistible host of invaders ;
and to-day their enemies were utterly destroyed. They
had experienced a deliverance that might rank with
the Exodus; and as at that former deliverance they
had spoiled the Egyptians, so now they had returned

---

[1] With R.V. marg.

[2] The identification of the valley of Berachah with the valley o
Jehoshaphat, close to Jerusalem and mentioned by Josephus, is a mere
theory, quite at variance with the topographical evidence.

laden with the plunder of Moab, Ammon, and Edom.
And all their neighbours were smitten with fear when
they heard of the awful ruin which Jehovah had brought
upon these enemies of Israel. No one would dare to
invade a country where Jehovah laid a ghostly ambush
of liers in wait for the enemies of His people. The
realm of Jehoshaphat was quiet, not because he was
protected by powerful allies or by the swords of his
numerous and valiant soldiers, but because Judah had
become another Eden, and cherubim with flaming
swords guarded the frontier on every hand, and "his
God gave him rest round about."

Then follow the regular summary and conclusion of
the history of the reign taken from the book of Kings,
with the usual alterations in the reference to further
sources of information. We are told here, in direct
contradiction to xvii. 6 and to the whole tenor of the
previous chapters, that the high places were not taken
away, another illustration of the slight importance the
chronicler attached to accuracy in details. He either
overlooks the contradiction between passages borrowed
from different sources, or else does not think it worth
while to harmonise his inconsistent materials.

But after the narrative of the reign is thus formally
closed the chronicler inserts a postscript, perhaps by
a kind of after-thought. The book of Kings narrates[1]
how Jehoshaphat made ships to go to Ophir for gold,
but they were broken at Ezion-geber; then Ahaziah
the son of Ahab proposed to enter into partnership
with Jehoshaphat, and the latter rejected his proposal.
As we have seen, the chronicler's theory of retribution
required some reason why so pious a king experienced

---

[1] 1 Kings xxii. 48, 49.

misfortune. What sin had Jehoshaphat committed to deserve to have his ships broken? The chronicler has a new version of the story, which provides an answer to this question. Jehoshaphat did not build any ships by himself; his unfortunate navy was constructed in partnership with Ahaziah; and accordingly the prophet Eliezer rebuked him for allying himself a second time with a wicked king of Israel, and announced the coming wreck of the ships. And so it came about that the ships were broken, and the shadow of Divine displeasure rested on the last days of Jehoshaphat.

We have next to notice the chronicler's most important omissions. The book of Kings narrates another alliance of Jehoshaphat with Jehoram, king of Israel, like his alliances with Ahab and Ahaziah. The narrative of this incident closely resembles that of the earlier joint expedition to Ramoth-gilead. As then Jehoshaphat marched out with Ahab, so now he accompanies Ahab's son Jehoram, taking with him his subject ally the king of Edom. Here also a prophet appears upon the scene; but on this occasion Elisha addresses no rebuke to Jehoshaphat for his alliance with Israel, but treats him with marked respect: and the allied army wins a great victory. If this narrative had been included in Chronicles, the reign of Jehoshaphat would not have afforded an altogether satisfactory illustration of the main lesson which the chronicler intended it to teach.

This main lesson was that the chosen people should not look for protection against their enemies either to foreign alliances or to their own military strength, but solely to the grace and omnipotence of Jehovah. One negative aspect of this principle has been enforced by the condemnation of Asa's alliance with Syria and

25

Jehoshaphat's with Ahab and Ahaziah. Later on the uselessness of an army apart from Jehovah is shown in the defeat of "the great host" of Joash by "a small company" of Syrians.[1] The positive aspect has been partially illustrated by the signal victories of Abijah and Asa against overwhelming odds and without the help of any foreign allies. But these were partial and unsatisfactory illustrations : Jehovah vouchsafed to share the glory of these victories with great armies that were numbered by the hundred thousand. And after all, the odds were not so very overwhelming. Scores of parallels may be found in which the odds were much greater. In the case of vast Oriental hosts a superiority of two to one might easily be counter-balanced by discipline and valour in the smaller army.

The peculiar value to the chronicler of the deliverance from Moab, Ammon, and the Meunim lay in the fact that no human arm divided the glory with Jehovah. It was shown conclusively not merely that Judah could safely be contented with an army smaller than those of its neighbours, but that Judah would be equally safe with no army at all. We feel that this lesson is taught with added force when we remember that Jehoshaphat had a larger army than is ascribed to any Israelite or Jewish king after David. Yet he places no confidence in his eleven hundred and sixty thousand warriors, and he is not allowed to make any use of them. In the case of a king with small military resources, to trust in Jehovah might be merely making a virtue of necessity ; but if Jehoshaphat, with his immense army, felt that his only real help was in his God, the example furnished an *à fortiori* argument which would conclusively show

---

[1] 2 Chron. xxiv. 24, peculiar to Chronicles.

that it was always the duty and privilege of the Jews to
say with the Psalmist, "Some trust in chariots, and
some in horses; but we will remember the name of
Jehovah our God."[1] The ancient literature of Israel
furnished other illustrations of the principle: at the Red
Sea the Israelites had been delivered without any
exercise of their own warlike prowess; at Jericho, as at
Jeruel, the enemy had been completely overthrown by
Jehovah before His people rushed upon the spoil;
and the same direct Divine intervention saved Jerusalem
from Sennacherib. But the later history of the Jews
had been a series of illustrations of enforced dependence
upon Jehovah. A little semi-ecclesiastical community
inhabiting a small province that passed from one great
power to another like a counter in the game of international politics had no choice but to trust in Jehovah,
if it were in any way to maintain its self-respect. For
this community of the second Temple to have had
confidence in its sword and bow would have seemed
equally absurd to the Jews and to their Persian and
Greek masters.

When they were thus helpless, Jehovah wrought
for Israel, as He had destroyed the enemies of
Jehoshaphat in the wilderness of Jeruel. The Jews
stood still and saw the working out of their deliverance;
great empires wrestled together like Moab, Ammon, and
Edom, in the agony of the death struggle: and over all
the tumult of battle Israel heard the voice of Jehovah,
"The battle is not yours, but God's; . . . set yourselves,
stand ye still, and see the deliverance of Jehovah with
you, O Judah and Jerusalem." Before their eyes there
passed the scenes of that great drama which for a time

---

[1] Psalm xx. 7.

gave Western Asia Aryan instead of Semitic masters.
For them the whole action had but one meaning:
without calling Israel into the field, Jehovah was
devoting to destruction the enemies of His people and
opening up a way for His redeemed to return, like
Jehoshaphat's procession, to the Holy City and the
Temple. The long series of wars became a wager
of battle, in which Israel, herself a passive spectator,
appeared by her Divine Champion ; and the assured
issue was her triumphant vindication and restoration
to her ancient throne in Zion.

After the Restoration God's protecting providence
asked no armed assistance from Judah. The mandates
of a distant court authorised the rebuilding of the
Temple and the fortifying of the city. The Jews
solaced their national pride and found consolation for
their weakness and subjection in the thought that their
ostensible masters were in reality only the instruments
which Jehovah used to provide for the security and
prosperity of His children.

We have already noticed that this philosophy of
history is not peculiar to Israel. Every nation has a
similar system, and regards its own interests as the
supreme care of Providence. We have seen, too, that
moral influences have controlled and checkmated
material forces; God has fought against the biggest
battalions. Similarly the Jews are not the only people
for whom deliverances have been worked out almost
without any co-operation on their own part. It was not
a negro revolt, for instance, that set free the slaves of
our colonies or of the Southern States. Italy regained
her Eternal City as an incidental effect of a great war
in which she herself took no part. Important political
movements and great struggles involve consequences

equally unforeseen and unintended by the chief actors
in these dramas, consequences which would seem to
them insignificant compared with more obvious results.
Some obscure nation almost ready to perish is given a
respite, a breathing space, in which it gathers strength ;
instead of losing its separate existence, it endures till
time and opportunity make it one of the ruling influences in the world's history : some Geneva or
Wittenberg becomes, just at the right time, a secure
refuge and vantage-ground for one of the Lord's
prophets. Our understanding of what God is doing in
our time and our hopes for what He may yet do will
indeed be small, if we think that God can do nothing
for our cause unless our banner flies in the forefront
of the battle, and the war-cry is " The sword of Gideon ! "
as well as " The sword of Jehovah ! " There will be
many battles fought in which we shall strike no blow
and yet be privileged to divide the spoil. We sometimes
" stand still and see the salvation of Jehovah."

The chronicler has found disciples in these latter
days of a kindlier spirit and more catholic sympathies.
He and they have reached their common doctrines by
different paths, but the chronicler teaches non-resistance
as clearly as the Society of Friends. " When you have
fully yielded yourself to the Divine teaching," he says,
" you will neither fight yourself nor ask others to fight
for you ; you will simply stand still and watch a Divine
providence protecting you and destroying your enemies."
The Friends could almost echo this teaching, not
perhaps laying quite so much stress on the destruction
of the enemy, though among the visions of the earlier
Friends there were many that revealed the coming judgments of the Lord ; and the modern enthusiast is still apt
to consider that his enemies, are the Lord's enemies and

to call the gratification of his own revengeful spirit a vindicating of the honour of the Lord and a satisfaction of outraged justice.

If the chronicler had lived to-day, the history of the Society of Friends might have furnished him with illustrations almost as apt as the destruction of the allied invaders of Judah. He would have rejoiced to tell us how a people that repudiated any resort to violence succeeded in conciliating savage tribes and founding the flourishing colony of Pennsylvania, and would have seen the hand of the Lord in the wealth and honour that have been accorded to a once despised and persecuted sect.

We should be passing to matters that were still beyond the chronicler's horizon, if we were to connect his teaching with our Lord's injunction, " Whosoever shall smite thee on thy right cheek, turn to him the other also." Such a sentiment scarcely harmonises with the three days' stripping of dead bodies in the wilderness of Jeruel. But though the chronicler's motives for non-resistance were not touched and softened with the Divine gentleness of Jesus of Nazareth, and his object was not to persuade his hearers to patient endurance of wrong, yet he had conceived the possibility of a mighty faith that could put its fortunes unreservedly into the hands of God and trust Him with the issues. If we are ever to be worthy citizens of the kingdom of our Lord, it can only be by the sustaining power and inspiring influence of a like faith.

When we come to ask how far the people for whom he wrote responded to his teaching and carried it into practical life, we are met with one of the many instances of the grim irony of history. Probably the chronicler's glowing vision of peaceful security, guarded on every hand by legions of angels, was partly inspired by the comparative prosperity of the time at which he wrote. Other considerations combine with this to suggest that the composition of his work beguiled the happy leisure of one of the brighter intervals between Ezra and the Maccabees.

Circumstances were soon to test the readiness of the Jews, in times of national danger, to observe the attitude of passive spectators and wait for a Divine deliverance. It was not altogether in this spirit that the priests met the savage persecutions of Antiochus. They made no vain attempts to exorcise this evil spirit with hymns, and psalteries, and harps, and trumpets; but the priest Mattathias and his sons slew the king's commissioner and raised the standard of armed revolt. We do indeed find indications of something like obedience to the chronicler's principles. A body of the revolted Jews were attacked on the Sabbath Day; they made no attempt to defend themselves: " When they gave them battle with all speed, they answered them not, neither cast they a stone at them, nor stopped the places where they lay hid, . . . and their enemies rose up against them on the sabbath, and slew them, with their wives, and their children, and their cattle, to the number of a thousand people."[1] No Divine intervention rewarded this devoted faith, nor apparently did the Jews expect it, for they had said, " Let us die all in our innocency; heaven and earth shall testify for us that ye put us to death wrongfully." This is, after all, a higher note than that of Chronicles: obedience may not bring invariable reward; nevertheless the faithful will

---

[1] 1 Macc. ii. 35-38.

not swerve from their loyalty. But the priestly leaders
of the people looked with no favourable eye upon this
offering up of human hecatombs in honour of the
sanctity of the Sabbath. They were not prepared to
die passively; and, as representatives of Jehovah and
of the nation for the time being, they decreed that
henceforth they would fight against those who attacked
them, even on the Sabbath Day. Warfare on these
more secular principles was crowned with that visible
success which the chronicler regarded as the manifest
sign of Divine approval; and a dynasty of royal priests
filled the throne and led the armies of Israel, and
assured and strengthened their authority by intrigues
and alliances with every heathen sovereign within their
reach.

CHAPTER V

JEHORAM, AHAZIAH, AND ATHALIAH: THE CON-SEQUENCES OF A FOREIGN MARRIAGE

2 CHRON. xxi.–xxiii

THE accession of Jehoram is one of the instances in which a wicked son succeeded to a conspicuously pious father, but in this case there is no difficulty in explaining the phenomenon : the depraved character and evil deeds of Jehoram, Ahaziah, and Athaliah are at once accounted for when we remember that they were respectively the son-in-law, grandson, and daughter of Ahab, and possibly of Jezebel. If, however, Jezebel were really the mother of Athaliah, it is difficult to believe that the chronicler understood or at any rate realised the fact. In the books of Ezra and Nehemiah the chronicler lays great stress upon the iniquity and inexpediency of marriage with strange wives, and he has been careful to insert a note into the history of Jehoshaphat to call attention to the fact that the king of Judah had joined affinity with Ahab. If he had understood that this implied joining affinity with a Phœnician devotee of Baal, this significant fact would not have been passed over in silence. Moreover, the names Athaliah and Ahaziah are both compounded with the sacred name Jehovah. A Phœnician Baal-worshipper may very well have been sufficiently eclectic to make such use of the name sacred to the family into which she married, but on the whole those names rather tell against the descent of their owners from Jezebel and her Zidonian ancestors.

We have seen that, after giving the concluding formula for the reign of Jehoshaphat, the chronicler adds a postscript narrating an incident discreditable to the king. Similarly he prefaces the introductory formula for the reign of Jehoram by inserting a cruel deed of the new king. Before telling us Jehoram's age at his accession and the length of his reign, the chronicler relates[1] the steps taken by Jehoram to secure himself upon his throne. Jehoshaphat, like Rehoboam, had disposed of his numerous sons in the fenced cities of Judah, and had sought to make them quiet and contented by providing largely for their material welfare : "Their father gave them great gifts : silver, gold, and precious things, with fenced cities in Judah." The sanguine judgment of paternal affection might expect that these gifts would make his younger sons loyal and devoted subjects of their elder brother ; but Jehoram, not without reason, feared that treasure and cities might supply the means for a revolt, or that Judah might be split up into a number of small principalities. Accordingly when he had strengthened himself he slew all his brethren with the sword, and with them those princes of Israel whom he suspected of attachment to his other victims. He was following the precedent set by Solomon when he ordered the execution of Adonijah ; and, indeed, the slaughter by a new sovereign of all those near relations who might possibly dispute his claim to the throne has usually

---

[1] xxi. 2–4, peculiar to Chronicles.

been considered in the East to be a painful but necessary and perfectly justifiable act, being, in fact, regarded
in much the same light as the drowning of superfluous
kittens in domestic circles. Probably this episode is
placed before the introductory formula for the reign
because until these possible rivals were removed
Jehoram's tenure of the throne was altogether unsafe.

For the next few verses[1] the narrative follows the
book of Kings with scarcely any alteration, and states
the evil character of the new reign, accounting for
Jehoram's depravity by his marriage with a daughter
of Ahab. The successful revolt of Edom from Judah
is next given, and the chronicler adds a note of his
own to the effect that Jehoram experienced these
reverses because he had forsaken Jehovah, the God
of his fathers.

Then the chronicler proceeds[2] to describe further
sins and misfortunes of Jehoram. He mentions
definitely, what is doubtless implied by the book of
Kings, that Jehoram made high places in the cities of
Judah[3] and seduced the people into taking part in a
corrupt worship. The Divine condemnation of the
king's wrong-doing came from an unexpected quarter and
in an unusual fashion. The other prophetic messages
specially recorded by the chronicler were uttered by
prophets of Judah, some apparently receiving their
inspiration for one particular occasion. The prophet
who rebuked Jehoram was no less distinguished a
personage than the great Israelite Elijah, who, according
to the book of Kings, had long since been translated

---

[1] Vv. 5-10; cf. 2 Kings viii. 17-22.
[2] xxi. 11-19, peculiar to Chronicles.
[3] So R.V. marg., with LXX. and Vulgate A.R.V. have "mountains,"
with Masoretic text.

to heaven. In the older narrative Elijah's work is exclusively confined to the northern kingdom. But the chronicler entirely ignores Elijah, except when his history becomes connected for a moment with that of the house of David.

The other prophets of Judah delivered their messages by word of mouth, but this communication is made by means of "a writing." This, however, is not without parallel: Jeremiah sent a letter to the captives in Babylon, and also sent a written collection of his prophecies to Jehoiakim.[1] In the latter case, however, the prophecies had been originally promulgated by word of mouth.

Elijah writes in the name of Jehovah, the God of David, and condemns Jehoram because he was not walking in the ways of Asa and Jehoshaphat, but in the ways of the kings of Israel and the house of Ahab. It is pleasant to find that, in spite of the sins which marked the latter days of Asa and Jehoshaphat, their "ways" were as a whole such as could be held up as an example by the prophet of Jehovah. Here and elsewhere God appeals to the better feelings that spring from pride of birth. *Noblesse oblige.* Jehoram held his throne as representative of the house of David, and was proud to trace his descent to the founder of the Israelite monarchy and to inherit the glory of the great reigns of Asa and Jehoshaphat; but this pride of race implied that to depart from their ways was dishonourable apostacy. There is no more pitiful spectacle than an effeminate libertine pluming himself on his noble ancestry.

Elijah further rebukes Jehoram for the massacre of

---

[1] Jer. xxix.: xxxvi.

his brethren, who were better than himself. They had all grown up at their father's court, and till the other brethren were put in possession of their fenced cities had been under the same influences. It is the husband of Ahab's daughter who is worse than all the rest ; the influence of an unsuitable marriage has already begun to show itself. Indeed, in view of Athaliah's subsequent history, we do her no injustice by supposing that, like Jezebel and Lady Macbeth, she had suggested her husband's crime. The fact that Jehoram's brethren were better men than himself adds to his guilt morally, but this undesirable superiority of the other princes of the blood to the reigning sovereign would seem to Jehoram and his advisers an additional reason for putting them out of the way ; the massacre was an urgent political necessity.

> "Truly the tender mercies of the weak,
> As of the wicked, are but cruel."

There is nothing so cruel as the terror of a selfish man. The Inquisition is the measure not only of the inhumanity, but also of the weakness, of the mediæval Church ; and the massacre of St. Bartholomew was due to the feebleness of Charles IX. as well as to the "revenge or the blind instinct of self-preservation"[1] of Mary de Medici.

The chronicler's condemnation of Jehoram's massacre marks the superiority of the standard of later Judaism to the current Oriental morality. For his sins Jehoram was to be punished by sore disease and by a great "plague" which would fall upon his people, and his

---

[1] Green's *Shorter History*, p. 404.

wives, and his children, and all his substance. From the following verses we see that "plague," here as in the case of some of the plagues of Egypt, has the sense of calamity generally, and not the narrower meaning of pestilence. This plague took the form of an invasion of the Philistines and of the Arabians "which are beside the Ethiopians." Divine inspiration prompted them to attack Judah; Jehovah stirred up their spirit against Jehoram. Probably here, as in the story of Zerah, the term Ethiopians is used loosely for the Egyptians, in which case the Arabs in question would be inhabitants of the desert between the south of Palestine and Egypt, and would thus be neighbours of their Philistine allies.

These marauding bands succeeded where the huge hosts of Zerah had failed; they broke into Judah, and carried off all the king's treasure, together with his sons and his wives, only leaving him his youngest son: Jehoahaz or Ahaziah. They afterwards slew the princes they had taken captive.[1] The common people would scarcely suffer less severely than their king. Jehoram himself was reserved for special personal punishment: Jehovah smote him with a sore disease; and, like Asa, he lingered for two years and then died. The people were so impressed by his wickedness that "they made no burning for him, like the burning of his fathers," whereas they had made a very great burning for Asa.[2]

---

[1] xxii. 1 *b*, peculiar to Chronicles.

[2] The Hebrew original of the A.R.V., "departed without being desired," is as obscure as the English of our versions. The most probable translation is, "He behaved so as to please no one." The A.R.V. apparently mean that no one regretted his death.

The chronicler's account of the reign of Ahaziah[1] does not differ materially from that given by the book of Kings, though it is considerably abridged, and there are other minor alterations. The chronicler sets forth even more emphatically than the earlier history the evil influence of Athaliah and her Israelite kinsfolk over Ahaziah's short reign of one year. The story of his visit to Jehoram, king of Israel, and the murder of the two kings by Jehu, is very much abridged. The chronicler carefully omits all reference to Elisha, according to his usual principle of ignoring the religious life of Northern Israel; but he expressly tells us that, like Jehoshaphat, Ahaziah suffered for consorting with the house of Omri: " His destruction or treading down was of God in that he went unto Jehoram." Our English versions have carefully reproduced an ambiguity in the original; but it seems probable that the chronicler does not mean that visiting Jehoram in his illness was a flagrant offence which God punished with death, but rather that, to punish Ahaziah for his imitation of the evil-doings of the house of Omri,[2] God allowed him to visit Jehoram in order that he might share the fate of the Israelite king.

The book of Kings had stated that Jehu slew forty-two brethren of Ahaziah. It is, of course, perfectly

---

[1] We need not discuss in detail the question of Ahaziah's age at his accession. The age of forty-two, given in 2 Chron. xxii. 2, is simply impossible, seeing that his father was only forty years old when he died. The Peshito and Arabic versions have followed 2 Kings viii. 26, and altered forty-two to twenty-two; and the LXX. reads twenty years. But twenty-two years still presents difficulties. According to this reading, Ahaziah, Jehoram's youngest son, was born when his father was only eighteen, and Jehoram having had several sons before the age of eighteen, had none afterwards.

[2] xxii. 7 *a*, peculiar to Chronicles.

allowable to take "brethren" in the general sense of
"kinsmen"; but as the chronicler had recently mentioned
the massacre of all Ahaziah's brethren, he avoids even
the appearance of a contradiction by substituting "sons
of the brethren of Ahaziah" for brethren. This
alteration introduces new difficulties, but these difficulties
simply illustrate the general confusion of numbers and
ages which characterises the narrative at this point. In
connection with the burial of Ahaziah, it may be noted
that the popular recollection of Jehoshaphat endorsed the
favourable judgment contained in the "writing of
Elijah": "They said" of Ahaziah, "He is the son of
Jehoshaphat, who sought Jehovah with all his heart."

The chronicler next narrates Athaliah's murder of
the seed royal of Judah and her usurpation of the throne
of David, in terms almost identical with those of the
narrative in the book of Kings. But his previous
additions and modifications are hard to reconcile with
the account he here borrows from his ancient authority.
According to the chronicler, Jehoram had massacred all
the other sons of Jehoshaphat, and the Arabians had
slain all Jehoram's sons except Ahaziah, and Jehu had
slain their sons; so that Ahaziah was the only living
descendant in the male line of his grandfather Jehoshaphat; he himself apparently died at the age of twenty-
three. It is intelligible enough that he should have a
son Joash and possibly other sons; but still it is
difficult to understand where Athaliah found "all the
seed royal" and "the king's sons" whom she put to
death. It is at any rate clear that Jehoram's slaughter
of his brethren met with an appropriate punishment:
all his own sons and grandsons were similarly slain,
except the child Joash.

The chronicler's narrative of the revolution by which

Athaliah was slain, and the throne recovered for the house of David in the person of Joash, follows substantially the earlier history, the chief difference being, as we have already noticed,[1] that the chronicler substitutes the Levitical guard of the second Temple for the bodyguard of foreign mercenaries who were the actual agents in this revolution.

A distinguished authority on European history is fond of pointing to the evil effects of royal marriages as one of the chief drawbacks to the monarchical system of government. A crown may at any time devolve upon a woman, and by her marriage with a powerful reigning prince her country may virtually be subjected to a foreign yoke. If it happens that the new sovereign professes a different religion from that of his wife's subjects, the evils arising from the marriage are seriously aggravated. Some such fate befell the Netherlands as the result of the marriage of Mary of Burgundy with the Emperor Maximilian, and England was only saved from the danger of transference to Catholic dominion by the caution and patriotism of Queen Elizabeth.

Athaliah's usurpation was a bold attempt to reverse the usual process and transfer the husband's dominions to the authority and faith of the wife's family. It is probable that Athaliah's permanent success would have led to the absorption of Judah in the northern kingdom. This last misfortune was averted by the energy and courage of Jehoiada, but in the meantime the half-heathen queen had succeeded in causing untold harm and suffering to her adopted country. Our own history furnishes numerous illustrations of the evil influences that come in the train of foreign queens. Edward II.

---

[1] Cf. p. 20

suffered grievously at the hands of his French queen ;
Henry VI.'s wife, Margaret of Anjou, contributed considerably to the prolonged bitterness of the struggle
between York and Lancaster; and to Henry VIII.'s
marriage with Catherine of Aragon the country owed
the miseries and persecutions inflicted by Mary Tudor.
But, on the other hand, many of the foreign princesses
who have shared the English throne have won the
lasting gratitude of the nation. A French queen of
Kent, for instance, opened the way for Augustine's
mission to England.

But no foreign queen of England has had the opportunities for mischief that were enjoyed and fully utilised
by Athaliah. She corrupted her husband and her
son, and she was probably at once the instigator of
their crimes and the instrument of their punishment.
By corrupting the rulers of Judah and by her own
misgovernment, she exercised an evil influence over the
nation ; and as the people suffered, not for their sins
only, but also for those of their kings, Athaliah brought
misfortunes and calamity upon Judah. Unfortunately
such experiences are not confined to royal families ; the
peace and honour, and prosperity of godly families in
all ranks of life have been disturbed and often destroyed
by the marriage of one of their members with a woman
of alien spirit and temperament. Here is a very
general and practical application of the chronicler's
objection to intercourse with the house of Omri.

CHAPTER VI

JOASH AND AMAZIAH

2 CHRON. xxiv.–xxv

FOR Chronicles, as for the book of Kings, the main interest of the reign of Joash is the repairing of the Temple ; but the later narrative introduces modifications which give a somewhat different complexion to the story. Both authorities tell us that Joash did that which was right in the eyes of Jehovah all the days of Jehoiada, but the book of Kings immediately adds that "the high places were not taken away : the people still sacrificed and burnt incense in the high places." [1] Seeing that Jehoiada exercised the royal authority during the minority of Joash, this toleration of the high places must have had the sanction of the high-priest. Now the chronicler and his contemporaries had been educated in the belief that the Pentateuch was the ecclesiastical code of the monarchy ; they found it impossible to credit a statement that the high-priest had sanctioned any other sanctuary besides the temple of Zion ; accordingly they omitted the verse in question.

In the earlier narrative of the repairing of the Temple

---

[1] Cf. xxv. 2 with 2 Kings xiv. 4, xxvi. 4 with 2 Kings xv. 4, xxvii. 2 with 2 Kings xv. 34, where similar statements are omitted by the chronicler.

the priests are ordered by Joash to use certain sacred dues and offerings to repair the breaches of the house; but after some time had elapsed it was found that the breaches had not been repaired: and when Joash remonstrated with the priests, they flatly refused to have anything to do with the repairs or with receiving funds for the purpose. Their objections were, however, overruled; and Jehoiada placed beside the altar a chest with a hole in the lid, into which "the priests put all the money that was brought into the house of Jehovah."[1] When it was sufficiently full, the king's scribe and the high-priest counted the money, and put it up in bags.

There were several points in this earlier narrative which would have furnished very inconvenient precedents, and were so much out of keeping with the ideas and practices of the second Temple that, by the time the chronicler wrote, a new and more intelligible version of the story was current among the ministers of the Temple. To begin with, there was an omission which would have grated very unpleasantly on the feelings of the chronicler. In this long narrative, wholly taken up with the affairs of the Temple, nothing is said about the Levites. The collecting and receiving of money might well be supposed to belong to them; and accordingly in Chronicles the Levites are first associated with the priests in this matter, and then the priests drop out of the narrative, and the Levites alone carry out the financial arrangements.

Again, it might be understood from the book of Kings that sacred dues and offerings, which formed the revenue of the priests and Levites, were diverted by

---

[1] 2 Kings xii. 9.

the king's orders to the repair of the fabric.   The chronicler was naturally anxious that there should be no mistake on this point ; the ambiguous phrases are omitted, and it is plainly indicated that funds were raised for the repairs by means of a special tax ordained by Moses.   Joash "assembled the priests and the Levites, and said to them, Go out into the cities of Judah, and gather of all Israel money to repair the house of your God from year to year, and see that ye hasten the matter.   Howbeit the Levites hastened it not."   The remissness of the priests in the original narrative is here very faithfully and candidly transferred to the Levites.   Then, as in the book of Kings, Joash remonstrates with Jehoiada, but the terms of his remonstrance are altogether different : here he complains because the Levites have not been required " to bring in out of Judah and out of Jerusalem the tax appointed by Moses the servant of Jehovah and by the congregation of Israel for the tent of the testimony," *i.e.,* the Tabernacle, containing the Ark and the tables of the Law.   The reference apparently is to the law[1] that when a census was taken a poll-tax of a half-shekel a head should be paid for the service of the Tabernacle. As one of the main uses of a census was to facilitate the raising of taxes, this law might not unfairly be interpreted to mean that when occasion arose, or perhaps even every year, a census should be taken in order that this poll-tax might be levied.   Nehemiah. arranged for a yearly poll-tax of a third of a shekel for the incidental expenses of the Temple.[2]   Here, however, the half-shekel prescribed in Exodus is intended ; and it should be observed that this poll-tax

---

[1] **Exod. xxx. 11-16.**   [2] **Neh. x. 32.**

was to be levied, not once only but "from year to year." The chronicler then inserts a note to explain why these repairs were necessary: "The sons of Athaliah, that wicked woman, had broken up the house of God; and also all the dedicated things of the house of Jehovah they bestowed upon the Baals." Here we are confronted with a further difficulty. All Jehoram's sons except Ahaziah were murdered by the Arabs in their father's life-time. Who are these "sons of Athaliah" who broke up the Temple? Jehoram was about thirty-seven when his sons were massacred, so that some of them may have been old enough to break up the Temple. One would think that "the dedicated things" might have been recovered for Jehovah when Athaliah was overthrown; but possibly, when the people retaliated by breaking into the house of Baal, there were Achans among them, who appropriated the plunder.

Having remonstrated with Jehoiada, the king took matters into his own hands; and he, not Jehoiada, had a chest made and placed, not beside the altar—such an arrangement savoured of profanity—but without at the gate of the Temple. This little touch is very suggestive. The noise and bustle of paying over money, receiving it, and putting it into the chest, would have mingled distractingly with the solemn ritual of sacrifice. In modern times the tinkle of threepenny pieces often tends to mar the effect of an impressive appeal and to disturb the quiet influences of a communion service. The Scotch arrangement, by which a plate covered with a fair white cloth is placed in the porch of a church and guarded by two modern Levites or elders, is much more in accordance with Chronicles. Then, instead of sending out Levites to collect the

tax, proclamation was made that the people themselves
should bring their offerings. Obedience apparently
was made a matter of conscience, not of solicitation.
Perhaps it was because the Levites felt that sacred
dues should be given freely that they were not forward to make yearly tax-collecting expeditions. At
any rate, the new method was signally successful.
Day after day the princes and people gladly brought
their offerings, and money was gathered in abundance.
Other passages suggest that the chronicler was not
always inclined to trust to the spontaneous generosity
of the people for the support of the priests and Levites ;
but he plainly recognised that free-will offerings are
more excellent than the donations which are painfully
extracted by the yearly visits of official collectors. He
would probably have sympathised with the abolition
of pew-rents.

As in the book of Kings, the chest was emptied at
suitable intervals ; but instead of the high-priest being
associated with the king's scribe, as if they were on
a level and both of them officials of the royal court, the
chief priest's *officer* assists the king's *scribe*, so that the
chief priest is placed on a level with the king himself.

The details of the repairs in the two narratives differ
considerably in form, but for the most part agree in
substance ; the only striking point is that they are
apparently at variance as to whether vessels of silver
or gold were or were not made for the renovated
Temple.

Then follows the account[1] of the ingratitude and
apostacy of Joash and his people. As long as Jehoiada
lived, the services of the Temple were regularly per-

---

[1] xxiv. 14-22, peculiar to Chronicles

formed, and Judah remained faithful to its God; but at last he died, full of days: a hundred and thirty years old. In his life-time he had exercised royal authority, and when he died he was buried like a king: " They buried him in the city of David among the kings, because he had done good in Israel and toward God and His house."[1] Like Nero when he shook off the control of Seneca and Burrhus, Joash changed his policy as soon as Jehoiada was dead. Apparently he was a weak character, always following some one's leading. His freedom from the influence that had made his early reign decent and honourable was not, as in Nero's case, his own act. The change of policy was adopted at the suggestion of the princes of Judah. King, princes, and people fell back into the old wickedness; they forsook the Temple and served idols. Yet Jehovah did not readily give them up to their own folly, nor hastily inflict punishment; He sent, not one prophet, but many, to bring them back to Himself, but they would not hearken. At last Jehovah made one last effort to win Joash back; this time He chose for His messenger a priest who had special personal claims on the favourable attention of the king. The prophet was Zechariah the son of Jehoiada, to whom Joash owed his life and his throne. The name was a favourite one in Israel, and was borne by two other prophets besides the son of Jehoiada. Its very etymology constituted an appeal to the conscience of Joash: it is compounded of the sacred name and a root meaning "to remember." The Jews were adepts at extracting from such a combination all its possible applications.

---

[1] Curiously enough, Jehoiada's name does not occur in the list of high-priests in 1 Chron. vi. 1-12.

The most obvious was that Jehovah would remember
the sin of Judah, but the recent prophets sent to recall
the sinners to their God showed that Jehovah also
remembered their former righteousness and desired to
recall it to them and them to it; they should remember
Jehovah. Moreover, Joash should remember the
teaching of Jehoiada and his obligations to the father
of the man now addressing him. Probably Joash did
remember all this when, in the striking Hebrew idiom,
"the spirit of God clothed itself with Zechariah the
son of Jehoiada the priest, and he stood above the
people and said unto them, Thus saith God: Why
transgress ye the commandments of Jehovah, to your
hurt? Because ye have forsaken Jehovah, He hath
also forsaken you." This is the burden of the prophetic utterances in Chronicles [1]; the converse is stated
by Irenæus when he says that to follow the Saviour
is to partake of salvation. Though the truth of
this teaching had been enforced again and again by
the misfortunes that had befallen Judah under apostate
kings, Joash paid no heed to it, nor did he remember
the kindness which Jehoiada had done him; that is to
say, he showed no gratitude towards the house of
Jehoiada. Perhaps an uncomfortable sense of obligation to the father only embittered him the more against
his son. But the son of the high-priest could not be
dealt with as summarily as Asa dealt with Hanani
when he put him in prison. The king might have
been indifferent to the wrath of Jehovah, but the son
of the man who had for years ruled Judah and
Jerusalem must have had a strong party at his back.

---

[1] I Chron. xxviii. 9; 2 Chron. vii. 19, xii. 5, xiii. 10, xv. 2, xxi. 10,
xxviii. 6, xxix. 6, xxxiv. 25.

Accordingly the king and his adherents conspired against Zechariah, and they stoned him with stones by the king's command. This Old Testament martyr died in a very different spirit from that of Stephen; his prayer was, not, "Lord, lay not this sin to their charge," but "Jehovah, look upon it and require it." His prayer did not long remain unanswered. Within a year the Syrians[1] came against Joash; he had a very great host, but he was powerless against a small company of the Divinely commissioned avengers of Zechariah. The tempters who had seduced the king into apostacy were a special mark for the wrath of Jehovah: the Syrians destroyed all the princes, and sent their spoil to the king of Damascus. Like Asa and Jehoram, Joash suffered personal punishment in the shape of "great diseases," but his end was even more tragic than theirs. One conspiracy avenged another: in his own household there were adherents of the family of Jehoiada: "Two of his own servants conspired against him for the blood of Zechariah, and slew him on his bed; and they buried him in the city of David, and not in the sepulchres of the kings."

The chronicler's biography of Joash might have been specially designed to remind his readers that the most careful education must sometimes fail of its purpose. Joash had been trained from his earliest years in the Temple itself, under the care of Jehoiada and of his aunt Jehoshabeath, the high-priest's wife. He had no doubt been carefully instructed in the religion and sacred history of Israel, and had been continually surrounded by the best religious influences of his age. For

---

[1] Cf. 2 Kings xii. 17, 18, of which this narrative is probably an adaptation.

Judah, in the chronicler's estimation, was even then the one home of the true faith. These holy influences had been continued after Joash had attained to manhood, and Jehoiada was careful to provide that the young king's harem should be enlisted in the cause of piety and good government. We may be sure that the two wives whom Jehoiada selected for his pupil were consistent worshippers of Jehovah and loyal to the Law and the Temple. No daughter of the house of Ahab, no "strange wife" from Egypt, Ammon, or Moab, would be allowed the opportunity of undoing the good effects of early training. Moreover, we might have expected the character developed by education to be strengthened by exercise. The early years of his reign were occupied by zealous activity in the service of the Temple. The pupil outstripped his master, and the enthusiasm of the youthful king found occasion to rebuke the tardy zeal of the venerable high-priest.

And yet all this fair promise was blighted in a day. The piety carefully fostered for half a life-time gave way before the first assaults of temptation, and never even attempted to reassert itself. Possibly the brief and fragmentary records from which the chronicler had to make his selection unduly emphasise the contrast between the earlier and later years of the reign of Joash; but the picture he draws of the failure of best of tutors and governors is unfortunately only too typical. Julian the Apostate was educated by a distinguished Christian prelate, Eusebius of Nicomedia, and was trained in a strict routine of religious observances; yet he repudiated Christianity at the earliest safe opportunity. His apostacy, like that of Joash, was probably characterised by base ingratitude. At Constantine's death the troops in Constantinople massacred nearly all the princes of the imperial family, and Julian, then only six years old, is said to have been saved and concealed in a church by Mark, Bishop of Arethusa. When Julian became emperor, he repaid this obligation by subjecting his benefactor to cruel tortures because he had destroyed a heathen temple and refused to make any compensation. Imagine Joash requiring Jehoiada to make compensation for pulling down a high place !

The parallel of Julian may suggest a partial explanation of the fall of Joash. The tutelage of Jehoiada may have been too strict, monotonous, and prolonged ; in choosing wives for the young king, the aged priest may not have made an altogether happy selection ; Jehoiada may have kept Joash under control until he was incapable of independence and could only pass from one dominant influence to another. When the high-priest's death gave the king an opportunity of changing his masters, a reaction from the too urgent insistence upon his duty to the Temple may have inclined Joash to listen favourably to the solicitations of the princes.

But perhaps the sins of Joash are sufficiently accounted for by his ancestry. His mother was Zibiah of Beersheba, and therefore probably a Jewess. Of her we know nothing further good or bad. Otherwise his ancestors for two generations had been uniformly bad. His father and grandfather were the wicked kings Jehoram and Ahaziah ; his grandmother was Athaliah ; and he was descended from Ahab, and possibly from Jezebel. When we recollect that his mother Zibiah was a wife of Ahaziah and had probably been selected by Athaliah, we cannot suppose that the element she contributed to his character would do much to counteract the evil he inherited from his father.

The chronicler's account of his successor Amaziah is
equally disappointing; he also began well and ended
miserably. In the opening formulæ of the history of
the new reign and in the account of the punishment of
the assassins of Joash, the chronicler closely follows the
earlier narrative, omitting, as usual, the statement that
this good king did not take away the high places.
Like his pious predecessors, Amaziah in his earlier and
better years was rewarded with a great army [1] and
military success; and yet the muster-roll of his forces
shows how the sins and calamities of the recent wicked
reigns had told on the resources of Judah. Jehoshaphat
could command more than eleven hundred and sixty
thousand soldiers; Amaziah has only three hundred
thousand.

These were not sufficient for the king's ambition; by
the Divine grace, he had already amassed wealth, in
spite of the Syrian ravages at the close of the preceding
reign: and he laid out a hundred talents of silver in
purchasing the services of as many thousand Israelites,
thus falling into the sin for which Jehoshaphat had
twice been reproved and punished. Jehovah, however,
arrested Amaziah's employment of unholy allies at the
outset. A man of God came to him and exhorted him
not to let the army of Israel go with him, because
" Jehovah is not with Israel"; if he had courage and
faith to go with only his three hundred thousand Jews,
all would be well, otherwise God would cast him down,
as He had done Ahaziah. The statement that Jehovah
was not with Israel might have been understood in a
sense that would seem almost blasphemous to the

---

[1] xxv. 5-13, peculiar to Chronicles, except that the account of the
war with Edom is expanded from the brief note in Kings. Cf. ver.
11 *f* with 2 Kings xiv. 7.

chronicler's contemporaries; he is careful therefore to explain that here "Israel" simply means "the children of Ephraim."

Amaziah obeyed the prophet, but was naturally distressed at the thought that he had spent a hundred talents for nothing : "What shall we do for the hundred talents which I have given to the army of Israel ? " He did not realise that the Divine alliance would be worth more to him than many hundred talents of silver; or perhaps he reflected that Divine grace is free, and that he might have saved his money. One would like to believe that he was anxious to recover this silver in order to devote it to the service of the sanctuary ; but he was evidently one of those sordid souls who like, as the phrase goes, "to get their religion for nothing." No wonder Amaziah went astray ! We can scarcely be wrong in detecting a vein of contempt in the prophet's answer : "Jehovah can give thee much more than this."

This little episode carries with it a great principle. Every crusade against an established abuse is met with the cry, "What shall we do for the hundred talents ? '—for the capital invested in slaves or in gin-shops ; for English revenues from alcohol or Indian revenues from opium ? Few have faith to believe that the Lord can provide for financial deficits, or, if we may venture to indicate the method in which the Lord provides, that a nation will ever be able to pay its way by honest finance. Let us note, however, that Amaziah was asked to sacrifice his own talents, and not other people's.

Accordingly Amaziah sent the mercenaries home ; and they returned in great dudgeon, offended by the slight put upon them and disappointed at the loss of prospective plunder. The king's sin in hiring Israelite mercenaries was to suffer a severer punishment than the loss of money. While he was away at war, his rejected allies returned, and attacked the border cities, [1] killed three thousand Jews, and took much plunder.

Meanwhile Amaziah and his army were reaping direct fruits of their obedience in Edom, where they gained a great victory, and followed it up by a massacre of ten thousand captives, whom they killed by throwing down from the top of a precipice. Yet, after all, Amaziah's victory over Edom was of small profit to him, for he was thereby seduced into idolatry. Amongst his other prisoners, he had brought away the gods of Edom; and instead of throwing them over a precipice, as a pious king should have done, "he set them up to be his gods, and bowed down himself before them, and burned incense unto them."

Then Jehovah, in His anger, sent a prophet to demand, "Why hast thou sought after foreign gods, which have not delivered their own people out of thine hand?" According to current ideas outside of Israel, a nation might very reasonably seek after the gods of their conquerors. Such conquest could only be attributed to the superior power and grace of the gods of the victors : the gods of the defeated were vanquished along with their worshippers, and were obviously incompetent and unworthy of further confidence. But to act like Amaziah—to go out to battle in the name of Jehovah, directed and encouraged by His prophet, to conquer by the grace of the God of Israel, and then to desert Jehovah of hosts, the Giver of victory, for

---

[1] In the phrase "from Samaria to Beth-horon," "Samaria" apparently means the northern kingdom, and not the city, *i.e.*, from the borders of Samaria ; the chronicler has fallen into the nomenclature of his own age.

the paltry and discredited idols of the conquered
Edomites—this was sheer madness. And yet as
Greece enslaved her Roman conquerors, so the victor
has often been won to the faith of the vanquished. The
Church subdued the barbarians who had overwhelmed
the empire, and the heathen Saxons adopted at last
the religion of the conquered Britons. Henry IV. of
France is scarcely a parallel to Amaziah: he went to
mass that he might hold his sceptre with a firmer
grasp, while the king of Judah merely adopted foreign
idols in order to gratify his superstition and love of
novelty.

Apparently Amaziah was at first inclined to discuss
the question: he and the prophet talked together; but
the king soon became irritated, and broke off the
interview with abrupt discourtesy: "Have we made
thee of the king's counsel? Forbear; why shouldest
thou be smitten?" Prosperity seems to have been
invariably fatal to the Jewish kings who began to reign
well; the success that rewarded, at the same time
destroyed their virtue. Before his victory Amaziah
had been courteous and submissive to the messenger of
Jehovah; now he defied Him and treated His prophet
roughly. The latter disappeared, but not before he
had declared the Divine condemnation of the stubborn
king.

The rest of the history of Amaziah—his presumptuous
war with Joash, king of Israel, his defeat and degradation,
and his assassination—is taken verbatim from the book
of Kings, with a few modifications and editorial notes
by the chronicler to harmonise these sections with the
rest of his narrative. For instance, in the book of
Kings the account of the war with Joash begins
somewhat abruptly: Amaziah sends his defiance before

any reason has been given for his action. The
chronicler inserts a phrase which connects his new
paragraph very suggestively with the one that goes
before. The former concluded with the king's taunt
that the prophet was not of his counsel, to which the
prophet replied that the king should be destroyed
because he had not hearkened to the Divine counsel
proffered to him. Then Amaziah "took advice"; *i.e.*, he
consulted those who were of his counsel, and the sequel
showed their incompetence. The chronicler also explains
that Amaziah's rash persistence in his challenge to
Joash "was of God, that He might deliver them into
the hand of their enemies, because they had sought
after the gods of Edom." He also tells us that the
name of the custodian of the sacred vessels of the
Temple was Obed-edom. As the chronicler mentions
five Levites of the name of Obed-edom, four of whom
occur nowhere else, the name was probably common
in some family still surviving in his own time. But,
in view of the fondness of the Jews for significant
etymology, it is probable that the name is recorded here
because it was exceedingly appropriate. "The servant
of Edom" suits the official who has to surrender his
sacred charge to a conqueror because his own king had
worshipped the gods of Edom. Lastly, an additional
note explains that Amaziah's apostacy had promptly
deprived him of the confidence and loyalty of his subjects; the conspiracy which led to his assassination
was formed from the time that he turned away from
following Jehovah, so that when he sent his proud
challenge to Joash his authority was already under-
mined, and there were traitors in the army which he
led against Israel. We are shown one of the means
used by Jehovah to bring about his defeat.

CHAPTER VII

UZZIAH, JOTHAM, AND AHAZ[1]

2 CHRON. xxvi.-xxviii.

AFTER the assassination of Amaziah, all the people of Judah took his son Uzziah, a lad of sixteen, called in the book of Kings Azariah, and made him king. The chronicler borrows from the older narrative the statement that " Uzziah did that which was right in the eyes of Jehovah, according to all that his father Amaziah had done." In the light of the sins attributed both to Amaziah and Uzziah in Chronicles, this is a somewhat doubtful compliment. Sarcasm, however, is not one of the chronicler's failings ; he simply allows the older history to speak for itself, and leaves the reader to combine its judgment with the statement of later tradition as best he can. But yet we might modify this verse, and read that Uzziah did good and evil, prospered and fell into misfortune, according to all that his father Amaziah had done, or an even closer parallel might be drawn between what Uzziah did and suffered and the chequered character and fortunes of Joash.

Though much older than the latter, at his accession Uzziah was young enough to be very much under

---

[1] For the discussion of the chronicler's account of Ahaz see Book III., Chap. VII.

the control of ministers and advisers ; and as Joash
was trained in loyalty to Jehovah by the high-priest
Jehoiada, so Uzziah " set himself to seek God during
the life-time " of a certain prophet, who, like the son of
Jehoiada, was named Zechariah, " who had understanding or gave instruction in the fear of Jehovah," [1] *i.e.*,
a man versed in sacred learning, rich in spiritual
experience, and able to communicate his knowledge,
such a one as Ezra the scribe in later days.

Under the guidance of this otherwise unknown
prophet, the young king was led to conform his private
life and public administration to the will of God. In
" seeking God," Uzziah would be careful to maintain
and attend the Temple services, to honour the priests
of Jehovah and make due provision for their wants ;
and " as long as he sought Jehovah God gave him
prosperity."

Uzziah received all the rewards usually bestowed
upon pious kings : he was victorious in war, and exacted
tribute from neighbouring states ; he built fortresses,
and had abundance of cattle and slaves, a large and
well-equipped army, and well-supplied arsenals. Like
other powerful kings of Judah, he asserted his supremacy over the tribes along the southern frontier of
his kingdom. God helped him against the Philistines,
the Arabians of Gur-baal, and the Meunim. He
destroyed the fortifications of Gath, Jabne, and Ashdod,
and built forts of his own in the country of the

---

[1] So R.V. marg., with LXX., Targum, Syriac and Arabic versions,
Talmud, Rashi, Kimchi, and some Hebrew manuscripts (Bertheau, i.
1). A.R.V., " had understanding in the visions " (R.V. vision) " of
God." The difference between the two Hebrew readings is very
slight. Vv. 5-20, with the exception of the bare fact of the leprosy
are peculiar to Chronicles.

Philistines. Nothing is known about Gur-baal; but the Arabian allies of the Philistines would be, like Jehoram's enemies "the Arabians who dwelt near the Ethiopians," nomads of the deserts south of Judah. These Philistines and Arabians had brought tribute to Jehoshaphat without waiting to be subdued by his armies; so now the Ammonites gave gifts to Uzziah, and his name spread abroad "even to the entering in of Egypt," possibly a hundred or even a hundred and fifty miles from Jerusalem. It is evident that the chronicler's ideas of international politics were of very modest dimensions.

Moreover, Uzziah added to the fortifications of Jerusalem; and because he loved husbandry and had cattle, and husbandmen, and vine-dressers in the open country and outlying districts of Judah, he built towers for their protection. His army was of about the same strength as that of Amaziah, three hundred thousand men, so that in this, as in his character and exploits, he did according to all that his father had done, except that he was content with his own Jewish warriors and did not waste his talents in purchasing worse than useless reinforcements from Israel. Uzziah's army was well disciplined, carefully organised, and constantly employed; they were men of mighty power, and went out to war by bands, to collect the king's tribute and enlarge his dominions and revenue by n w conquests. The war material in his arsenals is described at greater length than that of any previous king: shields, spears, helmets, coats of mail, bows and stones for slings. The great advance of military science in Uzziah's reign was marked by the invention of engines of war for the defence of Jerusalem; some, like the Roman *catapulta*, were for arrows, and others, like the *ballista*, to hurl huge stones. Though the Assyrian sculptures show us that battering-rams were freely employed by them against the walls of Jewish cities,[1] and the *ballista* is said by Pliny to have been invented in Syria,[2] no other Hebrew king is credited with the possession of this primitive artillery. The chronicler or his authority seems profoundly impressed by the great skill displayed in this invention; in describing it, he uses the root *hāshabh*, to devise, three times in three consecutive words. The engines were "*hishshebhōnôth mahāshebheth hôshēbh*"—"engines engineered by the ingenious." Jehovah not only provided Uzziah with ample military resources of every kind, but also blessed the means which He Himself had furnished; Uzziah "was marvellously helped, till he was strong, and his name spread far abroad." The neighbouring states heard with admiration of his military resources.

The student of Chronicles will by this time be prepared for the invariable sequel to God-given prosperity. Like David, Rehoboam, Asa, and Amaziah, when Uzziah "was strong, his heart was lifted up to his destruction." The most powerful of the kings of Judah died a leper. An attack of leprosy admitted of only one explanation: it was a plague inflicted by Jehovah Himself as the punishment of sin; and so the book of Kings tells us that "Jehovah smote the king," but says nothing about the sin thus punished. The chronicler was able to supply the omission: Uzziah had dared to go into the Temple and with irregular zeal to burn incense on the altar of incense. In so doing, he was violating the Law, which made the priestly office

---

[1] Cf. Ezek. xxvi. 9.
[2] Pliny, vii. 56 *apud* Smith's *Bible Dictionary.*

and all priestly functions the exclusive prerogative of the house of Aaron and denounced the penalty of death against any one who usurped priestly functions. [1] But Uzziah was not allowed to carry out his unholy design; the high-priest Azariah went in after him with eighty stalwart colleagues, rebuked his presumption, and bade him leave the sanctuary. Uzziah was no more tractable to the admonitions of the priest than Asa and Amaziah had been to those of the prophets. The kings of Judah were accustomed, even in Chronicles, to exercise an unchallenged control over the Temple and to regard the high-priests very much in the light of private chaplains. Uzziah was wroth; he was at the zenith of his power and glory; his heart was lifted up. Who were these priests, that they should stand between him and Jehovah and dare to publicly check and rebuke him in his own temple? Henry II.'s feelings towards Becket must have been mild compared to those of Uzziah towards Azariah, who, if the king could have had his way, would doubtless have shared the fate of Zechariah the son of Jehoiada. But a direct intervention of Jehovah protected the priests, and preserved Uzziah from further sacrilege. While his features were convulsed with anger, leprosy brake forth in his forehead. The contest between king and priest was at once ended; the priests thrust him out, and he himself hasted to go, recognising that Jehovah had smitten him. Henceforth he lived apart, cut off from fellowship alike with man and God, and his son Jotham governed in his stead. The book of Kings simply makes the general statement that Uzziah was buried with his fathers in the city of David; but the

---

[1] Num. xviii. 7 ; Exod. xxx. 7.

chronicler is anxious that his readers should not
suppose that the tombs of the sacred house of David
were polluted by the presence of a leprous corpse : he
explains that the leper was buried, not in the royal
sepulchre, but in the field attached to it.

The moral of this incident is obvious. In attempting
to understand its significance, we need not trouble
ourselves about the relative authority of kings and
priests ; the principle vindicated by the punishment of
Uzziah was the simple duty of obedience to an express
command of Jehovah. However trivial the burning
of incense may be in itself, it formed part of an
elaborate and complicated system of ritual. To interfere
with the Divine ordinances in one detail would mar
the significance and impressiveness of the whole Temple
service. One arbitrary innovation would be a precedent
for others, and would constitute a serious danger for a
system whose value lay in continuous uniformity.
Moreover, Uzziah was stubborn in disobedience. His
attempt to burn incense might have been sufficiently
punished by the public and humiliating reproof of the
high-priest. His leprosy came upon him because
when thwarted in an unholy purpose he gave way to
ungoverned passion.

In its consequences we see a practical application
of the lessons of the incident. How often is the
sinner only provoked to greater wickedness by the
obstacles which Divine grace opposes to his wrong-
doing ! How few men will tolerate the suggestion that
their intentions are cruel, selfish, or dishonourable !
Remonstrance is an insult, an offence against their
personal dignity ; they feel that their self-respect
demands that they should persevere in their purpose,
and that they should resent and punish any one who

has tried to thwart them. Uzziah's wrath was perfectly natural; few men have been so uniformly patient of reproof as not sometimes to have turned in anger upon those who warned them against sin. The most dramatic feature of this episode, the sudden frost of leprosy in the king's forehead, is not without its spiritual antitype. Men's anger at well-merited reproof has often blighted their lives once for all with ineradicable moral leprosy. In the madness of passion they have broken bonds which have hitherto restrained them and committed themselves beyond recall to evil pursuits and fatal friendships. Let us take the most lenient view of Uzziah's conduct, and suppose that he believed himself entitled to offer incense; he could not doubt that the priests were equally confident that Jehovah had enjoined the duty on them, and them alone. Such a question was not to be decided by violence, in the heat of personal bitterness. Azariah himself had been unwisely zealous in bringing in his eighty priests; Jehovah showed him that they were quite unnecessary, because at the last Uzziah "himself hasted to go out." When personal passion and jealousy are eliminated from Christian polemics, the Church will be able to write the epitaph of the *odium theologicum.*

Uzziah was succeeded by Jotham, who had already governed for some time as regent. In recording the favourable judgment of the book of Kings, "He did that which was right in the eyes of Jehovah, according to all that his father Uzziah had done," the chronicler is careful to add, "Howbeit he entered not into the temple of Jehovah"; the exclusive privilege of the house of Aaron had been established once for all. The story of Jotham's reign comes like a quiet and pleasant oasis in the chronicler's dreary narrative of wicked rulers, interspersed with pious kings whose piety failed them in their latter days. Jotham shares with Solomon the distinguished honour of being a king of whom no evil is recorded either in Kings or Chronicles, and who died in prosperity, at peace with Jehovah. At the same time it is probable that Jotham owes the blameless character he bears in Chronicles to the fact that the earlier narrative does not mention any misfortunes of his, especially any misfortune towards the close of his life. Otherwise the theological school from whom the chronicler derived his later traditions would have been anxious to discover or deduce some sin to account for such misfortune. At the end of the short notice of his reign, between two parts of the usual closing formula, an editor of the book of Kings has inserted the statement that " in those days Jehovah began to send against Judah Rezin the king of Syria and Pekah the son of Remaliah." This verse the chronicler has omitted ; neither the date [1] nor the nature of this trouble was clear enough to cast any slur upon the character of Jotham.

Jotham, again, had the rewards of a pious king : he added a gate to the Temple, and strengthened the wall of Ophel,[2] and built cities and castles in Judah ; he made successful war upon Ammon, and received from them an immense tribute—a hundred talents of silver, ten thousand measures of wheat, and as much barley—for three successive years. What happened

---

[1] Kimchi interprets " those days " as meaning " after the death of Jotham."

[2] The reference to the wall of Ophel is peculiar to Chronicles : indeed, Ophel is only mentioned in Chronicles and Nehemiah ; it was the southern spur of Mount Moriah (Neh. iii. 26, 27). Vv. 3 *b*-7 are also peculiar to Chronicles.

afterwards we are not told. It has been suggested
that the amounts mentioned were paid in three yearly
instalments, or that the three years were at the end
of the reign, and the tribute came to an end when
Jotham died or when the troubles with Pekah and
Rezin began.

We have had repeated occasion to notice that in his
accounts of the good kings the chronicler almost
always omits the qualifying clause to the effect that
they did not take away the high places. He does so
here; but, contrary to his usual practice, he inserts a
qualifying clause of his own: "The people did yet
corruptly." He probably had in view the unmitigated
wickedness of the following reign, and was glad to
retain the evidence that Ahaz found encouragement
and support in his idolatry; he is careful, however, to
state the fact so that no shadow of blame falls upon
Jotham.

The life of Ahaz has been dealt with elsewhere.
Here we need merely repeat that for the sixteen years
of his reign Judah was to all appearance utterly given
over to every form of idolatry, and was oppressed and
brought low by Israel, Syria, and Assyria.

CHAPTER VIII

HEZEKIAH: THE RELIGIOUS VALUE OF MUSIC

2 Chron. xxix.–xxxii.

THE bent of tne chronicler's mind is well illustrated by the proportion of space assigned to
ritual by him and by the book of Kings respectively.
In the latter a few lines only are devoted to ritual, and
the bulk of the space is given to the invasion of
Sennacherib, the embassy from Babylon, etc., while
in Chronicles ritual occupies about three times as
many verses as personal and public affairs.

Hezekiah, though not blameless, was all but perfect
in his loyalty to Jehovah. The chronicler reproduces
the customary formula for a good king: "He did that
which was right in the eyes of Jehovah, according to
all that David his father had done"; but his cautious
judgment rejects the somewhat rhetorical statement
in Kings that "after him was none like him among all
the kings of Judah, nor any that were before him."

Hezekiah's policy was made clear immediately after
his accession. His zeal for reformation could tolerate
no delay; the first month[1] of the first year of his reign

---

[1] This is usually understood as Nisan, the first month of the ecclesiastical year.

saw him actively engaged in the good work.[1] It was no light task that lay before him. Not only were there altars in every corner of Jerusalem and idolatrous high places in every city of Judah, but the Temple services had ceased, the lamps were put out, the sacred vessels cut in pieces, the Temple had been polluted and then closed, and the priests and Levites were scattered. Sixteen years of licensed idolatry must have fostered all that was vile in the country, have put wicked men in authority, and created numerous vested interests connected by close ties with idolatry, notably the priests of all the altars and high places. On the other hand, the reign of Ahaz had been an unbroken series of disasters; the people had repeatedly endured the horrors of invasion. His government as time went on must have become more and more unpopular, for when he died he was not buried in the sepulchres of the kings. As idolatry was a prominent feature of his policy, there would be a reaction in favour of the worship of Jehovah, and there would not be wanting true believers to tell the people that their sufferings were a consequence of idolatry. To a large party in Judah Hezekiah's reversal of his father's religious policy would be as welcome as Elizabeth's declaration against Rome was to most Englishmen.

Hezekiah began by opening and repairing the doors of the Temple. Its closed doors had been a symbol of the national repudiation of Jehovah; to reopen them

---

[1] xxix. 3–xxxi. 21 (the cleansing of the Temple and accompanying feast, Passover, organisation of the priests and Levites) are substantially peculiar to Chronicles, though in a sense they expand 2 Kings xviii 4–7, because they fulfil the commandments which Jehovah commanded Moses.

was necessarily the first step in the reconciliation of Judah to its God, but only the first step. The doors were open as a sign that Jehovah was invited to return to His people and again to manifest His presence in the Holy of holies, so that through those open doors Israel might have access to Him by means of the priests. But the Temple was as yet no fit place for the presence of Jehovah. With its lamps extinguished, its sacred vessels destroyed, its floors and walls thick with dust and full of all filthiness, it was rather a symbol of the apostacy of Judah. Accordingly Hezekiah sought the help of the Levites. It is true that he is first said to have collected together priests and Levites, but from that point onward the priests are almost entirely ignored.

Hezekiah reminded the Levites of the misdoings of Ahaz and his adherents and the wrath which they had brought upon Judah and Jerusalem; he told them it was his purpose to conciliate Jehovah by making a covenant with Him; he appealed to them as the chosen ministers of Jehovah and His temple to co-operate heartily in this good work.

The Levites responded to his appeal apparently rather in acts than words. No spokesman replies to the king's speech, but with prompt obedience they set about their work forthwith; they arose, Kohathites, sons of Merari, Gershonites, sons of Elizaphan, Asaph, Heman, and Jeduthun—the chronicler has a Homeric fondness for catalogues of high-sounding names—the leaders of all these divisions are duly mentioned. Kohath, Gershon, and Merari are well known as the three great clans of the house of Levi; and here we find the three guilds of singers—Asaph, Heman, and Jeduthun—placed on a level with the older clans. Elizaphan was apparently a division of the clan Kohath,[1] which, like the guilds of singers, had obtained an independent status. The result is to recognise seven divisions of the tribe.

The chiefs of the Levites gathered their brethren together, and having performed the necessary rites of ceremonial cleansing for themselves, went in to cleanse the Temple; that is to say, the priests went into the holy place and the Holy of holies and brought out "all the uncleanness" into the court, and the Levites carried it away to the brook Kidron : but before the building itself could be reached eight days were spent in cleansing the courts, and then the priests went into the Temple itself and spent eight days in cleansing it, in the manner described above. Then they reported to the king that the cleansing was finished, and especially that "all the vessels which King Ahaz cast away" had been recovered and reconsecrated with due ceremony. We were told in the previous chapter that Ahaz had cut to pieces the vessels of the Temple, but these may have been other vessels.

Then Hezekiah celebrated a great dedication feast; seven bullocks, seven rams, seven lambs, and seven he-goats were offered as a sin-offering for the dynasty,[2] for the Temple, for Judah, and (by special command of the king) for all Israel, *i.e.* for the northern tribes as well as for Judah and Benjamin. Apparently this sin-offering was made in silence, but afterwards the king set the Levites and priests in their places with their musical instruments, and when the burnt offering began

---

[1] Exod. vi. 18, 22 ; Num. iii. 30, mention Elizaphan as a descendant of Kohath.

[2] So Strack-Zockler, i, 1.

"the song of Jehovah began with the trumpets together with the instruments of David king of Israel. And all the congregation worshipped, and the singers sang, and the trumpeters sounded," and all this continued till the burnt offering was finished.

When the people had been formally reconciled to Jehovah by this representative national sacrifice, and thus purified from the uncleanness of idolatry and consecrated afresh to their God, they were permitted and invited to make individual sacrifices, thank-offerings and burnt offerings. Each man might enjoy for himself the renewed privilege of access to Jehovah, and obtain the assurance of pardon for his sins, and offer thanksgiving for his own special blessings. And they brought offerings in abundance : seventy bullocks, a hundred rams, and two hundred lambs for a burnt offering ; and six hundred oxen and three thousand sheep for thank-offerings. Thus were the Temple services restored and reinaugurated ; and Hezekiah and the people rejoiced because they felt that this unpremeditated outburst of enthusiasm was due to the gracious influence of the Spirit of Jehovah.

The chronicler's narrative is somewhat marred by a touch of professional jealousy. According to the ordinary ritual,[1] the offerer flayed the burnt offerings ; but for some special reason, perhaps because of the exceptional solemnity of the occasion, this duty now devolved upon the priests. But the burnt offerings were abundant beyond all precedent ; the priests were too few for the work, and the Levites were called in to help them, "for the Levites were more upright in heart to purify themselves than the priests." Apparently even in the

---

[1] Lev. i. 6.

second Temple brethren did not always dwell together
in unity.

Hezekiah had now provided for the regular services
of the Temple, and had given the inhabitants of Jerusalem
a full opportunity of returning to Jehovah; but the
people of the provinces were chiefly acquainted with
the Temple through the great annual festivals. These,
too, had long been in abeyance; and special steps had to
be taken to secure their future observance. In order
to do this, it was necessary to recall the provincials to
their allegiance to Jehovah. Under ordinary circumstances the great festival of the Passover would have
been observed in the first month, but at the time
appointed for the paschal feast the Temple was still
unclean, and the priests and Levites were occupied in its
purification. But Hezekiah could not endure that the
first year of his reign should be marked by the omission
of this great feast. He took counsel with the princes
and public assembly—nothing is said about the priests
—and they decided to hold the Passover in the second
month instead of the first. We gather from casual
allusions in vv. 6–8 that the kingdom of Samaria had
already come to an end; the people had been carried into
captivity, and only a remnant were left in the land.[1]
From this point the kings of Judah act as religious heads
of the whole nation and territory of Israel. Hezekiah
sent invitations to all Israel from Dan to Beersheba.
He made special efforts to secure a favourable response
from the northern tribes, sending letters to Ephraim
and Manasseh, i.e., to the ten tribes under their leadership. He reminded them that their brethren had gone

---

[1] According to 2 Kings xviii. 10, Samaria was not taken till the
sixth year of Hezekiah's reign. It is not necessary for an expositor of
Chronicles to attempt to harmonise the two accounts.

into captivity because the northern tribes had deserted the Temple ; and held out to them the hope that, if they worshipped at the Temple and served Jehovah, they should themselves escape further calamity, and their brethren and children who had gone into captivit, should return to their own land.

" So the posts passed from city to city through the country of Ephraim and Manasseh, even unto Zebulun." Either Zebulun is used in a broad sense for all the Galilean tribes, or the phrase " from Beersheba to Dan " is merely rhetorical, for to the north, between Zebulun and Dan, lay the territories of Asher and Naphtali. It is to be noticed that the tribes beyond Jordan are nowhere referred to ; they had already fallen out of the history of Israel, and were scarcely remembered in the time of the chronicler.

Hezekiah's appeal to the surviving communities of the northern kingdom failed : they laughed his messengers to scorn, and mocked them ; but individuals responded to his invitation in such numbers that they are spoken of as " a multitude of the people, even many of Ephraim and Manasseh, Issachar and Zebulun." There were also men of Asher among the northern pilgrims.[1]

The pious enthusiasm of Judah stood out in vivid contrast to the stubborn impenitence of the majority of the ten tribes. By the grace of God, Judah was of one heart to observe the feast appointed by Jehovah through the king and princes, so that there was gathered in Jerusalem a very great assembly of worshippers, surpassing even the great gatherings which the chronicler had witnessed at the annual feasts.

---

[1] Cf. xxx. 11, 18.

But though the Temple had been cleansed, the Holy City was not yet free from the taint of idolatry. The character of the Passover demanded that not only the Temple, but the whole city, should be pure. The paschal lamb was eaten at home, and the doorposts of the house were sprinkled with its blood. But Ahaz had set up altars at every corner of the city; no devout Israelite could tolerate the symbols of idolatrous worship close to the house in which he celebrated the solemn rites of the Passover. Accordingly before the Passover was killed these altars were removed.[1]

Then the great feast began; but after long years of idolatry neither the people nor the priests and Levites were sufficiently familiar with the rites of the festival to be able to perform them without some difficulty and confusion. As a rule each head of a household killed his own lamb; but many of the worshippers, especially those from the north, were not ceremonially clean: and this task devolved upon the Levites. The immense concourse of worshippers and the additional work thrown upon the Temple ministry must have made extraordinary demands on their zeal and energy.[2] At first apparently they hesitated, and were inclined to abstain from discharging their usual duties. A passover in a month not appointed by Moses, but decided on by the civil authorities without consulting the priesthood, might seem a doubtful and dangerous innovation. Recollecting Azariah's successful assertion of hierarchical

---

[1] xxx. 14; cf. 2 Kings xviii. 4. The chronicler omits the statement that Hezekiah destroyed Moses's brazen serpent, which the people had hitherto worshipped. His readers would not have understood how this corrupt worship survived the reforms of pious kings and priests who observed the law of Moses.

[2] Cf. xxix. 34, xxx. 3.

prerogative against Uzziah, they might be inclined to attempt a similar resistance to Hezekiah. But the pious enthusiasm of the people clearly showed that the Spirit of Jehovah inspired their somewhat irregular zeal; so that the ecclesiastical officials were shamed out of their unsympathetic attitude, and came forward to take their full share and even more than their full share in this glorious rededication of Israel to Jehovah.

But a further difficulty remained: uncleanness not only disqualified from killing the paschal lambs, but from taking any part in the Passover; and a multitude of the people were unclean. Yet it would have been ungracious and even dangerous to discourage their new-born zeal by excluding them from the festival; moreover, many of them were worshippers from among the ten tribes, who had come in response to a special invitation, which most of their fellow-countrymen had rejected with scorn and contempt. If they had been sent back because they had failed to cleanse themselves according to a ritual of which they were ignorant, and of which Hezekiah might have known they would be ignorant, both the king and his guests would have incurred measureless ridicule from the impious northerners. Accordingly they were allowed to take part in the Passover despite their uncleanness. But this permission could only be granted with serious apprehensions as to its consequences. The Law threatened with death any one who attended the services of the sanctuary in a state of uncleanness.[1] Possibly there were already signs of an outbreak of pestilence; at any rate, the dread of Divine punishment for sacrilegious presumption would distress the whole assembly and

---

[1] Lev. xv. 31.

mar their enjoyment of Divine fellowship. Again it is no priest or prophet, but the king, the Messiah, who comes forward as the mediator between God and man. Hezekiah prayed for them, saying, "Jehovah, in His grace and mercy,[1] pardon every one that setteth his heart to seek Elohim Jehovah, the God of his fathers, though he be not cleansed according to the ritual of the Temple. And Jehovah hearkened to Hezekiah, and healed the people," *i.e.*, either healed them from actual disease or relieved them from the fear of pestilence.

And so the feast went on happily and prosperously, and was prolonged by acclamation for an additional seven days. During fourteen days king and princes, priests and Levites, Jews and Israelites, rejoiced before Jehovah; thousands of bullocks and sheep smoked upon the altar; and now the priests were not backward: great numbers purified themselves to serve the popular devotion. The priests and Levites sang and made melody to Jehovah, so that the Levites earned the king's special commendation. The great festival ended with a solemn benediction: "The priests[2] arose and blessed the people, and their voice was heard, and their prayer came to His holy habitation, even unto heaven." The priests, and through them the people, received the assurance that their solemn and prolonged worship had met with gracious acceptance.

We have already more than once had occasion to

---

[1] So Bertheau, i. 1, slightly paraphrasing.

[2] A.R.V., with Masoretic text, "the priests the Levites"; LXX., Vulg. Syr., "the priests and the Levites." The former is more likely to be correct. The verse is partly an echo of Deut. xxvi. 15, so that the chronicler naturally uses the Deuteronomic phrase "the priests the Levites"; but he probably does so unconsciously, without intending to make any special claim for the Levites: hence I have omitted the word in the text.

consider the chronicler's main theme : the importance of the Temple, its ritual, and its ministers. Incidentally and perhaps unconsciously, he here suggests another lesson, which is specially significant as coming from an ardent ritualist, namely the necessary limitations of uniformity in ritual. Hezekiah's celebration of the Passover is full of irregularities : it is held in the wrong month ; it is prolonged to twice the usual period ; there are amongst the worshippers multitudes of unclean persons, whose presence at these services ought to have been visited with terrible punishment. All is condoned on the ground of emergency, and the ritual laws are set aside without consulting the ecclesiastical officials. Everything serves to emphasise the lesson we touched on in connection with David's sacrifices at the threshing-floor of Ornan the Jebusite : ritual is made for man, and not man for ritual. Complete uniformity may be insisted on in ordinary times, but can be dispensed with in any pressing emergency ; necessity knows no law, not even the Torah of the Pentateuch. Moreover, in such emergencies it is not necessary to wait for the initiative or even the sanction of ecclesiastical officials ; the supreme authority in the Church in all its great crises resides in the whole body of believers. No one is entitled to speak with greater authority on the limitations of ritual than a strong advocate of the sanctity of ritual like the chronicler ; and we may well note, as one of the most conspicuous marks of his inspiration, the sanctified common sense shown by his frank and sympathetic record of the irregularities of Hezekiah's passover. Doubtless emergencies had arisen even in his own experience of the great feasts of the Temple that had taught him this lesson ; and it says much for the healthy tone of the Temple community in his day that he does not attempt to reconcile the practice of Hezekiah with the law of Moses by any harmonistic quibbles.

The work of purification and restoration, however, was still incomplete : the Temple had been cleansed from the pollutions of idolatry, the heathen altars had been removed from Jerusalem, but the high places remained in all the cities of Judah.   When the Passover was at last finished, the assembled multitude, " all Israel that were present," set out, like the English or Scotch Puritans, on a great iconoclastic expedition.   Throughout the length and breadth of the Land of Promise, throughout Judah and Benjamin, Ephraim and Manasseh, they brake in pieces the sacred pillars, and hewed down the Asherim, and brake down the high places and altars ; then they went home.

Meanwhile Hezekiah was engaged in reorganising the priests and Levites and arranging for the payment and distribution of the sacred dues.   The king set an example of liberality by making provision for the daily, weekly, monthly, and festival offerings.   The people were not slow to imitate him ; they brought firstfruits and tithes in such abundance that four months were spent in piling up heaps of offerings.

" Thus did Hezekiah throughout all Judah ; and he wrought that which was good, and right, and faithful before Jehovah his God ; and in every work that he began in the service of the Temple, and in the Law, and in the commandments, to seek his God, he did it with all his heart, and brought it to a successful issue."

Then follow an account of the deliverance from Sennacherib and of Hezekiah's recovery from sickness, a reference to his undue pride in the matter of the embassy from Babylon, and a description of the prosperity of his reign, all for the most part abridged

from the book of Kings.   The prophet Isaiah, however,
is almost ignored.   A few of the more important
modifications deserve some little attention.   We are
told that the Assyrian invasion was " after these things
and this faithfulness," in order that we may not forget
that the Divine deliverance was a recompense for
Hezekiah's loyalty to Jehovah.   While the book of
Kings tells us that Sennacherib took all the fenced
cities of Judah, the chronicler feels that even this
measure of misfortune would not have been allowed to
befall a king who had just reconciled Israel to Jehovah,
and merely says that Sennacherib purposed to break
these cities up.

The chronicler [1] has preserved an account of the
measures taken by Hezekiah for the defence of his
capital : how he stopped up the fountains and watercourses outside the city, so that a besieging army might
not find water, and repaired and strengthened the
walls, and encouraged his people to trust in Jehovah.

Probably the stopping of the water supply outside
the walls was connected with an operation mentioned at
the close of the narrative of Hezekiah's reign : " Hezekiah
also stopped the upper spring of the waters of Gihon,
and brought them straight down on the west side of
the city of David." [2]   Moreover, the chronicler's statements are based upon 2 Kings xx. 20, where it is
said that "Hezekiah made the pool and the conduit
and brought water into the city."   The chronicler was
of course intimately acquainted with the topography
of Jerusalem in his own days, and uses his knowledge
to interpret and expand the statement in the book of
Kings.   He was possibly guided in part by Isa. xxii.

---

[1] xxxii. 2–8, peculiar to Chronicles.   [2] xxxii. 30.

9, 11, where the " gathering together the waters of the
lower pool" and the "making a reservoir between the
two walls for the water of the old pool" are mentioned
as precautions taken in view of a probable Assyrian
siege. The recent investigations of the Palestine
Exploration Fund have led to the discovery of aqueducts,
and stoppages, and diversions of watercourses which
are said to correspond to the operations mentioned
by the chronicler. If this be the case, they show a
very accurate knowledge on his part of the topography
of Jerusalem in his own day, and also illustrate his
care to utilise all existing evidence in order to obtain
a clear and accurate interpretation of the statements
of his authority.

The reign of Hezekiah appears a suitable opportunity to introduce a few remarks on the importance
which the chronicler attaches to the music of the
Temple services. Though the music is not more prominent with him than with some earlier kings, yet in
the case of David, Solomon, and Jehoshaphat other
subjects presented themselves for special treatment ;
and Hezekiah's reign being the last in which the music
of the sanctuary is specially dwelt upon, we are able
here to review the various references to this subject.
For the most part the chronicler tells his story of the
virtuous days of the good kings to a continual accom-
paniment of Temple music. We hear of the playing
and singing when the Ark was brought to the house
of Obed-edom ; when it was taken into the city of
David ; at the dedication of the Temple ; at the battle
between Abijah and Jeroboam ; at Asa's reformation ;
in connection with the overthrow of the Ammonites,
Moabites, and Meunim in the reign of Jehoshaphat ; at
the coronation of Joash ; at Hezekiah's feasts ; and

again, though less emphatically, at Josiah's passover. No doubt the special prominence given to the subject indicates a professional interest on the part of the author. If, however, music occupies an undue proportion of his space, and he has abridged accounts of more important matters to make room for his favourite theme, yet there is no reason to suppose that his actual statements overrate the extent to which music was used in worship or the importance attached to it. The older narratives refer to the music in the case of David and Joash, and assign psalms and songs to David and Solomon. Moreover, Judaism is by no means alone in its fondness for music, but shares this characteristic with almost all religions.

We have spoken of the chronicler so far chiefly as a professional musician, but it should be clearly understood that the term must be taken in its best sense. He was by no means so absorbed in the technique of his art as to forget its sacred significance; he was not less a worshipper himself because he was the minister or agent of the common worship. His accounts of the festivals show a hearty appreciation of the entire ritual; and his references to the music do not give us the technical circumstances of its production, but rather emphasise its general effect. The chronicler's sense of the religious value of music is largely that of a devout worshipper, who is led to set forth for the benefit of others a truth which is the fruit of his own experience. This experience is not confined to trained musicians; indeed, a scientific knowledge of the art may sometimes interfere with its devotional influence. Criticism may take the place of worship; and the hearer, instead of yielding to the sacred suggestions of hymn or anthem, may be distracted by his æsthetic judgment as to the

merits of the composition and the skill shown by its
rendering. In the same way critical appreciation of
voice, elocution, literary style, and intellectual power
does not always conduce to edification from a sermon.
In the truest culture, however, sensitiveness to these
secondary qualities has become habitual and automatic,
and blends itself imperceptibly with the religious consciousness of spiritual influence. The latter is thus
helped by excellence and only slightly hindered by
minor defects in the natural means. But the very
absence of any great scientific knowledge of music
may leave the spirit open to the spell which sacred
music is intended to exercise, so that all cheerful and
guileless souls may be "moved with concord of sweet
sounds," and sad and weary hearts find comfort in
subdued strains that breathe sympathy of which words
are incapable.

Music, as a mode of utterance moving within the
restraints of a regular order, naturally attaches itself
to ritual. As the earliest literature is poetry, the
earliest liturgy is musical. Melody is the simplest
and most obvious means by which the utterances of
a body of worshippers can be combined into a seemly
act of worship. The mere repetition of the same words
by a congregation in ordinary speech is apt to be
wanting in impressiveness or even in decorum; the
use of tune enables a congregation to unite in worship
even when many of its members are strangers to each
other.

Again, music may be regarded as an expansion of
language : not new dialect, but a collection of symbols
that can express thought, and more especially emotion,
for which mere speech has no vocabulary. This new
form of language naturally becomes an auxiliary of

religion. Words are clumsy instruments for the expression of the heart, and are least efficient when they undertake to set forth moral and spiritual ideas. Music can transcend mere speech in touching the soul to fine issues, suggesting visions of things ineffable and unseen.

Browning makes Abt Vogler say of the most enduring and supreme hopes that God has granted to men, "'Tis we musicians know"; but the message of music comes home with power to many who have no skill in its art.

CHAPTER IX

MANASSEH: REPENTANCE AND FORGIVENESS

2 CHRON. xxxiii.

IN telling the melancholy story of the wickedness of Manasseh in the first period of his reign, the chronicler reproduces the book of Kings, with one or two omissions and other slight alterations. He omits the name of Manasseh's mother; she was called Hephzi-bah—"My pleasure is in her." In any case, when the son of a godly father turns out badly, and nothing is known about the mother, uncharitable people might credit her with his wickedness. But the chronicler's readers were familiar with the great influence of the queen-mother in Oriental states. When they read that the son of Hezekiah came to the throne at the age of twelve and afterwards gave himself up to every form of idolatry, they would naturally ascribe his departure from his father's ways to the suggestions of his mother. The chronicler is not willing that the pious Hezekiah should lie under the imputation of having taken delight in an ungodly woman, and so her name is omitted.

The contents of 2 Kings xxi. 10–16 are also omitted; they consist of a prophetic utterance and further particulars as to the sins of Manasseh; they are virtually replaced by the additional information in Chronicles.

From the point of view of the chronicler, the history

444

of Manasseh in the book of Kings was far from satisfactory. The earlier writer had not only failed to provide materials from which a suitable moral could be deduced, but he had also told the story so that undesirable conclusions might be drawn. Manasseh sinned more wickedly than any other king of Judah : Ahaz merely polluted and closed the Temple, but Manasseh "built altars for all the host of heaven in the two courts of the Temple," and set up in it an idol. And yet in the earlier narrative this most wicked king escaped without any personal punishment at all. Moreover, length of days was one of the rewards which Jehovah was wont to bestow upon the righteous ; but while Ahaz was cut off at thirty-six, in the prime of manhood, Manasseh survived to the mature age of sixty-seven, and reigned fifty-five years.

However, the history reached the chronicler in a more satisfactory form. Manasseh was duly punished, and his long reign fully accounted for.[1] When, in spite of Divine warning, Manasseh and his people persisted in their sin, Jehovah sent against them " the captains of the host of the king of Assyria, which took Manasseh in chains, and bound him with fetters,[2] and carried him to Babylon."

The Assyrian invasion referred to here is partially confirmed by the fact that the name of Manasseh occurs amongst the tributaries of Esarhaddon and his successor, Assur-bani-pal. The mention of Babylon as his place of captivity rather than Nineveh may be accounted for by supposing that Manasseh was taken

---

[1] xxxiii. 11-19, peculiar to Chronicles.

[2] So R.V.: A.V., "among the thorns "; R.V. marg., "with books." if so in a figurative sense. Others take the word as a proper name : Hôhîm.

prisoner in the reign of Esarhaddon. This king of
Assyria rebuilt Babylon, and spent much of his time
there. He is said to have been of a kindly disposition,
and to have exercised towards other royal captives the
same clemency which he extended to Manasseh. For
the Jewish king's misfortunes led him to repentance :
"When he was in trouble, he besought Jehovah his God,
and humbled himself greatly before the God of his
fathers, and prayed unto him." Amongst the Greek
Apocrypha is found a " Prayer of Manasses," doubtless
intended by its author to represent the prayer referred
to in Chronicles. In it Manasseh celebrates the Divine
glory, confesses his great wickedness, and asks that his
penitence may be accepted and that he may obtain
deliverance.

If these were the terms of Manasseh's prayers,
they were heard and answered ; and the captive
king returned to Jerusalem a devout worshipper and
faithful servant of Jehovah. He at once set to work
to undo the evil he had wrought in the former period
of his reign. He took away the idol and the heathen
altars from the Temple, restored the altar of Jehovah
and re-established the Temple services. In earlier
days he had led the people into idolatry ; now he
commanded them to serve Jehovah, and the people
obediently followed the king's example. Apparently
he found it impracticable to interfere with the high
places ; but they were so far purified from corruption
that, though the people still sacrificed at these illegal
sanctuaries, they worshipped exclusively Jehovah, the
God of Israel.

Like most of the pious kings, his prosperity was
partly shown by his extensive building operations.
Following in the footsteps of Jotham, he strengthened

or repaired the fortifications of Jerusalem, especially about Ophel. He further provided for the safety of his dominions by placing captains, and doubtless also garrisons, in the fenced cities of Judah. The interest taken by the Jews of the second Temple in the history of Manasseh is shown by the fact that the chronicler is able to mention, not only the "Acts of the Kings of Israel," but a second authority : "The History of the Seers." The imagination of the Targumists and other later writers embellished the history of Manasseh's captivity and release with many striking and romantic circumstances.

The life of Manasseh practically completes the chronicler's series of object-lessons in the doctrine of retribution ; the history of the later kings only provides illustrations similar to those already given. These object-lessons are closely connected with the teaching of Ezekiel. In dealing with the question of heredity in guilt, the prophet is led to set forth the character and fortunes of four different classes of men. First [1] we have two simple cases : the righteousness of the righteous shall be upon him, and the wickedness of the wicked shall be upon him. These have been respectively illustrated by the prosperity of Solomon and Jotham and the misfortunes of Jehoram, Ahaziah, Athaliah, and Ahaz. Again, departing somewhat from the order of Ezekiel—"When the righteous turneth away from his righteousness, and committeth iniquity, and doeth according to all the abominations of the wicked man, shall he live ? None of his righteous deeds that he hath done shall be remembered ; in his trespass that he hath trespassed and in his sin that he hath

---

[1] Ezek. xviii. 20.

sinned he shall die"—here we have the principle that in Chronicles governs the Divine dealings with the kings who began to reign well and then fell away into sin : Asa, Joash, Amaziah, and Uzziah.

We reached this point in our discussion of the doctrine of retribution in connection with Asa. So far the lessons taught were salutary : they might deter from sin ; but they were gloomy and depressing : they gave little encouragement to hope for success in the struggle after righteousness, and suggested that few would escape terrible penalties of failure. David and Solomon formed a class by themselves ; an ordinary man could not aspire to their almost supernatural virtue. In his later history the chronicler is chiefly bent on illustrating the frailty of man and the wrath of God. The New Testament teaches a similar lesson when it asks, "If the righteous is scarcely saved, where shall the ungodly and sinner appear ?"[1] But in Chronicles not even the righteous is saved. Again and again we are told at a king's accession that he " did that which was good and right in the eyes of Jehovah"; and yet before the reign closes he forfeits the Divine favour, and at last dies ruined and disgraced.

But this sombre picture is relieved by occasional gleams of light. Ezekiel furnishes a fourth type of religious experience : " If the wicked turn from all his sins that he hath committed, and keep all My statutes, and do that which is lawful and right, he shall live ; he shall not die. None of his transgressions that he hath committed shall be remembered against him ; in his righteousness that he hath done he shall live. Have I any pleasure in the death of the wicked, saith the

---

Lord Jehovah, and not rather that he should return from his way and live?"[1] The one striking and complete example of this principle is the history of Manasseh. It is true that Rehoboam also repented, but the chronicler does not make it clear that his repentance was permanent. Manasseh is unique alike in extreme wickedness, sincere penitence, and thorough reformation. The reformation of Julius Cæsar or of our Henry V., or, to take a different class of instance, the conversion of St. Paul, was nothing compared to the conversion of Manasseh. It was as though Herod the Great or Cæsar Borgia had been checked midway in a career of cruelty and vice, and had thenceforward lived pure and holy lives, glorifying God by ministering to their fellow-men. Such a repentance gives us hope for the most abandoned. In the forgiveness of Manasseh the penitent sinner receives assurance that God will forgive even the most guilty. The account of his closing years shows that even a career of desperate wickedness in the past need not hinder the penitent from rendering acceptable service to God and ending his life in the enjoyment of Divine favour and blessing. Manasseh becomes in the Old Testament what the Prodigal Son is in the New: the one great symbol of the possibilities of human nature and the infinite mercy of God.

The chronicler's theology is as simple and straightforward as that of Ezekiel. Manasseh repents, submits himself, and is forgiven. His captivity apparently had expiated his guilt, as far as expiation was necessary. Neither prophet nor chronicler was conscious of the moral difficulties that have been found in so simple a

---

[1] Ezek. xviii. 21-23.

plan of salvation. The problems of an objective atonement had not yet risen above their horizon.

These incidents afford another illustration of the
necessary limitations of ritual. In the great crisis of
Manasseh's spiritual life, the Levitical ordinances played
no part ; they moved on a lower level, and ministered to
less urgent needs. Probably the worship of Jehovah
was still suspended during Manasseh's captivity ; none
the less Manasseh was able to make his peace with God.
Even if they were punctually observed, of what use were
services at the Temple in Jerusalem to a penitent
sinner at Babylon ? When Manasseh returned to Jerusalem, he restored the Temple worship, and offered
sacrifices of peace-offerings and of thanksgiving ;
nothing is said about sin-offerings. His sacrifices were
not the condition of his pardon, but the seal and token
of a reconciliation already effected. The experience of
Manasseh anticipated that of the Jews of the Captivity :
he discovered the possibility of fellowship with Jehovah,
far away from the Holy Land, without temple, priest,
or sacrifice. The chronicler, perhaps unconsciously
already foreshadows the coming of the hour when men
should worship the Father neither in the holy mountain of Samaria nor yet in Jerusalem.

Before relating the outward acts which testified the
sincerity of Manasseh's repentance, the chronicler devotes a single sentence to the happy influence of forgiveness and deliverance upon Manasseh himself.
When his prayer had been heard, and his exile was at
an end, *then* Manasseh knew and acknowledged that
Jehovah was God. Men first begin to know God
when they have been forgiven. The alienated and
disobedient, if they think of Him at all, merely have
glimpses of His vengeance and try to persuade them-

selves that He is a stern Tyrant. By the penitent
not yet assured of the possibility of reconciliation God
is chiefly thought of as a righteous Judge. What
did the Prodigal Son know about his father when
he asked for the portion of goods that fell to him or
while he was wasting his substance in riotous living?
Even when he came to himself, he thought of the
father's house as a place where there was bread
enough and to spare ; and he supposed that his father
might endure to see him living at home in permanent
disgrace, on the footing of a hired servant. When he
reached home, after he had been met a great way off
with compassion and been welcomed with an embrace,
he began for the first time to understand his father's
character. So the knowledge of God's love dawns
upon the soul in the blessed experience of forgiveness ;
and because love and forgiveness are more strange
and unearthly than rebuke and chastisement, the sinner
is humbled by pardon far more than by punishment ;
and his trembling submission to the righteous Judge
deepens into profounder reverence and awe for the
God who can forgive, who is superior to all vindictiveness, whose infinite resources enable Him to blot
out the guilt, to cancel the penalty, and annul the
consequences of sin.

> "There is forgiveness with Thee,
> That Thou mayest be feared."[1]

The words that stand in the forefront of the Lord's
Prayer, " Hallowed be Thy name," are virtually a
petition that sinners may repent, and be converted, and
obtain forgiveness.

---

[1] Psalm cxxx. 4, probably belonging to about the same period as
Chronicles.

In seeking for a Christian parallel to the doctrine expounded by Ezekiel and illustrated by Chronicles, we have to remember that the permanent elements in primitive doctrine are often to be found by removing the limitations which imperfect faith has imposed on the possibilities of human nature and Divine mercy. We have already suggested that the chronicler's somewhat rigid doctrine of temporal rewards and punishments symbolises the inevitable influence of conduct on the development of character. The doctrine of God's attitude towards backsliding and repentance seems somewhat arbitrary as set forth by Ezekiel and Chronicles. A man apparently is not to be judged by his whole life, but only by the moral period that is closed by his death. If his last years be pious, his former transgressions are forgotten; if his last years be evil, his righteous deeds are equally forgotten. While we gratefully accept the forgiveness of sinners, such teaching as to backsliders seems a little cynical; and though, by God's grace and discipline, a man may be led through and out of sin into righteousness, we are naturally suspicious of a life of "righteous deeds" which towards its close lapses into gross and open sin. "Nemo repente turpissimus fit." We are inclined to believe that the final lapse reveals the true bias of the whole character. But the chronicler suggests more than this: by his history of the almost uniform failure of the pious kings to persevere to the end, he seems to teach that the piety of early and mature life is either unreal or else is unable to survive as body and mind wear out. This doctrine has sometimes, inconsiderately no doubt, been taught from Christian pulpits; and yet the truth of which the doctrine is a misrepresentation supplies a correction of the former principle

that a life is to be judged by its close. Putting aside
any question of positive sin, a man's closing years
sometimes seem cold, narrow, and selfish when once
he was full of tender and considerate sympathy ; and
yet the man is no Asa or Amaziah who has deserted
the living God for idols of wood and stone. The man
has not changed, only our impression of him. Unconsciously we are influenced by the contrast between his
present state and the splendid energy and devotion oɪ
self-sacrifice that marked his prime; we forget that
inaction is his misfortune, and not his fault; we
overrate his ardour in the days when vigorous action
was a delight for its own sake ; and we overlook the
quiet heroism with which remnants of strength are still
utilised in the Lord's service, and do not consider that
moments of fretfulness are due to decay and disease
that at once increase the need of patience and diminish
the powers of endurance. Muscles and nerves slowly
become less and less efficient ; they fail to carry to the
soul full and clear reports of the outside world ; they are
no longer satisfactory instruments by which the soul can
express its feelings or execute its will. We are less
able than ever to estimate the inner life of such by that
which we see and hear. While we are thankful for the
sweet serenity and loving sympathy which often make
the hoary head a crown of glory, we are also entitled
to judge some of God's more militant children by their
years of arduous service, and not by their impatience of
enforced inactivity.

If our author's statement of these truths seem unsatisfactory, we must remember that his lack of a doctrine
of the future life placed him at a serious disadvantage.
He wished to exhibit a complete picture of God's
dealings with the characters of his history, so that

their lives should furnish exact illustrations of the working of sin and righteousness. He was controlled and hampered by the idea that underlies many discussions in the Old Testament: that God's righteous judgment upon a man's actions is completely manifested during his earthly life. It may be possible to assert an *eternal* providence; but conscience and heart have long since revolted against the doctrine that God's justice, to say nothing of His love, is declared by the misery of lives that might have been innocent, if they had ever had the opportunity of knowing what innocence meant. The chronicler worked on too small a scale for his subject. The entire Divine economy of Him with whom a thousand years are as one day cannot be even outlined for a single soul in the history of its earthly existence. These narratives of Jewish kings are only imperfect symbols of the infinite possibilities of the eternal providence. The moral of Chronicles is very much that of the Greek sage, "Call no man happy till he is dead"; but since Christ has brought life and immortality to light through the Gospel, we no longer pass final judgment upon either the man or his happiness by what we know of his life here. The decisive revelation of character, the final judgment upon conduct, the due adjustment of the gifts and discipline of God, are deferred to a future life. When these are completed, and the soul has attained to good or evil beyond all reversal, then we shall feel, with Ezekiel and the chronicler, that there is no further need to remember either the righteous deeds or the transgressions of earlier stages of its history.

CHAPTER X

THE LAST KINGS OF JUDAH

2 Chron. xxxiv.–xxxvi.

WHATEVER influence Manasseh's reformation exercised over his people generally, the taint of idolatry was not removed from his own family. His son Amon succeeded him at the age of two-and-twenty. Into his reign of two years he compressed all the varieties of wickedness once practised by his father, and undid the good work of Manasseh's later years. He recovered the graven images which Manasseh had discarded, replaced them in their shrines, and worshipped them instead of Jehovah. But in his case there was no repentance, and he was cut off in his youth.

In the absence of any conclusive evidence as to the date of Manasseh's reformation, we cannot determine with certainty whether Amon received his early training before or after his father returned to the worship of Jehovah. In either case Manasseh's earlier history would make it difficult for him to counteract any evil influence that drew Amon towards idolatry. Amon could set the example and perhaps the teaching of his father's former days against any later exhortations to righteousness. When a father has helped to lead his children astray, he cannot be sure that he will carry them with him in his repentance.

After Amon's assassination the people placed his son Josiah on the throne. Like Joash and Manasseh, Josiah was a child, only eight years old. The chronicler follows the general line of the history in the book of Kings, modifying, abridging, and expanding, but introducing no new incidents ; the reformation, the repairing of the Temple, the discovery of the book of the Law, the Passover, Josiah's defeat and death at Megiddo, are narrated by both historians. We have only to notice differences in a somewhat similar treatment of the same subject.

Beyond the general statement that Josiah " did that which was right in the eyes of Jehovah" we hear nothing about him in the book of Kings till the eighteenth year of his reign, and his reformation and putting away of idolatry is placed in that year. The chronicler's authorities corrected the statement that the pious king tolerated idolatry for eighteen years. They record how in the eighth year of his reign, when he was sixteen, he began to seek after the God of David ; and in his twelfth year he set about the work of utterly destroying idols throughout the whole territory of Israel, in the cities and ruins of Manasseh, Ephraim, and Simeon, even unto Naphtali, as well as in Judah and Benjamin. Seeing that the cities assigned to Simeon were in the south of Judah, it is a little difficult to understand why they appear with the northern tribes, unless they are reckoned with them technically to make up the ancient number.

The consequence of this change of date is that in Chronicles the reformation precedes the discovery of the book of the Law, whereas in the older history this discovery is the cause of the reformation. The chronicler's account of the idols and other apparatus of

false worship destroyed by Josiah is much less detailed
than that of the book of Kings. To have reproduced
the earlier narrative in full would have raised serious
difficulties. According to the chronicler, Manasseh had
purged Jerusalem of idols and idol altars ; and Amon
alone was responsible for any that existed there at the
accession of Josiah : but in the book of Kings Josiah
found in Jerusalem the altars erected by the kings
of Judah and the horses they had given to the sun.
Manasseh's altars still stood in the courts of the
Temple ; and over against Jerusalem there still remained the high places that Solomon had built for
Ashtoreth, Chemosh, and Milcom. As the chronicler in
describing Solomon's reign carefully omitted all mention
of his sins, so he omits this reference to his idolatry.
Moreover, if he had inserted it, he would have had to
explain how these high places escaped the zeal of the
many pious kings who did away with the high places.
Similarly, having omitted the account of the man of
God who prophesied the ruin of Jeroboam's sanctuary at
Bethel, he here omits the fulfilment of that prophecy.

The account of the repairing of the Temple is
enlarged by the insertion of various details as to the
names, functions, and zeal of the Levites, amongst
whom those who had skill in instruments of music
seem to have had the oversight of the workmen. We
are reminded of the walls of Thebes, which rose out
of the ground while Orpheus played upon his flute.
Similarly in the account of the assembly called to hear
the contents of the book of the Law the Levites are
substituted for the prophets. This book of the Law is
said in Chronicles to have been given by Moses, but
his name is not connected with the book in the parallel
narrative in the book of Kings.

The earlier authority simply states that Josiah held a great passover; Chronicles, as usual, describes the festival in detail. First of all, the king commanded the priests and Levites to purify themselves and take their places in due order, so that they might be ready to perform their sacred duties. The narrative is very obscure, but it seems that either during the apostacy of Amon or on account of the recent Temple repairs the Ark had been removed from the Holy of holies. The Law had specially assigned to the Levites the duty of carrying the Tabernacle and its furniture, and they seem to have thought that they were only bound to exercise the function of carrying the Ark; they perhaps proposed to bear it in solemn procession round the city as part of the celebration of the Passover, forgetting the words of David [1] that the Levites should no more carry the Tabernacle and its vessels. They would have been glad to substitute this conspicuous and honourable service for the laborious and menial work of flaying the victims. Josiah, however, commanded them to put the Ark into the Temple and attend to their other duties.

Next, the king and his nobles provided beasts of various kinds for the sacrifices and the Passover meal. Josiah's gifts were even more munificent than those of Hezekiah. The latter had given a thousand bullocks and ten thousand sheep; Josiah gave just three times as many. Moreover, at Hezekiah's passover no offerings of the princes are mentioned, but now they added their gifts to those of the king. The heads of the priesthood provided three hundred oxen and two thousand six hundred small cattle for the priests, and the chiefs of the Levites five hundred oxen and five thousand small

---

[1] 1 Chron. xxiii. 26, peculiar to Chronicles.

cattle for the Levites. But numerous as were the victims at Josiah's passover, they still fell far short of the great sacrifice [1] of twenty-two thousand oxen and a hundred and twenty thousand sheep which Solomon offered at the dedication of the Temple.

Then began the actual work of the sacrifices : the victims were killed and flayed, and their blood was sprinkled on the altar ; the burnt offerings were distributed among the people ; the Passover lambs were roasted, and the other offerings boiled, and the Levites " carried them quickly to all the children of the people." Apparently private individuals could not find the means of cooking the bountiful provision made for them ; and, to meet the necessity of the case, the Temple courts were made kitchen as well as slaughterhouse for the assembled worshippers. The other offerings would not be eaten with the Passover lamb, but would serve for the remaining days of the feast.

The Levites not only provided for the people, for themselves, and the priests, but the Levites who ministered in the matter of the sacrifices also prepared for their brethren who were singers and porters, so that the latter were enabled to attend undisturbed to their own special duties ; all the members of the guild of porters were at the gates maintaining order among the crowd of worshippers ; and the full strength of the orchestra and choir contributed to the beauty and solemnity of the services. It was the greatest Passover held by any Israelite king.

Josiah's passover, like that of Hezekiah, was followed by a formidable foreign invasion ; but whereas

---

[1] 2 Chron. vii. 5. The figures are peculiar to Chronicles ; 1 Kings viii. 5 says that the victims could not be counted

Hezekiah was rewarded for renewed loyalty by a triumphant deliverance, Josiah was defeated and slain. These facts subject the chronicler's theory of retribution to a severe strain. His perplexity finds pathetic expression in the opening words of the new section, "After all this," after all the idols had been put away, after the celebration of the most magnificent Passover the monarchy had ever seen. After all this, when we looked for the promised rewards of piety—for fertile seasons, peace and prosperity at home, victory and dominion abroad, tribute from subject peoples, and wealth from successful commerce—after all this, the rout of the armies of Jehovah at Megiddo, the flight and death of the wounded king, the lamentation over Josiah, the exaltation of a nominee of Pharaoh to the throne, and the payment of tribute to the Egyptian king. The chronicler has no complete explanation of this painful mystery, but he does what he can to meet the difficulties of the case. Like the great prophets in similar instances, he regards the heathen king as charged with a Divine commission. Pharaoh's appeal to Josiah to remain neutral should have been received by the Jewish king as an authoritative message from Jehovah. It was the failure to discern in a heathen king the mouthpiece and prophet of Jehovah that cost Josiah his life and Judah its liberty.

The chronicler had no motive for lingering over the last sad days of the monarchy; the rest of his narrative is almost entirely abridged from the book of Kings. Jehoahaz, Jehoiakim, Jehoiachin, and Zedekiah pass over the scene in rapid and melancholy succession. In the case of Jehoahaz, who only reigned three months, the chronicler omits the unfavourable judgment recorded in the book of Kings; but he repeats it for the other three,

even for the poor lad of eight[1] who was carried away
captive after a reign of three months and ten days. The
chronicler had not learnt that kings can do no wrong ;
on the other hand, the ungodly policy of Jehoiachin's
ministers is labelled with the name of the boy-sovereign.

Each of these kings in turn was deposed and carried
away into captivity, unless indeed Jehoiakim is an
exception. In the book of Kings we are told that he
slept with his fathers, *i.e.*, that he died and was buried
in the royal tombs at Jerusalem, a statement which
the LXX. inserts here also, specifying, however, that
he was buried in the garden of Uzza. If the pious
Josiah were punished for a single error by defeat and
death, why was the wicked Jehoiakim allowed to reign
till the end of his life and then die in his bed ? The
chronicler's information differed from that of the
earlier narrative in a way that removed, or at any rate
suppressed the difficulty. He omits the statement that
Jehoiakim slept with his fathers, and tells us [2] that
Nebuchadnezzar bound him in fetters to carry him to
Babylon. Casual readers would naturally suppose
that this purpose was carried out, and that the Divine
justice was satisfied by Jehoiakim's death in captivity ;
and yet if they compared this passage with that in
the book of Kings, it might occur to them that after
the king had been put in chains something might have
led Nebuchadnezzar to change his mind, or, like
Manasseh, Jehoiakim might have repented and been
allowed to return. But it is very doubtful whether
the chronicler's authorities contemplated the possibility
of such an interpretation ; it is scarcely fair to credit

---

[1] Jehoiachin. The ordinary reading in 2 Kings xxiv. 8 makes him
eighteen.

xxxvi. 6 *b*, peculiar to Chronicles.

them with all the subtle devices of modern commentators.

The real conclusion of the chronicler's history of the
kings of the house of David is a summary of the sins
of the last days of the monarchy and of the history of
its final ruin in xxxvi. 14–20.[1] All the chief of the priests
and of the people were given over to the abominations
of idolatry ; and in spite of constant and urgent admonitions from the prophets of Jehovah, they hardened
their hearts, and mocked the messengers of God, and
despised His words, and misused His prophets, until
the wrath of Jehovah arose against His people, and
there was no healing.

However, to this peroration a note is added that the
length of the Captivity was fixed at seventy years, in
order that the land might " enjoy her sabbaths." This
note rests upon Lev. xxv. 1–7, according to which
the land was to be left fallow every seventh year. The
seventy years' captivity would compensate for seventy
periods of six years each during which no sabbatical
years had been observed. Thus the Captivity, with the
four hundred and twenty previous years of neglect,
would be equivalent to seventy sabbatical periods.
There is no economy in keeping back what is due to
God.

Moreover, the editor who separated Chronicles from
the book of Ezra and Nehemiah was loath to allow the
first part of the history to end in a gloomy record of
sin and ruin. Modern Jews, in reading the last chapter
of Isaiah, rather than conclude with the ill-omened
words of the last two verses, repeat a previous portion
of the chapter. So here to the history of the ruin of

---

[1] Mostly peculiar to Chronicles.

Jerusalem the editor has appended two verses from the opening of the book of Ezra, which contain the decree of Cyrus authorising the return from the Captivity. And thus Chronicles concludes in the middle of a sentence which is completed in the book of Ezra: "Who is there among you of all his people? Jehovah his God be with him, and let him go up. . . ."

Such a conclusion suggests two considerations which will form a fitting close to our exposition. Chronicles is not a finished work; it has no formal end; it rather breaks off abruptly like an interrupted diary. In like manner the book of Kings concludes with a note as to the treatment of the captive Jehoiachin at Babylon: the last verse runs, "And for his allowance there was a continual allowance given him of the king, every day a portion, all the days of his life." The book of Nehemiah has a short final prayer: "Remember me, O my God, for good"; but the preceding paragraph is simply occupied with the arrangements for the wood offering and the first-fruits. So in the New Testament the history of the Church breaks off with the statement that St. Paul abode two whole years in his own hired house, preaching the kingdom of God. The sacred writers recognise the continuity of God's dealings with His people; they do not suggest that one period can be marked off by a clear dividing line or interval from another. Each historian leaves, as it were, the loose ends of his work ready to be taken up and continued by his successors. The Holy Spirit seeks to stimulate the Church to a forward outlook, that it may expect and work for a future wherein the power and grace of God will be no less manifest than in the past. Moreover, the final editor of Chronicles has shown himself un-willing that the book should conclude with a gloomy record of sin and ruin, and has appended a few lines to remind his readers of the new life of faith and hope that lay beyond the Captivity. In so doing, he has echoed the key-note of prophecy: ever beyond man's transgression and punishment the prophets saw the vision of his forgiveness and restoration to God.

1983-84 TITLES

Code	Author	Title	Price
0104	MacDonald, Donald	Biblical Doctrine of Creation and the Fall: Genesis 1-3	18.95
1401	Bennett, William H.	An Exposition of the Books of Chronicles	17.50
1903	Cox, Samuel	The Pilgrim Psalms: An Exposition of the Songs of Degrees	9.50
2703	Wright, Charles H. H.	Studies in Daniel's Prophecy	13.95
3202	Kirk, Thomas	Jonah: His Life and Mission	12.95
4503	Olshausen, Hermann	Studies in the Epistle to the Romans	16.50
8803	Westcott, Frederick B.	The Biblical Doctrine of Justification	15.25
8804	Salmond, S. D. F.	The Biblical Doctrine of Immortality	26.95
9516	Harris, John	The Teaching Methods of Christ: Characteristics of Our Lord's Ministry	16.75
9517	Blaikie, William G.	The Public Ministry of Christ	13.25
9518	Laidlaw, John	Studies in the Miracles of Our Lord	14.75

TITLES CURRENTLY AVAILABLE

Code	Author	Title	Price
0101	Delitzsch, Franz	A New Commentary on Genesis (2 vol.)	30.50
0102	Blaikie, W. G.	Heroes of Israel	19.50
0103	Bush, George	Genesis (2 vol.)	29.95
0201	Murphy, James G.	Commentary on the Book of Exodus	12.75
0202	Bush, George	Exodus	22.50
0203	Dolman, D. & Rainsford, M.	The Tabernacle (2 vol. in 1)	19.75
0301	Kellogg, Samuel H.	The Book of Leviticus	21.00
0302	Bush, George	Leviticus	10.50
0401	Bush, George	Numbers	17.95
0501	Cumming, John	The Book of Deuteronomy	16.00
0601	Blaikie, William G.	The Book of Joshua	15.75
0602	Bush, George	Joshua & Judges (2 vol. in 1)	17.95
0603	Kirk, Thomas & Lang, John	Studies in the Book of Judges (2 vol. in 1)	17.75
0701	Cox, S. & Fuller, T.	The Book of Ruth (2 vol. in 1)	14.75
0901	Blaikie, William G.	First Book of Samuel	16.50
0902	Deane, W. J. & Kirk, T.	Studies in the First Book of Samuel (2 vol. in 1)	19.00
0903	Blaikie, William G.	Second Book of Samuel	15.00
1101	Farrar, F. W.	The First Book of Kings	19.00
1201	Farrar, F. W.	The Second Book of Kings	19.00
1301	Kirk, T. & Rawlinson, G.	Studies in the Books of Kings (2 vol. in 1)	20.75
1701	Raleigh, Alexander	The Book of Esther	9.75
1801	Gibson, Edgar Charles	The Book of Job (available December)	10.00
1802	Green, William H.	The Argument of the Book of Job Unfolded	13.50
1901	Dickson, David	A Commentary on the Psalms (2 vol.)	32.50
1902	MacLaren, Alexander	The Psalms (3 vol.)	45.00
2001	Wardlaw, Ralph	Book of Proverbs (3 vol.)	45.00
2101	MacDonald, James M.	The Book of Ecclesiastes	15.50
2102	Wardlaw, Ralph	Exposition of Ecclesiastes	16.25
2201	Durham, James	An Exposition on the Song of Solomon	17.25
2301	Kelly, William	An Exposition of the Book of Isaiah	15.25
2302	Alexander, Joseph	Isaiah (2 vol.)	29.95
2401	Orelli, Hans C. von	The Prophecies of Jeremiah	15.25
2601	Fairbairn, Patrick	An Exposition of Ezekiel	18.50
2701	Pusey, Edward B.	Daniel the Prophet	19.50
2702	Tatford, Frederick Albert	Daniel and His Prophecy	9.25
3001	Cripps, Richard S.	A Commentary on the Book of Amos	13.50
3201	Burns, Samuel C.	The Prophet Jonah	11.25
3801	Wright, Charles H. H.	Zechariah and His Prophecies	24.95
4001	Morison, James	The Gospel According to Matthew	24.95
4101	Alexander, Joseph	Commentary on the Gospel of Mark	16.75
4102	Morison, James	The Gospel According to Mark	21.00
4201	Kelly, William	The Gospel of Luke	18.50
4301	Brown, John	The Intercessory Prayer of Our Lord Jesus Christ	11.50
4302	Hengstenberg, E. W.	Commentary on the Gospel of John (2 vol.)	34.95
4401	Alexander, Joseph	Commentary on the Acts of the Apostles (2 vol. in 1)	27.50
4402	Gloag, Paton J.	A Critical and Exegetical Commentary on the Acts of the Apostles (2 vol.)	29.95
4403	Stier, Rudolf E.	Words of the Apostles	18.75
4502	Moule, H. C. G.	The Epistle to the Romans	16.25
4601	Brown, John	The Resurrection of Life	15.50
4602	Edwards, Thomas C.	A Commentary on the First Epistle to the Corinthians	18.00
4603	Jones, John Daniel	Exposition of First Corinthians 13	9.50
4801	Ramsey, William	Historical Commenatry on the Epistle to the Galatians	17.75
4802	Brown, John	An Exposition of the Epistle of Paul to the Galatians	16.00
4901	Westcott, Brooke F.	St. Paul's Epistle to the Ephesians (available December)	10.50
4902	Pattison, R. & Moule, H.	Exposition of Ephesians: Lessons in Grace and Godliness (2 vol. in 1)	14.75
5001	Johnstone, Robert	Lectures on the Book of Philippians	18.25
5102	Westcott, F. B.	The Epistle to the Colossians	7.50
5103	Eadie, John	Colossians	10.50
5104	Daille, Jean	Exposition of Colossians	24.95
5401	Liddon, H. P.	The First Epistle to Timothy	6.00
5601	Taylor, Thomas	An Exposition of Titus	20.75
5801	Delitzsch, Franz	Commentary on the Epistle to the Hebrews (2 vol.)	31.50
5802	Bruce, A. B.	The Epistle to the Hebrews	17.25
5803	Edwards, Thomas C.	The Epistle to the Hebrews	13.00
5901	Johnstone, Robert	Lectures on the Epistle of James	16.50
5902	Mayor, Joseph B.	The Epistle of St. James	20.25
5903	Stier, Rudolf E.	Commentary on the Epistle of James	10.25
6201	Lias, John J.	The First Epistle of John	15.75
6202	Morgan, J. & Cox S.	The Epistles of John (2 vol. in 1)	22.95
6501	Manton, Thomas	An Exposition of the Epistle of Jude (available December)	14.00
6601	Trench, Richard C.	Commentary on the Epistles to the Sever Churches	8.50
7000	Tatford, Frederick Albert	The Minor Prophets (3 vol.)	44.95
7001	Orelli, Hans C. von	The Twelve Minor Prophets	15.50
7002	Alford, Dean Henry	The Book of Genesis and Part of the Book of Exodus	12.50
7003	Marbury, Edward	Obadiah and Habakkuk	23.95
7004	Adeney, Walter	The Books of Ezra and Nehemiah	13.00
7101	Mayor, Joseph B.	The Epistle of St. Jude & The Second Epistle of Peter	16.50
7102	Lillie, John	Lectures on the First and Second Epistles of Peter	19.75
7103	Hort, F. J. A. & Hort, A. F.	Expository and Exegetical Studies	29.50
7104	Milligan, George	St. Paul's Epistles to the Thessalonians	12.00
7105	Stanley, Arthur P.	Epistles of Paul to the Corinthians	20.95
7106	Moule, H. C. G.	Colossian and Philemon Studies	12.00
7107	Fairbairn, Patrick	The Pastoral Epistles	17.25
7108	Cox, S. & Drysdale, A. H.	The Epistle to Philemon (2 vol. in 1)	9.25

TITLES CURRENTLY AVAILABLE